HOLMAN
Old
Testament
Commentary

HOLMAN
Old
Testament
Commentary

*Nahum, Habakkuk, Zephaniah,
Haggai, Zechariah, Malachi*

GENERAL EDITOR

Max Anders

AUTHOR

Stephen R. Miller

HOLMAN
REFERENCE

NASHVILLE, TENNESSEE

Bible versions used in this book:

Unless otherwise stated all Scripture citation is from the HOLY BIBLE, NEW INTERNATIONAL VERSION®. Copyright © 1973, 1978, 1984 by International Bible Society. Used by permission of Zondervan Publishing House. All Rights Reserved. The "NIV" and "New International Version" trademarks are registered in the United States Patent and Trademark Office by International Bible Society. Use of either trademark requires the permission of International Bible Society.

Scripture quotations marked HCSB, are taken from the *Holman Christian Standard Bible*, ® copyright © 1999, 2000, 2002, 2003 by Holman Bible Publishers. Used by permission.

Scripture citations marked NASB are from the New American Standard Bible. © The Lockman Foundation, 1960, 1962, 1968, 1971, 1973, 1975, 1977. Used by permission.

Scripture citations marked NKJV are from The New King James Version, copyright © 1979, 1980, 1982, Thomas Nelson, Inc., Publishers.

Scripture citations marked NLT are from the Holy Bible, New Living Translation, copyright ©1996. Used by permission of Tyndale House Publishers, Inc., Wheaton, Illinois 60189. All rights reserved.

Scripture citations marked NRSV are from the New Revised Standard Version of the Bible, copyright © 1989 by the Division of Christian Education of the National Council of Churches of Christ in the United States of America. Used by permission. All rights reserved.

Scripture citations marked RSV are from the *Revised Standard Version* of the Bible copyright 1946, 1952, © 1971, 1973 by the National Council of the Churches of Christ in the U.S.A. and used by permission.

The King James Version

ISBN 978–0–8054–9478–5
Dewey Decimal Classification: 224.9
Subject Heading: BIBLE. O.T. MINOR PROPHETS

Nahum-Malachi /Stephen R. Miller
p.   cm. — (Holman Old Testament commentary)
Includes bibliographical references. (p.).
ISBN
1. Bible. O.T. Nahum—Commentaries.   2. Bible. O.T. Habakkuk—Commentaries.   3. Bible. O.T. Zephaniah—Commentaries.   4. Bible. O.T. Haggai—Commentaries.   5. Bible. O.T. Zechariah—Commentaries.   6. Bible. O.T. Malachi—Commentaries.   I. Title.   II. Series.

—dc21

7 8 9 10 11 12   19 18 17 16 15

*I*n honor of my parents,
Roy and Nell Miller,
and my wife's parents,
Arch and Emily Farmer.

"But as for you, continue in what
you have learned and have become
convinced of, because you know
those from whom you learned it,
and how from infancy you have
known the holy Scriptures, which
are able to make you wise for salvation through faith in Christ Jesus"
(2 Tim. 3:14–15).

Contents

Editorial Preface ix
Holman Old Testament Commentary Contributors xi
Holman New Testament Commentary Contributors. . . . xii

Nahum 1
  If God Is for Us! 1
Nahum 2–3
  The Fall of Evil Empires 29
Habakkuk 1–2
  Life's Mysteries 51
Habakkuk 3
  True Worship 73
Zephaniah 1–3
  Things That Never Change 91
Haggai 1–2
  A Call to Commitment 113
Zechariah 1–2
  God Cares for You! 133
Zechariah 3
  God Forgives 157
Zechariah 4
  God Empowers 175
Zechariah 5–6
  Sin's Devastation and Defeat 193
Zechariah 7–8
  Motivation Matters 215
Zechariah 9–10
  The King Is Coming! 237
Zechariah 11
  Prophecy of the Rejected Shepherd 263
Zechariah 12–14
  Israel's Future 283

Contents

Malachi 1
    God's Love and Our Response 309
Malachi 2:1–16
    Always Faithful 331
Malachi 2:17–4:6
    How Are You Treating God? 351

    Glossary. 371
    Bibliography 375

Editorial Preface

Today's church hungers for Bible teaching, and Bible teachers hunger for resources to guide them in teaching God's Word. The Holman Old Testament Commentary provides the church with the food to feed the spiritually hungry in an easily digestible format. The result: new spiritual vitality that the church can readily use.

Bible teaching should result in new interest in the Scriptures, expanded Bible knowledge, discovery of specific scriptural principles, relevant applications, and exciting living. The unique format of the Holman Old Testament Commentary includes sections to achieve these results for every Old Testament book.

Opening quotations stimulate thinking and lead to an introductory illustration and discussion that draw individuals and study groups into the Word of God. "In a Nutshell" summarizes the content and teaching of the chapter. Verse-by-verse commentary answers the church's questions rather than raising issues scholars usually admit they cannot adequately solve. Bible principles and specific contemporary applications encourage students to move from Bible to contemporary times. A specific modern illustration then ties application vividly to present life. A brief prayer aids the student to commit his or her daily life to the principles and applications found in the Bible chapter being studied. For those still hungry for more, "Deeper Discoveries" take the student into a more personal, deeper study of the words, phrases, and themes of God's Word. Finally, a teaching outline provides transitional statements and conclusions along with an outline to assist the teacher in group Bible studies.

It is the editors' prayer that this new resource for local church Bible teaching will enrich the ministry of group, as well as individual, Bible study, and that it will lead God's people truly to be people of the Book, living out what God calls us to be.

Holman Old Testament Commentary Contributors

Vol. 1 Genesis
ISBN 978-0-8054-9461-7
Kenneth O. Gangel and Stephen Bramer

Vol. 2 Exodus, Leviticus, Numbers
ISBN 978-0-8054-9462-4
Glen Martin

Vol. 3 Deuteronomy
ISBN 978-0-8054-9463-1
Doug McIntosh

Vol. 4 Joshua
ISBN 978-0-8054-9464-8
Kenneth O. Gangel

Vol. 5 Judges, Ruth
ISBN 978-0-8054-9465-5
W. Gary Phillips

Vol. 6 1 & 2 Samuel
ISBN 978-0-8054-9466-2
Stephen Andrews

Vol. 7 1 & 2 Kings
ISBN 978-0-8054-9467-9
Gary Inrig

Vol. 8 1 & 2 Chronicles
ISBN 978-0-8054-9468-6
Winfried Corduan

Vol. 9 Ezra, Nehemiah, Esther
ISBN 978-0-8054-9469-3
Knute Larson and Kathy Dahlen

Vol. 10 Job
ISBN 978-0-8054-9470-9
Stephen J. Lawson

Vol. 11 Psalms 1-72
ISBN 978-0-8054-9471-6
Steve J. Lawson

Vol. 12 Psalms 73-150
ISBN 978-0-8054-9481-5
Steve J. Lawson

Vol. 13 Proverbs
ISBN 978-0-8054-9472-3
Max Anders

Vol. 14 Ecclesiastes, Song of Songs
ISBN 978-0-8054-9482-2
David George Moore and Daniel L. Akin

Vol. 15 Isaiah
ISBN 978-0-8054-9473-0
Trent C. Butler

Vol. 16 Jeremiah, Lamentations
ISBN 978-0-8054-9474-7
Fred C. Wood and Ross McLaren

Vol. 17 Ezekiel
ISBN 978-0-8054-9475-4
Mark F. Rooker

Vol. 18 Daniel
ISBN 978-0-8054-9476-1
Kenneth O. Gangel

Vol. 19 Hosea, Joel, Amos, Obadiah, Jonah, Micah
ISBN 978-0-8054-9477-8
Trent C. Butler

Vol. 20 Nahum, Habakkuk, Zephaniah, Haggai, Zechariah, Malachi
ISBN 978 0-8054-9478-5
Stephen R. Miller

Holman New Testament Commentary Contributors

Vol. 1 Matthew
ISBN 978-0-8054-0201-8
Stuart K. Weber

Vol. 2 Mark
ISBN 978-0-8054-0202-5
Rodney L. Cooper

Vol. 3 Luke
ISBN 978-0-8054-0203-2
Trent C. Butler

Vol. 4 John
ISBN 978-0-8054-0204-9
Kenneth O. Gangel

Vol. 5 Acts
ISBN 978-0-8054-0205-6
Kenneth O. Gangel

Vol. 6 Romans
ISBN 978-0-8054-0206-3
Kenneth Boa and William Kruidenier

Vol. 7 1 & 2 Corinthians
ISBN 978-0-8054-0207-0
Richard L. Pratt Jr.

Vol. 8 Galatians, Ephesians, Philippians, Colossians
ISBN 978-0-8054-0208-7
Max Anders

Vol. 9 1 & 2 Thessalonians, 1 & 2 Timothy, Titus, Philemon
ISBN 978-0-8054-0209-4
Knute Larson

Vol. 10 Hebrews, James
ISBN 978-0-8054-0211-7
Thomas D. Lea

Vol. 11 1 & 2 Peter, 1, 2, 3 John, Jude
ISBN 978-0-8054-0210-0
David Walls & Max Anders

Vol. 12 Revelation
ISBN 978-0-8054-0212-4
Kendell H. Easley

Holman Old Testament Commentary

Twenty volumes designed for Bible study and teaching to enrich the local church and God's people.

Series Editor	Max Anders
Managing Editor	Steve Bond
Project Editor	Dean Richardson
Product Development Manager	Ricky D. King
Marketing Manager	Stephanie Huffman
Executive Editor	David Shepherd
Page Composition	TF Designs, Greenbrier, TN

Nahum 1

If God Is for Us!

I. INTRODUCTION
Life Without God

II. COMMENTARY
A verse-by-verse explanation of the chapter.

III. CONCLUSION
Will the Real God Please Stand Up!
An overview of the principles and applications from
the chapter.

IV. LIFE APPLICATION
Does God Make a Difference?
Melding the chapter to life.

V. PRAYER
Tying the chapter to life with God.

VI. DEEPER DISCOVERIES
Historical, geographical, and grammatical enrichment of the commentary.

VII. TEACHING OUTLINE
Suggested step-by-step group study of the chapter.

VIII. ISSUES FOR DISCUSSION
Zeroing the chapter in on daily life.

"Without God, mankind quickly degenerates into the subhuman."

P a u l   J o h n s o n

PROPHECY PROFILE

- The prophecy is brief, consisting of only three chapters and forty-seven verses.
- The prophecy is severe in tone. Nahum pronounced a scathing message of judgment on the city of Nineveh, the capital of the Assyrian Empire.
- The prophecy is focused. Almost every verse in the book deals in some way with the destruction of Nineveh.
- The prophecy is composed in majestic style with many beautiful poetic and stylistic devices.
- The prophecy was written to comfort God's people and assure them that their Assyrian tormentor would soon be punished.
- Theme: Nineveh will be destroyed and God's people delivered as a result of the righteous vengeance of God.
- God's truth for us is that our God reigns and will have the last word against evil.
- Two points are relevant for dating Nahum's prophecy: (1) Nahum referred to the fall of Thebes (3:8; Heb. *No-Amon*) before the armies of Ashurbanipal (668–627 B.C.) as a past event. This took place in 663 B.C., so the book must have been written after that time. (2) The prophet spoke of the fall of Nineveh in 612 B.C. as future but imminent. Thus the prophet delivered this message some time between 663 B.C. and 612 B.C., probably around 625 B.C.

AUTHOR PROFILE: NAHUM THE PROPHET

- Nahum was a prophet of the Lord who preached to the Southern Kingdom (Judah).
- His name means "comforter" or "consolation." The idea of comfort fits the theme of the book well, for Nahum comforted the people of Judah by prophesying Nineveh's downfall.

- No personal information is known about Nahum except that he was from Elkosh, a town in Judah.

- Nahum lived in the seventh century B.C. under Assyrian domination.

- Nahum was a literary genius whose work ranks as one of the literary masterpieces of the writing prophets.

READER PROFILE: THE NATION OF JUDAH

- Nahum's letter is addressed to his countrymen, the people of Judah.

- By Nahum's day the Northern Kingdom (Israel) had fallen to Assyria (721 B.C.). Although the Southern Kingdom (Judah) survived, it remained a vassal state of the evil Assyrian Empire until the fall of Nineveh in 612 B.C.

- The nation of Judah consisted primarily of the tiny tribe of Benjamin and the much larger tribe of Judah.

- Judah had suffered under the oppressive Assyrian regime for approximately one hundred years.

I N   A   N U T S H E L L

*I*n chapter 1 Nahum announces that the Lord has decreed the destruction of Nineveh, the capital of the evil Assyrian Empire. The prophet begins by setting forth the credentials of the God who has made such a bold pronouncement. The Lord is just, mighty, and will not leave the guilty unpunished. His holy nature and omnipotence ensure that Nineveh, and all evil empires, will crumble. Yet the Lord loves his people. He is good to them, protects them, and cares for them. Divine judgment on Nineveh will free God's people from oppression and will be a cause for celebration among the godly.

If God Is for Us!

Life Without God

Alexander Zaichenko grew up in Moscow, Russia, during the height of the cold war. A brilliant scholar, he became an economic adviser to the Gorbachev and Yeltsin governments. He was raised in an absolutely atheistic home and never met a Christian. Yet from a very early age, Alexander knew something was missing from his life. His parents were atheists and never talked about religion. His teachers at school only mentioned religion in the most disparaging ways. Still he wondered about the meaning of life and the purpose of human existence. Once he dared to ask his professor what our purpose for being is if we are only here for a little while and have no future. Rather than answering the question, the professor sternly rebuked Alexander for asking such a question. Yet Alexander continued to ponder the purpose of life and who God is, the One atheists kept denouncing.

He tried to find religious materials to read yet found that impossible. Finally, in 1979 he was able to purchase a Bible on the black market. Alexander took the Bible home and opened it to the Gospel of Matthew. At first, it did not seem interesting at all.

He read through the genealogy and birth of Jesus, the appearance of John the Baptist, and Jesus' early ministry. "I thought maybe the atheists were right," he later said.

But something happened when he read chapter 5. His mind and feelings changed as he read Jesus' Sermon on the Mount. "It took my breath away, and I started reading the Bible every day," he was quoted as saying in an article in *Christian Herald* magazine.

The more he read, the more he understood. The spiritual turning point came when he gave his life to the Lord Jesus Christ. "I considered myself a Christian, even though there were no Christians around me."

Two years later he got married, and he and his wife began studying the Bible together. "We also started searching for a church," he says. The Russian Orthodox Church's ritual wasn't satisfying, so "we decided to look for a Protestant church, which I had read about in atheist literature."

Four years passed before he was able to find an underground church where he and his wife could attend. Alexander said he found the church in an unusual way. He called the government office and said that a foreign visitor was coming to Moscow and desired to attend a Protestant church. He asked where one might be found. When he checked the location on the map, he found that in an effort to prevent people from finding the church, the Communists had omitted the street from the map.

Alexander was a secret Christian for many years. In December 1990, while being interviewed on nationwide Russian television, the reporter shocked him by asking about rumors that he had become a Christian. At that time Communism had not fallen in Russia, and Christians were being persecuted. In spite of the danger, Zaichenko bravely disclosed to the world that he was a follower of Christ. When he went to work the next day, he really did not know what to expect. To his surprise he suffered no open persecution, and as a matter of fact, several of his colleagues privately indicated they were interested in knowing about his faith.

Zaichenko has a Ph.D. in economics and headed a government-private enterprise program on economic reform under the Russian government's cabinet of ministers. He also served as an adviser to former Soviet president Mikhail Gorbachev. Zaichenko emphasized that Russia's economic prosperity is linked with the moral and ethical values of free evangelical Christianity. He contended that Christian values are essential to building a free economy and a civilized state.

Incredibly, by the grace and power of God, the "iron curtain" fell. Alexander is now able to worship freely. Best of all, he has joy and fulfillment because he has found the true God. He knows how hopeless and empty life can be without him. On the other hand, life with God is filled with hope for the future and confidence and joy in this life. The prophet Nahum knew that very well.

In this first chapter of his book, Nahum pronounces judgment upon Nineveh, Assyria's leading city. Assyria had caused untold suffering for Judah and the world of that day. God had not been asleep, and the time had come for judgment to fall. Finally, justice would be carried out.

Nahum's message is also one of hope and deliverance for God's people. The Northern Kingdom (ten northern tribes) had been totally annihilated by Assyria. Over fifty thousand captives had been dragged away from their homes to other lands. Judah (the two tribes in the south) survived but had lived "under the thumb" of Assyria for a hundred years. Now God promised that soon their oppressor would be destroyed. This was cause for celebration.

Before Nahum described the destruction of Nineveh, he presented a panoramic view of the greatness and majesty of God. The Lord makes the bold assertion that Nineveh would be destroyed. For one hundred years the Assyrians had ruled the world and crushed little Judah. Could this powerful foe really be defeated? The answer was a resounding yes! It was possible because Israel's God cared about the plight of his people and had the power to carry out his threats against Nineveh. This was a great comfort to Nahum's audience. As we turn our attention to the magnificent picture of God that Nahum paints, we will appreciate more than ever our great God. We can exclaim with the apostle Paul, "What, then, shall we say in response to this? If God is for us, who can be against us?" (Rom. 8:31).

The minor prophets of the Old Testament are often overlooked or ignored, especially little books like Nahum. But this short prophecy contains a powerful message for our modern age. In its pages we find God's promise that his people will be delivered from tyranny and justice will be meted out. Read and appreciate the timeless message of this Old Testament book.

II. COMMENTARY

If God Is for Us!

MAIN IDEA: *Our omnipotent God is able to deliver his people and defeat our persecutors, no matter how powerful they appear to be.*

A Introducing the Prophecy of Our Great God (1:1)

SUPPORTING IDEA: *God's prophet testifies about the Lord's greatness to warn the wicked to repent and to assure God's people of deliverance.*

1:1. Nahum's prophecy is designated an **oracle** in the NIV (also NASB, NRSV) and a "burden" (heavy message) in the KJV and NKJV. "Oracle" or "burden" may stand at the head of individual prophecies (Isa. 13:1; 14:28; 15:1; 17:1; Ezek. 12:10; Zech. 9:1; 12:1) or whole books, as in the case of Nahum (Hab. 1:1; Mal. 1:1).

Although Nahum preached his message to his fellow countrymen in Judah, the barbs of his severe message were directed toward the Assyrians. **Nineveh** was the leading city of Assyria at this time. Over one hundred years earlier, a reluctant Jonah had traveled the approximately five hundred miles to Nineveh and preached to its citizens. Jonah described Nineveh as "a very important city—a visit required three days" (Jonah 3:3). Evidently, Nineveh was so large that it took three days to see the place. In the Book of Jonah, God also declared the city to be extremely corrupt ("its wickedness has come up before me," Jonah 1:2), so much so that God was about to wipe it off the face of the earth (Jonah 3:4). Then Nineveh experienced one of the greatest revivals in history. From the king on down, people repented of their sin, and the city was spared (Jonah 3:5–10). God is indeed a merciful God. Yet soon after Jonah's visit, the city went back to its old ways, and wickedness became rampant once more. Now God decreed Nineveh's destruction through the prophet Nahum. This time God's judgment would be carried out.

Nahum's **book** was not like a modern book but rather was a scroll. Scrolls were produced from either papyrus or animal skins. Papyrus was similar to our paper and was made from the papyrus plant. Of course, scrolls made from animal skins were more durable. Few books written on papyrus have survived, whereas more manuscripts written on animal skins have been preserved. The Dead Sea Scrolls (dating from about 200 B.C. to A.D. 70), found mostly at Qumran (near Israel's Dead Sea), were written on animal skins.

This scroll contained a record of **the vision** that the prophet received from God. The Hebrew word rendered *vision* is derived from a verb that means "to see." When we think of a vision, we usually think of something seen by other than normal sight, possibly in a dream or trance. For example, Daniel had a vision in which he saw animals rising out of the sea (Dan. 7:3), and John saw a beast with ten horns and seven heads (Rev. 13:1). However, in the Old Testament a vision may also refer to a prophetic revelation generally, and that is the meaning here. Nahum's book contains a revelation from God to the prophet. Isaiah (1:1) and Obadiah (1:1) are also prophetic books that came through visions.

As we have noted previously, the name **Nahum** means "comfort" or "consolation." The prophet's message was indeed a comfort to the people of Judah who were told that their persecutor would soon be judged. Nahum was an **Elkoshite**, denoting his place of origin. There are several traditions about the location of the town of Elkosh. Jerome (fourth century A.D.) claimed that he was shown a town in Galilee (possibly el-Kauzeh or Capernaum) as the biblical Elkosh. Most likely, Elkosh was an unknown village situated in the southern part of ancient Judah.

B A Just God (1:2–3a)

SUPPORTING IDEA: *God's holy nature and love for his people demand that the wicked be brought to justice.*

1:2. The first two verses set the tone for Nahum's entire message. God will judge Nineveh and deliver his people. He must do so, for his justice demands that sin be punished and the righteous defended. Surprisingly, one whole book of the Bible is devoted to the destruction of a single heathen city. First, God's judgment will come because he is a **jealous** God. In the Bible the term *jealous* has both positive and negative connotations. Negatively, it may denote sinful human envy. But when speaking of God, the term *jealousy* may be used to express God's demand for faithfulness and his zealous protection of those he loves.

Second, God is an **avenging God** who **takes vengeance** (repeated later in the verse), another frequently misunderstood concept. Three times in this one verse God is said to be a deity who takes revenge. Some interpreters have taken these kinds of passages to suggest that the Old Testament God is an angry, vindictive being who is all wrath and no love. Nothing could be further from the truth.

The words translated "avenging" and "takes vengeance" come from the same Hebrew root (*naqam*). This root, with its derivatives, is used about seventy times in the Old Testament. The concept of divine vengeance must be understood in the light of Old Testament teaching about the holiness and justice of God and its effect on human beings as sinners. Rightly understood, divine vengeance is a necessary aspect of the history of redemption. We are warned not to take vengeance in our own hands (Lev. 19:18; Deut. 32:35). Most uses of *naqam* designate God as the source of vengeance. Deuteronomy 32:35 is the classic passage: "It is mine to avenge; I will repay."

God cannot be true to his character of holiness and justice if he allows sin and rebellion to go unpunished. The prophets emphasized the day of the Lord's vengeance (Isa. 34:8; 61:2; 63:4) as times in history when

> the Lord sets the record straight. . . . The Bible balances the fury of God's vengeance against the sinner with greatness of his mercy on those whom he redeems from sin. God's vengeance must never be viewed apart from his purpose to show mercy. He is not only the God of wrath but must be the God of wrath in order for his mercy to have meaning. . . . He avenges his people in the sense that he becomes their champion against the common enemy (Ps. 94) (Harris, Archer, and Waltke, TWOT, 2:599).

Thus God's vengeance is not flying off the handle in a fit of anger but a measured and just response to the evil actions of those who oppose him and his people.

Third, God is described as a God of **wrath.** The English word *wrath* is a translation of the Hebrew noun *chema,* meaning "heat, hot displeasure, indignation, anger, or wrath." It is derived from a verb that indicates heat. Much of what has been said about God's vengeance seems relevant to the wrath of God. God's righteous anger is poured out on evildoers and those who have harmed his people. This is the meaning in this passage. God's vengeance and wrath are not directed toward his children but toward **his foes** and **his enemies**. God's enemies are also the enemies of his people—the Assyrians who had oppressed Israel for a hundred years. We may take comfort in knowing that we have a defender who cares about us. He has all power and will defend us. Our enemies are his enemies. We can trust God.

1:3a. Lest someone get the wrong impression, Nahum quickly emphasized that God is not quick to judge. As the apostle John said, "God is love" (1 John 4:16). God is not some tyrant looking over the balcony of heaven with a lightning bolt waiting to zap people. In Ezekiel 18:32 the Lord declares: "For I take no pleasure in the death of anyone, declares the Sovereign LORD. Repent and live!" An even stronger affirmation of this fact is found in Ezekiel 33:11, "Say to them, 'As surely as I live, declares the Sovereign LORD, I take no pleasure in the death of the wicked, but rather that they turn from their ways and live. Turn! Turn from your evil ways! Why will you die, O house of Israel?'"

Our God is patient with sinners and is in no rush to pour out his wrath (**slow to anger**). In the Hebrew text, "slow to anger" is literally "long of nostrils," evidently referring to the flaring of the nostrils by an animal (such as a bull) when angry. Nahum's language is reminiscent of the Sinai experience (Exod. 34:6; Num. 14:18). God's restraint is born of meekness and not of weakness, as indicated by the contrast with his **great power**. Yet his patience is not forever: "Then the LORD said, 'My Spirit will not contend with man forever'" (Gen. 6:3), and, "A man who remains stiff-necked after many rebukes will suddenly be destroyed—without remedy" (Prov. 29:1). His power guarantees that he **will not leave the guilty unpunished** (a translation of the verb *niqqah*, "to acquit, pronounce innocent"). If there is no repentance, God's judgment will come because he cannot allow sin to go unpunished. If he overlooked unrepentant sin, he would not be just.

An Omnipotent God (1:3b–6)

SUPPORTING IDEA: *Our God has all power and can be trusted to care for his children and bring the wicked to justice.*

1:3b. Nineveh's doom is certain because the one who promises their judgment is the omnipotent God of the universe. The God who spoke the universe into existence and sustains it by his will is an unimaginably powerful being. No force in heaven or earth can resist him. **The whirlwind and the storm** are awesome displays of nature's power. A person only needs to view the aftermath of a tornado to confirm the magnitude of its destruction. These figures often express God's coming judgment (Ps. 83:15; Isa. 29:6). *Whirlwind* also appears in Hosea 8:7 in a judgment context. God is described as walking on the **clouds**, a figure that suggests his sovereignty over all of nature.

In his classic hymn, "O Worship the King," Sir Robert H. Grant reflects this imagery:

> O tell of His might, O sing of His grace,
> Whose robe is the light, whose canopy space!
> His chariots of wrath the deep thunderclouds form,
> And dark is His path on the wings of the storm.

1:4. God gave the command, and the Red Sea and the Jordan River dried up (Exod. 14:21–31; Josh. 3:7–17). **Bashan** was known for its plush pasturelands (Deut. 32:14; Ezek. 39:18). David spoke of the "strong bulls of Bashan" that surrounded him (Ps. 22:12). These bulls were large and strong because they grazed on the abundant vegetation in Bashan. **Carmel** is the mountain where Elijah met the prophets of Baal (1 Kgs. 18:19). Located near the Mediterranean coast, it overlooks the modern Israeli city of Haifa. It attains a maximum elevation of about 1,750 feet. Carmel, meaning "garden" or "fruitful field," was proverbial for its beauty, a garden spot. **Lebanon** also was noted for magnificent forests (Isa. 60:13), particularly its "cedars of Lebanon" (Judg. 9:15; Isa. 2:13). Yet a harsh word from Israel's God could make these beauty spots **wither** and **fade.**

1:5. Before the omnipotent God, the **mountains quake** and **the hills melt away** and **the earth trembles** (see also Judg. 5:4–5; 2 Sam. 22:8,16; Job 28:9; Pss. 46:6; 77:18; Joel 3:16). Like nature, humanity will be terrified at God's **presence** when they encounter him. The psalmist observed: "An oracle is within my heart concerning the sinfulness of the wicked: There is no fear of God before his eyes" (Ps. 36:1; see also Ps. 55:19). The apostle Paul concluded his graphic description of sin in the Epistle to the Romans with these words: "There is no fear of God before their eyes" (Rom. 3:18). Presently, evildoers do not fear God, but when they finally come face-to-face with him, they will cry out to the mountains and the rocks, "Fall on us and hide us from the face of him who sits on the throne and from the wrath of the Lamb!" (Rev. 6:16).

1:6. Nahum's questions demand a negative answer. None can survive the burning **anger** of God's **wrath** which will be **poured out like fire.** The word

indignation is a synonym for *anger* in this context and is sometimes translated "wrath" in the NIV (e.g., Isa. 13:5; Jer. 10:10; 50:25). Even huge boulders **are shattered before him**. Nahum's admonitions are a warning to Nineveh to repent in order to avoid the wrath of Israel's powerful God. It is futile to resist.

Ⓓ A Good God (1:7–8)

SUPPORTING IDEA: *The goodness of God assures that he will care for his children and punish those who seek to harm us.*

1:7. Sometimes the prophets are thought of as preachers of doom and gloom. Yet this is far from the truth. Usually following messages of judgment, the prophets delivered an encouraging message of comfort and love for the faithful. For example, Isaiah, after delivering a stinging rebuke to Israel in chapter 1, quickly added a beautiful word of comfort in chapter 2 (Isa. 2:2–4). Nahum follows this pattern. **The LORD is good** to his people. He loves them and has good things in store for them now and in the life to come. God protects us by being a **refuge in times of trouble**. When life seems too much to bear, we may run to God who wraps his loving arms around us and keeps us safe through the storm.

The phrase **cares for** is literally "knows" and points to the experiential relationship that exists between God and his children. This relationship forms the basis for God's care and concern. We must remember that when we suffer hardships and pain, God sees and God cares for us. Some day, Christ will come and put an end to evil, disease, and death. The well-known little children's prayer, "God is great. God is good. Let us thank him for our food," is simple but extremely profound. God is indeed great, and he is indeed good beyond our comprehension. We should be thankful.

1:8. God's goodness does not mean that he will not bring his foes (and his people's foes) to justice. Often we hear people say, "God is too good to punish anyone." Actually, the opposite is true. God is too good *not* to punish sin. God is so holy and so just that he cannot allow unrepentant sin to go unpunished. If God allowed Adolph Hitler to go unpunished for the millions of lives he slaughtered, God would not be just. But he is just, and sin will be punished. Like an **overwhelming flood**, God's wrath will sweep the wicked away.

Nahum may have had in mind the great flood of Noah's day, the destruction of Pharaoh's army by the returning sea, or the torrents that rushed through the usually dry riverbeds in Israel known as wadis. When the rains fell, these wadis would fill up quickly, and water would rush through them, sweeping everything in their path away, including any unfortunate travelers who happened to be camping near them. The object of God's wrath is **Nineveh**. Although not specifically named in the Hebrew text (note the brackets around the name *Nineveh* in the NIV), Nahum has already identified Nineveh as the foe in the book's opening verse. Nineveh's greatness would come crashing to an end, and God would **pursue** them **into darkness**, evidently a figure for death (1 Sam. 2:9; Ps. 88:12).

𝔼 An Invincible God (1:9–12a)

SUPPORTING IDEA: *Resistance is futile because God is invincible.*

1:9. Nineveh did not go quietly, yet their resistance against Israel's omnipotent God was futile. Whatever they plotted **against the LORD** would fail. We are reminded of the psalmist's words:

> Why do the nations rebel and the peoples plot in vain? The kings of the earth take their stand and the rulers conspire together against the LORD and against His Anointed One: "Let us tear off their chains and free ourselves from their restraints." The One enthroned in heaven laughs; the Lord ridicules them. Then He speaks to them in His anger and terrifies them in His wrath (Ps. 2:1–5 HCSB).

About one hundred years earlier, Assyria's King Sennacherib had challenged the Lord. This resulted in his own destruction and that of his army (Isa. 37:9–38). Nineveh would have no **second** opportunity this **time** to oppose God, for he would completely destroy them.

1:10. Nineveh's complete destruction is foretold with three figures: thorns, drunkenness, and stubble. The exact translation of the verse is debated, but the thrust is clear. Nineveh will be utterly destroyed. Most likely the verse means that Nineveh will be overpowered like **thorns** and **dry stubble** are utterly consumed by fire, and the great Assyrian army will be as weak as a helpless **drunk**.

1:11. The **one** who comes from **Nineveh** and **plots evil against the LORD and counsels wickedness** is the king of Assyria. Some commentators understand Nahum to be speaking of Sennacherib (705–681 B.C.), a particularly evil king from Assyria's past. In 701 B.C. he devastated the land of Judah, destroying forty-seven fortified cities, including Lachish. If not for God's supernatural intervention, he would have annihilated Jerusalem (2 Kgs. 18:13–19:37). Nahum could also have had in mind the current king of Nineveh. He designed evil and wickedness against the true God and his people. "Wickedness" is literally the Hebrew word *beliyaal* (also 1:15 and about twenty other times in the Old Testament), a noun that means "without worth." The term indicates a total lack of moral worth or principle. During the intertestamental period, Belial, a variant of *beliyaal*, became a title for Satan, the father of lies and lawlessness. This word appears in the New Testament with this meaning (2 Cor. 6:15).

1:12a. God now officially pronounces Nineveh's doom. Nahum makes clear that this message is not merely his personal verdict by using the formula so frequent in the prophets (but only here in Nahum)—**this is what the LORD says** (appearing about four hundred times in the KJV as the famous "thus saith the LORD"). Nineveh had human help (**allies**) and its citizens were **numerous**; still they would be destroyed and **pass away** with other evil empires into the graveyard of history. **Cut off** is a translation of a Hebrew word that normally speaks of shearing sheep (Gen. 31:19; Isa. 53:7).

A Saving God (1:12b–15)

SUPPORTING IDEA: *Our God will save us from all who would harm us.*

1:12b. Now God turns his attention to his precious people, **Judah**. No longer does God speak in the third person (**they**) as he did when addressing Nineveh but speaks directly to Judah. In terms similar to Isaiah 40:1–2, the Lord speaks comforting words to his people. Because of their sin, God had **afflicted** them with the rod of Assyria, but now Assyria would be judged, and Judah would no longer be afflicted. The years of suffering under Assyria's oppression had come to an end. God must destroy Nineveh because of his great love for his people. Judah had suffered under Assyria's tyranny for too long, and this mistreatment of God's people must stop. Here we find a theological principle that cannot be violated. God loves his people and will not allow evil empires or individuals to oppress them forever. He loves us too much!

1:13. Nineveh's destruction will be a blessing to God's people, who will be freed from Assyrian oppression. Nahum used two pictures to illustrate his point. First, Assyria's destruction would be for Judah like a heavy wooden **yoke** being removed from the neck of an ox. Second, Judah would experience freedom from oppression like a prisoner released from **shackles** in a dungeon. Of course, God delivered Judah from Assyria, but the human instrument that he used was the Babylonian king, Nabopolassar, who, with the help of the Medes, conquered Assyria in 612 B.C. Judah was free! What a blessing!

When Communism fell in Russia, it was a blessing for Christians throughout that land. They were finally free from Communist persecution.

1:14. Now God addressed Nineveh directly. For ancient peoples, having **no descendants** to carry on their name was one of the greatest tragedies imaginable (Deut. 7:24; 29:20; 1 Sam. 24:21). This meant that Nineveh's people would be forgotten forever. Assyrian kings would go to great lengths to preserve their names, carving them on stone building inscriptions. Ashurbanipal invoked a curse on anyone who dared to remove his name. Yet the God of Israel himself determined that these wicked kings would be without successors or offspring. Nineveh boasted that its **gods** were invincible and more powerful than those of any nation. Sennacherib, as the representative of Assyrian deities, boasted that no foreign god, including the God of Israel, could stand against him (Isa. 36:18–20; 37:10–13). Yet the Lord God declared that he would throw Assyria's gods on the trash heap and level their temples. This would be a fitting punishment for Assyria since it had desecrated the temples and gods of a host of other nations.

God even proclaimed that he would **prepare** Assyria's **grave**. If the tomb was ready, Nineveh's demise must be at hand. Nineveh deserved to be discarded, for it was **vile**, a translation of a Hebrew word meaning, "be slight, swift, trifling, of little account." Morally, the people of Nineveh had been "weighed on the scales and found wanting" (Dan. 5:27). Egyptian tomb paintings depict the souls of the departed being weighed on scales to see if they deserve to enter paradise. The persecutor of God's people would be completely destroyed. God's people had no fear that they would rise and harm them again.

1:15. When Nineveh falls, God's people will celebrate. They would celebrate not out of revenge but because justice would be accomplished and their oppression would be over. The **one who brings good news** in this context was the messenger who arrived with the report of Nineveh's defeat. In ancient times modern means of communication like television and radio did not exist. They depended on messengers who would run throughout the countryside bearing important messages. Apparently, this messenger stood on tops of the **mountains** so that all could hear as he shouted his message (Isa. 40:9). He proclaimed **peace** since the armies of Assyria would come no more.

Judah should show its gratitude to God by keeping the feasts (Passover and others) and fulfilling **vows** made to the Lord. Judah was now free to celebrate its feasts with great joy since the **wicked** (Nineveh) would no longer **invade** them because they had been **completely destroyed**. Similarly, God's people would celebrate the destruction of the evil world power that will persecute believers in the end times (Rev. 18:19–19:7). When evil empires fall today, believers celebrate because their evil and oppression of God's people have ceased.

> **MAIN IDEA REVIEW:** *Our omnipotent God is able to deliver his people and defeat our persecutors, no matter how powerful they appear to be.*

III. CONCLUSION

Will the Real God Please Stand Up!

Our world is a very religious place. Surveys show that Americans are more interested in spiritual things now than ever. People in our world believe in countless gods and religious systems. Hinduism teaches that there are thousands of manifestations of God. Jesus, they claim, is merely one of them. Over one billion people worship Allah, the god of Islam. Primitive peoples still worship spirits and idols. I heard a missionary tell of seeing a poor woman offer a chicken as a blood sacrifice, hoping that her god would send rain to water the parched land.

In America people think of themselves as much more sophisticated than that. Yet reflect on what Americans have believed. Hundreds of people left California to follow a charismatic religious figure named Jim Jones. He led the people into heresy and eventually persuaded (or forced) the whole group to commit suicide on November 18, 1978, in Jonestown, Guyana, by drinking cyanide-laced Kool-Aid. David Koresh convinced a group of people called the Branch Davidians that he was the Messiah, and most of them paid for that deception with their lives as their compound in Waco, Texas, burned to the ground in April 1993. In March 1997 Marshall Applewhite of the Heaven's Gate cult led thirty-nine people to commit suicide in Rancho Santa Fe, California, with the promise that they would be transported to a spaceship of aliens supposedly hidden behind the Hale-Bopp comet!

More surprising than what people won't believe is what they will believe! Many other examples could be given. Yet all of these people were religious. They believed in God. But merely believing in God is not good enough. We must believe in the God of the Bible—the God whom Nahum describes. As Christians we know there is only one true God who eternally exists as three persons—Father, Son, and Holy Spirit. Repentance and faith in God's Son, Jesus Christ, bring pardon from sin and assurance that we will spend eternity with God.

PRINCIPLES

- The God of the Bible is the only true God.
- God raises up messengers to testify to the world of his greatness.
- Because the Lord is just, he cannot allow the guilty to go unpunished.
- The Lord is patient, giving individuals and nations ample opportunity to repent and be spared.
- God's power is incomprehensible and irresistible.
- The Lord is good and will protect his people.
- False gods cannot save or deliver their worshipers from the Lord God.
- God will always triumph over evil forces.
- When God delivers his people from evil individuals and nations, they will rejoice.

APPLICATIONS

- Beware of those who would encourage you to worship any god other than the true God of the Bible.
- False gods are dangerous, cannot save, and lead their followers to destruction.
- Name several examples of false gods in our world today.
- List ways that God has demonstrated his power and reality in your life.
- If you have never repented of your sin and received Christ as your Lord and Savior, do so now and experience the joy of knowing the Lord God.
- God's power and absolute sovereignty ensure that he can protect and deliver his children.
- Pray that others might find the joy of knowing the true God.

IV. LIFE APPLICATION

Does God Make a Difference?

British historian Paul Johnson relates that one Sunday morning he woke up filled with anger toward someone who had wrongly criticized him. He had planned to write an article in the press lashing out at his tormentor. It was

Sunday, and he decided that before he wrote his rebuttal, he would attend church. The sermon was on anger. As the pastor spoke, God convicted him of his wrong attitude. He did not write the article.

Johnson said that among his reasons for believing in God is the fact that it made him a better person than he would be otherwise. Johnson said that Evelyn Waugh, the gifted curmudgeon, was once asked how he could behave as he did and still be a Christian. Waugh replied with grim sincerity, "Madam, I may be as bad as you say, but believe me, were it not for my religion, I would scarcely be a human being."

Johnson has covered some of the biggest stories in history in his twenty-eight books, including *The History of Christianity* (1976), *The History of the Jews* (1987), *The Intellectuals* (1988), *The Birth of the Modern* (1991), and *Modern Times* (1983). He is under no illusions about human nature, which he characterizes as being like Jekyll and Hyde. When he began to write *The History of Christianity,* he wondered if his faith would survive a careful examination of Christians over the last two thousand years.

> I went on to write the book, and emerged from that experience with my faith strengthened. I discovered that the calamities of mankind during the Christian centuries occurred not because men and women practiced Christianity but because they failed to do so. Bad as it was *with* religion, mankind would be infinitely worse off without it.

In his book *Modern Times,* he covers the period from World War I to the early 1980s. This was the first era since the birth of Christianity in which most leaders of major states were guided by post-Christian ethics. In an article in *Reader's Digest,* Johnson said he found this era

> unique in its cruelty, destructiveness and depravity . . . While writing *Modern Times,* I formed the unshakable conviction that man without God is a doomed creature. The history of the twentieth century proves the view that as the vision of God fades, we first become mere clever monkeys; then we exterminate one another.

Does God make a difference? The answer is a resounding yes! A proper belief in God and obedience to his Word make for better individuals and a better society. A world without God would be a very frightening place.

V. PRAYER

O Lord, thank you for the privilege of knowing you. Thank you that you are such a wonderful God and that we can trust you completely. Thank you that you loved the world so much that you sent your Son Jesus Christ to die for us so that we could know you. Remind us that there are millions of people in our nation and billions around the world who do not know you. Help us to care more for those who live in the darkness of paganism and sin. Show us what we can do to share the gospel with a lost world. In the name of Jesus Christ we pray. Amen.

VI. DEEPER DISCOVERIES

A. Oracle or Burden? (1:1)

Nahum's prophecy is designated an "oracle" in the NIV (also NASB, NRSV) and a "burden" (heavy message) in the KJV. Which is correct? The Hebrew word is *massa'*, a noun derived from a Hebrew root meaning "to lift up" or "carry," and may describe a heavy load or burden that is lifted up or carried. *Massa'* is translated in many ways in the NIV, including "oracle" (twenty-seven times), "oracles" (one time), "burden" (eight times), and "load" (seven times). If "oracle" is correct, the idea could be a lifting up of the voice to deliver a word from God, that is, an "oracle" or "message" (NLT). The KJV (and NKJV) translators rendered the word in its basic sense as "burden." Either "oracle" or "burden" is possible. If "burden" is correct, the idea would be that Nahum's message is a "heavy" message, filled with judgment and woe for the wicked.

B. The City of Nineveh (1:1)

Nineveh is one of the most important foreign cities mentioned in the Bible. In the NIV the name "Nineveh" appears twenty-two times (Gen. 10:11,12; 2 Kgs. 19:36; Isa. 37:37; Jonah 1:2; 3:2,3 [twice],4,6,7; 4:11; Nah. 1:1,8,11,14; 2:1,8; 3:7; Zeph. 2:13; Matt. 12:41; Luke 11:32) and "Ninevites" twice (Jonah 3:5; Luke 11:30). Nineveh was the greatest of the capitals of the ancient Assyrian Empire, which flourished from about 800 to 612 B.C. It was located on the Tigris River in northeastern Mesopotamia, near the city of Mosul in northern Iraq.

According to Genesis 10:9–12, Nineveh was one of the cities established by Nimrod. God sent the reluctant prophet Jonah there in the eighth century B.C. Jonah called it a "great city" (1:2; 4:11; cp. 3:3) and added that "a visit required three days," presumably to visit all the sights. The phrase "more than a hundred and twenty thousand people who cannot tell their right hand from their left" (4:11) has been interpreted to refer to children (resulting in a total population of about 600,000) or to describe the citizens of Nineveh as spiritually blind. The city was magnificent, as the following description from the *Holman Illustrated Bible Dictionary* makes clear:

> Sennacherib (704–681 B.C.) built the enormous southwest palace at Quyundjiq. We observe on his reliefs captive Philistines, Tyrians, Aramaeans, and others working under the supervision of the king himself. His "palace which has no equals" covered five acres and had 71 rooms, including two large halls 180 feet long and 40 feet wide. He boasted that the materials for the palace included "fragrant cedars, cypresses, doors banded with silver and copper . . . painted brick . . . curtain pegs of silver and copper, alabaster, breccia, marble, ivory." The rooms were embellished with 9,880 feet of sculptured reliefs, depicting Assyrian victories over enemy cities, including the Judean city of Lachish, captured in 701 B.C. Sennacherib's city was enclosed by eight miles of walls with fifteen gates. It had gardens and parks, watered by a thirty-mile-long aqueduct.
>
> Ashurbanipal (668–628 B.C.), the last great Assyrian king, built the northern palace with its magnificent reliefs of royal lion hunts. He amassed a library of 20,000 tablets, which contained important literary epics, magical and omen collections, royal archives and letters.

In 612 B.C. the Babylonians and Medes joined forces to conquer Nineveh. By 500 B.C. the prophet's words "Nineveh is laid waste" (Nah. 3:7 KJV) were echoed by the Greek historian Herodotus, who spoke of the Tigris as "the river on which the town of Nineveh formerly stood."

The ruins of Nineveh have been located at Quyundjiq in Iraq. About 1850 the Englishman A. H. Layard discovered Sennacherib's palace there. Hormuz Rassam found Ashurbanipal's palace and his great library in 1853. Nineveh was indeed a splendid city. What a pity that because of its wickedness it was destroyed.

C. The Divine Name (1:2)

When "LORD" appears in the Scripture in all capital letters, it represents the Hebrew name of God pronounced Yahweh or Jehovah. The pronunciation of this name is not completely certain since the Hebrew Scriptures were originally written without vowels. The consonants are transliterated into English as *YHWH*. To further complicate the problem, the Jews eventually quit pronouncing this divine name altogether, fearing that they might misuse it and bring God's wrath upon themselves (Exod. 20:7). Instead they substituted *Adonai* (Lord, sovereign) whenever the divine name was read. This is still the practice in the Jewish community today.

When vowels were added to the Hebrew Bible about A.D. 500, those for *Adonai* were attached to the consonants *YHWH*, resulting in the name *Jehovah* (*J=Y* and *V=W*). Since there are instances where the abbreviated name *Yah* occurs separately as "LORD" (Exod. 15:2) and since *Yah* (or *Yahu*) appears as a theophoric ending on many Hebrew names (e.g., Isaiah, Jeremiah, Obadiah), it seems rather certain that the first part of *YHWH* is pronounced *Yah*. Most scholars believe the next vowel is *e*, thus *Yahweh*.

Yahweh comes from a root (*hawah*) meaning "to be, become." According to most scholars, the significance of the name is "the one who is," indicating that the Lord is the existing, unchangeable, eternal one. This very name declared to the world that Israel's God was the only true and living God. Other gods were mere aberrations.

What is the significance of this for us? We may take comfort in the fact that the eternal, unchangeable "I AM" (Exod. 3:14) God of the Old Testament is still with us today. He is ever present in our time of need. He never changes. He is "the same yesterday and today and forever" (Heb. 13:8). His love never fails. Just as he cared for his people in Nahum's day, he cares for us. He is still the only true and living God. Only he can save, since only he exists. Isaiah declared: "This is what the LORD says—Israel's King and Redeemer, the LORD Almighty: I am the first and I am the last; apart from me there is no God" (Isa. 44:6).

D. A Jealous God (1:2)

In the Bible the term *jealous* has both positive and negative connotations. Negatively it may denote sinful human envy. "When Rachel saw that she was not bearing Jacob any children, she became jealous of her sister" (Gen. 30:1). Joseph's "brothers were jealous of him" (Gen. 37:11), and "Saul kept a jealous eye on David" (1 Sam. 18:9). This kind of jealousy is wrong and brings misery even to our loved ones.

On the other hand, in Nahum and in many other passages of Scripture, the Lord is declared to be a "jealous God." On first reflection jealousy seems unbecoming to God. Is God petty or envious in some way? Certainly not! How could God be jealous? There is nothing that anyone could possess that he would envy. God owns the universe! God's jealousy is righteous and holy. The first instance where God declared himself to be "a jealous God" was at Sinai (Exod. 20:5). There God entered into a covenant relationship with Israel. In the Old Testament this relationship is often compared to that of a husband and a wife. For example, the prophet Hosea's tumultuous marriage to his wife Gomer is compared to God's relationship with Israel (Hos. 1:2; 2:1–2; 3:1–5). Figuratively, God was Israel's husband, and Israel was his wife. Israel's unfaithfulness was described in terms of acts committed by an unfaithful wife. "Have you seen what faithless Israel has done? She has gone up on every high hill and under every spreading tree and has committed adultery there" (Jer. 3:6; the hills and trees were places of idolatry).

The most graphic description of Israel's idolatry as adulterous behavior is found in Ezekiel 23. Thus God, like a jealous husband with an unfaithful wife, is brokenhearted when his people forsake him for idols.

God's jealousy also refers to his watchful concern for his people Israel and his determination to punish those who have harmed them—like a caring husband who vigilantly guards his wife and responds forcefully to anyone who attempts to harm her. Ezekiel prophesied:

> Therefore prophesy concerning the land of Israel and say to the mountains and hills, to the ravines and valleys: "This is what the Sovereign LORD says: I speak in my jealous wrath because you have suffered the scorn of the nations. Therefore this is what the Sovereign LORD says: I swear with uplifted hand that the nations around you will also suffer scorn" (Ezek. 36:6–7).

Joel also declared: "Then the LORD will be jealous for his land and take pity on his people" (Joel 2:18; cp. Zech. 1:14; 8:2). This latter concept is the meaning of God's jealousy in Nahum. God had seen the atrocities committed against Israel by the Assyrians. Now like a loving husband, he was ready to defend his bride.

E. Nahum, a Student of the Bible (1:2)

Nahum clearly was a student of God's Word. Throughout his oracle we discover numerous allusions to other Bible passages. Compare the examples on the following page.

Other illustrations could be cited, but the point is clear. Nahum was a man who loved the Word of God. The Scriptures were his guide and the basis for his belief system. One reason God chose Nahum to be his spokesman was his love for and knowledge of the Bible. Nahum is a model for us. We should spend much time in the Word. Not only should we read the Bible; like Nahum we should allow its principles to govern our worldview. A love of the Word is also a characteristic of the blessed person (Ps. 1:1–2).

F. The Lord Is Good (1:7)

On September 11, 2001, the most horrific crime in its two-hundred-year history was committed against the United States. About twenty terrorists hijacked planes and flew them into the twin towers of the New York World Trade Center and the Pentagon, killing more than three thousand innocent men, women, and children. Only by God's grace, other sites filled with innocent people around the country were not destroyed. The question that has been asked over and over is, "Where was God?" The implication is, If God exists and he is good, how could such a thing happen?

Where was God? God showed his goodness in a myriad of ways. First, the four planes involved together could carry over 1,000 passengers but only 266 were aboard. Second, God was comforting the terrified passengers on those flights and giving them the ability to stay calm. Family members who talked to loved ones on the hijacked planes reported that they seemed amazingly calm. One family member recited the Lord's Prayer with her husband. Third, God put incredible courage into the hearts of many people on United Airlines Flight 93. They gave their lives in Pennsylvania for the sake of hundreds in Washington. Fourth, the World Trade Center held over 50,000 workers, but only around 20,000 were at the towers when the first jet hit. This was a miracle in itself. After the impacts, the buildings stood long enough for more than 15,000 of these workers to escape to safety. Fifth, God used this tragedy to bring a nation together in ways virtually unprecedented. Finally, this tragedy has led many people to see their need for God and turn to Christ for salvation.

Bad things still happen even to God's people, but God is good. Some day Christ will return, and evil will come to an end. The apostle Paul called

"The LORD is a jealous and avenging God" (Nah. 1:2).	"You shall not bow down to them [other gods] or worship them; for I, the LORD your God, am a jealous God, punishing the children for the sin of the fathers to the third and fourth generation of those who hate me" (Exod. 20:5).	"Do not worship any other god, for the LORD, whose name is Jealous, is a jealous God" (Exod. 34:14).
"The LORD takes vengeance on his foes and maintains his wrath against his enemies" (Nah. 1:2).	"When I sharpen my flashing sword and my hand grasps it in judgment, I will take vengeance on my adversaries and repay those who hate me" (Deut. 32:41).	"But those who hate him he will repay to their face by destruction; he will not be slow to repay to their face those who hate him" (Deut. 7:10).
"The LORD is slow to anger and great in power; the LORD will not leave the guilty unpunished" (Nah. 1:3).	"And he passed in front of Moses, proclaiming, 'The LORD, the LORD, the compassionate and gracious God, slow to anger, abounding in love and faithfulness, maintaining love to thousands, and forgiving wickedness, rebellion and sin. Yet he does not leave the guilty unpunished; he punishes the children and their children for the sin of the fathers to the third and fourth generation'" (Exod. 34:6–7).	"The LORD is slow to anger, abounding in love and forgiving sin and rebellion. Yet he does not leave the guilty unpunished; he punishes the children for the sin of the fathers to the third and fourth generation" (Num. 14:18).
"His way is in the whirlwind and the storm, and clouds are the dust of his feet" (Nah. 1:3).	"See, the storm of the LORD will burst out in wrath, a whirlwind swirling down on the heads of the wicked" (Jer. 23:19).	"See, the LORD is coming with fire, and his chariots are like a whirlwind; he will bring down his anger with fury, and his rebuke with flames of fire" (Isa. 66:15).
"He rebukes the sea and dries it up" (Nah. 1:4).	"Then Moses stretched out his hand over the sea, and all that night the LORD drove the sea back with a strong east wind and turned it into dry land. The waters were divided" (Exod. 14:21).	"Listen to the words of the LORD. . . . As soon as the priests who carry the ark of the LORD—the Lord of all the earth—set foot in the Jordan, its waters flowing downstream will be cut off and stand up in a heap" (Josh. 3:9,13).
"He rebukes the sea and dries it up; he makes all the rivers run dry. Bashan and Carmel wither and the blossoms of Lebanon fade" (Nah. 1:4).	"The land mourns and wastes away, Lebanon is ashamed and withers; Sharon is like the Arabah, and Bashan and Carmel drop their leaves" (Isa. 33:9).	"He said: 'The LORD roars from Zion and thunders from Jerusalem; the pastures of the shepherds dry up, and the top of Carmel withers'" (Amos 1:2).

Christ's return our "blessed hope—the glorious appearing of our great God and Savior, Jesus Christ" (Titus 2:13).

G. The One Who Brings Good News (1:15)

The "one who brings good news" in Nahum 1:15 is the messenger who arrived with the report of Nineveh's defeat. In Isaiah 21:9 we have a similar description of a messenger bringing news of an evil city's fall: "Look, here comes a man in a chariot with a team of horses. And he gives back the answer: 'Babylon has fallen, has fallen! All the images of its gods lie shattered on the ground!'" Babylon was the capital of the Babylonian Empire. Like Assyria before it, Babylonia was mighty. Like Assyria, the Babylonians oppressed the Jews, destroying Jerusalem and deporting tens of thousands of its citizens into exile in 586 B.C. And like Nineveh, Babylon fell at the Lord's command for its wickedness. These evil empires have fallen, and we can be sure it is only a matter of time before those of our day will topple as well.

Comparable language is also used to describe the fall of a future empire. This Babylon, symbolic of the evil world system in the last days, will oppress God's people on an unprecedented scale. In Revelation 14:8 an angel announced the good news of its fall: "A second angel followed and said, 'Fallen! Fallen is Babylon the Great, which made all the nations drink the maddening wine of her adulteries.'" Also in Revelation 18:1–2, we read: "After this I saw another angel with great authority coming down from heaven, and the earth was illuminated by his splendor. He cried in a mighty voice: 'It has fallen, Babylon the Great has fallen! She has become a dwelling for demons, a haunt for every unclean spirit, a haunt for every unclean bird, and a haunt for every unclean and despicable beast'" (HCSB).

Like believers in Nahum's day, the saints will celebrate the destruction of this future evil kingdom. "Rejoice over her, heaven: saints, apostles and prophets; because God has executed your judgment on her!" (Rev. 18:20 HCSB; see also 19:1–8).

Nahum's admonition also has parallels to that of Isaiah 52:7: "How beautiful on the mountains are the feet of those who bring good news, who proclaim peace, who bring good tidings, who proclaim salvation, who say to Zion, 'Your God reigns!'" In Romans 10:15 Paul quoted Isaiah to describe those who proclaim the gospel to a lost world.

H. Idolatry in Ancient Assyria (1:14)

Assyria's main gods were the king of their pantheon, Ashur, and the goddess of love and war, Ishtar. Other gods included Ninurta (warfare and hunting), Adad (storm god), Sin (moon god), and Shamash (sun god), and many other lesser deities. Each god had its own temples and priests that ministered to them. Assyrian kings, being superstitious, did not want to offend any deity, so they heavily subsidized the temples of each, primarily by looting other nations. Religion affected every area of Assyrian life. "Nearly every Assyrian royal annal describing military campaigns includes the statement 'by the command of Ashur' as the justification for war." In ancient times a war was not merely a contest of nations but of the gods of those nations. When a nation defeated another, it was believed its gods were superior to those of the defeated people. Consequently, gods of the vanquished were destroyed and their temples desecrated. Idols were "toppled over and disfigured, with heads and limbs cut off" (Walton, Matthews, and Chavalas, BBCOT, 789).

VII. TEACHING OUTLINE

A. INTRODUCTION

1. Lead Story: Life Without God

2. Context: In the first chapter of Nahum, the prophet identifies Nineveh as the subject of his prophecy. Nineveh was the leading city of Assyria, one of the most brutal and merciless empires in the annals of human history. The Assyrians have been called the Nazis of their day. Moreover, God's people had suffered mightily at the hands of the Assyrians. In 722–721 B.C. the Assyrians had destroyed the Northern Kingdom (Israel) and taken thousands of captives away to other lands. Foreigners were brought in, and they intermarried with the few Jews allowed to remain in the land. From this union came the mixed race known as the Samaritans of Jesus' day. The Southern Kingdom (Judah) did not escape Assyria's brutality. In 701 B.C. the Assyrian king Sennacherib invaded the Southern Kingdom, slaughtering thousands of Jews and taking many captives. Only the Lord's supernatural intervention preserved Jerusalem and Judah from annihilation (Isa. 36–37). Although the nation of Judah was not totally

destroyed by the Assyrians, gradually they came to be dominated by Assyria and suffered from their oppressive policies.

3. Transition: In this book, Nahum pronounces judgment upon a wicked empire. Assyria had harmed many nations, including God's people in Judah. Now the time had come for the Lord to deliver his people and give Nineveh its just recompense. Could the God of Israel really bring Nineveh to justice? Nahum answers this question by presenting a beautiful description of Israel's God at the very beginning of his prophecy (1:2–12a) and concludes with God's promise to deliver his people (1:12b–15). His is an omnipotent and invincible God. Nineveh would be no match for him. When God delivers his people, they will rejoice (1:13–15). Nahum reminds all the oppressed and mistreated that "there is a God in heaven" (Dan. 2:28) who cares. He is willing and able to deliver us.

B. COMMENTARY

1. Introducing the Prophecy of Our Great God (1:1)
2. A Just God (1:2–3a)
3. An Omnipotent God (1:3b–6)
4. A Good God (1:7–8)
5. An Invincible God (1:9–12a)
6. A Saving God (1:12b–15)

C. CONCLUSION: WILL THE REAL GOD PLEASE STAND UP!

VIII. ISSUES FOR DISCUSSION

1. Do we, as many people claim, all worship the same God? What characteristics distinguish the God of the Bible from the deities of other religions?
2. What are some false gods in today's world? How might you help adherents of other religions see the truth of Christianity?
3. How does knowing God make a difference in your life? What attitudes, actions, and habits do you have that show the world you truly know God?

4. Since God has all power, how do we explain suffering and injustice in our world? What has Christ done, and what will he do, to end the effects of sin?

5. What did Nahum mean by designating the Lord as "a jealous and avenging God"?

Nahum 2–3

The Fall of Evil Empires

I. INTRODUCTION
Death of a Tyrant

II. COMMENTARY
A verse-by-verse explanation of these chapters.

III. CONCLUSION
Is Judgment Christian?

An overview of the principles and applications from these chapters.

IV. LIFE APPLICATION
The Cure for Crime

Melding these chapters to life.

V. PRAYER
Tying these chapters to life with God.

VI. DEEPER DISCOVERIES
Historical, geographical, and grammatical enrichment of the commentary.

VII. TEACHING OUTLINE
Suggested step-by-step group study of these chapters.

VIII. ISSUES FOR DISCUSSION
Zeroing these chapters in on daily life.

Quote

"*Man* is unjust, but God is just; and finally justice triumphs."

H e n r y   W a d s w o r t h   L o n g f e l l o w

Nahum 2–3

 I N   A   N U T S H E L L

In chapters 2–3 Nahum predicts and describes in graphic detail the coming judgment of Nineveh. The prophet declares that Nineveh's fate is sealed because the holy, omnipotent Lord is against them. God will judge them for their sins, which include enslaving nations and the practice of witchcraft. No amount of preparation can save them from their doom. The nations have felt the sting of Nineveh's cruelty and will rejoice at the news of the city's fall.

The Fall of Evil Empires

I. INTRODUCTION

Death of a Tyrant

*N*icolae Ceausescu became secretary-general of Romania's Communist Party in 1965. In 1967 he was elected president of the state council and then president of the republic in 1974. His regime was the most brutally repressive in the old Soviet Union. Countless numbers of innocent victims suffered under his rule. He was particularly harsh with Christians. In the 1970s, he accepted ten thousand Bibles from the West in a ploy to acquire most-favored-nation status from the U.S. Congress. Rather than permitting the Bibles to be distributed to his people, he sent them to a paper mill where they were turned into toilet tissue.

By 1989 the tide of democracy had swept through other Communist countries. Russia's Communist government was falling, yet Ceausescu remained firm. His security forces became more vigilant. Most Romanians were afraid to stand up to the regime, and those who did paid a heavy price.

Far away from Bucharest in the remote city of Timisoara lived the pastor of a tiny church. His name was Laszlo Tokes. Laszlo's father had also been a minister but was stripped of his church position for speaking out against Ceausescu's government. Like his father, Laszlo had been in trouble for his outspoken rhetoric and had been demoted from pastor to assistant pastor for it. He was sent to distant Timisoara with the warning to keep quiet. But six months after his arrival, the old pastor died and Laszlo inherited his post. He began to teach the Bible and speak out against Ceausescu's reign of terror once more.

As the congregation swelled from a few dozen worshipers to more than two thousand, Laszlo began to draw national and even international attention. Radio Free Europe, the Voice of America, and the BBC began broadcasting news of the pastor's defiance back into Romania. Concerned authorities decided to reassign Laszlo to an even more remote village that was accessible only over rutted wagon tracks. Surely in that desolate place his voice would not be heard. But Laszlo defied the authorities and refused to go. On July 24 a clandestine interview with Laszlo was aired on Hungarian television, viewable in the western half of Romania. Millions of Romanians saw the program.

Now Laszlo knew it would be either death or a miracle. Police squads crowded the entrance of his church, and police posted round-the-clock guards outside the church building. The deadline for Laszlo's forced departure from Timisoara was set for December 15. Yet support for the pastor continued to grow across the country. On December 15, several hundred members of his congregation gathered outside the pastor's apartment. They formed a human chain around the church and refused to leave. On December 16 other Romanians joined the parishioners. By nightfall the crowd had surged to more than five thousand people linking hands around the church building.

The greatly outnumbered police were unable to disperse the crowd. Suddenly, someone began to shout, "Down with dictatorship! Down with Ceausescu!" Things began to get out of hand. Finally, reinforcements arrived, and the police forced the crowd to move. Laszlo and his wife were arrested as he stood by the church altar, holding his Bible in his hands. The couple was forcibly driven to Mineu, and their home was surrounded by police.

Though the pastor had been taken away, the demonstrations in Timisoara did not stop. Hundreds of thousands of Romanian citizens joined the rebellion. Tanks and armored personnel carriers were called in against the defenseless citizens. Seventy-three people were killed, and many others were wounded. Finally, the killing stopped when the army refused to fire on the crowds any longer.

Yet Timisoara was only the beginning. A wave of unrest was spreading across the country. On the morning of December 21, 1989, Ceausescu appeared on the balcony of the Communist Party building in Bucharest to try to calm the situation. Over one hundred thousand Romanians gathered before him. As he was speaking, suddenly somewhere from the back of the crowd rose the cry, "Timisoara!" Someone else shouted, "Murderer!" Within hours Bucharest exploded into chaos. Uncontrollable demonstrations broke out all over the capital. When the army joined the crowds, Ceausescu knew the end had come. Four days later, on Christmas day, Ceausescu and his evil wife, Elena, were tried and executed for crimes against the Romanian people.

Far away in Mineu, Pastor Laszlo Tokes looked out his window. His jailers had vanished. A dictator and his evil empire had fallen. They were free!

Dictators like Ceausescu are not a new phenomenon. Tyrants and their evil empires have existed throughout history. Nahum the prophet lived under just such a regime. The great Assyrian Empire, one of the cruelest in history, controlled Judah.

In chapters 2–3, Nahum pronounced judgment upon Nineveh, Assyria's leading city, in graphic terms. Assyria had caused untold suffering for Judah and the world of that day. God had not been asleep, and the time had come for judgment to fall. Finally, justice would be carried out.

Nahum's message was also one of hope and deliverance for the nations and for God's people specifically. The Northern Kingdom (ten northern tribes) had been totally annihilated by Assyria. Over fifty thousand captives had been dragged away from their homes to other lands. Judah (the two tribes in the south) survived but had lived under the thumb of Assyria for one hundred years. Now God promised that soon their oppressor would be destroyed. This was cause for rejoicing. Just as Romania was finally freed from their evil leader, soon Judah would be free from Assyria's tyranny.

II. COMMENTARY

The Fall of Evil Empires

> **MAIN IDEA:** *Nations and empires built on wickedness and oppression will fall, and God's people will be delivered.*

A God's Love and Nineveh's Fall (2:1–2)

> **SUPPORTING IDEA:** *Because God loves his people, he will send an "attacker" against Nineveh, their oppressor.*

Nineveh will fall because the Lord is a jealous God (1:2). He loves his people and jealously watches over them. In order to free his people, Assyria's power had to be broken. Therefore, God would send an army against Nineveh to this end. Nahum's message was delivered in Jerusalem, not Nineveh. Though it is possible that the prophet's warning made its way to Nineveh, the primary audience consisted of the poor and oppressed in Judah who suffered under Assyrian domination. They would have been heartened by news of the fall of their tormentors.

2:1. For more than one hundred years, Assyria had waged hostile campaigns against other nations. Now the tables had turned, and God announced plans to send an **attacker** against them. *Attacker* is literally "one who scatters or shatters," a common figure for a victorious king (Ps. 68:1; Isa. 24:1; Jer. 52:8). Divine judgment is not merely an abstract principle but manifests itself in reality, and the means of carrying out the threats of chapter 1 are now explained. A military coalition of the Babylonians and Medes was the advancing foe.

In 614 B.C. Cyaxerxes, king of the Medes, had waged war against Nineveh but was able to subdue only a portion of its suburbs. A Babylonian-Median alliance finally defeated Nineveh in April/May 612 B.C. Nahum mockingly challenged Nineveh to do all it could to prepare for war such as guarding **the fortress** and watching **the road**. The phrase translated **brace yourselves** means literally "to gird the loins," a practice of tying the robe up around the waist in order to run or in this case to fight. Assyrian kings had prepared well for a siege. Sennacherib had spent six years building an armory that occupied forty acres in the city, and Esarhaddon expanded it. The armory contained weapons necessary for the protection and extension of the Assyrian empire: chariots, horses, armor, bows, arrows, quivers, and equipment. Easy movement of Assyrian troops was assured on the royal road, enlarged by Sennacherib to a width of seventy-eight feet. In spite of all these material resources, the Assyrian Empire sank into oblivion because the God of Israel was against them.

In verse 1 we observe the military language that anticipates the more detailed description of the battle to follow and Nahum's use of imperatives to emphasize the need for urgency.

2:2. The Lord made a comforting promise to the people of Judah. In stark contrast to the bleak future of Nineveh, the prospects for Judah were bright. God promised to **restore the splendor of Jacob**. That was good news. Politically, economically, and militarily, Judah could not even be considered a second-class nation in Nahum's day. The glory days of David and Solomon were long gone. Yet with Nineveh's fall, Assyrian domination would end and renewed prosperity would ensue. **Jacob** and **Israel** (usually synonymous; Gen. 32:28; 1 Kgs. 18:31; 2 Kgs. 17:34; Hos. 12:12) both refer to God's people as a whole. The two names are used for emphasis. Often the nation of Israel is represented by the figure of a vine in Scripture (Gen. 49:22; Isa. 5:1–7).

𝔹 Description of Nineveh's Fall (2:3–10)

SUPPORTING IDEA: *Nahum describes the defeat and plunder of Nineveh in graphic language.*

2:3–4. Now the predicted onslaught against Nineveh (1:14–15; 2:1) is described in all its frightening detail. Ancient Nineveh encompassed an area of about 1,800 acres with an estimated population of up to 300,000 people. Yet the invaders were at the gates of the proud city and soon would be wreaking havoc within its walls. Median soldiers carried red **shields** and wore scarlet uniforms. As **chariots storm through the streets** plowing through ranks of soldiers or civilians, their **metal** fittings or ornamentation flashed like **flaming torches**. They raced around the city as fast as **lightning**.

2:5. Nahum may mean that the king of Assyria (Sin-Shar-Ishkun, ruler at the time of Nineveh's fall) called up his elite forces to defend the city, yet they **stumble** from weakness; they rushed to the **city wall** to protect it, but to no avail. However, most commentators understand the verse to describe the invading Medes and Babylonians as they rushed the city wall. In this case, the **protective shield** (literally, "covering"; Exod. 25:20; Ezek. 28:14,16) seems to be a technical term denoting the besiegers' defensive equipment. Apparently, the corpses of the enemy would be so numerous that the invaders would stumble over them as they advanced (Nah. 3:3).

2:6. This brief verse (only five Hebrew words) marks a turning point in the battle. Now the enemy has entered the city and even reached the royal palace. The Tigris River flowed near Nineveh's walls, and two of its tributaries, the Khosr and the Tebiltu, passed through the city itself. The **river gates** controlled the flow of the rivers into the city. Mention of these sluice gates may indicate the rivers were at flood stage and had damaged a portion of the wall, permitting easier access into the city. It is also possible that the enemy may have deliberately opened the gates in order to flood the city. The Assyrians, themselves, had flooded other cities in order to destroy them.

Nineveh's principal palaces at this time included Sennacherib's residence, the alleged "palace with no equal." Beautifully decorated with cedar and cypress wood, bronze lions, colossal bulls of white marble, and many sculptured reliefs, the palace's main hall measured approximately 40 feet by 150 feet.

2:7. Assyria had taken the inhabitants of countless cities into exile. Now God had **decreed** that it was their turn. The KJV understood the Hebrew word translated *decreed* to be a proper noun, "Huzzab," evidently a queen attended by her maids. No queen by this name is found in historical records, and the majority of modern translations render the term as "decreed" or "fixed."

Tiglath-Pileser III (744–727 B.C.) instituted a policy of mass deportations to reduce local nationalistic feelings. Conquered people were carried into exile to live in lands vacated by other conquered exiles. In 721 B.C. Assyria took the citizens of Samaria (capital of the Northern Kingdom) into exile. Captives from other lands were brought in to intermingle with the Israelites who remained. Some of these people intermarried and produced the mixed race called the Samaritans, prominent in the New Testament period. **Slave** girls wailed **and beat upon their breasts** as signs of distress, realizing they were to be taken into exile. The cooing of **doves** made a sound similar to moaning. Mourning slave girls (cp. Ezek. 7:16) is a common figure in Ancient Near Eastern literature and appears on Assyrian wall carvings depicting the anguish of their captives.

2:8. Nineveh's defenses are compared to either irrigation water **draining** from a **pool** (useless) or **water** gushing through the breaches in a dam (troops deserting their posts). The latter is the idea in the second half of the verse. Rather than heed the order to **stop**, the frightened soldiers ran for their lives, afraid even to look back lest they be overtaken by the invaders.

2:9–10. Nineveh's wealth from its looting of the nations was incalculable. Assyrian kings boasted of the plunder taken in war, and nations that submitted were drained of their wealth by the exaction of heavy tribute (tax). During the seventh century, Nineveh had become the richest city in the Ancient Near East. Now the nations would **plunder** it of its **silver**, **gold**, and accumulated **wealth**. As the Median and Babylonian soldiers ravaged the city, its citizens were terrified. Four expressions capture the horror of the situation—**hearts melt, knees give way, bodies tremble, every face grows pale.**

ⓒ Reasons for Nineveh's Fall (2:11–3:4)

SUPPORTING IDEA: *Nineveh will fall because their great sinfulness has turned the omnipotent God of Israel against them.*

2:11–12. Nineveh is compared to a ferocious lion that had slaughtered its victims and filled its lair with its **prey.** Assyria had attacked its innocent victims without **fear** like a roving pride of lions. Who could challenge them? Now they would experience the terror they had inflicted on many others. The lion metaphor is appropriate as a designation for Nineveh, since its kings often compared their awesome power to that of lions (e.g., Sennacherib) and engaged in lion hunts. Lions were kept in its game parks and were frequently depicted in Assyrian reliefs and decorations. Statues of winged lions adorned Assyrian palaces. Assyria had been represented in the Old Testament as a lion by Isaiah (Isa. 5:29–30) and Jeremiah (Jer. 50:17). Nahum mockingly asked, **Where now is the lions' den . . . ?**, an allusion to the fact that their capital, Nineveh, had been destroyed.

2:13. In this verse we encounter one of the most terrifying phrases in the Bible. **I am against you** is found at least ten times in Ezekiel (5:8; 13:8; 21:3; 26:3; 28:22; 29:3,10; 35:3; 38:3; 39:1) as well as in Jeremiah (50:31; 51:25) and later in Nahum (3:5). Human foes may be overcome, but when God turns against a nation, there is no escape. The NIV omits the introductory word *behold*, so common in the Old Testament, but this interjection is in the Hebrew text and calls special attention to God's threat. Three times in this verse, the pronoun "I" is used to highlight the personal involvement of the LORD **Almighty.** Assyria's vast array of **chariots** would be burned, her soldiers (**young lions**) killed, and her wealth (**prey**) plundered. **Messengers,** like the field commander of the arrogant Sennacherib (2 Kgs. 18:17–25), would no longer be sent to demand capitulation, extort tribute, or blaspheme the Lord (2 Kgs. 19:22; Isa. 37:4,6).

3:1. **Woe** is a translation of Hebrew *hoy,* which appears fifty-one times in the Old Testament. In the NIV it is rendered as "woe" (thirty-six times), "alas" (five times), "come" (four times), "ah" (three times), "oh" (two times), and "awful" (one time). Fifty of its occurrences are in the prophets. Six times it denotes mourning for the dead (e.g., 1 Kgs. 13:30); forty times it entails negative warnings or threats of God's punishment (Isa. 5:8–24; 10:1–3; Mic. 2:1–4; Amos 5:18–20; Hab. 2:9–19), as in this verse (only use in Nahum). Nineveh was indeed a **city of blood.** Its atrocities are proverbial (see "Deeper Discoveries"). They had shed this blood in their merciless (and gleeful) massacre of foreign peoples, their **victims** (literally, "prey," 2:12). **Full of lies** probably means "deception." Sennacherib's offer of courteous treatment to the besieged citizens of Jerusalem if they surrendered (2 Kgs. 18:31) was disingenuous in light of his actions at Lachish, a Jewish fortress defeated in the same campaign (2 Kgs. 18:14,17; 19:8). Nineveh was filled with **plunder** from its looting of other nations (2:9).

3:2–3. Nahum returned to his vivid portrayal of the coming battle of Nineveh (2:3–10). These two verses are inserted between verses 1 and 4, both of which describe Assyria's wickedness. Apparently, the prophet sandwiched this gory scene here for effect and as a warning about the wages of sin. Verse 2 depicts the charioteers as they furiously plowed through the Ninevites (2:3–4) and verse 3 the **charging cavalry** slashing the enemy with **swords** and brandishing **spears.** Four different terms are used to emphasize the enormity of the carnage in verse 3. **Corpses** of fallen Ninevites would be piled so high the invaders would stumble over them (2:5). Reading Nahum's graphic description, one can almost hear the sounds of battle. In Babylonian historical documents, we find a reference to the barbaric manner in which residents in a suburb of Nineveh were slaughtered.

3:4. A further explanation of the sins that will bring Nineveh's downfall is now given. Three times in this verse Nineveh's harlotry is emphasized—**harlot, prostitution,** and **wanton lust** (also from the same root, meaning "to commit fornication" or "play the harlot"). The harlot is an apt image of Nineveh's wickedness for several reasons.

First, Assyria had an insatiable lust for power and wealth that caused it to murder for hire and launch campaigns against innocent nations.

Second, like a prostitute enticing a client, Nineveh lured nations into unholy alliances by promising aid and then attempted to enslave them (Ahaz's alliance with Assyria, 2 Kgs. 16:7–18).

Third, Nineveh's commercial and military success attracted nations to adopt its idols and occult practices (spiritual adultery, Jer. 3:6,9; Hos. 1:2). While in Damascus meeting with the Assyrian king, Tiglath-Pileser III, Ahaz was impressed with a pagan altar (more likely Assyrian rather than Aramean) and ordered a copy constructed in the temple precincts at Jerusalem (2 Kgs. 16:1–14). Evidently, Ahaz felt if such a great king worshiped this god, he would worship it as well. Assyria committed spiritual adultery by worshiping gods like Asshur and goddesses like Ishtar in place of the Lord. Yet they seemed to go beyond that. **Sorceries** and **witchcraft** (same Hebrew word in both instances) could be symbolic of seductive and corrupting influences but likely indicate Nineveh's involvement in the occult. Certainly, Nineveh practiced sorcery and witchcraft, as did Babylon (Dan. 2:2). In some manner, the Assyrians may have used these methods in an attempt to control nations.

Ⅾ The Disgrace of Nineveh's Fall (3:5–7)

SUPPORTING IDEA: *Sin will bring shame and disgrace to Nineveh.*

3:5–7. The Lord repeated the ominous refrain of 2:13: **I am against you.** Nineveh had been described as a seductive harlot in the previous verses, and now she will receive a punishment fitting a prostitute. Like a prostitute (Ezek. 16:35–39; Hos. 2:3), Nineveh's **nakedness** would be exposed to the **nations** she had oppressed. This penalty was doubly appropriate since the Assyrians literally stripped the vanquished and forced them to march into captivity naked. Prostitutes in ancient times were also publicly shamed, and all kinds of **filth** were thrown at them. Both in ancient and modern times, a nation's defeat is a terrible disgrace. Those who saw this once-attractive harlot would flee in disgust and shock. Nineveh would be totally disgraced before the nations and exposed for the wretch that it was. When the city lay **in ruins**, no one would **mourn** or **comfort** her. Rather, the world's people would rejoice that Nineveh's cruelties against them had ended (3:19).

⊞ The Certainty of Nineveh's Fall (3:8–18)

SUPPORTING IDEA: *Just as certainly as the Lord has brought evil cities of the past to justice, Nineveh will fall in spite of its resistance.*

3:8. Some people might question Nahum's bold prediction that mighty Nineveh would fall. The city seemed invincible. Yet Nahum proclaimed that Nineveh's fall was certain. Other seemingly impregnable cities had fallen, and Nineveh would be no different. Nahum singled out the once-great city of **Thebes**, the magnificent capital city of Upper Egypt, as an example. The Hebrew-rendered Thebes is *No Amon*, meaning literally "city of Amon." Amon (or Amun) was the sun god, chief of the Egyptian gods at the time. It was named Thebes by the Greeks, who knew it also as Diospolis ("heavenly city").

The famous temples of Karnak and Luxor, the avenue of sphinxes, and numerous other lasting monuments were erected in and around Thebes. Famous Egyptian monarchs like Rameses II, Thutmosis III, and Tutankhamun ("King Tut") were buried in the tombs located in its Valley of the Kings. Most of these tombs contained rooms with carved and painted scenes and hieroglyphic texts. Tutankhamun's tomb, discovered in 1922, contained more than five thousand items buried with the young king. Except for Queen Hatshepsut, royal wives were buried to the south in the Valley of the Queens.

Thebes is mentioned four other times in the Old Testament (Jer. 46:25; Ezek. 30:14–16). Ancient Thebes was located about 450 miles south of present-day Cairo. Like Nineveh, Thebes was situated on a river (the **Nile**) and surrounded by **water**, an excellent defensive posture.

3:9. Cush, which included most of modern Sudan and northern Ethiopia, controlled **Egypt** at the time of the destruction of Thebes. **Put** (south of Egypt, probably Somalia) and **Libya** (west) were **allies** and provided added security for Thebes.

3:10. Thebes had everything in its favor, yet in 663 B.C. it fell before the forces of the Assyrian king, Ashurbanipal. The Assyrian soldiers were merciless. Helpless **infants** were slaughtered (Hos. 13:16; also see Ps. 137:9; Isa. 13:16,18; Hos. 10:14) at the most conspicuous places (**the head of every street**). They gambled for the prized slaves, the Thebian **nobles**, and **put in chains** the city's **great men**. The citizens were then marched off **into exile**. Such atrocities! Could there be any doubt that Nineveh must be destroyed?

3:11. If mighty Thebes could fall in such dramatic fashion, no hope remained for Nineveh. Nahum concluded by warning Nineveh that like Thebes it would become weak, like a **drunk**, and run in fear from the enemy.

Interestingly, the Greek historian Diodorus Siculus (about 90–21 B.C.) reports that the Assyrians were involved in a drunken orgy when the city was attacked (similar to Belshazzar's drunken party the night Babylon fell, Dan. 5:1–2,30–31). **You will go into hiding** may also be translated, "thou shalt be hid" (KJV) or "you will be hidden" (NKJV, NASB). Following the latter translation, some commentators have understood Nahum to be prophesying the disappearance of Nineveh from history.

Even the location of the ancient city was unknown until about 1850 when A. H. Layard positively identified an obscure ruin in the Iraqi desert (Quyundjiq) as the site of ancient Nineveh. Ashurbanipal (669–628 B.C.) had collected a library of twenty thousand tablets, containing literary epics, magical and omen collections, royal archives and letters. This important library was found in Nineveh's ruins in 1853.

3:12–13. Just as **ripe fruit** falls easily from a **shaken** tree, Nineveh's defenses would succumb quickly to the enemy. Assyrian soldiers, once ferocious as lions (2:11–12), would be overcome with fear in the face of their attackers and become weak as **women** (cp. Isa. 19:16; Jer. 50:37; 51:30). Fortresses would not stand against the onslaught. Enemy troops would **pour** through **gates** that are **wide open** (possibly opened by destructive floodwaters; see 2:6) and set **fire** to the city, including its gates with their locking **bars**. Archaeologists attest to the fact that Nineveh was burned by the enemy.

3:14–15. Nahum ironically challenged the Ninevites to prepare fully for the **siege**: (1) store up plenty of **water**, (2) reinforce **defenses**, and (3) bake enough **clay** bricks to **repair** breaches in the walls. Yet in the midst of their fortified city, **fire** and **sword** would sweep through and **consume** them like a horde of **grasshoppers** (probably a kind of "locust," NKJV, NASB, NRSV). Archaeologists have confirmed that fire was instrumental in the destruction of Nineveh's palaces. Greek tradition details that the king of Nineveh committed suicide by setting fire to his palace and dying in the flames. Nineveh had a large population for that day, about three hundred thousand; yet Nahum exhorted them to **multiply** even more, **like locusts**! Locusts have an unusual ability to reproduce, with swarms reaching into the millions or billions. Even if Nineveh's people were as numerous as the locusts, they would still be overcome because the Lord God had decreed it.

3:16. Nineveh's countless **merchants** navigated the Tigris River all the way to the sea where they did business with the Phoenicians. By their commercial activities, the land became rich. The latter part of the verse may mean either that the merchants would take their wares and flee the city or that the invading army would plunder the wealth accumulated by Nineveh's lucrative trade, probably the latter (2:9–10). Like **locusts** the invaders would **strip the land** bare and disappear (**fly away**).

3:17. Locusts serve as another point of comparison. Locusts are inactive when **cold**, but once the sun's heat warms their wings, **they fly away.** Like locusts, Nineveh's leadership would run for their lives, leaving the city to the Medes and Babylonians. Ancient sources report that Assyria's nobility did indeed take flight. Nahum displayed his marvelous literary artistry by the varied use of the locust figure: as a destructive invading army, the great number of Nineveh's citizens, and the flight of Nineveh's leaders.

3:18. The final verses of the book are similar to a dirge or funeral song for Assyria's demise. Nahum now addressed the **king of Assyria** directly. The battle is over, and the monarch is informed that Assyria's leaders and nobility are dead. Further resistance is pointless. In the previous verse Assyria's leaders were compared to locusts, now to **shepherds.** In the Old Testament, all kinds of leaders were designated shepherds (Num. 27:17; Isa. 44:28; Jer. 17:16; 23:1; Ezek. 34:2–23; 37:24; Zech. 10:2–3; 11:5). Assyrian kings also referred to themselves as shepherds. **Slumber** or sleep is a well-known figure for physical death in Scripture (Ps. 76:5; Isa. 26:19; Dan. 12:2; John 11:11–14). Without shepherds, the **people** scatter like sheep wandering aimlessly on the **mountains.** Refugees commonly seek out hiding places in mountainous regions that are more inaccessible for large armies. For two thousand years, Assyria had existed as a nation. At its height, it ruled a large portion of the Near East. Now it had totally disintegrated and lost its independent character.

F Joy over Nineveh's Fall (3:19)

SUPPORTING IDEA: *Judah and other nations oppressed by Nineveh's tyranny will rejoice at the fall of their oppressor.*

3:19. Assyria's **wound** was incurable, and her **injury** was **fatal.** In spite of the failed attempt by King Ashur-uballit (612–609 B.C.) to keep the dynasty alive in Haran, Assyria would pass from the stage of world history into the graveyard of nations. Like Humpty Dumpty, the nation could never be put together again, a fact confirmed by archeology. Yet there would be no mourning or sorrow over her demise. Assyria had inflicted **endless cruelty** on surrounding nations, and the world was glad to see her go. **Everyone who hears the news** of her destruction will rejoice (1:15).

MAIN IDEA REVIEW: *Nations and empires built on wickedness and oppression will fall, and God's people will be delivered.*

III. CONCLUSION

Is Judgment Christian?

Today there are many people who feel that judgment is somehow incompatible with the love of Christ. They contend, "The Old Testament prophets went too far! Why can't these prophets of doom be kind and loving like Jesus?" First, Nahum included messages of hope and comfort for God's people (1:7,12–13,15; 2:2; 3:19), as did the other prophets. Their messages are doom and gloom only for the wicked. Second, Jesus himself issued some of the most scathing pronouncements of judgment in the Bible (e.g., Matt. 23:33). Yet Jesus loved us enough to shed his blood and die in agony on the cross so we could go to heaven.

Moreover, the doctrines of God's love and his wrath are not incompatible. When terrorists took the lives of over three thousand innocent men, women, and children in their attacks on the Pentagon and the World Trade Center in New York City on September 11, 2001, many thoughtful Christians grappled with the tension between God's love and punishment of these criminals. Yet it is because God is loving and holy that he must punish evil. As a righteous judge, he cannot permit the wicked to go free. As a loving God, he must defend his people from nations and individuals who harm them. This involves judgment.

Both these truths are found in Nahum's prophecy. Nahum declared in no uncertain terms that God would severely punish evil Nineveh. On the other hand, God loves his people and will deliver them by removing their oppressor.

PRINCIPLES

- Though God is loving, he also judges sin.

- Because the Lord is just, he cannot allow the guilty to go unpunished. No empire or individual can resist or escape the judgment of our omnipotent God.

- The Lord loves his people and will deliver them from their oppressors.

- The fall of evil forces is a cause for joy among God's people.

APPLICATIONS

- Nations and individuals should not be deceived into thinking that their sin will go unpunished.
- God is merciful and is willing to forgive penitent nations and individuals, just as years earlier God had spared those in Nineveh who repented at Jonah's preaching.
- The only way to escape God's judgment is to repent of your sins and receive Jesus Christ as Lord and Savior.
- Persecuted Christians should rejoice to know that God has not forgotten them and that some day he will deliver them and judge their tormentors.
- Praise the Lord for that joyous, future time when Christ will appear and rid the earth of all oppression and sin.
- Pray for persecuted believers.

IV. LIFE APPLICATION

The Cure for Crime

What causes crime? Researchers have been debating this issue for years. Standard answers are: poverty, racism, social alienation, lenient judges, not enough prisons, poor parenting. Certainly all of these are contributing factors but not the root cause. For example, if poverty causes crime, why was the crime rate so low during the Depression, when over a quarter of the population had no income at all? Or why did crime rise in the affluent eighties and nineties? Charles Colson, the founder of Prison Fellowship Ministries, writes:

> Last year I met with the minister of internal affairs in the Soviet Union. He was surprisingly candid about his country's crime crisis— a 38 percent increase in a single year.
>
> The Soviet people, he told me, are being driven to crime by political and economic hardship. No, I told him, that's not it. Your problem is not economic or political, Mr. Minister; it is spiritual.
>
> You only need to read your own Russian writer Fyodor Dostoevsky, I told him. Dostoevsky wrote a brilliant novel called *The Brothers Karamazov*, a story about three brothers who debate the source of evil in the world. Finally one brother cries out, "If there is no God, then everything is permitted!"

That's your problem, I told the Soviet minister: seventy years of atheism. The Soviet state has pounded it into the people's heads that there is no God . . . and the people have concluded that therefore everything is permitted.

Without God, there is no restraint on our baser impulses.

Crime becomes inevitable.

Then I told the Soviet official about Prison Fellowship, and the way it brings the Word of God into the prisons. He looked across the table at me and he said, "Mr. Colson, you're right. That's what we need in the Soviet Union" (Colson, *A Dance with Deception*, Word Publishing, 1993, pp. 201–202).

Charles Colson *is* right. The only thing that will produce a civil society is a proper fear of God. People must understand what Nahum taught us long ago: there is a God who sees and judges sin. Some day everyone will give account to God for every word, deed, and thought. Thus we should be careful how we live.

Since there is a day of judgment, believers should be busy sharing the knowledge of God with others. We must tell our friends, coworkers, neighbors, and relatives that God loves them. Yet we must not fail to warn them that there is another side to God. If they do not turn from their sin, they will face God's wrath (John 3:36). Are you concerned about the fact that millions of people every year plunge into eternity without God? Do you have a desire to see people delivered from an eternity in hell? Then share Christ with them while there is still time.

V. PRAYER

O Lord, thank you that in America we are free to worship you as our conscience dictates. Remind us that there are many people throughout the world today who do not have that privilege. They are being oppressed and even put to death by those antagonistic to your Son, Jesus Christ. Help us not to forget to pray for these Christian brothers and sisters. Lord, deliver them from evil individuals and regimes as you delivered Nahum's people long ago. Thank you for the blessed hope of Jesus' coming again and the time when the meek "will inherit the earth." In the name of Christ we pray. Amen.

VI. DEEPER DISCOVERIES

A. Ancient Chariots (2:3–4)

Chariots were used widely in Mesopotamia before 3000 B.C. and were brought into Canaan and Egypt by the Hyksos about 1800–1600 B.C. A pair of horses pulled these two-wheeled vehicles that were made of various kinds of wood with fittings of leather and metal (bronze, iron). Functioning primarily as mobile firing platforms in battles, they were also used for hunting, for transportation of dignitaries, and in state and religious ceremonies. Egyptian chariots are the first to be mentioned in the Bible (Gen. 41:43; 46:29; 50:9), but the Philistines (Judg. 1:19; 4:3,13–17; 1 Sam. 13:5–7) and Israelites also possessed them (1 Kgs. 4:26; 9:15–19; 10:28–29). Assyrian records indicate that Ahab brought two thousand chariots into the Battle of Qarqar in 853 B.C. King Sennacherib of Assyria (2 Kgs. 18:13; 19:9,16,20,36) is depicted in his chariot.

B. The Palace of Nineveh (2:6)

Of Nineveh's principal palaces in the seventh century B.C., Sennacherib's residence (built between 703 and 691 B.C.), the so-called "palace with no equal" (now known as the Southwest Palace), is the most celebrated. Its huge complex of 71 interconnected rooms (including 2 large halls 180 feet long and 40 feet wide) and courts is estimated at 1,635 by 786 feet (an area large enough to fit 25 football fields). Massive white marble statues of winged bulls (some of which are now at the University of Chicago Oriental Museum) presented a menacing spectacle as one approached the throne room. Bronze lions, detailed reliefs of military battles, and carved limestone facades also decorated the area. Archaeologists began excavating this palace about 1850 and still have not uncovered it all.

C. "The LORD Almighty" (2:13)

"The LORD Almighty" is more literally, "the LORD of hosts." This divine name occurs over two hundred times in the Old Testament, often in a judgment context. Basically "hosts" refers to armies. It may signify any arrayed army (Judg. 4:2), the inhabitants of heaven (1 Kgs. 22:19), or the celestial bodies (Deut. 4:19). Apparently, the name designates the Lord as the captain of heaven's armies, who at his command stand ready to defend the righteous and destroy the wicked. Nineveh had no idea that their greatest foe was not the Medes and the Babylonians, but "the LORD of hosts." This same mighty God jealously watches over his people today, his angelic hosts always prepared to come to our aid.

D. The City of Blood (3:1)

Nahum described Nineveh as "the city of blood," and Assyrian atrocities have been abundantly confirmed by archaeological discoveries. In a bronze relief (a picture etched into metal or stone), Shalmaneser III (858–824 B.C.) displays a prisoner impaled on a stick with his hands and feet cut off. In another portion of the relief, three stakes are depicted, each with eight male heads, standing erect like human totem poles. Esarhaddon (680–669 B.C.) is depicted holding two captives with ropes attached to rings through their lower lips. Proud of his ghastly deeds, King Ashurbanipal (668–627 B.C.) had the following record of his atrocities forever etched in stone. Two Elamite prisoners are tied to the ground with ropes and stakes, while two Assyrians skin them alive, an unimaginably horrible way to die. Another scene shows an Assyrian carrying a head with a rope. In the same picture below, an Assyrian soldier holds the head of a prisoner while another tears out his tongue. A different Assyrian relief depicts the scribes of King Sennacherib (704–681 B.C.) matter-of-factly counting the heads of the enemy dead.

In 701 B.C. Sennacherib invaded Judah and, except for divine intervention, would certainly have captured Jerusalem (2 Kgs. 18:13–19:37). During the same campaign the Assyrian king besieged and defeated the Jewish fortress of Lachish (2 Kgs. 18:14,17; 19:8). So thrilled was Sennacherib at this victory that he had the battle inscribed on his palace wall (covering seventy linear feet) at Nineveh. In this relief Jewish soldiers are depicted fighting from the walls while the Assyrians move their war machines into position. Around the outside of the besieged city, captured Judahites are depicted impaled on stakes. Such cruelty, even against God's people! Is it any wonder that Nahum described Nineveh as "the city of blood"? How could God's judgment fail to be poured out on such evil?

E. The Destruction of Nineveh (3:7,18–19)

Under Sennacherib (704–681 B.C.) and his successors, Assyria rose to unrivaled prominence as a political power. In Sennacherib's time, Nineveh was enclosed by eight miles of walls with fifteen gates. Gardens and parks were watered by a thirty-mile-long aqueduct. Yet within eighty years the empire had spiraled downward until it totally disintegrated. The destruction of its capital city, Nineveh, was so complete that its very location was lost from memory until the middle of the nineteenth century. Herodotus, the Greek historian, in the fifth century B.C. spoke of the Tigris as "the river on which the town of Nineveh formerly stood."

Nineveh's demise came when the Babylonians and Medes joined forces and attacked the city in 612 B.C. Nahum 2:6 suggests that the opening of sluice gates contributed in some manner to its demise. According to the ancient Greek historian Diodorus, the river flooded and knocked down part of the wall of Nineveh, contributing to the city's defeat. Records from ancient Babylon mention that after a siege of three months the city fell and was turned "into ruin-hills and heaps of debris." Sinsharishkun, its king, perished. Lucian (about A.D. 120–180), a Greek writer, declared: "Nineveh has perished, and there is no trace left where it once was."

A. H. Layard, one of Nineveh's excavators, remarked:

> We have been fortunate enough to acquire the most convincing and lasting evidence of that magnificence, and power, which made Nineveh the wonder of the ancient world, and her fall the theme of the prophets, as the most signal instance of divine vengeance. Without the evidence that these monuments afford, we might also have doubted that the great Nineveh ever existed, so completely has she become "a desolation and a waste" (Maier, 135–136).

Nineveh was destroyed, just as Nahum had predicted. God's Word never fails!

F. Sleep as a Figure for Death (3:18)

"Slumber" or sleep is a figure of speech used frequently in the Bible to designate physical death (Ps. 76:5; Isa. 26:19; Dan. 12:2; John 11:11–14; Acts 7:60; 1 Cor. 15:51; 1 Thess. 4:13). These passages lend no support to the theories of some groups that persons who die are annihilated or experience "soul sleep." Scripture is clear that when the spirit of a believer leaves the body, it goes directly into the presence of the Lord (2 Cor. 5:8; Phil. 1:21–23). Likewise, when the spirit of an unbeliever departs, it goes immediately to a place of conscious torment (Luke 16:22–31). Thus, this sleep refers exclusively to the body's inactivity at death. What a blessing to know that immediately upon our exodus from this world, we will open our eyes in a better world. Best of all, we will see our Lord and Savior Jesus Christ in all his glory.

G. Rejoicing over Nineveh's Fall (3:19)

When Nineveh was destroyed, the world rejoiced. This may sound harsh, but the celebration was not mean-spirited vindictiveness but a fitting response to the fall of a tyrant. When Adolph Hitler and the evil Nazi Third Reich fell at the end of World War II, America and the world celebrated. We have all seen the pictures of people celebrating in New York's Time Square when news was heralded that the war was over. Our nation rejoiced because an empire that had murdered and oppressed millions of innocent people had ended. For the same reason the world rejoiced in 612 B.C. when news reached them of Nineveh's fall.

VII. TEACHING OUTLINE

A. INTRODUCTION

1. Lead Story: Death of a Tyrant
2. Context: In chapters 2–3 Nahum describes in vivid terms the destruction of Nineveh which took place at the hands of the Babylonians and the Medes in 612 B.C. The prophet explains the reasons for Nineveh's destruction. God's people had suffered under Assyrian oppression, and their tormentor had to be eliminated to release them from bondage. God declared that he was against Nineveh and would judge the nation of Assyria because of its extreme sinfulness. The fall of this proud empire would be disgraceful and certain, with no one to save them. When Nineveh fell, all those who had been oppressed by Assyria for so many years would rejoice.
3. Transition: As we look at chapters 2–3, we see Nahum setting forth the spiritual law that evil individuals and empires must fall. God's reputation as a just God and the defender of his people depends on it. Assyria had harmed many nations, including God's people in Judah. Now the time had come for the Lord to deliver them and give Nineveh its just recompense. Though evil empires may flourish temporarily, Nahum assures us that our God is not asleep. There will be a payday for the wicked. The effects of sin are graphically portrayed

in Nahum's description of Nineveh's fall. Yet Nahum's prophecy is not negative, but a positive message of hope for all who suffer under the tyranny of their "Nineveh."

B. COMMENTARY

1. God's Love and Nineveh's Fall (2:1–2)
2. Description of Nineveh's Fall (2:3–10)
3. Reasons for Nineveh's Fall (2:11–3:4)
4. The Disgrace of Nineveh's Fall (3:5–7)
5. The Certainty of Nineveh's Fall (3:8–18)
6. Joy over Nineveh's Fall (3:19)

C. CONCLUSION: IS JUDGMENT CHRISTIAN?

VIII. ISSUES FOR DISCUSSION

1. How do you reconcile the fact that God is love and yet judges sin?
2. What are some reasons why God judges sin?
3. What is the danger of denying the biblical teaching of divine judgment?
4. Do you think that most unbelievers feel that God will punish them for their sin? How can you warn the lost of their condition without being offensive?
5. How can we help believers who live in areas of the world where they are persecuted for their faith by an evil regime?

Habakkuk 1–2

Life's Mysteries

I. INTRODUCTION
The Question of Why?

II. COMMENTARY
A verse-by-verse explanation of these chapters.

III. CONCLUSION
Life's Little Mysteries

An overview of the principles and applications from these chapters.

IV. LIFE APPLICATION
If God Exists, Why Is There Evil?

Melding these chapters to life.

V. PRAYER
Tying these chapters to life with God.

VI. DEEPER DISCOVERIES
Historical, geographical, and grammatical enrichment of the commentary.

VII. TEACHING OUTLINE
Suggested step-by-step group study of these chapters.

VIII. ISSUES FOR DISCUSSION
Zeroing these chapters in on daily life.

| Quote |

"*A* genuine faith resolves the mystery of life

by the mystery of God."

R e i n h o l d   N i e b u h r

PROPHECY PROFILE

- Like many of the minor prophets, Habakkuk is brief, consisting of only three chapters and fifty-six verses.
- The book consists of two units: chapters 1–2 and chapter 3. Each unit begins by ascribing the material to Habakkuk the prophet and is distinct in content.
- In chapters 1–2, Habakkuk grapples with two mysteries: (1) Why does God allow evil to go unpunished in Judah? (2) How could a righteous God use Babylon to judge sin in Judah since Babylon was far more wicked than Judah?
- In chapter 3, the prophecy concludes with a magnificent hymn of praise to the sovereign God. In spite of the difficult days ahead, Habakkuk would continue to praise the Lord, confident that God was just and good.
- Traditionally, the entire book has been ascribed to Habakkuk. A clear unity of subject matter, theme, vocabulary, and perspective supports this view.
- Habakkuk was written late in the seventh century B.C. Evidence for dating the prophecy is as follows: The prophet describes the Babylonians as being a formidable enemy (1:6–10). This would indicate that Nineveh had fallen (612 B.C.) and Babylon was now the world power. The book must have been written before Babylon's first invasion of Judah (605 B.C.) since this event is spoken of as future. However, the tone of the book indicates that Babylon's invasion is imminent. Therefore, the book was composed during the reign of Judah's evil King Jehoiakim, shortly before 605 B.C.

- The prophecy was a favorite of the people who penned the Dead Sea Scrolls.
- Habakkuk's declaration that "the righteous [or "just"] will live by his faith" (2:4) was a central element of the apostle Paul's theology (Rom. 1:17; Gal. 3:11) and later Protestant Reformers. Thus a so-called "minor" prophet had a major influence on later generations.

AUTHOR PROFILE: HABAKKUK THE PROPHET

- Habakkuk was a prophet of the late seventh century B.C., a contemporary of Jeremiah, Nahum, and Zephaniah.
- Habakkuk's name most likely signifies "embraced" or "embracer." Possibly the idea is that the prophet was "embraced" by the Lord as his child and messenger.
- Habakkuk was a unique prophet because he did not speak for God to the people but rather spoke to God about his people.
- The Book of Habakkuk reveals the prophet to be a courageous and deeply spiritual man. Otherwise, nothing of a personal nature is known about him. One later Jewish tradition makes him a priest of the tribe of Levi. The apocryphal work Bel and the Dragon (written approximately a century before Christ) tells about Habakkuk being taken to Babylon by an angel to feed Daniel while he was in the lions' den. This account is clearly fictional.
- Habakkuk uses dialogue as the primary method for presenting his material. He asks questions, and the Lord responds.

READER PROFILE: THE NATION OF JUDAH

- Habakkuk's message addressed conditions in his country, ancient Judah.
- By Habakkuk's day the Northern Kingdom (Israel) had fallen to Assyria (721 B.C.). Although the Southern Kingdom (Judah) survived, it remained a vassal state of the evil Assyrian Empire until the fall of Nineveh in 612 B.C. Egypt then dominated Judah until Babylon defeated Pharaoh Neco II at the Battle of Carchemish in 605 B.C. Babylon immediately moved to subdue Judah and the

surrounding area. Judah then became a vassal state of the Babylonian Empire.

- The nation of Judah consisted primarily of the tiny tribe of Benjamin and the much larger tribe of Judah.
- Habakkuk had witnessed Judah fall from a spiritual high point under King Josiah (640–609 B.C.) to the depths of wickedness under Josiah's son, King Jehoiakim (609–597 B.C.).

Habakkuk 1–2

 IN A NUTSHELL

In chapters 1–2 Habakkuk grapples with two mysteries: Why does God allow evil to go unpunished in Judah? and How could a righteous God use Babylon, a nation far more wicked, to judge Judah? God graciously gives the prophet insight about these mysteries. The section ends with a strong denunciation of sin in the form of five "woe" judgments.

Life's Mysteries

I. INTRODUCTION

The Question of Why?

*C*indy Lipscomb and June Bonnin had met only two years before, but they quickly became best friends. They shared a profound faith in Christ and had daughters about the same age. Cindy had three daughters: Rainey, 10, Lacey, 8, and Jesse Anne, 5. June had a daughter, Ashley, 8, and a granddaughter, Jessica, 12. They enjoyed being together. For spring break they decided to take a train trip to Chicago on Amtrak's famous City of New Orleans. They went to the top of Chicago's Sears Tower, visited the children's museum, and shopped. What stories the little girls would have to tell their school friends the next week!

On the return trip all seemed peaceful as the train quietly sped down the track on that cold March night in 1999. Cindy's family was assigned a sleeping car in the back of the train; June's family was in the front. The older girls wanted to have a slumber party together, so Rainey and Lacey kissed their mom goodnight and went off to be with the Bonnins in the front of the train. Less than an hour later, about fifty miles south of Chicago, the train slammed into a truck loaded with steel. The horrendous impact (heard miles away) derailed all but three of the railroad cars, leaving the cars strewn around the tracks like an accordion. One engine split in half. Flames engulfed the front cars.

Frantically, Cindy made her way toward her daughters. "I wanted to die when I saw the flames because I knew. It was either lay down and die or pray, and I just sat down and prayed," Cindy said. When it was all over, eleven people were dead, including Rainey, Lacey, June Bonnin, and June's granddaughter Jessica. Miraculously, Bonnin's eight-year-old daughter, Ashley, was able to crawl out of the wreckage, just as the door of the train (now turned over) came crashing down, severing her foot and lower leg.

When we hear of such tragic events, even the most devout can't help but wonder why. Of the two hundred people on the train, why did these sweet little girls and a godly mother perish? After all, they were committed Christians. Ironically, June Bonnin had just seemed to win a four-year battle with cancer. Why would she now die like this? Why couldn't they all providentially have been in the rear sleeping car rather than the front? Why couldn't the accident have been an hour earlier? Then at least Rainey and Lacey would have survived. Why didn't the trucker stop?

What good could possibly come from such a tragedy? Much is unclear, but some things are evident. Cindy, her husband Matt Lipscomb, and June Bonnin's husband Max gave a beautiful testimony for Christ throughout the ordeal as they were interviewed by the local and national media, including the national television networks. The funeral was broadcast live on Memphis television. Christ received great glory, and undoubtedly many people came to faith in Jesus through their testimony. Still, much remains a mystery.

Habakkuk came face-to-face with some of life's mysteries as well. In this little prophecy we will come to learn more about the ways of God and our attitude in every circumstance of life.

II. COMMENTARY

Life's Mysteries

MAIN IDEA: *Life is filled with mysteries, but we can trust our holy and just God to act fairly and faithfully.*

A The Prophetic Introduction (1:1)

SUPPORTING IDEA: *Habakkuk's prophecy is an important message from God that will help us better understand the mysteries of life.*

1:1. Prophetic books usually begin with an introductory verse or verses supplying the name of the writer and other pertinent details. The Book of Habakkuk provides only the most essential information. We are told that the prophecy is a message from God related by an otherwise unknown Old Testament **prophet** named **Habakkuk**. His historical setting is not indicated, though this may be determined from the book's contents.

Like Nahum and Malachi, Habakkuk designated his prophecy as an **oracle** ("burden," KJV). (For a discussion of the word *oracle*, see the "Commentary" discussion on Nahum 1:1 and the "Deeper Discoveries" section for Nahum 1.) **Received** is a translation of the Hebrew word *chazah*, which literally means "to see." The term may indicate seeing with the physical eyes, perceiving, or seeing prophetically—either a literal vision or a prophetic revelation. Here the latter is the idea. God opened Habakkuk's spiritual eyes to receive a divine message. Isaiah also "saw" (*chazah*) an "oracle" (Isa. 13:1). Sometimes prophets were even called God's "seers" (1 Sam. 9:9). Habakkuk was a spiritually perceptive person who was in tune with God. For this reason God chose him to receive a message to share with his countrymen.

Ⓑ Mystery 1: How Can God Permit Evil? (1:2–11)

SUPPORTING IDEA: *Habakkuk cannot understand how a holy God could permit wickedness in Judah, but God assures him that he will punish sin.*

1:2. The Book of Habakkuk begins in a unique way with a question for God. Habakkuk rather boldly asked God why he tolerates sin. Initially, we may be a little shocked, but God was not offended by Habakkuk's inquiry. Neither is God insulted when we come to him with our questions. As a matter of fact, God is probably offended when we go everywhere else looking for answers except to him. God may not always give us all the information that we would like to have, but he is never offended if we ask in a reverent spirit. Barker and Bailey comment, "The very fact that Habakkuk took his complaints to God can help believers to be honest in prayer, taking all our burdens to the Lord. Habakkuk's experience shows that God is willing to hear our needs and to help us deal with our problems" (Barker and Bailey, 293).

How long, a phrase that occurs sixty-five times in the Bible, often expresses anguish over God's perceived delay in bringing justice. David exclaimed:

> LORD, how long will You continually forget me? How long will You hide Your face from me? How long will I store up anxious concerns within me, agony in my mind every day? How long will my enemy dominate me? Consider me and answer, LORD, my God. Restore brightness to my eyes; otherwise, I will sleep in death (Ps. 13:1–3 HCSB; see also Pss. 6:3; 35:17; 79:5; 94:3).

Habakkuk was disturbed that God seemed to be oblivious to or unconcerned about the rampant evil in Judah. Apparently he had been pleading with God for **help**, but no help had come. It appeared that God was not even listening. Habakkuk began to feel that God did not care about what was happening. God's people were being mistreated, and the wicked were prospering. Where was the holy God who lit up Mount Sinai with fire when he gave the Ten Commandments? Why had God not come in and zapped the wicked with a bolt of lightning? Judah was overrun with crime. The Hebrew word rendered **violence** (*chamas*) may refer to injurious language or harsh treatment but is used specifically of physical violence. Godly people were being harmed by these thugs, and yet God had not intervened to **save** them.

1:3. In the previous verse Habakkuk asked "how long" this would go on. Here he asked God **why** it was happening. The prophet used six terms to describe the evils prevalent in Judean society—**injustice, wrong, destruction, violence, strife,** and **conflict.** The word *injustice* is a translation of a Hebrew noun meaning "trouble, sorrow, or wickedness." In Hebrew thought wickedness inevitably leads to trouble and hardship. Verse 4 makes clear that Judah's wickedness involved injustice. Righteous people were being mistreated by the powerful in court. The Hebrew word rendered "wrong" is also suggestive of suffering due to mistreatment. Evildoers were destroying the righteous and undermining Judean society. Kaiser points out:

> Five times in this brief book Habakkuk decries the overwhelming presence of violence (1:2,3,9; 2:8,17). Noah used the same word to describe the society in his day, which God found necessary to destroy with the flood (Gen. 6:11). The violence was the manifestation of the meaner, baser, and more selfish instincts of the haughty persons against the weaker elements of their culture (cp. Amos 3:10; Jer. 6:7) (Kaiser, *Mastering the Old Testament,* 153).

When society's values begin to break down, strife and conflict result. The Hebrew word translated strife may also suggest wide-scale legal action, since it was the normal word for a lawsuit.

1:4. The problems in Judah's court system were many. First, courts evidently were overwhelmed with the sheer number of lawsuits, as is the case in America today. Second, **the law is paralyzed** means that judges were not following Israel's law code in administering sentences. Third, judges were rendering unjust decisions, probably because they were being bribed by the wealthy. The **wicked** trapped the **righteous** by forcing them into court on trumped-up charges where unjust judges rendered decisions against them. Then the wealthy were able to take their property, possessions, and sometimes even receive the family as their slaves. Naboth was just such a recipient of this kind of injustice. He lost his property and his life when Jezebel instigated a kangaroo court in order to obtain his vineyard for her wicked husband, King Ahab (1 Kgs. 21:1–16).

Habakkuk likely penned his prophecy just after godly King Josiah's death in 609 B.C., in the reign of his wicked son, Jehoiakim. Judah had experienced one of its greatest spiritual awakenings only a dozen years before (621 B.C.)

during Josiah's reign (2 Kgs. 22:8–20). Now with Jehoiakim in charge, the wicked gained the upper hand, and the whole nation was in peril. How quickly things had changed! This illustrates the imperative of godly political leadership and the necessity of believers participating in the political process.

1:5. Habakkuk seemed to think that God had been asleep on the job, but God makes clear that he has seen all that has gone on and will intervene. As a matter of fact, God is going to act so decisively that Habakkuk and his countrymen (**you**, plural in the Hebrew) will be shocked. When the prophet learned God's intentions, he was stunned. His horror precipitated a second inquiry (1:12–17). Here we are reminded of a comforting fact—God is at work in our world. Sometimes it may appear as if the world is out of control, but our God is watching and working in many ways to bring about his purposes.

God told the prophet to open his eyes and look on the world scene. What was happening? Babylon was on the move. Nabopolassar had defeated Nineveh in 612 B.C. and had quickly solidified his empire. The Babylonian beast was hungry for prey and would soon be at the gates of Jerusalem. Habakkuk should have been able to discern this.

1:6. The Lord was **raising up the Babylonians** for his purpose. What was that purpose? Though not specifically stated here, it may be inferred from the following: Habakkuk pleaded with God to deal with wickedness in Judah. God responded by informing the prophet that the Babylonians were coming to wreak havoc on the nations. That Habakkuk understood the point—God would use Babylon to punish wickedness in Judah—is evidenced by his next inquiry (1:12–17). Moreover, in verse 12 Habakkuk acknowledged that God had ordained Babylon to "execute judgment" and "to punish." The Hebrew word rendered "Babylonians" is *kasdim* and is more literally "Chaldeans" (KJV, NKJV, NASB, NRSV). Strictly speaking, the Chaldeans were an ethnic group who succeeded in dominating Babylonia, but the term came to represent the Babylonians generally, as here.

What was this nation like that God was going to use to punish Judah? Babylon was incredibly evil, even worse than the wicked people in Judah that Habakkuk had been complaining about. In verses 6–11, God himself described the Babylonians in the harshest terms. They were **ruthless** (literally, "bitter"). An example was their treatment of the Judean king, Zedekiah. Nebuchadnezzar killed all of Zedekiah's sons before him and then gouged out his eyes (2 Kgs. 25:7). The last thing Zedekiah saw was his children massacred! The Babylonians were **impetuous**, in a hurry, apparently referring to their sudden and swift conquests of other nations. They waged offensive wars because of their greed for other lands.

1:7. The Babylonians were **feared and dreaded** by the world's peoples. Who wouldn't fear a **people** as cruel as these? They were lawless, doing as they pleased.

1:8–11. Babylon had an irresistible military force. Nebuchadnezzar was a military genius with a well-equipped and highly motivated army. Of course, soldiers in that day were inspired to fight well by the fact that they were paid from the booty taken from conquered cities—no conquests, no pay. Habakkuk was an artist with words, and he described Babylon's forces in very picturesque terms—**swifter than leopards, fiercer than wolves, fly like a vulture, like a desert wind, gather prisoners like sand, sweep past like the wind.** These figures emphasize the ferocity, swiftness, cruelty, and fearlessness of Babylon's army.

The phrase **come bent on violence** is ironic. In Judah the wicked had committed violence against their fellow Jews (1:2–3). Now they would reap what they had sown, because Babylon would heap violence on them. God had warned his people centuries before that if they turned away from his law, he would send an enemy nation to judge them. "The LORD will bring a nation against you from far away, from the ends of the earth, like an eagle swooping down, a nation whose language you will not understand" (Deut. 28:49). Wright comments:

> The Babylonians were God's instrument to punish Judah, much like Cyrus, the pagan king of Persia, would be God's instrument to bring Judah back to their homeland (cp. Isa. 45:1). Although used by God, the Babylonians made no pretext of recognizing His divine hand in world affairs (Wright, 71).

To the Babylonians, their power was **their god**, their supreme concern. Finally, God called the Babylonians **guilty men** who stood condemned in the eyes of the heavenly judge.

Ⓒ Mystery 2: How Can God Use a Pagan Nation to Punish Judah? (1:12–2:20)

SUPPORTING IDEA: *Habakkuk is puzzled about how a just God can use Babylon to judge Judah. Babylon is much more wicked. God explains that after using Babylon to judge Judah, he will then punish Babylon.*

What surprised Habakkuk was not the coming judgment, but the agent of that judgment. How could God be just and use a wicked nation like Babylon to punish Judah? Sure, Judah was bad. Habakkuk recognized that fact in his first complaint to God. However, they may have been bad, but they were not as bad as Babylon. God, you are not being fair! This dilemma leads to Habakkuk's second inquiry. How can God use evil Babylon to punish Judah?

1:12. The prophet based his second question on the character of God. God is eternally **holy.** How then could he use a wicked nation like Babylon **to execute judgment** on and **to punish** Judah? During the cold war Americans would have been just as appalled if someone had told them that God was planning to use the old Soviet Union or the Chinese Communists to judge the United States for its sins! **Holy One** is also found in 3:3 and is Isaiah's favorite characterization of Israel's God (thirty times). The pronoun **my** emphasizes Habakkuk's personal relationship with **God.** Habakkuk also addressed the LORD as his **Rock,** a figure for security and protection. This figure for God, so common in the Psalms (e.g., Pss. 18:2,31; 19:14; 28:1; 95:1), is found only here in the minor prophets.

Two points are relevant about the prophet's affirmation, **we will not die.** First, mighty Babylon could easily have annihilated tiny Judah, but Habakkuk was confident this would not happen because his omnipotent God would not allow it. Second, although the coming judgment was deserved, Habakkuk knew that God would keep his covenant promises to Israel that his people would never be totally destroyed.

1:13. Here is one of the great verses in the Bible on God's holiness. Not only does God hate sin; he is repulsed at the very sight of it: **your eyes are too pure to look on evil!** Habakkuk was perplexed. Since God hates sin so intensely, why did he **tolerate the treacherous,** and why was he seemingly **silent** when the **wicked** oppressed the **righteous?** This is a dilemma that persecuted and mistreated believers everywhere face. Habakkuk probably had in mind both the wicked in Judah and the Babylonians, but primarily the latter.

1:14–17. In these verses the prophet compared the oppressed to defenseless **fish** caught in the net of their **wicked foe,** who lived **in luxury** at their expense. Ironically, rather than giving glory to God for victory, the oppressor worshiped **his net.** That Habakkuk's primary focus was on Babylon is clear in verse 17 by his reference to **destroying nations without mercy** (cp. 1:6).

2:1. Habakkuk had cried out to God about this mystery of evil, and he knew God would answer. Like a sentinel perched high in his watchtower scanning the horizon for signs of an enemy army, the prophet stood ready with great anticipation to hear what God would say to him. Elsewhere in the prophets we encounter the figure of the watchman on the wall (Isa. 21:11–12; Ezek. 3:17; 33:2,6; Hos. 9:8).

2:2. God spoke to his waiting servant and told Habakkuk to **write down the revelation**. The word *revelation* is a translation of the Hebrew *chazon*, which means literally, "something seen." The term may refer to a visionary experience or as in this case to receiving (seeing) a prophetic revelation. **Tablets** were most likely made of baked clay which, once dried, preserved the writing. **Herald** is literally "the one calling out, proclaiming, or reading." Either the herald reads the message and then runs to share it or proclaims it as he is running. Some have taken **run** to represent the reader as living in obedience to the message, yet the former interpretation seems preferable. In summary, God's message was to be clearly recorded, preserved, and proclaimed to all.

2:3. Habakkuk was told to **wait** patiently. Though it may take a while, the following prophecy of Babylon's doom would **certainly** be fulfilled at the **appointed time**. The prophet had asked how God could use such a wicked nation to punish Judah. In the following verses God explained to the prophet that after he has used Babylon as his instrument of judgment on Judah and other nations, he will judge Babylon for its sins. God is just after all. The word **end** may refer not only to the termination of Babylon's savage rule, but to the eschatological end when God's victory over wickedness is complete.

2:4–5. In these verses God sets forth the wicked character of Babylon. They were filled with pride, inspired by evil **desires**, deceived by **wine**, **greedy**, and they assaulted innocent **peoples**. Like the **grave** and **death**, Babylon is **never satisfied** (cp. Prov. 27:20) with its conquest and looting of the nations.

In the midst of this horrid description of Babylon, we find one of the most important verses in the Bible. Theologically, the brief proclamation (only three words in the Hebrew text), **but the righteous will live by his faith**, cannot be overemphasized. It goes to the heart of God's method of salvation and of living the Christian life. Both are by faith. Initially, we receive eternal life by faith and then live daily by faith. In context Habakkuk's use of this affirmation contrasts the righteous and the wicked. The wicked trusted in their own might and would perish, while the righteous trusted in the true God and would live. Certainly, faith in God brings eternal life, but Habakkuk may also have been reassuring the faithful that God would spare their lives during the coming Babylonian invasion.

2:6–14. In verses 6–20 God pronounced five woe (Heb. *hoy*) judgments on the wicked. This section is not extraneous material, but it forms an integral part of God's answer to Habakkuk's questions, primarily the latter: "How can God use wicked Babylon to punish Judah?" In these verses God makes clear that when Babylon has served its purpose, it will also experience God's wrath. The message takes the form of a **taunt** spoken by the nations who suffered at the hands of the Babylonians. When Babylon falls, these nations will rejoice. Although Babylon is the primary target of these woes, all the wicked, whether in ancient Judah or in our modern world, are forewarned. Wright remarks: "These five woe oracles provide a look at the social injustices of Habakkuk's day. Each contained a reversal of fortunes, a common prophetic theme (Mic. 2:2–5; Nah. 3:8–15; cp. 1 Sam. 2:5–8; Matt. 19:30)" (Wright, 75).

The following are the five big sins that Habakkuk singled out for condemnation: greed (2:6–8), exploitation of others (2:9–11), crimes against humanity (2:12–14), drunkenness (2:15–17), and idolatry (2:18–20). Babylon greedily acquired wealth at the expense of innocent nations, built its kingdom **by unjust gain**, and the magnificent capital city of Babylon **with bloodshed** (cp. v. 17). After Babylon fell to the Medo-Persian Empire in 539 B.C., captive nations did **plunder** their captor.

Another of the Bible's special gems is found in verse 14. Attempts of the wicked to build their empires on greed and violence will not succeed because such endeavors are an affront to a holy God. **The nations exhaust themselves for nothing** because the LORD **Almighty** (traditionally, "LORD of hosts") whose law they have rejected and whose glory they have denied will win the war. Resistance is futile. Whether the wicked like it or not, **the earth will be filled with the knowledge of the glory of the LORD, as the waters cover the sea.** Now our world is filled with sin, crime, oppression, injustice, and tyrants, but some day the King will come and a new day will dawn. Then the light of the true God will shine across the globe, and Jesus Christ will receive the glory he deserves (Phil. 2:5–11).

2:15–17. In verse 15 drunkenness is connected with immorality (**that he can gaze on their naked bodies**), and they often go hand in hand. An example of Babylon's drunkenness and immorality is found in the account of Belshazzar's feast (Dan. 5). With the Medo-Persian armies camped outside Babylon's gates, Belshazzar arrogantly held a drunken orgy and blasphemed the God of Israel. That night Belshazzar was killed and the city fell, bringing to an end the great Babylonian Empire. For its **violence** and murder, Babylon would receive another kind of **cup** to **drink**. This cup would not be filled with wine but with the wrath of God (Jer. 25:15; Rev. 16:19).

2:18–20. Babylon was a center of idolatry. Marduk, Nabu, Sin, and Ishtar were some of the city's most prominent deities. Archaeologists have uncovered about fifty pagan temples in the ruins of the city. According to the Greek historian Herodotus, there was a gold statue of Marduk in Babylon (at least as early as the time of Cyrus) which stood eighteen feet high. Habakkuk poked fun at the absurdity of idolatry. An idol was merely a man-made **creation** of wood usually overlaid with **gold** or **silver**. The phrase **teaches lies** means that idols deceived and deluded their followers into believing they could save them. Idols could not **speak**, had no **life** in them, and could not **give guidance**.

False gods of today may not be made of wood, stone, silver, and gold, but they are just as worthless and just as useless to save. By contrast, Habakkuk worshiped a living God who rules the universe from his heavenly throne. Earth's inhabitants should bow their heads in reverential silence before him. Because our God lives, he can save from sin and deliver in time of need.

> **MAIN IDEA REVIEW:** *Life is filled with mysteries, but we can trust our holy and just God to act fairly and faithfully.*

III. CONCLUSION

Life's Little Mysteries

Life is filled with little everyday mysteries, according to Douglas B. Smith in an article in the *Reader's Digest*. For example, why does a bride always stand on the groom's left? Why are most pencils hexagonal? Why is an expensive but nonproductive possession called a "white elephant"? Most people have no idea. Brides began standing on the groom's left during the days when men sometimes captured women from neighboring villages. The groom wanted his sword hand free—the right one—during the wedding to fight off a possible attack by the bride's relatives or jealous suitors. Nine hexagonal pencils can be made from the same amount of wood as eight round ones. Thus pencils are hexagonal because they are cheaper to produce and also less likely to roll off a desk. If displeased with members of his court, the king of Siam purportedly gave them white elephants to ruin them. The animals were sacred and were not permitted to work but still had to be maintained.

Wouldn't it be wonderful if all of life's mysteries were as simple to solve as these? They are not. Habakkuk's prophecy makes clear that although we may not always understand what happens, God is good, just, and loving. He knows what he is doing, and we can trust him to do the right thing.

PRINCIPLES

- Faithfulness in prayer will be rewarded with insight.
- Life is filled with mysteries that necessitate faith in a loving God.
- God is fully aware of wickedness in our world and will judge in due time.
- God sometimes uses unlikely instruments to accomplish his purposes.
- God is not offended when we come to him with our questions.
- Our omniscient God is the proper source for help when seeking to understand life's mysteries.
- Faith is the key to eternal life and daily Christian living.
- God's Word will certainly be fulfilled.
- Empires built on greed, exploitation, and violence will be destroyed.
- Some day the knowledge of the true God will pervade the whole earth.
- Drunkenness harms individuals and nations.
- Idolatry is foolish since only the living God can cleanse from sin, provide strength for daily living, and bestow eternal life.

APPLICATIONS

- Determine to trust God even when you do not understand why.
- Seek God's face in the midst of doubts or fears you may have.
- Wait on God for answers to your questions.
- Name examples of modern nations that have built their empires by violence and oppression.
- If you have never put your faith in Christ, ask him now to forgive your sins and give you eternal life.
- Determine to live daily by faith in God's Word.
- Thank the Lord that some day the knowledge of God will fill the earth.
- Spread the knowledge of the Lord now by sharing the gospel of Jesus Christ with someone.
- Examine other Bible passages on the dangers of strong drink (e.g., Prov. 23:29–35; 31:4–7).

IV. LIFE APPLICATION

If God Exists, Why Is There Evil?

Several years ago my son-in-law took a course in philosophy at a local university. On the first day of the course, the teacher walked to the board and wrote:

> God is good.
> God has all power.
> There is evil in the world.
> Therefore, there is no God!

In other words, how could a loving God allow crime, pain, suffering, and death if he has the power to prevent them? Since these evils exist, God could not exist.

We would disagree with such logic, but the fact is the problem of evil has been one of the most difficult philosophical and theological questions throughout the ages. Theologians refer to the attempt to explain how God can be just and still allow evil as *theodicy*. Like the philosophy professor, many people have given up on God because of it. While visiting homes in his area, a pastor knocked on a strange door. A young woman opened the door. He told her who he was and that he wanted to talk to her about God's love. At this she became belligerent and slammed the door in his face. Out of curiosity the tenacious pastor knocked once more. When the woman opened the door, he said, "Lady, I am leaving, but before I go, would you please tell me why you are so angry?" At this the woman burst into tears and cried out, "Why did God let my baby die?"

These kinds of heartbreaks can shake people's faith. What is the biblical response to the problem of evil? Evil entered the world when Adam and Eve sinned. Sin not only affected the human race but all of creation. Since human beings have free will, they may choose to do evil.

Renowned theologian J. I. Packer provides the following helpful summary:

> Of the evils that infect God's world (moral and spiritual perversity, waste of good, and the physical disorders and disruptions of a spoiled cosmos), it can summarily be said: God permits evil (Acts 14:16); he punishes evil with evil (Ps. 81:11–12; Rom. 1:26–32); he

brings good out of evil (Gen. 50:20; Acts 2:23; 4:27–28; 13:27; 1 Cor. 2:7–8); he uses evil to test and discipline those he loves (Matt. 4:1–11; Heb. 12:4–14); and one day he will redeem his people from the power and presence of evil altogether (Rev. 21:27; 22:14–15) (Packer, *Concise Theology*, Wheaton, Ill.: Tyndale House, 1993, p. 56).

Moreover, let us remember that Christianity is unique in that God did something astounding: he became a human being like us. He knows what we face in this world, and he suffers with us during our times of sadness and pain. He also suffered for us. British pastor John R. W. Stott asserts: "I could never myself believe in God, if it were not for the cross. . . . He laid aside his immunity to pain. He entered our world of flesh and blood, tears and death. He suffered for us" (Stott, *The Cross of Christ*, Downers Grove, Ill.: InterVarsity Press, 1986, pp. 335–36).

V. PRAYER

O Lord, there are many things that we do not understand and may never understand until we meet you in heaven. When we confront heartbreaks, apparent injustices, and other earthly evils, help us to remember that you loved us enough to send your Son Jesus to die for us. Therefore, we know that whatever happens, we can trust you. We can take refuge in the truth of Romans 8:28, "We know that all things work together for the good of those who love God: those who are called according to His purpose" (HCSB). Amen.

VI. DEEPER DISCOVERIES

A. The Relevance of Habakkuk's "Oracle" (1:1)

Some people feel that the Bible is out of date and irrelevant, but nothing could be further from the truth. The more I study the Scriptures, the more impressed I am with just how relevant the Bible is for today's world. All the issues that we moderns face are dealt with in its pages. Habakkuk's prophecy is over twenty-six hundred years old, yet as God's message it provides answers to questions that are being asked by people all over the world. Barker and Bailey comment:

Can any book be more up to date than one which questions the prosperity of the wicked and the demise of the righteous? Habakkuk asked the questions the suffering people of his day were asking. How can the wicked prosper? How can God not answer when the righteous suffer? More importantly, he was not content to hear human philosophies about these questions. He asked God to answer these questions (Barker and Bailey, 287).

We might add that Habakkuk teaches us the importance of faith and how to attain life (2:4).

B. The Neo-Babylonian Empire (1:6)

Habakkuk predicted the Babylonian invasion of Judah. The following is a historical overview of this empire that had such a dramatic impact on God's people.

- The Neo-Babylonian Empire (centered in the area of modern Iraq) dominated the world during the time of Habakkuk's prophecy.
- Nabopolassar founded the Neo-Babylonian Empire and reigned from 626 to 605 B.C.
- In 612 B.C., with the help of the Medes, the Babylonians sacked the Assyrian capital Nineveh.
- World domination was solidified when Babylonian forces under the crown prince Nebuchadnezzar routed Pharaoh Neco II and his Egyptian troops at Carchemish in 605 B.C. (Jer. 46:2–12).
- Nabopolassar's son, Nebuchadnezzar II (605–562 B.C.), became the greatest king of the Neo-Babylonian period.
- Babylon invaded Judah three times. In 605 B.C., Daniel and his friends were taken captive to Babylon. In March 597 B.C., King Jehoiachin and about ten thousand others were deported, including the prophet Ezekiel. In the summer of 586 B.C., the Babylonians brought an end to the nation of Judah, totally destroying Jerusalem and the temple.
- Later kings of this empire were Amel-Marduk (562–560 B.C.), Neriglissar (560–556 B.C.), Labashi-Marduk (556 B.C.), and Nabonidus (556–539 B.C.), whose son Belshazzar served as coregent (Dan. 5).
- The city of Babylon fell to the Medo-Persian armies of Cyrus the Great in October 539 B.C., bringing an end to the short-lived Neo-

Babylonian Empire. Accounts of the fall of Babylon were recorded by the prophet Daniel (Dan. 5) and the ancient Greek historians Herodotus and Xenophon.

- Marduk was the most prominent god in Babylon and was given the epithet Bel (equivalent to the Canaanite term Baal), meaning "lord." Marduk's son Nabu (the Nebo in Isa. 46:1) was considered the god of writing and scribes and became especially exalted in the Neo-Babylonian Period.

- Ishtar, goddess of the morning and evening star (the Greek Aphrodite and Roman Venus), was also an important goddess to the Babylonians.

C. Waiting on God (2:1)

Like a watchman on a wall, Habakkuk stood at his post and waited for God to speak. Wright correctly remarks:

Waiting for God to answer prayer is one of the most difficult tasks Christians face. The saints of the Bible often waited for God, agonizing over their circumstances in the meantime. The most poignant cries for divine action are found in the Book of Psalms. Sometimes the psalmist accused God of hiding His face even though His people had done nothing wrong (e.g., Ps. 27:7–9). The psalmists counsel their readers to wait for God with confidence, knowing He will answer in the end (Ps. 27:14) (Wright, 73).

Habakkuk's patience was rewarded with an answer from God, and so will ours be. Jesus promised: "Keep asking, and it will be given to you. Keep searching, and you will find. Keep knocking, and the door will be opened to you. For everyone who asks receives, and the one who searches finds, and to the one who knocks, the door will be opened" (Matt. 7:7–8 HCSB).

D. "The Righteous Will Live by His Faith" (2:4)

Habakkuk's declaration that "the righteous [or "just"] will live by his faith" (2:4) was a central element of the apostle Paul's theology (Rom. 1:17; Gal. 3:11) and is also quoted in the Epistle to the Hebrews. Armerding summarizes its New Testament usage:

Habakkuk's message, the core of which is found in 2:4, forms a basic point in three New Testament books. Paul, in Romans 1:17, introduced his gospel as one of salvation by faith, as opposed to salvation by works, and cited Habakkuk 2:4 "the righteous will live by his faith"—as [Old Testament] support for his argument. Galatians 3:11–12 sets forth faith as the antithesis of law or legal salvation, and again Habakkuk 2:4 serves as a proof-text. Finally, in an intriguing passage from Hebrews 10:37–38, Habakkuk 2:3–4 is again quoted; but the context focuses on the pending arrival of the fulfillment of the vision and the identification of the Hebrews with those who have faith and thus persevere under pressure (Armerding, 495).

Justification by faith was also the theme that inspired Martin Luther to nail his ninety-five theses to the door of the castle church in Wittenberg, Germany, on October 31, 1517, thereby launching the Protestant Reformation, one of history's greatest religious awakenings.

Kaiser has a good discussion of the Hebrew word, 'emunah, and concludes that it is best rendered "faith" (NIV, KJV, NKJV, NASB, NRSV) rather than "faithfulness" in this context (Kaiser, *Mastering the Old Testament*, 169–71). However, faith and faithfulness cannot be separated because faithfulness is the outward manifestation of inward faith.

VII. TEACHING OUTLINE

A. INTRODUCTION

1. Lead Story: The Question of Why?
2. Context: In chapters 1–2 of Habakkuk, the prophet asks God two very puzzling questions. First, Habakkuk wants to know why God permitted evil to exist in Judah. God explains that he would use Babylon to punish the wicked in Judah for their sins. This led to the prophet's second question, How could God use Babylon, a much more wicked nation, to judge Judah? Again, God graciously responds by showing Habakkuk that after Babylon had served its purpose, it too would be judged, particularly in the "woe" judgment section (2:6–20).
3. Transition: As we listen to Habakkuk's questions and God's answers, we learn that a holy God sees and will punish sin. We learn that God

may use unusual means to bring about his purposes. In the "woe" judgment section, Habakkuk warns against five deadly sins that we should especially avoid. They are common today.

B. COMMENTARY

1. The Prophetic Introduction (1:1)
2. Mystery 1: How Can God Permit Evil? (1:2–11)
3. Mystery 2: How Can God Use a Pagan Nation to Punish Judah? (1:12–2:20)

C. CONCLUSION: LIFE'S LITTLE MYSTERIES

VIII. ISSUES FOR DISCUSSION

1. What light does the Book of Habakkuk shed on the fact that sometimes wicked people seem to prosper? Name some current examples of people (or nations) who have committed crimes or atrocities and yet seem to be doing well. What is their ultimate fate?
2. How can you reconcile the fact that God is love and yet evil exists in our world?
3. How did the apostle Paul apply Habakkuk's words, "The righteous will live by his faith" (2:4), in Romans 1:17 and Galatians 3:11? What does this show about God's way of salvation and how we should live the Christian life?
4. Read Habakkuk 2:18–20. Name several contrasts between the false gods (religions) of our modern world and the Christian God.

Habakkuk 3

True Worship

I. **INTRODUCTION**
If This Is Worship, Count Me Out!

II. **COMMENTARY**
A verse-by-verse explanation of the chapter.

III. **CONCLUSION**
Worship Is a Transitive Verb

An overview of the principles and applications from the chapter.

IV. **LIFE APPLICATION**
Why Do You Go to Church?

Melding the chapter to life.

V. **PRAYER**
Tying the chapter to life with God.

VI. **DEEPER DISCOVERIES**
Historical, geographical, and grammatical enrichment of the commentary.

VII. **TEACHING OUTLINE**
Suggested step-by-step group study of the chapter.

VIII. **ISSUES FOR DISCUSSION**
Zeroing the chapter in on daily life.

"*The* truest expression of trust in a great God will always be worship."

J . I . Packer

Habakkuk 3

 IN A NUTSHELL

In spite of the coming disaster, Habakkuk concludes his prophecy with a hymn of worship for his sovereign God. In his prayer of praise, we find instruction in worship that is relevant for today.

True Worship

I. INTRODUCTION

If This Is Worship, Count Me Out!

*D*evotees of various religions worship in different ways. One of the most intriguing religious celebrations is held in India.

> Snake worship still forms an important part of popular religion in many regions of India. One day in the year—around the beginning of August—is devoted to a "festival of the serpents," when, it is believed, cobras will not bite anyone. The festival, which is called Naga Panchami (the words means "snake" and "fifth"), falls on the fifth day of the Hindu month of Shravan, which runs from early July to early August.
>
> On that day live cobras, or their images, are worshiped. Sometimes the snakes are handled by devotees of the cult. Snake worshipers also ritually feed sacred cobras reared in special shrines and even leave out milk as an offering to wild cobras in places frequented by them (*Strange Stories, Amazing Facts*, ed. Carol Alway, Pleasantville, NY: The Reader's Digest Association, Inc, 1976, p. 311).

Probably the most famous of these Naga Panchami festivals is held in Battis Shirala, a tiny village in the hills of Sanglis. Young people begin to catch the snakes a month earlier and put them in clay pots. On the day of the feast, youths dressed in bright-colored clothing carry the snake-filled pots through the village. Loud music accompanies the procession. Throughout the day the snakes are worshiped at local temples. The next day the snakes are released unharmed. If this is worship, I think I'll pass!

Habakkuk concludes his book with a magnificent prayer that illustrates the character of true worship. According to Kaiser: "Habakkuk's response to God's revelation of answers to the probing questions he had set before his Lord was to worship God with an exalted combination prayer and hymn. It was the prophet's 'amen' to what he had been told" (Kaiser, *Mastering the Old Testament*, 189). The importance of worship to the Christian life can hardly be overstated. John Stott maintains, "Worship is the highest and noblest activity of which man, by the grace of God, is capable" (Water, 1140). Yet A. W. Tozer believes that "we have lost the art of worship" (Water, 1141).

We talk much about worship in our churches, but many Christians probably could not give an accurate definition of it. Some people associate worship with a certain ritual or a behavior tradition. Worship styles often become divisive in our churches.

What is worship? The English word *worship* is a combination of two Old English terms meaning "worthy" (or "worth") and "ship." Thus, worship is respect and service that we offer to God because we believe he is worthy of it. Although the specific word *worship* is not mentioned in this chapter, Habakkuk sets forth a general framework that is instructive for public and private religious worship today.

II. COMMENTARY

True Worship

MAIN IDEA: *True worship focuses on our glorious God and produces greater faith, joy, and strength in the believer.*

A Elements of Worship (3:1)

SUPPORTING IDEA: *Habakkuk's doxology illustrates that prayer and music are important elements of worship.*

3:1. Habakkuk labeled his doxology a **prayer** to God. In the Old Testament there are at least a dozen Hebrew words for "pray" and "prayer." *Tephillah,* the term found here, is the most general and most common. It is found seventy-seven times in the Old Testament, most often in the Psalms (thirty-two times). *Tephillah* comes from a verb (*palal*) that means "to intervene, interpose, pray."

Richards summarizes:

> While the root meaning is uncertain, it may emphasize (1) a call to God to assess a need presented and act on it, (2) the dependence and humility of the one praying, or (3) an appeal for a divine decision. . . . These words [the noun and verb] are used of personal and corporate prayer with the sense of requesting intervention (Nu 21:7), of entreaty (1 Sa 2:1), of confession (2 Ch 33:18–19), and of thanksgiving (Ne 11:17) (Richards, *Expository Dictionary of Bible Words,* 497).

Prayer is essential in worship since it is through prayer that we communicate with God. We speak to God and he speaks to us. Unger and White point out: "Also, since the verb form ["pray"] can have a reciprocal meaning between subject and object, it may emphasize the fact that prayer is basically communication, which always has to be two-way in order to be real" (Unger and White, 303).

A second important element of worship is music. Habakkuk's prayer is unique in the prophets because it is set to music. Like Habakkuk 3, five psalms are specifically called "prayers" in their superscription (Pss. 17; 86; 90; 102; 142). "In these uses *tephillah* means a prayer set to music and sung in the formal worship service. In Ps. 72:20 the word describes all the psalms or 'prayers' of Psalms 1–72, only one of which is specifically called a 'prayer' (17:1)" (Unger and White, 303–304).

The meaning of **shigionoth** is uncertain but probably is some kind of musical notation. First, the only other use of the term in the Bible is the singular form in the title of Psalm 7: "A *shiggaion* of David, which he sang to the Lord concerning Cush, a Benjamite." Clearly, the term is connected to a psalm that David sang. Second, at the close of Habakkuk's hymn, the music leader was instructed to accompany the singing of it with "stringed instruments" (3:19).

Wright further explains:

> The word *Shigionoth* is an untranslated Hebrew word that may indicate the tone or mood in which his prayer was intended to be sung in ancient Israelite Temple worship. If so, it is analogous to terms such as *andante* or *moderato* which are often found at the beginning of written musical compositions today. . . . Similar musical terms appear in various biblical psalms and are sometimes translated into English (e.g., Ps 5:1; 6:1; 7:1; 45:1, etc.) (Wright, 77).

Thus, Habakkuk 3 may be classified as a prayer hymn sung by the people of Israel in worship.

Music is not a peripheral enterprise but an integral part of worship. Songs should lift our spirits and proclaim a message that is biblically sound. Too often this is not the case. We should remember that the purpose of our music is not merely to make us "feel" good, but to glorify God. C. S. Lewis warns, "Nothing should be done or sung or said in church which does not aim directly or indirectly either at glorifying God or edifying the people or both" (Water, 1140). Congregational singing is an opportunity for all to participate in public worship. Everyone cannot preach the sermon or sing the solos, but all can join in praising God through song. God does not care if we have a beautiful singing voice. He only wants to hear us praise him. Francis Schaeffer declares: "One day all Christians will join in a doxology and sing God's praises with perfection. But even today, individually and corporately, we are not only to sing the doxology, but to be the doxology" (Water, 739).

Other key elements of worship are studying the Bible and giving. Habakkuk's high regard for Scripture is evident throughout this brief hymn from his many allusions to earlier biblical books (e.g., Pss. 18; 68; 77; Exod. 15; Deut. 33).

B Attitude in Worship (3:2)

SUPPORTING IDEA: *True worship is possible only when we approach God with a right attitude.*

3:2. Attitude is vitally important in worship. Jesus made this clear: "Yet a time is coming and has now come when the true worshipers will worship the Father in spirit and truth, for they are the kind of worshipers the Father seeks. God is spirit, and his worshipers must worship in spirit and in truth" (John 4:23–24). For us to worship properly, we must have a right spirit or attitude.

Habakkuk approached God in a spirit of reverential **awe**. For NIV's **fame**, other English versions have "speech" (KJV, NKJV), "report" (NASB), or "renown" (NRSV). Literally, the Hebrew word means "hearing" or "report." Either the prophet has in mind God's "speech" or "report" about the coming discipline of Judah and destruction of Babylon (chs. 1–2), or the "report" of God's greatness exhibited by his past mighty **deeds**. In light of what follows in this and later verses, the report of God's great deeds of the past seem to be in view. Thus, "fame" seems to capture the idea well. Habakkuk is praising God for his wondrous acts, particularly those associated with Israel's preservation and deliverance during the exodus period. The prophet did not experience these wonders firsthand but had heard of them from the Bible record. When Habakkuk considered all the great deeds of his God, he was overwhelmed. Like Billy Graham's crusade vocalist, George Beverly Shea, Habakkuk had to proclaim, "How Great Thou Art!"

As Habakkuk pondered the greatness of the Lord and how he had so mightily delivered Israel in times past by his wondrous deeds, he cried out for God to **renew them in our day, in our time make them known.** In the Hebrew text both "in our day" and "in our time" are literally "in the midst of the years." If he was referring to God's promise to discipline Judah and destroy Babylon, the prophet seems to be requesting a prompt fulfillment (1:5). If, as is more likely, Habakkuk was speaking of the great deliverance of Israel in the past, he was imploring God to do it again! Habakkuk had heard of God's wonders, but he longed to see them with his own eyes. We should not be content just to hear of the greatness of God; we should desire to have a personal encounter with him.

Habakkuk knew that the promised **wrath** (the Babylonian invasion) would come on Judah, but he pleaded with God to **remember mercy**. Kaiser rightly notes: "He could pray this way since he knew from previous revelation that God's nature was to be merciful, full of compassion and abundant in His loving-kindness (Exod. 34:6)" (Kaiser, *Mastering the Old Testament,* 193). Moreover, God had promised that Israel would never cease to exist as a nation, thus wrath for Judah's ungodly but mercy for the righteous remnant that included saints like Habakkuk, Daniel, Jeremiah, and Ezekiel.

Often we think of prayer as asking God for things, but Habakkuk offered only two petitions in his entire prayer—deliverance and mercy. Most of his prayer centered on praising God.

Focus of Worship (3:3–15)

SUPPORTING IDEA: *True worship focuses on the person and character of God.*

The proper focus of worship must always be on God, but what is the true God like? In verses 3–15 Habakkuk presented several characteristics of God in the form of a magnificent theophany (appearance of God). Some scholars divide the text into two separate theophanies, but the majority seem to be correct in identifying this as one theophany with two parts. Verses 3–7 describe God's great acts of the past, particularly those done in connection with the exodus; verses 8–15 portray the Lord as a warrior who will bring future deliverance (though still using some exodus terminology). The whole section is highly poetic, and not surprisingly the prophet used language and literary forms typical of the Book of Psalms.

3:3. Habakkuk depicted God as coming from **Teman** and **Mount Paran.** Teman was an oasis town (and possibly also a region) in mountainous Edom (Seir), southeast of Judah (Obad. 9; Amos 1:12). According to Deuteronomy 33:2, Mount Paran was another name for Mount Sinai. Habakkuk deliberately connected God's holiness with Sinai, for it was there that the Lord appeared in fire and commanded: "I am the LORD who brought you up out of Egypt to be your God; therefore be holy, because I am holy" (Lev. 11:45). The sun, moon, and stars (**heavens**) paled in light of the **glory** (Heb. *hod,* "glory, splendor, majesty") of the Lord as he passed by. God's **praise** (here a virtual synonym for "glory") also **filled the earth**. Outside the Book of Psalms, **Selah** occurs only in this chapter (vv 3,9,13). Though the meaning of the term is uncertain, it most likely indicates a musical break or a pause for reflection. Kaiser observes:

> This hymn traces the steps over which God led Israel as she journeyed to take possession of the land of Canaan. We move from Sinai to Edom as Israel is poised to enter the Promised Land. Through this hymn we relive the far-reaching effects of the glory of God in times past (Kaiser, *Mastering the Old Testament*, 179).

3:4. Now God's **splendor** is compared to a **sunrise.** The flashing **rays** (literally, "horns") are reminiscent of the rays that shone around Moses' face as he descended from Mount Sinai (Exod. 34:29–30,35). In the Exodus passages, Moses' "face was radiant" is literally Moses' "face was horned." Of course, the horns symbolized the rays shining forth from his face after being in God's presence. Based on a literal reading of Exodus 34, Michelangelo sculpted a statue with horns protruding from Moses' head! This famous sculpture now stands in the Church of Saint Peter in Chains, in Rome. **Rays flashed from his hand** was "a typical pose of divine warrior storm gods in the ancient Near East . . . with bolts of lightning in an upraised hand" (Walton, Matthews, and Chavalas, BBCOT, 793). Habakkuk was applying this imagery to the true ruler of the storms, the Lord.

Our God is glorious beyond imagination. Paul says that our King "lives in unapproachable light, whom no one has seen or can see" (1 Tim. 6:16). God warned Moses, "You cannot see my face, for no one may see me and live" (Exod. 33:20). God's glory elicits worship.

> Glory befits God because of His majesty, while lowliness befits man because it unites us with God. If we realize this, rejoicing in the glory of the Lord, we too, like St. John the Baptist, will begin to say unceasingly, "He must increase, but we must decrease" (cp. John 3:30) (Diadochos of Photiki, in Water, 1139).

3:5–6. God's great power is emphasized in this passage. He passes through like a mighty king accompanied by a vast retinue with **plague** and **pestilence,** his servants, ready to strike at his command. The Lord released plagues on Egypt to free his people (Exod. 9:3,15). The **earth** shakes in his presence, and a glance from the Lord makes **the nations tremble** and **mountains** crumble. They melt, but he is **eternal.** The psalmist exclaimed: "Long ago You established the earth, and the heavens are the work of Your hands.

They will perish, but You will endure; all of them will wear out like clothing. You will change them like a garment, and they will pass away. But You are the same, and Your years will never end" (Ps.102:25–27 HCSB).

3:7. The **tents of Cushan** and the **dwellings of Midian** trembled **in anguish** (literally "quaked, quivered") as the earth shook in the presence of the Lord. Midian was a land in the northwestern Arabian peninsula east of the Gulf of Aqabah. Cushan may be a longer form of Cush, which normally designated the nation of "Ethiopia." In this context the association with tents and the parallelism with Midian suggests Cushan was a Bedouin tribe in the same vicinity as Midian or in the nearby Sinai peninsula. Moses' Cushite wife (Num. 12:1) was likely from this area. Wright points out: "The four places mentioned in Habakkuk 3:3,7 are all in the wilderness through which Moses led the people of Israel on their journey from Egypt to Canaan" (Wright, 78).

Nearby Cushan and Midian knew of God's mighty acts on Israel's behalf at the exodus and in the wilderness and were terrified. Armerding concludes: "The imagery of vv. 6–7 again recalls the earthquake and volcanic upheaval at Mount Sinai (e.g., Exod 19:18; Judg 5:4–5), thus echoing v. 3 in its clear allusion to Sinai, and so framing the intervening verses and providing a specific context for their interpretation" (Armerding, 527).

As with his glory, God's incomprehensible power is a call to fall before him and worship. Our Milky Way galaxy alone contains approximately two hundred billion stars, and scientists tell us there are billions of galaxies in the universe! Isaiah exclaims: "Lift your eyes and look to the heavens: Who created all these? He who brings out the starry host one by one, and calls them each by name. Because of his great power and mighty strength, not one of them is missing" (Isa. 40:26; cp. Ps. 147:4). Such an awesome God is worthy of our respect and total commitment. Stephen Charnock declares, "All worship is shot wrong that is not directed to, and conducted by, the thoughts of the power of God, whose assistance we need" (Water, 1139).

3:8. Habakkuk posed several rhetorical questions that expect a negative answer. No, God was not **angry with the rivers, streams**, or **sea** (cp. v. 12). Allusions to God's dividing the Red Sea (Exod. 14:21–31; 15:1–21) and the Jordan River (Josh. 3:7–4:24) seem likely here. Evidently, the Lord's **chariots** are thunderclouds since verses 9–10 depict the earth as flooded with torrents of water. We find this same imagery in Psalm 104:3, "He makes the clouds his chariot and rides on the wings of the wind." Baal, the Canaanite fertility deity, was a serious religious threat to Israel for centuries, especially during the time of Ahab and Jezebel. Baal was touted as the lord of the rain and storms, and "Rider of the Clouds" was a favorite designation for Baal in pagan literature.

Habakkuk was probably issuing a direct attack on this false god, asserting that it is the Lord God who is truly sovereign over nature.

3:9–10. The two Hebrew words rendered **many arrows** may be translated in a wide variety of ways as is evident from the English versions. Literally the text reads, "curses [or "oaths"] of shafts" [or "rods, staves, shafts, tribes"]. In context with **bow**, the NIV is probably correct in seeing a curse of shafts or arrows here. At God's command his thunderclouds flood the earth, a possible allusion to Noah's flood. Kaiser aptly remarks: "The warrior described in this text certainly is no ordinary soldier. His weapons and the scope of His battle are cosmic. No mortal or earthly power will be able to withstand His assaults" (Kaiser, *Mastering the Old Testament,* 183).

3:11. The phrase **sun and moon stood still** may suggest an eclipse, the account of the supernatural cessation of these heavenly bodies in Joshua's day (Josh. 10:12–14), or the storm's obscuring them. In context of the thunder clouds and floods, the latter seems most likely. Armerding informs us:

> Such an interruption of the created order typically accompanies the judgment of God, as here (vv. 12–16); and this judgment, culminating in the eschatological Day of the Lord, is characterized consistently by darkness (e.g., Exod. 10:21–22; 14:20; Eccl. 12:2; Isa. 13:10; 24:23; Jer. 4:23,28; Joel 2:2,10,31; 3:15; Amos 5:18–20; 8:9; Zeph. 1:15; Matt. 24:29; 27:45; Luke 23:45; Rev. 6:12; 8:12; 9:2; 22:5) (Armerding, 529–30).

3:12. Now we see the target of God's wrath—not nature (v. 8) but the earth's wicked. God makes plain to Habakkuk that none will escape retribution for their wicked deeds. Justice is certain. **Earth** and **nations** seem to indicate a universal scope. Thus, this judgment moves beyond the historical punishment of Judah and Babylon to God's **wrath** on all nations at the climax of history.

3:13. God's war with the nations is also intended **to deliver** his **people** from the wicked. **Anointed one** is Hebrew *mashiach,* messiah, and has been interpreted in a number of ways. Some have identified this anointed one as a past leader of Israel, such as Moses at the exodus. Many evangelicals believe this is a reference to the Messiah. However, in what sense would the Messiah need to be saved? According to Blue, "By preserving the people of Israel (delivering them from Egypt and then later from Babylonian Captivity), God maintained the line for the Messiah" (Blue, 1520).

In parallel with **to deliver your people,** the phrase **to save your anointed one** could conceivably be a reference to God's people, though admittedly the term is not found elsewhere in the Old Testament in this sense. The passage could also mean to save "with" your anointed one (cp. KJV, NKJV) and could therefore indicate that this deliverance would be accomplished by the Messiah. However, the point is clear: God will deliver his saints in spectacular fashion (most likely, at Messiah's second coming).

The identification of **the leader of the land of wickedness** (Pharaoh, Babylonian ruler, eschatological figure) depends on one's interpretation of the historical setting of the deliverance in the preceding. Blue explains the metaphor, **stripped him from head to foot**: "The figure in the Hebrew is that of a building from which the gable is ripped off and then the entire structure demolished, so that the foundations are laid bare" (Blue, 1520). Although Babylon's leader would certainly be **crushed** (Dan. 5), so will the leader of evil at Christ's return (Rev. 19:19–20).

3:14–15. Confidently, the forces of the evil king storm forth to destroy the **wretched** (poor, oppressed). Like a mighty warrior God intervenes, overpowering their evil leader, even slaying him **with his own spear**. Habakkuk described the Lord's great eschatological triumph over the wicked in language (**trampled the sea**; **churning the great waters**) reminiscent of God's destruction of Pharaoh's army at the Red Sea (Exod. 14:23–28).

In verses 8–15 we encounter an awesome display of God's judgment on a wicked world. Why does God react so? Earlier Habakkuk explained, "Your eyes are too pure to look on evil; you cannot tolerate wrong" (1:13). We worship a holy God. He hates the very sight of wickedness. Because he is holy, we may be confident that prayers for justice will be answered. The wicked will be punished, and the righteous will be vindicated. Because he is holy, we must be clean in order to enter his presence for fellowship (Ps. 24:3–4).

Ⓓ Results of Worship (3:16–19)

SUPPORTING IDEA: *True worship deepens our faith in God and gives joy and strength even in the midst of difficult circumstances.*

3:16. First, worship deepens our faith. Habakkuk's reaction to the theophany he had witnessed was extreme terror. He had heard of God's "fame" (v. 2), but when he received this brief glimpse of the glory, power, and holiness of God, he was overwhelmed (cp. the apostle John's experience, Rev. 1:17; also Daniel, Dan. 10:4–9). He realized that no power (including Babylon) could stand against his mighty God. Moreover, he knew that the holy "Judge of all the earth" would "do right" (Gen. 18:25). He was confident that God would not allow Judah's invader to escape. Payday (**the day of calamity**) would surely come for Babylon. **Wait patiently**, however, suggests that Babylon's judgment might take a while.

3:17–18. Second, worship brings joy regardless of circumstances. This verse is one of the most touching in all of Scripture. Habakkuk depicted an economy in shambles! Failed crops and no livestock were curses forewarned by Moses if Israel was unfaithful to God's covenant (Deut. 28:15–24). Everything that so many people believe provides security, satisfaction, and happiness had disappeared. Nevertheless, the prophet had joy because his joy was in the Lord. Everything was gone, but God was still there. Habakkuk was still saved (**God my Savior**, literally, "the God of my salvation"). The prophet was echoing the attitude of the psalmist, "Whom have I in heaven but you? And earth has nothing I desire besides you" (Ps. 73:25). Thomas Traherne, a seventeenth-century English clergyman, wrote, "Till you can sing and rejoice and delight in God as misers do in gold, and kings in scepters, you can never enjoy the world" (Water, 1141). Habakkuk could also **rejoice** because the theophany he had just witnessed reminded him that his omnipotent God would triumph in the end. There was a better world coming.

3:19. Third, worship provides **strength** for living. Habakkuk's strength, and ours, came from the **Sovereign Lord** of the universe. Like a **deer** able to tread safely upon the rocky cliffs without falling, Habakkuk was safe and secure in God. The prophet clearly had in mind Psalm 18:32–33 and its parallel passage, 2 Samuel 22:33–34. The last two lines of this verse are found in Psalm 18:33 and 2 Samuel 22:34, and strength is alluded to in Psalm 18:32 and 2 Samuel 22:33. Wright comments:

> According to its superscription, Psalm 18 was written after the Lord had delivered David from all of his enemies. The psalm presents David as a mighty and successful warrior, triumphant over his many foes. Habakkuk drew on the life of David to express his confidence in God's ability to see him through whatever troubles lay ahead (Wright, 79).

Habakkuk concluded the chapter with a notation for the congregational music leader, instructing him that this prayer hymn was to be played on **stringed instruments** (see also "Commentary" discussion on 3:1). Music was an important part of ancient Israel's worship services. The note, **for the director of music**, elsewhere is found only in the Psalms (fifty-five times).

MAIN IDEA REVIEW: *True worship focuses on our glorious God and produces greater faith, joy, and strength in the believer.*

III. CONCLUSION

Worship Is a Transitive Verb

D. A. Carson reminds us that worship is a transitive verb, that is, it has a direct object—God.

> We do not meet to worship (i.e., to experience worship); we aim to worship *God*. "Worship the Lord your God, and serve him only": there is the heart of the matter. . . . If you seek experiences of worship, you will not find them; if you worship the living God, you will experience something of what is reflected in the Psalms. Worship is a transitive verb, and the most important thing about it is the direct object (Carson, *Worship: Adoration and Action*, Wipf and Stock Publishers, 2002, p. 15).

Carson is right. True worship must focus on God and nothing else. But not just any god will do. Our world is filled with people who are religious. The nineteen hijackers who crashed three jets into the World Trade Center and the Pentagon on September 11, 2001, were extremely religious. They believed in God, yet they believed in a false god, a god who commanded murder. The object of our faith must be the real God—the God of the Bible. Only he exists. Only he can save. Habakkuk tells us that all we need to have real joy, peace, and satisfaction is found in him.

PRINCIPLES

- Prayer and music are important elements in worship.
- We should not be content just to hear of the greatness of God; we should desire to know him by experience.
- The proper attitude for worship is reverential awe.
- The only object worthy of our worship is the true God described in the Bible.
- Contemplating God's glory, power, and holiness inspires us to worship him.
- When we engage in true worship, we will experience increased faith, joy, and strength.
- True joy does not come from material possessions but from knowing God.

- Like Israel's rescue at the Red Sea, our omnipotent God will triumph over evil and deliver his saints at the climax of history.

APPLICATIONS

- Determine to worship God faithfully each day by having a quiet time with him.
- Be faithful to the public worship services of your church.
- Ask God to act mightily for his glory in our day.
- Practice focusing on the glory of God rather than the world and its material possessions.
- Worship God by participating in congregational singing at your church. Try singing a hymn or praise song to the Lord as part of your personal quiet time.
- Praise the Lord that he will some day bring an end to evil.
- Follow Habakkuk's example of submitting to God's sovereign plan.

IV. LIFE APPLICATION

Why Do You Go to Church?

In his *Encyclopedia of 7,700 Illustrations* (Rockville, Md.: Assurance Publishers, 1979, p. 1651), Paul Tan records the story of a visiting minister who was substituting for the famed pastor Henry Ward Beecher.

A large audience had assembled to hear the popular pastor. At the appointed hour, the visiting minister entered the pulpit. Learning that Beecher was not to preach, several began to move toward the doors. The visiting minister stood and called out, "All who have come here today to worship Henry Ward Beecher may now withdraw from the church! All who have come to worship God, keep your seats!" No one then left.

Do you go to church to worship God or for some other reason? Sometimes people complain about their pastor's preaching or their church's music. As important as these may be, we do not go to church for the pastor or the music leader. We attend church to worship God. If we come in a right spirit, we will meet God, and that is what matters.

V. PRAYER

O Lord, thank you for the privilege of worshiping you. Help us to be faithful in practicing this privilege both in our private and corporate worship life. When we are tempted to fear life's circumstances, remind us that we are eternally secure in our glorious, omnipotent, and holy God. Let our focus always be on you, our source of true joy and strength, and not the world. In Christ's name we pray. Amen.

VI. DEEPER DISCOVERIES

A. God's Nature as Presented in Habakkuk 3

Habakkuk 3 presents a magnificent portrait of God. Barker and Bailey provide an excellent summary of major teachings about God's nature in this chapter. God is:

- famous so that people talk about what he has done for them (3:2).
- active with deeds that silence people awestruck (3:2).
- a God of wrath (3:2,12).
- one who comes to his needy people from his ancient dwelling place (3:3).
- the glorious one whose acts bring forth praise that fills the universe (3:3).
- so splendid in appearance that he dims the dawning sun (3:4).
- powerful (3:4).
- in control of all diseases (3:5).
- in control of all history, all nature, and all people (3:6–7).
- willing and able to show his anger against sinful people as exemplified in the exodus from Egypt (3:8–15).
- in control of all the chaotic waters and deeps (3:8–10).
- one who uses even the heavenly bodies for his purposes (3:11).
- our Savior from the enemy and the protector of our anointed leader (3:13,16).
- the source of all our strength (3:19) (Barker and Bailey, 285).

To the above, we may add that God is our source of joy (3:18). God is truly wonderful, deserving of our worship.

B. Prophet (3:1)

Twice in the book (1:1; 3:1) Habakkuk describes himself as a "prophet" (Heb. *navi'*). *Navi'* is very common, appearing 316 times in the Old Testament. Its derivation is disputed, and R. D. Culver summarizes scholarly opinion as follows:

> Actually the views of the derivation are four. (1) From an Arabic root, . . . "to announce," hence "spokesman" . . . . (2) From a Hebrew root, . . . "to bubble up," hence pour forth words. . . . (3) From an Akkadian root . . . "to call," hence one who is called [by God] . . . hence one who felt called of God. (4) From an unknown Semitic root (Harris, Archer, and Waltke, TWOT, 2:544).

Regardless of its origin, the meaning of *navi'* as an authorized spokesman is clear from its usage. Prophets were divinely inspired as God's spokesmen to communicate his will to the people and often to disclose the future to them.

Key criteria for recognizing a genuine prophet are as follows: (1) True prophets spoke only in the name of the Lord (Deut. 13:1–5; 18:20); (2) their prophecies were always fulfilled (Deut. 18:21–22); (3) they had a holy character (2 Kgs. 4:9); and (4) sometimes their prophecies were authenticated by signs or miracles (1 Kgs. 18:36–39).

Throughout Israel's history, false prophets were a threat to the spiritual well-being of the nation (e.g., Hananiah, Jer. 28:15–16). Today our world is also filled with false prophets who lead literally billions astray, and Jesus warned that it would get worse as his return approaches (Matt. 24:24). These modern counterfeits may be recognized by examining their character and actions in light of the above criteria, as Jesus also emphasized (Matt. 7:20).

C. *Selah* (3:3,9,13)

Selah appears three times in this chapter (3:3,9,13). Elsewhere, it is found only in the Book of Psalms (seventy-one times), highlighting the chapter's affinity with the poetic material of the Psalms. Scholars have advanced numerous theories about its meaning. Blue has a good discussion:

> What is generally considered another musical notation, *Selah* (Hab. 3:3,9,13), probably indicates a pause in the song. (In the NIV *Selah* is in the right hand margin, whereas in other versions it is within the verses.) . . . The Hebrew verb from which the term comes means "to exalt," "to lift up." It may mean a pause (a) to elevate to a

higher key or increase the volume, (b) to reflect on what has been sung and exalt the Lord in praise, or (c) to lift up certain instruments for something like a trumpet fanfare (Blue, 1518).

In conclusion, since *selah* appears only in the Psalms and in Habakkuk 3, which is specifically identified as a song (v. 19), we may safely assume that the term is in fact a musical notation. The etymology, "to lift up," suggests that an elevation of the music is intended, probably to a higher key or volume. "Maskil" (e.g., Pss. 32:1; 42:1) and "miktam" (e.g., Pss. 16:1; 56:1) appear only in the Book of Psalms and are also probable musical notations of uncertain meaning.

D. The Importance of Public Worship (3:19)

The notation at the end of the chapter ("For the director of music. On my stringed instruments.") indicates that Habakkuk's prayer was intended to be sung in Israel's public worship services (also see "Commentary" discussion of *shigionoth* on 3:1). Certainly private worship is vital, but we cannot afford to neglect corporate worship. John Stott asserts:

> Whenever we fail to take public worship seriously, we are less than the fully biblical Christians we claim to be. We go to church for the preaching, some of us say, not for the praise. Evangelism is our speciality, not worship. In consequence either our worship services are slovenly, perfunctory, mechanical and dull or, in an attempt to remedy this, we go to the opposite extreme and become repetitive, unreflective and even flippant (Water, 1140).

Many church members are less than faithful to the public worship services of their church, but the writer of the Letter to the Hebrews exhorts us: "Let us not give up meeting together, as some are in the habit of doing, but let us encourage one another—and all the more as you see the Day approaching" (Heb. 10:25).

VII. TEACHING OUTLINE

A. INTRODUCTION

1. Lead Story: If This Is Worship, Count Me Out!

2. Context: Habakkuk concludes his book with a beautiful little prayer hymn to God. Notations at the beginning and end of the chapter indicate that this prayer was set to music and sung in Israel's temple worship. Most of the chapter is a magnificent description of a theophany. Habakkuk had "heard" of God's "fame"; now he witnesses for himself the glory, power, and holiness of the Lord. Habakkuk's experience deepened his faith and led him to rejoice in the Lord in spite of the impending disaster—the Babylonian invasion.

3. Transition: In this chapter we will learn more about true worship. Habakkuk emphasizes that the focus of all true worship is God himself. Like the prophet, our faith will be strengthened, and we will learn to rejoice in God in spite of circumstances. Brother Lawrence, a seventeenth-century monk, wrote: "We should dedicate ourselves to becoming in this life the most perfect worshipers of God we can possibly be, as we hope to be through all eternity" (Water, 1140).

B. COMMENTARY

1. Elements of Worship (3:1)
2. Attitude in Worship (3:2)
3. Focus of Worship (3:3–15)
4. Results of Worship (3:16–19)

C. CONCLUSION: WORSHIP IS A TRANSITIVE VERB

VIII. ISSUES FOR DISCUSSION

1. Habakkuk tells of God's mighty deeds of the past. What are some things that God has done in recent years to show his glory to our generation?

2. Discuss ways to improve your private worship time with God. Suggest a worship model for a typical quiet time.

3. How would you rate public worship services in the average church today? Do you believe that God is the focus of most worship services? If not, what is? What could be done to make our public worship more meaningful and exciting?

4. How could Habakkuk have such faith and joy in the face of disaster? Discuss ways that Habakkuk's experience may be applied to believers today.

Zephaniah 1–3

Things That Never Change

I. INTRODUCTION
Beloit College Mind-set List

II. COMMENTARY
A verse-by-verse explanation of these chapters.

III. CONCLUSION
The Richest Person in History

An overview of the principles and applications from these chapters.

IV. LIFE APPLICATION
Titanic's Unheeded Warnings

Melding these chapters to life.

V. PRAYER
Tying these chapters to life with God.

VI. DEEPER DISCOVERIES
Historical, geographical, and grammatical enrichment of the commentary.

VII. TEACHING OUTLINE
Suggested step-by-step group study of these chapters.

VIII. ISSUES FOR DISCUSSION
Zeroing these chapters in on daily life.

"*M*ost of the change we think we see in life

is due to truths being in and out of favor."

R o b e r t   F r o s t

PROPHECY PROFILE

- The "day of the LORD" is the overriding theme of Zephaniah's prophecy.
- The book may be divided into two major divisions: prophecies of judgment (1:1–3:8) and prophecies of blessing (3:9–20).
- Zephaniah is generally dated about 625 B.C. Three key factors in dating the prophecy are: (1) in the heading Zephaniah reports that he prophesied during the reign of King Josiah (640–609 B.C.), (2) the prophet anticipates the fall of Nineveh (612 B.C.) as a future event, and (3) according to Zephaniah 1:4–6, pagan idolatry was prevalent in Judah. Since Josiah's reforms (about 622–621 B.C.) mostly eliminated such practices (2 Kgs. 22–23), the book may be dated before 621 B.C., about 625 B.C.
- The prophecy is a call for Judah to repent or face God's wrath.
- Besides Amos, Zephaniah is the only minor prophet to include a section containing prophecies against foreign nations.
- Zephaniah's predictions involved an immediate judgment on Judah carried out by Babylon (605–586 B.C.) and the ultimate judgment of the world at the end of the age (day of the Lord).
- Zephaniah has been called the least known of all the minor prophets.
- The key verse of the book is Zephaniah's exhortation to "seek the LORD" in 2:3.

AUTHOR PROFILE: ZEPHANIAH THE PROPHET

- Zephaniah's name means "the Lord hides," apparently suggesting that the Lord hides his followers for their protection.

- According to the prophecy's heading, Zephaniah prophesied during the reign of King Josiah (640–609 B.C.).
- He apparently lived in Jerusalem (cp. 1:4,10–11).
- His prophetic activity may have been instrumental in stirring King Josiah to his reforms (cp. 2 Chr. 34:1–7).
- Zephaniah was a contemporary of Nahum and Jeremiah.
- If Zephaniah's ancestor named in the opening verse was the famous King Hezekiah, the prophet was a member of the royal family.

READER PROFILE: THE NATION OF JUDAH

- Zephaniah's prophecy is addressed to his countrymen, the people of Judah.
- Jerusalem was the capital of Judah.
- Judah was a vassal state of the evil Assyrian Empire until the fall of Nineveh in 612 B.C.
- The nation of Judah consisted primarily of the tiny tribe of Benjamin and the much larger tribe of Judah.
- Idolatry and various other sins were rampant when Zephaniah issued his prophecies. The moral decay reflected in the book grew out of Manasseh's fifty-year reign (697–642 B.C.).

Zephaniah 1–3

IN A NUTSHELL

Zephaniah prophesies the coming day of the Lord—a time of judgment on the wicked and blessing for the righteous. Historically, he warns Judah and other nations that a day of the Lord will come for them if they do not repent. He pleads with his wayward nation to seek the Lord in repentance before it is too late. He concludes by prophesying the judgment of all nations on the eschatological day of the Lord and the subsequent blessings of the righteous in the glorious messianic kingdom. Both God's judgment of sin and future blessings on his people rest on his unchangeable character.

Things That Never Change

I. INTRODUCTION

Beloit College Mind-set List

Each year Beloit College in Beloit, Wisconsin, compiles what it calls its Mind-set List to help faculty understand the perspective of incoming freshmen. Following are excerpts from two recent lists:

Class of 2002

1. They have no meaningful recollection of the Reagan era and did not know he had ever been shot.
2. They were preteen when the Persian Gulf War was waged.
3. There has been only one pope.
4. They were preteen when the Soviet Union broke apart and do not remember the Cold War.
5. They do not remember the space shuttle *Columbia* blowing up.
6. Their lifetime has always included AIDS.
7. They never had a polio shot and likely do not know what it is.
8. They have never owned a record player.
9. They have always had an answering machine.
10. They have always had cable television.
11. There have always been VCRs.
12. The Vietnam War is as ancient history to them as WWI, WWII, or even the Civil War.

Class of 2005

1. IBM Selectrics are antiques.
2. Hard copy has nothing to do with a TV show; a browser is not someone relaxing in a bookstore; a virus does not make humans sick; and a mouse is not a rodent (and there is no proper plural for it).
3. They were born the same year as the PC and the Mac.
4. Boeing has not built the 727 since they were born.
5. They have always used e-mail.
6. The precise location of the *Titanic* has always been known.
7. Volkswagen Beetles have always had engines in the front.
8. Major newspapers have always been printed in color.

Makes you think, doesn't it? I typed my doctoral dissertation on one of those antique IBM Selectrics! We live in a rapidly changing world. The changes in technology that have taken place since I was in college are mind-boggling. Yet many changes in our society have not been progress but regress. When I was a boy, people could not have imagined that television content and moral standards could sink so low and that crime rates could soar so high.

Many things change, but some things always remain the same. Spiritual truth is as valid today as ever. Although Zephaniah lived more than twenty-six hundred years ago, his prophecy contains a timely message for our modern world. In this book we will discover that God's holy character, his righteous demands, his promises, and, sadly, human nature never change.

II. COMMENTARY

Things That Never Change

MAIN IDEA: *God does not change. He is a jealous God who demands that we worship him alone and a holy God who requires that we be holy. He is merciful and forgives, but unrepentant sin will bring his judgment. For the penitent God promises a glorious future.*

A God's Prophet (1:1)

SUPPORTING IDEA: *Zephaniah warns his generation to turn from their sin and seek the Lord.*

1:1. Zephaniah provides a brief introduction to his great prophecy. He makes plain that this message is not just his opinion but is, in fact, **the word of the LORD.** Here we have a strong claim for the divine inspiration of Scripture. Since the prophecy is God's word, it must be obeyed. Three other men in the Old Testament (a priest, a postexilic Judean, and a Levite) were called Zephaniah. The name means "the Lord hides," apparently suggesting that the Lord hides his followers for their protection.

Zephaniah's introduction is unusual in that he is the only prophet to trace his ancestry through four generations. If the **Hezekiah** in his list is the king by that name, Zephaniah was descended from one of Judah's most revered rulers. He would also have been distantly related to the reigning king, **Josiah** (640–609 B.C.). Josiah's father **Amon** (642–640 B.C.) ruled only two years before being assassinated in a palace revolt (2 Kgs. 21:19–23). Amon was the son of the wicked Manasseh and followed his father in his idolatrous ways. The wickedness addressed by Zephaniah grew out of these previous administrations.

B God's Unchanging Demand for Worship (1:2–18)

SUPPORTING IDEA: *God demands that his creation worship him rather than false gods.*

When asked which was the greatest commandment, Jesus responded by quoting Deuteronomy 6:5: "Love the Lord your God with all your heart and with all your soul and with all your mind. This is the first and greatest commandment" (Matt. 22:37–38). If this is the greatest commandment, it seems reasonable that to disobey it would be the greatest sin. Our Creator made us for himself and demands that we give to him our undivided love and devotion. God is jealous (see v. 18; 3:8) of our worship. Yet many people in ancient Judah had turned away from the true God to idols. In verses 2–18 Zephaniah warned that God's response to idolatry would be certain and severe judgment. God's demand that humanity worship him, and him exclusively, has not changed, and neither has the penalty for such disobedience.

1:2–3. Immediately, Zephaniah gets to the main theme of his message: God will judge sin. **I will sweep away** is literally, "removing [or "gathering"], I will make an end of." Human life (that is, the wicked) and even animals will perish in this cataclysm. All that will be left of the **wicked** will be piles of **rubble**. The scope (**face of the earth**) and extent of this destruction can only point to the eschatological judgment of the world (Isa. 13:9–12). As Kaiser notes: "Just as all creation had been corrupted since the Fall, so all creation would now be involved in the divine visitation: man, beasts of the land, birds of the air, and creatures of the sea. This would be a universal judgment" (Kaiser, *Mastering the Old Testament,* 216).

1:4. Zephaniah began with a warning of God's judgment on all nations during the future day of the Lord. Now he narrows his focus to Judah. Not only will the wicked in pagan nations be judged, but the wicked in Judah will be as well. **Stretch out** the **hand** is a threatening gesture, like a mighty warrior preparing to strike (2:13; Ps. 138:7; Ezek. 14:9; 25:7,16). At the exodus the Lord had stretched out his hand against Egypt: "So I will stretch out my hand and strike the Egyptians with all the wonders that I will perform among them. After that, he will let you go" (Exod. 3:20). Now he warned that he would strike **Judah** and its capital, **Jerusalem**.

God was angry with his people because they had been unfaithful and worshiped other gods. They had broken the first two of God's Ten Commandments:

"I am the LORD your God, who brought you out of Egypt, out of the land of slavery. You shall have no other gods before me. You shall not make for yourself an idol in the form of anything in heaven above or on the earth beneath or in the waters below. You shall not bow down to them or worship them; for I, the LORD your God, am a jealous God" (Exod. 20:2–5a).

Several types of religious apostasy are singled out in verses 4–6. **Baal** worship had been a stumbling block throughout Israel's history (especially under Ahab and Jezebel, 1 Kgs. 16:30–32) and was still raising its ugly head. Supposedly, this Canaanite deity brought fertility to crops and families. Baal worship involved the worst forms of depravity—religious prostitution and sexual orgies. God vowed to eradicate Baal worship and Baal's **priests** from the land.

1:5–6. Worship of the heavenly bodies had also made inroads into Judah. Devotees would ascend to their rooftops and **bow down** before the sun, moon, and stars. Others in Judah attempted to have it both ways. They tried to worship both the Lord and false gods. **Molech** (or possibly, "their king," another reference to Baal) was a pagan deity of Ammon (1 Kgs. 11:7). The most detestable practice imaginable, child sacrifice, was associated with worship of this god (Lev. 18:21; 20:2; 2 Kgs. 23:10). Recent archaeological evidence indicates that child sacrifice was practiced in ancient Ammon. These people in Judah had turned away **from following the** LORD and had chosen to **seek** counsel from pagan gods, rather than from the true source of wisdom and salvation.

The paganism rampant in Judah was a reflection of its past political leadership. Josiah, who became king at eight years of age, had not yet instituted his religious reforms; and the influence of King Manasseh, whose reign had ended less than twenty years before, was still being felt. Manasseh had set new heights in promoting idolatry and is specifically said to have practiced the forms of paganism mentioned in these verses, even offering his own son as a burnt offering (2 Kgs. 21:3–6). Godly political leadership is imperative.

1:7–9. All are to **be silent** (Amos 6:10; 8:3; Hab. 2:20; Zech. 2:13) in reverential awe of the **Sovereign** LORD of the universe. Silence is also appropriate when one considers the horror of what is about to come upon the earth (Rev. 8:1). Those to be judged are portrayed here as invited guests who will also serve as the **sacrifice**. Specifically, the guests were political leaders and others who worshiped false gods. The phrase **clad in foreign clothes** represents the pagan lifestyles adopted by the Judeans, which included wearing different types of clothing. Observant Jews wore tassels of twisted cords fastened to the four corners of their outer garments as a reminder of covenant obligations (Num. 15:38–39; Deut. 22:12; cp. Zech. 8:23). Apparently, these idolatrous

Jews refused to wear these. **Avoid stepping on the threshold** likely refers to the Philistine superstition reflected in 1 Samuel 5:5. The NIV's **the temple of their gods** could also be rendered, "the house of their masters." Hebrew *adon* may refer to either a human or divine "master" or "lord." In context, divine lords or "gods" seems best.

1:10–11. On that day is found over thirty times in the prophets and four times in Zephaniah (1:9–10; 3:11,16). All four of Zephaniah's references speak of the day of the Lord (cp. 1:7). Everyone in Jerusalem will be in mourning when God's judgment falls. Wright observes: "Zephaniah 1:10–11 attests to the prophet's intimate knowledge of the topography of his city. Like the old city of Jerusalem today, Zephaniah's Jerusalem was built on and around several hills. The city's Fish Gate was located near the northwest corner of the Temple mount, and the second quarter encompassed a higher hill within the city to the west. The 'Mortar' (NASB) or 'Maktesh' (NKJV) [NIV, 'market district'] was the valley between the two where the merchants and traders congregated. The entire city was ringed by higher hills. The unique topography of Jerusalem, accurately described in Zephaniah 1:10–11, allowed a loud cry to echo around the city and reverberate through its valleys, sending an alarm to all the inhabitants" (Wright, 84). Presumably, the **Fish Gate** was so named because a fish market was located there.

1:12–13. Verses 12–18 provide a horrifying account of the destruction of Jerusalem and its inhabitants in the coming judgment. God is depicted as searching **Jerusalem with lamps** to find every last one of the guilty. Many people in Jerusalem were **complacent**, thinking the Lord would **do nothing**. They were about to be stunned. Hannah explains the metaphor of **wine left on its dregs** as follows: "The analogy of wine left on its dregs suggests that the nation had become spiritually polluted. Wine allowed to ferment for a long time forms a hard crust and the liquid becomes syrupy, bitter, and unpalatable. Instead of removing the dregs of daily pollution, Judah had become hardened and indifferent to God" (Hannah, 1527). **Their wealth** and property would be taken away.

1:14–16. Zephaniah declared that the **day of the LORD** was **near. The cry** (literally, "voice, sound") on the approaching day of judgment **will be bitter**, either speaking of the wailing of those in Judah or the terrifying noise of the approaching enemy army. Elsewhere, the Hebrew word rendered **shouting** appears only in Isaiah 42:13, where it means to raise a battle cry against enemies. In light of its usage in Isaiah, **the shouting of the warrior** is best understood as the battle cry of Judah's invaders. The **day** of the Lord will be a time of **wrath** with its accompanying **anguish, trouble,** and other woes. Joel also spoke of this day as one of darkness, gloom, clouds, and blackness (Joel 2:2; see also Amos 5:18,20). **Trumpet and battle cry** were familiar elements of war. God's immediate judgment on Judah would come in the form of the Babylonian armies. The devastation and loss of life during the siege and fall of Jerusalem to Nebuchadnezzar in 586 B.C. were horrific. The city and its great temple were leveled, and survivors were carted off into captivity.

1:17–18. The phrase **walk like blind men** suggests helplessness. The reason for this judgment is set forth—**they have sinned against the** LORD. The Babylonians in Judah's day could not be bought (Ezek. 7:19), and neither could God. Zephaniah moved fluidly between the historical judgment of Judah by the Babylonians and the future punishment of the **whole world.** The fact that the historical manifestation of the day of the Lord occurred is proof that the future judgment would surely come. **Jealousy** describes God's attitude toward spiritual unfaithfulness. In Exodus 34:14, we read: "Do not worship any other god, for the LORD, whose name is Jealous, is a jealous God." God is jealous of our devotion and worship, and judgment is the result of failure to acknowledge him as Lord and Savior.

Ⓒ God's Unchanging Mercy (2:1–3)

SUPPORTING IDEA: *God is merciful and will spare the repentant on the day of judgment.*

2:1. Zephaniah's description of God's wrath on Judah, and ultimately all the earth, is overwhelming. Yet in this section we see God's loving heart. Zephaniah called on the people to seek the Lord, for the prophet knew that God is merciful and will forgive. Micah proclaims: "Who is a God like you, who pardons sin and forgives the transgression of the remnant of his inheritance? You do not stay angry forever but delight to show mercy" (Mic. 7:18). The apostle Peter adds that the Lord " is patient with you, not wanting any to perish, but all to come to repentance" (2 Pet. 3:9 HCSB). God loves the world (John 3:16) and is willing to show mercy to any who repent and believe. This has not changed throughout the ages.

Zephaniah sent out a call for the people to **gather together** (repeated for emphasis) for a time of national repentance. Joel issued a similar call during a time of national crisis: "Put on sackcloth, O priests, and mourn; wail, you who minister before the altar. Come, spend the night in sackcloth, you who minister before my God; for the grain offerings and drink offerings are withheld from the house of your God. Declare a holy fast; call a sacred assembly.

Summon the elders and all who live in the land to the house of the LORD your God, and cry out to the LORD" (Joel 1:13–14).

Here the Hebrew for **nation** is *goy*, a term usually reserved for the heathen nations. When applied to God's people, it often is intended as a rebuke. Zephaniah was implying that Judah was acting like the heathen. The NIV's **shameful** has also been translated "undesirable" (NKJV). Either meaning would be suitable, but most commentators seem to prefer "shameful" or "shameless."

2:2. Zephaniah pleaded with the nation to repent because God's judgment was approaching swiftly like light **chaff** driven by the wind. **Before** is repeated three times in the verse, emphasizing the urgency to repent quickly because it would soon be too late. The words **sweeps on, fierce anger,** and **wrath** emphasize the severity of the threat.

2:3. Now Zephaniah issued a call to **seek the LORD** (cp. Amos 5:5,14). The people were to **humble** themselves before God and obey his command to repent. They should demonstrate their sincerity by forsaking their sin and seeking **righteousness.** Perhaps then their lives would be spared during the coming Babylonian invasion (like Jeremiah, Daniel, and Ezekiel). Certainly, they would escape the final judgment (Rev. 20:11–15).

Ⅾ God's Unchanging Justice (2:4–15)

SUPPORTING IDEA: *God is just and will not allow nations that have mistreated his people to go unpunished.*

Besides Amos, Zephaniah is the only minor prophet to include prophecies against foreign nations. Each of these nations had committed offenses against God's people at some point in Israel's history and deserved judgment. Justice must be done because God is just. As justice was meted out to the ancient foes of his people, so God's justice will faithfully be carried out today.

Zephaniah singled out three nearby nations (Philistia, Moab, and Ammon) and two distant nations (Cush = Ethiopia and Assyria) for condemnation. Their location at all four points of the compass—Philistia (west), Moab and Ammon (east), Ethiopia (south), and Assyria (north)—seems to suggest that they represented all the world's nations.

2:4–7. When David came to the throne, Israel had been locked in a life-and-death struggle with the Philistines for more than century. They were a threat to the very existence of Israel as a nation. With God's help David's forces finally gained the upper hand in several key battles (2 Sam. 5:17–25; 8:1). Philistia was located on the coastal plain of the Mediterranean Sea in ancient Canaan north of modern Tel Aviv south to the Gaza strip. **Kerethite** refers to peoples from Crete who lived in Philistia. Zephaniah predicted the extinction of Philistia's peoples with Judah gaining their territory. Four of the five major Philistine cities are mentioned in order from south to north. Goliath's hometown of Gath (1 Sam. 17:4,23) was situated farther to the east and is omitted.

According to Wright, "Archaeological evidence suggests that ancient Gath (Tell es-Safi) was destroyed in the mid-eighth century B.C. This coincides with an attack on the city by Judah's King Uzziah described in 2 Chronicles 26:6. Biblical and Assyrian records listing the Philistine cities from about the middle of the eighth century B.C. on, fail to mention Gath, further corroborating Uzziah's destruction of the city (e.g., Jer. 25:20; Amos 1:6–8; Zeph. 2:4; Zech. 9:5–7)" (Wright, 85). The name Palestine is derived from "Philistine."

2:8–11. Moab was positioned to the south of Ammon, and both were located to Judah's east. Since they were positioned on the borders of Israel and Judah, conflict was inevitable. Amos tells of one sordid incident when the Ammonites "ripped open the pregnant women of Gilead" (Amos 1:13). These nations were opportunistic and now **made threats against** Judah. Apparently, they felt that Judah had deteriorated politically to the point that they could defeat them and take **their land**. The Lord God took boasts against his people personally for two reasons. First, he was jealously protective of his people. Second, the ancients believed that the nation with the greatest god(s) would prevail. Therefore, Moab and Ammon were directly challenging the Lord by asserting that Molech and Chemosh were more powerful.

In verse 11 the Lord promised to demonstrate his supremacy over these false deities by destroying their idols. Ultimately, all **nations** of the earth would **worship him**, thus proving that the Lord is the earth's greatest, and only, God. This wonderful promise will be fulfilled at Christ's return. For their impudence the Lord vowed to make Moab **like Sodom** and Ammon **like Gomorrah**, a terrifying fate (Gen. 19:24–25).

2:12. Cush was a nation situated south of Egypt roughly equivalent to modern Sudan and Ethiopia ("Cushites," NIV; "Ethiopians," KJV, NKJV, NASB, NRSV). Ethiopians fought with Pharaoh Shishak against Rehoboam (2 Chr. 12:3), and the Ethiopian general Zerah attacked Asa, king of Judah (2 Chr. 14:9). For a time (during Egypt's twenty-fifth dynasty), Ethiopians ruled over both Egypt and Ethiopia. Ethiopia would not escape God's judgment (cp. Isa. 18; Ezek. 30).

2:13–15. Assyria, located to the **north**, had harshly oppressed Judah for a hundred years. So complete would be the destruction of Assyria's magnificent palaces and buildings that **desert** birds and **wild beasts** would make their homes in their desolate ruins. Zephaniah referred to Nineveh as the **carefree city** because its people felt safe and secure within its great walls. Assyria's pride is expressed by the words, **I am, and there is none besides me.** Yet, at about this very time, the king who would destroy Nineveh, Nabopolassar, assumed the throne in Babylon (626 B.C.). Within fourteen years Zephaniah's prophecy of Nineveh's overthrow would be fulfilled (612 B.C.). God hates pride.

E God's Unchanging Moral Law (3:1–7)

SUPPORTING IDEA: *God's moral law never changes, and those who disobey it will be punished.*

We live in what has been labeled a postmodern culture where absolutes are considered out of date. Yet the Bible teaches there are indeed absolutes. Contrary to popular opinion God's moral law does not change. God's moral standards cannot change because they come from the unchangeable holy character of God himself. A few years ago one church had a sign that read, "Just because it's legal doesn't make it right." How true! Society may change, but God never does. In this section we discover that, sadly, human nature does not change either. Humanity continues to violate God's moral requirements. We will also discover that the sins of Zephaniah's day are the sins of our modern world. In reality, little has changed in more than twenty-six hundred years.

3:1–2. The description of **the city** clearly indicates Jerusalem, and in verse 7 this city is contrasted with the "nations" of verse 6. Once more Zephaniah pronounced divine judgment (**woe**, cp. Hab. 2) on Jerusalem for its many sins. In 1:2–18 the focus was on Jerusalem's idolatry; in 3:1–7 at least ten sins are cited: oppression of others (v. 1), rebellion against God (v. 1), spiritual defilement (v. 1), disobedience (v. 2), lack of trust in the Lord (v. 2), wickedness of rulers (v. 3), corrupt religious leaders (v. 4), injustice, by contrast with a just God (v. 5), lack of shame (v. 5), and refusal to heed God's warnings to repent (vv. 6–7). What an indictment!

Zephaniah had invited the people to "seek the LORD" (2:3), but they refused to **draw near to . . . God.** Judah had moved, not God. Like a loving father, the Lord still longed for his people to return to him (Joel 2:12; Zech. 1:3).

3:3–4. In these verses Judah's corrupt leaders are addressed. Her political leaders' oppressive behavior is compared to that of **roaring lions** and **evening wolves** who ferociously devoured their prey (cp. Mic. 3:9–10). According to Wright, "Zephaniah's use of 'evening wolves' (3:3; cp. Hab. 1:8) to describe Judah's judges was particularly sinister. Wolves habitually lay low throughout the day until dusk, striking when other animals are tired and ready to bed down for the night. They usually descend in packs, tearing their prey and gorging themselves on flesh. Jesus described false prophets as 'ravenous wolves' (Matt. 7:15 RSV), and the apostle Paul referred to false teachers as 'fierce wolves' not sparing the flock (Acts 20:29 RSV)" (Wright, 87).

Degradation among the people often reflects a failure of spiritual leadership. Not surprisingly, Zephaniah declared that apostasy among Judah's spiritual leaders was rampant. The word **treacherous** essentially denotes unfaithfulness in dealings with God or other people. These **prophets** were probably guilty of unfaithfulness in both areas. **Priests** were to teach **the law** (Ezra 7:12; 2 Chr. 15:3), but these had violated **the law** and profaned **the sanctuary**, evidently by their idolatry (Zeph. 1:4–5) and by offering blemished animals.

3:5–7. Zephaniah's reference to God's unfailing **justice** is a veiled rebuke of the injustice prevalent in Judah. God is **righteous**. By contrast Judah was **unrighteous**, but the people were unashamed of their sin. Mark Twain quipped, "Man is the only animal that blushes. Or needs to." Judah needed to blush but felt **no shame** (2:1; Jer. 8:12). Such an attitude is indicative of a decadent society. God's destruction of sinful **nations** was a warning to Jerusalem of the consequences of sin. Rather than repent, they were **eager to act corruptly**. Certainly, they should have learned from the destruction of the Northern Kingdom (Israel) by the Assyrians less than one hundred years before (2 Kgs. 18:9–12; Jer. 3:6–8). Yet Judah would not heed God's warning.

▐F▐ God's Unchanging Penalty for Unrepentant Sin (3:8)

SUPPORTING IDEA: *The penalty for unrepentant sin is certain judgment.*

3:8. Now Zephaniah moves from the historical circumstances of ancient Judah to the eschatological judgment of the **whole world** in the great day of the Lord (1:2–3). Not only Judah, but all sinful **nations** would undergo the unwavering penalty for sin—God's **wrath, fierce anger**, and **the fire** of his **jealous anger**. Assembling and gathering nations for judgment is language similar to that of the prophet Joel (3:2). **Stand up to testify** depicts God in a court of law presenting his case against these rebellious peoples. They would be found guilty. The term *jealous* at the end of the verse is often associated with idolatry and suggests that their sin is worshiping other gods.

The phrase **wait for me** is not a promise but a threat. God's penalty for unrepentant sin is judgment. It may take a while, but it is an unchanging and certain reality. Friedrich von Logau's often repeated saying is absolutely correct: "Though the mills of God grind slowly, yet they grind exceeding small; though with patience He stands waiting, with exactness grinds He all."

Ⓖ God's Unchanging Promise of a Better World (3:9–20)

SUPPORTING IDEA: *For the righteous God promises a glorious new world in the future.*

3:9. Thankfully, the Book of Zephaniah ends with a wonderful message of hope for the Gentile nations (3:9–10) and Judah (3:11–20). God has promised that a better world is coming some day, and he will never go back on his word. The word **then** is pivotal, indicating that blessing is now possible since sin has been purged.

God's choice of Israel was never intended to suggest that he did not love all the world's peoples. Israel was not to keep the truth of God to itself but was to spread the news throughout the earth. Many Gentiles, like Naaman the Syrian (2 Kgs. 5:15–17), worshiped the Lord during Old Testament times. In verse 9 Zephaniah informs us that some day all **peoples** will worship the Lord. God will **purify** their **lips** so they will no longer call on false gods but will **call on the name of the LORD**. Together they will **serve** the true God.

3:10. The **scattered people** who would come to Jerusalem to worship might be Jewish exiles dispersed as far as **Cush**, Gentiles, or a combination of Gentiles and dispersed Jews. Considering the universal language of verse 9, the latter view seems correct. Previously denounced (2:12), Cush is now mentioned in a positive light. Apparently, this nation is named because of its remote location and indicates that peoples from the farthest regions of the earth will worship the Lord.

3:11–13. The phrase **that day** refers to the day of the Lord and reveals that this time will include blessing as well as judgment. Jesus Christ (Messiah) himself will usher in this glorious new world at his second coming. Finally, the earth will experience what God always intended. Zephaniah outlined the blessed conditions in the messianic kingdom: sin's removal (vv. 11–13), joy (v. 14), security (vv. 15–17), no sorrow (v. 18), deliverance from oppressors (v. 19), a regathering (v. 20a), and honor (v. 20b).

Many scholars believe Zephaniah was describing the millennium (literally, "thousand years," Rev. 20:4) when Christ would rule as King on the earth. Primarily, this section was directed toward the Jewish people, but except for the promise of national regathering (v. 20), all these blessings apply to Gentile believers as well. The wicked would be removed from Jerusalem (**holy hill**; Ps. 2:6; Dan. 9:16,20; Joel 2:1; 3:17), and the city would now be filled with **the meek and humble, who trust in the name of the** LORD (contrast 3:2). Finally, Jesus' prophecy will be fulfilled: "Blessed are the meek, for they will inherit the earth" (Matt. 5:5).

3:14–17. Christ's presence and blessing will bring inexpressible joy and absolute security to his people. Never again need believers **fear** because **the** LORD, **the King of Israel**, is with them. The phrase **hands hang limp** is a figure of extreme terror (Jer. 6:24; 50:43). In 1:4 God had fought against Judah; now the one who is **mighty to save** will defend them.

3:18–20. Verse 18 is difficult, as evidenced by the divergent translations in the English versions. In light of the regathering predicted in verses 19–20, verse 18 may be taken as God's promise to **remove** the sorrow of exiled Jews who were unable to participate in the **feasts**. Observing the feasts had been a **burden** for the wicked (and **a reproach**, either displeasing to God or a disgrace) but would be a joy for the redeemed. God will judge those who had **oppressed** his people and bring **home** all those who had been dispersed to other lands. Rather than being weak and disgraced, they will be honored by **all the peoples of the earth**. What a contrast between the opening and concluding verses of this prophecy!

> **MAIN IDEA REVIEW:** *God does not change. He is a jealous God who demands that we worship him alone and a holy God who requires that we be holy. He is merciful and forgives, but unrepentant sin will bring his judgment. For the penitent God promises a glorious future.*

III. CONCLUSION

The Richest Person in History

According to *Forbes* magazine's sixteenth annual ranking of billionaires, Microsoft's Bill Gates is the world's richest person with $52.8 billion. Yet Gates's wealth is dwarfed by the person whom Guinness World Records names the richest in history—John D. Rockefeller. In 1913 Rockefeller's fortune was worth $900 million, which is the equivalent of almost $190 billion today. Happily, Rockefeller was a Christian. By 1922 he had given away a billion dollars to family members and charity, keeping just $20 million for himself.

In this life, wealth can provide a measure of protection, but all the money in the world cannot save from sin or buy heaven. Zephaniah prophesied that the day of the Lord is coming when the wicked will be judged. He warned: "Neither their silver nor their gold will be able to save them on the day of the LORD's wrath" (1:18). The Babylonians in Judah's day could not be bought (Ezek. 7:19); neither can God. How may we escape judgment and be part of the wonderful messianic kingdom described in 3:9–20? Zephaniah tells us in 2:3, "Seek the LORD." God is willing to forgive our sin and welcome us into his family. Then the day of the Lord will not be "darkness and gloom" (1:15) but joy and gladness (3:14).

PRINCIPLES

- God demands that we worship him alone rather than the false gods of this world.
- Someday God's judgment will fall on an unrepentant world.
- God is merciful and invites us to seek him and escape judgment.
- God is just and will punish those who mistreat his people.
- Humanity should obey God's unchanging moral law.
- The penalty for unrepentant sin is certain judgment.
- God has promised his followers a wonderful future with him.

APPLICATIONS

- God's judgment is an incentive for us to share our faith with others.
- Read Zephaniah 2:3 and identify characteristics of those people who please God in this passage.
- Name countries where believers are being oppressed today.
- List sins mentioned in the Book of Zephaniah that are prevalent today.
- Praise the Lord for the promise of our glorious future with Christ.
- List characteristics of the messianic age described in Zephaniah 3:9–20.

IV. LIFE APPLICATION

Titanic's Unheeded Warnings

The "unsinkable" *Titanic* sped through the icy Atlantic waters on the moon-less night of April 14, 1912, in spite of at least six ice warnings received from other ships that very day. According to *Great Mysteries of the Past* both the *Caronia* and *Baltic* had sent messages alerting Captain E. J. Smith. At least twice, the *Californian* sent messages. "Three large icebergs" was the first warning from that ship's operator. "Say, old man," he radioed in the evening, from a point nineteen miles away, "we are stuck here, surrounded by ice." A testy Jack Phillips snapped back, "Keep out. Shut up. You're jamming my signal. I'm working on Cape Race" . . . From the Cape Race operator in Newfoundland, Phillips was receiving messages for the important passengers aboard his ship. . . . The water temperature fell rapidly from 43 degrees Fahrenheit to slightly below freezing in only a few hours—always an indication in northerly water that ice might be floating near. Yet the *Titanic* neither slowed nor turned southward to avoid the danger zone into which it was entering.

At 11:40 p.m. the iceberg was sighted. At 2:20 a.m. the *Titanic* slid beneath the water, breaking in two as it fell thirteen thousand feet to the bottom of the ocean floor. Over fifteen hundred lives were lost. *Titanic* would not heed the warning (*Great Mysteries of the Past*, Pleasantville, N.Y.: The Reader's Digest Association, Inc, 1991, p. 415).

Zephaniah issued a warning to ancient Judah. It was a warning they did not heed, and like the *Titanic* they paid the price. The Babylonian armies destroyed Jerusalem and its great temple, then carted Judah's inhabitants off into exile. The prophet's warning is just as relevant for nations and individuals in our time who have rejected the true God. Like the *Titanic* they are moving rapidly toward disaster, and Zephaniah's call to "seek the Lord" is their only hope. Let us pray that they heed the warning!

V. PRAYER

O Lord, you have made us for yourself, and we give our lives to you as our Lord and Savior. Thank you for loving us enough to forgive our sins and to save us from judgment. Help us to be faithful in sharing Christ with others so that they will "not perish but have eternal life" (John 3:16). We look forward to that day when all the world will acknowledge your Son Jesus as Lord. Thank you that you have in store for your children a wonderful future world where peace, joy, and righteousness will prevail. In Jesus' name we pray. Amen.

VI. DEEPER DISCOVERIES

A. Zephaniah's Name (1:1)

Zephaniah's name means "the Lord hides," apparently suggesting that the Lord hides his followers for their protection. In the same vein the psalmist declared: "For in the day of trouble he will keep me safe in his dwelling; he will hide me in the shelter of his tabernacle and set me high upon a rock" (Ps. 27:5; see also Pss. 31:20; 32:7; 64:2). Zephaniah was born during the reign of Manasseh, one of the most evil men in the Old Testament. In 2 Kings 21:16 we are told that "Manasseh also shed so much innocent blood that he filled Jerusalem from end to end." Jewish tradition, seemingly reflected in Hebrews 11:37, says that Manasseh even martyred the great prophet Isaiah. Zephaniah's name may indicate God's protection during this dangerous time. In light of 2:3 (believers "sheltered"), the name may also be a subtle promise to the repentant of protection from God's wrath.

B. Zephaniah's Ancestry (1:1)

Zephaniah traced his ancestry through four generations, a fact that is unique among the prophets. Zechariah named two generations (Zech. 1:1), whereas Isaiah, Jeremiah, Ezekiel, Hosea, Joel, and Jonah listed only their father's name. Eight prophets provide no specific genealogical information (Daniel, Amos, Obadiah, Micah, Nahum, Habakkuk, Haggai, and Malachi).

Kaiser offers the following explanation of Zephaniah's extended genealogy: "The most plausible reason for the genealogy is that the author wanted to make clear that he was a Jew even though his father's name was 'Cushi,' meaning 'Ethiopian.' There is a strong chance that his father was a foreigner, but Jewish nevertheless, just as the thousands of recent Ethiopian immigrants to Israel are foreigners yet Jewish. As Moses prescribed in Deuteronomy 23:8, in Zephaniah's time if a Jewish woman married a foreigner, the offspring of that union could not be accepted into the Jewish community until a pure Jewish pedigree was established for at least three generations. Zephaniah demonstrated such a pedigree" (Kaiser, *Mastering the Old Testament*, 207).

Other commentators, probably correctly, hold that Zephaniah traced his lineage back four generations to demonstrate his relationship to the great

King Hezekiah, who died about 686 B.C. If so, Zephaniah was a member of the royal family and was descended from one of Judah's most revered kings. With the likely exception of Daniel, Zephaniah was the only known Old Testament prophet of royal blood and of such high social prominence. He was also distantly related to the ruling King Josiah (640–609 B.C.). Perhaps Zephaniah felt the connection to the respected Hezekiah would help his message gain a wider audience.

C. Worship of the Starry Host (1:5)

Worship of astral deities was pervasive in ancient times. In Egypt the sun god Re was the dominant deity, and pharaohs often included his name in their title (e.g., Rameses II). In the fourteenth century B.C., Pharaoh Akhenaton, also called Amenhotep IV (the famed King Tutankhamun's father-in-law), even attempted to force the Egyptians to worship the sun god, Aton, exclusively. The sun god was also worshiped in Sumeria, ancient India, during the later periods of Roman history, by the plains Indians of North America, and by early civilizations in Mexico and Peru. The Aztecs offered human sacrifices to the sun gods. In Japan the sun goddess, Amaterasu, was worshiped as the supreme ruler of the universe, and the sun symbol still represents Japan.

Other heavenly bodies were worshiped as well. Thoth, the moon god, was revered as the Egyptian god of learning, and pharaohs were named after him (Thutmose I, II, III). Nut was the Egyptian sky goddess. Babylonian Sin, the moon god, was worshiped with his wife Ningal in temples at Ur and Harran. Judah had become enamored with the gods of these powerful and prosperous pagan nations and had adopted their gods, foolishly hoping that these deities would bless them.

Ancient peoples were in awe of these heavenly bodies, yet today we know that they are only spheres of fiery gases or earthlike materials. In spite of our modern scientific knowledge, astrology has gained a wide following, and horoscopes appear in most major newspapers in America. Usually modern astrologers deny that the celestial bodies are deities, but they still erroneously claim that the planets and stars in some way determine or affect human destiny. Not only is such belief not supported by scientific evidence; it is spiritually dangerous and unbiblical (Isa. 47:13; Jer. 10:2).

D. "The Day of the LORD" (1:7,14)

The day of the Lord is a major theological theme in the Old Testament and the focal point of Zephaniah's prophecy. The exact phrase, "day of the LORD," appears sixteen times in the Old Testament (Isa. 13:6,9; Ezek. 13:5; 30:3; Joel 1:15; 2:1,11,31; 3:14; Amos 5:18,20; Obad. 15; Zeph. 1:7,14; Zech. 14:1; Mal. 4:5), but references to the day of the Lord are much more extensive. Often the day of the Lord is simply spoken of as "the day," "that day," or "in that day." Zephaniah wrote the full phrase three times (1:7,14[twice]), but referred to the "day of the LORD" another seventeen times by using the following expressions: "on the day" (1:8; 2:3), "on that day" (1:9,10; 3:11,16), "that day" (1:15; 2:2), "a day" (1:15[five times],16), and "the day" (1:18; 2:2; 3:8).

Examination of the Book of Zephaniah reveals the following truths about the day of the Lord: (1) At that time Gentile nations will be judged (1:2–3,18; 3:8). (2) The wicked in Israel will be judged (1:4–18). (3) This judgment will be carried out by the Lord, portrayed as a mighty and just warrior-judge (1:2–9,12,17–18; 3:8). (4) Ultimately, the day will be eschatological (1:2–3,18; 3:8). However, historical judgments were often associated with the day of the Lord, apparently as acts that prefigure the future, universal judgment. For example, Zephaniah 1:4–18 probably has relevance both to the Babylonian destruction and the end times. (5) People may escape this judgment by repentance (2:2–3). (6) Universal judgment will be followed by a glorious age in which the Lord will dwell with the righteous (3:9–20). All the earth's people will then worship the true God (2:11; 3:9–10). (7) Since it encompasses both the final judgment and the messianic age, the day of the Lord is obviously not a twenty-four-hour day but a period of time.

In the New Testament the phrase, "day of the Lord," appears in Acts 2:20; 1 Corinthians 5:5; 2 Corinthians 1:14; 1 Thessalonians 5:2; 2 Thessalonians 2:2; 2 Peter 3:10. Other abbreviated references to the day of the Lord, such as "the Day" (e.g., 1 Cor. 3:13; Heb. 10:25), could be cited. Later New Testament revelation associates this day with Jesus Christ's second coming (1 Cor. 1:8; 2 Cor. 1:14; Phil. 1:6,10; 1 Thess. 5:2; 2 Pet. 3:10).

VII. TEACHING OUTLINE

A. INTRODUCTION

1. Lead Story: Beloit College Mind-set List
2. Context: Zephaniah is probably the most neglected of all the prophets. He wrote his book during the early reign of godly King Josiah (640–609 B.C.), likely about 625 B.C. Habakkuk prophesied approximately twenty years later. Zephaniah lived in the Southern Kingdom

(Judah) and addressed the idolatry and wickedness prevalent in that day. The moral decay reflected in the book grew out of the evil reigns of Manasseh (697–642 B.C.) and his son Amon (642–640 B.C.). Zephaniah's preaching was probably instrumental in preparing the way for the great religious reformation under Josiah (about 622–621 B.C.). The overriding theme of the prophecy is "the day of the LORD," a time of judgment for the wicked and blessing for the righteous.

3. Transition: Zephaniah's message is unchanging truth. God demands that we worship him rather than the false gods of our world. Today's idols may not be Baal and Molech, but our world is filled with idolatry just the same. Multitudes worship the gods of materialism, humanism, secularism, pleasure, and false religion. Such rejection of the true God will bring the same results as in Zephaniah's day— judgment. Yet God's merciful character is unchanging. He stands ready to forgive. For all those who will come to him, God promises a glorious future.

B. COMMENTARY

1. God's Prophet (1:1)
2. God's Unchanging Demand for Worship (1:2–18)
3. God's Unchanging Mercy (2:1–3)
4. God's Unchanging Justice (2:4–15)
5. God's Unchanging Moral Law (3:1–7)
6. God's Unchanging Penalty for Unrepentant Sin (3:8)
7. God's Unchanging Promise of a Better World (3:9–20)

C. CONCLUSION: THE RICHEST PERSON IN HISTORY

VIII. ISSUES FOR DISCUSSION

1. What right does the God of the Bible have to demand that we worship him, and him alone?
2. Do you think that God's judgment of a lost world should be a motivation for witnessing? Explain.
3. How is God's love revealed in the Book of Zephaniah?
4. What are some characteristics of the messianic kingdom described in Zephaniah 3:9–20?

Haggai 1–2

A Call to Commitment

I. **INTRODUCTION**
Hero of United Airlines Flight 93

II. **COMMENTARY**
A verse-by-verse explanation of these chapters.

III. **CONCLUSION**
The Chicken and the Pig

An overview of the principles and applications from these chapters.

IV. **LIFE APPLICATION**
Martyr for Christ

Melding these chapters to life.

V. **PRAYER**
Tying these chapters to life with God.

VI. **DEEPER DISCOVERIES**
Historical, geographical, and grammatical enrichment of the commentary.

VII. **TEACHING OUTLINE**
Suggested step-by-step group study of these chapters.

VIII. **ISSUES FOR DISCUSSION**
Zeroing these chapters in on daily life.

" *N*o reserve, no retreat, and no regrets."

W i l l i a m   B o r d e n

PROPHECY PROFILE

- The Book of Haggai (only thirty-eight verses) follows Obadiah as the second shortest book in the Old Testament, yet it is packed with spiritual truth.

- Haggai was the first of the postexilic prophetic books.

- Haggai's literary style is simple and direct prose.

- The prophecy consists of an introduction and four brief messages, each beginning with "the word of the LORD came" (1:3; 2:1,10,20). These four messages are dated specifically, and all were delivered within four months of each other in 520 B.C. (the second year of Darius I). According to our present calendar, Haggai's first prophecy was delivered on August 29, the second on October 17, and the third and fourth on December 18.

- Ezra records the historical background for this prophecy and specifically mentions Haggai in Ezra 5:1–2 and 6:14–15.

- The purpose of Haggai's message was to encourage the people to commit themselves to finish work on the temple. Work on the temple began soon after the first Jews returned from exile (538/7 B.C.), but after the foundation had been laid, it halted due to opposition from Judah's enemies (Ezra 4:1–5,24). Haggai proclaimed that the time had come to complete the task. The people obeyed his message and finished the temple four years later.

AUTHOR PROFILE: HAGGAI THE PROPHET

- Haggai's name means "festal" or "festive." Possibly he was given this name because he was born on an Israelite feast day.

- Like seven other prophets, Haggai provides no information about his parentage or genealogy. Other than his name, we know nothing about his personal life.
- Haggai evidently returned from Babylon with Zerubbabel.
- He was the first prophet to preach in Jerusalem after the exile.
- On the basis of Haggai 2:3, some interpreters believe that Haggai had seen Solomon's temple before its destruction by the Babylonians in 586 B.C.—sixty-six years before. If so, he must have been over seventy years of age.
- Haggai affirmed the divine authority of his messages with phrases like, "This is what the LORD Almighty says," at least twenty-five times in his two short chapters.
- Some manuscripts of the ancient Greek version of the Old Testament called the Septuagint attribute Psalms 137 and 145–148 to Haggai and/or Zechariah, whereas the Latin Vulgate assigns Psalms 125–126 and 145–147 to Haggai and/or Zechariah.
- Haggai was a contemporary of the prophet Zechariah.
- Haggai was a man of courage and commitment.

READER PROFILE: THE POSTEXILIC NATION OF JUDAH

- In 539 B.C. Babylon fell to the Medo-Persian armies of Cyrus the Great (cp. Dan. 5). From this point until its defeat by Alexander the Great in a series of battles (334–331 B.C.), the Medo-Persian Empire dominated the world. Judah became a province of the empire and was ruled by a governor appointed by the Medo-Persians. Cyrus was a benevolent ruler who permitted the exiled Jews (and other peoples) to return to their homeland. Haggai and his fellow countrymen had now returned to Judah and were in the process of rebuilding the country.
- Haggai's prophecy was directed to this postexilic group of Jewish believers who had been in the land almost twenty years. Zerubbabel, the governor, and Joshua, the high priest, are specifically addressed in the book (1:1; 2:2,21).
- Conditions were difficult for the returnees, yet they were filled with joy at being back in the land of Abraham, Isaac, and Jacob (Ps. 126:1–3).

- Haggai's message makes clear that the people had become preoccupied with their own material interests and had neglected God's work.

Haggai 1

IN A NUTSHELL

The prophet Haggai calls on his countrymen to finish the task of rebuilding the temple which they had started about sixteen years earlier. The threat of outside intervention has passed, but the people show little interest in finishing God's house. Haggai recognizes the problem as a lack of spiritual commitment to God. He points out that the people's lack of blessing is directly related to their lack of commitment. The people repent and begin the work of rebuilding. God assures them that, unlike before, the work will be completed. God even promises that this second temple will eventually be greater than Solomon's temple! Haggai concludes the book with a prophecy of God's triumph over all earth's kingdoms.

A Call to Commitment

I. INTRODUCTION

Hero of United Airlines Flight 93

*U*nited Airlines Flight 93 took off from Newark Airport for San Francisco at 8:43 a.m. with forty-four people on board. Less than five minutes later a hijacked American Airlines jet crashed into the north tower of the World Trade Center. By 9:32 a.m. the flight recorder indicated that the hijackers (four in all) had taken control of Flight 93.

Seated in the rear of the jet, a young man named Todd Beamer picked up a phone and reached operator Lisa Jefferson. He described one hijacker who appeared to have a bomb and two bodies lying on the floor outside the cockpit. At 9:35 a.m. the plane suddenly made a U-turn in the direction of Washington, D.C. Because of a delay in taking off, passengers were alerted that the World Trade Center and Pentagon had been hit by hijackers. They knew their plane was turning back toward Washington as a flying missile, possibly to kill thousands of innocent people.

Beamer and a group of other brave passengers knew what they had to do. Todd, an evangelical Christian, asked Jefferson to promise to tell his family how much he loved them and then asked her to say the Lord's Prayer with him. Jefferson said Todd's last words were, "Are you guys ready? OK. Let's roll." He put the phone down. A chorus of screams and yells were overheard over the phones, then silence. Within minutes the plane went down in a field near Shanksville, Pennsylvania, a dark cloud of smoke rising from the crater created by the crash. It was 10:10 a.m. Authorities believe that the terrorists' target was either the White House or the Capitol building.

Todd's life was short, but he made his mark. Later his wife Lisa made this remarkable statement: "Some people live their whole lives, long lives, without having left anything behind. My sons will be told their whole lives that their father was a hero." Todd's battle cry, "Let's roll," has become part of American vernacular. Todd Beamer and his comrades gave their lives to save others. What commitment!

The prophet Haggai also talked about commitment. He called on his fellow Jews in ancient Israel to commit themselves to serve the Lord. Today's believers should heed Haggai's call as well. Planet Earth is in chaos, and its only hope is Christ. In order to reach the world with God's message of love, peace, and forgiveness, Christians must commit themselves to follow Christ at any cost. Now let us hear what Haggai has to say to us in this wonderful little treasure written more than twenty-five hundred years ago.

II. COMMENTARY

A Call to Commitment

MAIN IDEA: *Individuals and nations committed to God will be blessed. God promises victory for them in this life and in the world to come.*

🅰 A Committed Prophet and an Uncommitted People (1:1–2)

SUPPORTING IDEA: *God accepts no excuses for lack of commitment.*

1:1. Haggai's prophecy is very brief but precisely dated. Since Judah no longer had a king, the book was dated according to the reign of a foreign ruler. **Darius** I (522–486 B.C.) was the third in the line of Medo-Persian monarchs, following Cyrus and his son, Cambyses II. His **second year** stretched from spring 520 B.C. to spring 521 B.C. The **sixth month** was called Elul and spanned portions of our August and September. The **first day** of that month in 520 B.C. was August 29. The New Moon festival was held on the first day of the month (Num. 10:10; 28:11; Ps. 81:3; Isa. 1:13–14; Hos. 2:11; Amos 8:5), and probably a large crowd had gathered for the holiday. Haggai took advantage of this opportunity to address his fellow countrymen.

The word of the LORD came appears over one hundred times in the Old Testament, including five times in Haggai (1:1,3; 2:1,10,20). The phrase is a strong affirmation of the divine inspiration of the Bible. Historically, the phrase is of great importance as well. This was the first recorded instance after the return from the Babylonian exile of an authentic word from God coming through a prophet to the people. Haggai's name is derived from the Hebrew word for "festival" (*chag*) and apparently means "festal" or "festive." Possibly he was so named because he was born on a feast day. Other than Haggai's name, we have no biographical information about him. Frequently, the prophets identify their fathers' names, but like seven other prophets (Daniel, Amos, Obadiah, Micah, Nahum, Habakkuk, and Malachi), Haggai provides no specific genealogical information. Here he merely refers to himself as **the prophet** (also in 1:3; 2:1,10), and in 1:13 as "the LORD's messenger." Evidently Haggai was so well-known to his contemporaries that no further identification was necessary.

Zerubbabel ("seed of Babylon") was the grandson of King Jehoiachin (1 Chr. 3:17) and had been appointed **governor of Judah** by the Persian government. **Joshua** was the spiritual leader of the postexilic community, the **high priest** of the line of Zadok. Like Zerubbabel, Joshua (a common name in ancient Israel; also spelled *Jeshua*) returned from the Babylonian exile (Ezra 2:2). **Jehozadak,** Joshua's father, was the high priest deported to Babylon from Jerusalem in 586 B.C. (1 Chr. 6:15). Addressing these leaders by name probably emphasized their responsibility to lead the people to take the right action.

1:2. The prophet made clear that ultimately this message was not his but that of God himself. **The LORD Almighty** (traditionally, "the LORD of hosts") occurs fourteen times in the Book of Haggai and emphasizes God's power and might.

Haggai begins by quoting an apparently popular saying among the people, **The time has not yet come for the LORD's house to be built.** This pious sounding rhetoric was nothing more than an excuse not to follow the Lord. In reality many of the people had become so obsessed with their own lives that they had little time for the things of God. Moreover, in the following verses Haggai related that they selfishly would rather spend their money on lavish homes than the house of God.

We may observe the dramatic contrast between the problems addressed in the postexilic community and those faced by their counterparts before the exile. Zephaniah, for example, preached against rampant idolatry, oppression of the poor, evil leaders, injustice, and apostate prophets and priests. Haggai did not mention any of these matters, for the fire of the exile had purged the nation of such flagrant sins. Rather, he focused on the people's lack of spiritual commitment, specifically their neglect of the task of rebuilding the temple.

B A Rebuke for Lack of Commitment and the People's Repentance (1:3-15)

SUPPORTING IDEA: *Haggai points out that many of his nation's ills are because of a lack of commitment to God. The people immediately repent of their lack of commitment and determine to obey God.*

1:3-4. The first of Haggai's four sermons is introduced by the characteristic phrase, **the word of the LORD came.** The prophet's question to the people is convicting. Should you be living in luxury while God's **house** lies in ruins? Of course not! The Hebrew word translated **paneled** (literally, "covered") in verse 4 occurs only five times elsewhere in the Old Testament. In context a covering of the stone in the interior of the home with paneled wood seems to be the meaning (cp. Jer. 22:14).

1:5. The phrase **give careful thought** (literally, "set your heart") is a favorite expression of Haggai (1:5,7; 2:15,18[twice]). Here and in verse 7, he asked the people to think about the direction of their lives (**ways**). Not building the temple was not the problem; it was merely an external symptom. The problem was much deeper—an uncommitted life. Haggai's prophecy is often used to encourage giving, particularly to building programs. Admittedly, when observing a church building in disrepair, it is easy to question the commitment of the church members. However, the problem is not the building; it is the heart. The principles that Haggai set forth reach far beyond a building program. They extend to God's work and spiritual things generally. How important are the things of God to us? What are our priorities?

1:6. Haggai called on the people to look around and observe what was happening. Their crops were not producing; therefore, they did not have enough to **eat** and **drink**. Their clothing was insufficient to keep them **warm**, and there always seemed to be too much month at the end of the paycheck. In verses 9–11, Haggai made clear that these dismal economic conditions were the result of divine chastening for disobedience (cp. Lev. 26:18–20; Deut. 28:38–40). The people were not being blessed because of their selfishness and lack of commitment to God. Certainly, God's blessing includes much more than the material. God's fellowship, inward peace, and joy are far more important. However, all the missed blessings that Haggai pointed to in this verse are material in nature. Perhaps Haggai felt that this would be the most obvious to the people and in their lethargic spiritual condition may have commanded their attention more readily. However, this verse and many others in the Bible show that God does indeed bless his children materially for their faithfulness (Matt. 6:33).

1:7. Once more God called on the people to think about what they were doing. The call to self-examination implies an invitation to repentance.

1:8. This verse begins the first positive part of Haggai's message to the people. He had told them what they should not do; now he tells them what they should do. He followed the negative with a positive message—a good lesson for modern preachers and teachers. Haggai urged his countrymen to focus on God's work (specifically, the building of his temple) rather than themselves.

The prophet's exhortation involved three imperatives: **go up**, **bring down**, and **build**. Stone for temple construction was readily available in Jerusalem. The quarry from which the stones were cut for Solomon's temple and this second temple may be visited in Jerusalem today. However, **timber** for the beams, roof, and inside paneling of the building had to be brought in from a distance. For Solomon's temple cedar was acquired from Lebanon (1 Kgs. 5:6–10). About fifteen years before Haggai's message, the returnees had once more brought in cedar from Lebanon for the temple (Ezra 3:7). Perhaps these materials had been used for private homes, because God instructed them to **go up into the mountains** and cut more wood for the building. Whether they brought lumber from Lebanon or used timber from within the country is unknown. Their sad economic condition may have necessitated the latter.

God stated that completion of the new temple would please and honor him. The temple symbolized God's presence with his people, and it was the place where they could gather to worship him. Such worship pleased the Lord. A place of worship would also honor God because it would demonstrate to the nations that his followers felt he was worthy of their commitment and worship.

1:9–11. Verses 9–11 are the divine commentary on verses 4–6. What had previously been implied is now specifically stated. Judah's people were not being blessed because of their selfishness and disobedience of God. Crops, vineyards, and olive trees (**oil**) languished for lack of rain, a divine judgment for sin (Deut. 28:22–23).

1:12. Seldom in history has a spiritual reformation been so immediate and complete. From the leaders (**Zerubbabel**, **Joshua**) to the **whole remnant of the people**, they repented of their sin and committed themselves to obey **the voice of the LORD their God**. Often prophets had met with indifference, mocking, hostility, and even martyrdom (2 Chr. 24:20–22; cp. Matt. 23:35). How refreshing it is to find such a welcome response to God's word. What was the difference between Haggai's audience and that of many preexilic prophets? These people **feared the LORD**. Apparently, they were true believers who had allowed the things of the world to turn their hearts. Once confronted with their sin, they repented.

1:13. When Judah's people repented, God was quick to express the fact that his fellowship and blessing would now return to them (**I am with you**). God loves his people and is always willing to forgive. With forgiveness comes all the blessings of God on our lives. God's promise to be with his people also encouraged them. His presence and power would assure the success of the daunting task that lay ahead.

1:14–15. God touched the hearts of the people and their leaders, and they began work on the temple. Construction began on September 21, 520 B.C., only twenty-three days (cp. 1:1) after Haggai's sermon! Such a short delay before beginning the work was amazing, but even that may be explained by the fact that they were in a harvest month (of figs, grapes, and pomegranates) and also needed time to prepare for the building project.

Ⅽ Commitment and Courage (2:1–9)

> **SUPPORTING IDEA:** *The people and their leaders are told to follow the Lord courageously, because his power will ensure their protection and success.*

2:1. Haggai's second message is marked by the characteristic phrase, **the word of the LORD came**, and a new date (October 17, 520 B.C.). Following God takes courage. Fifteen years earlier, this same group had been forced to shut down work on the temple because of opposition from enemies and slanderous accusations made against them to the Persian authorities (Ezra 4:1–5). In Nehemiah's day (about eighty years later), enemies of the Jews even threatened to kill those people who were rebuilding Jerusalem's wall (Neh. 4:11). In this section God calmed their fears by assuring them that their efforts would be successful because of his greatness and power.

2:2–3. Solomon's temple was truly a wonder of the ancient world. Available to King Solomon was an immeasurable cache of gold, silver, fine stone, marble, and other valuable materials for its construction (1 Chr. 29:1–8). It took almost two hundred thousand workmen approximately seven years to build (1 Kgs. 5:13–16; 6:38). Perched high on Mount Moriah, the temple was an impressive sight. Now the whole nation consisted of only a little group of fifty thousand returnees with very limited resources. To returnees who had seen Solomon's magnificent temple the new structure seemed **like nothing** (cp. Zech. 4:10). As a matter of fact, when the foundation was laid about sixteen years earlier, they wept while others shouted for joy (Ezra 3:10–13).

2:4–5. How could such a small group do such a great work? Three times—to **Zerubbabel, Joshua,** and all the **people**—God proclaimed, **Be strong.** They could accomplish the task because God was with them (see 1:13). Yes, the work was too great for them but not for **the LORD Almighty.** Not by mere human power but by God's might, their temple would be built (cp. Zech. 4:6). At Sinai the Lord had promised in his covenant with Israel to be their God. Therefore, they did not need to **fear** their enemies or the magnitude of the task.

2:6. God shook the earth at Sinai (Exod. 19:18); the second time he will **shake** the universe—nature and nations. God's eschatological judgment is described in terms of an earthquake ("shake"; Isa. 2:21; Ezek. 38:20; Hag. 2:21–22). Jesus predicted that at his return to earth "the heavenly bodies will be shaken" (Matt. 24:29). The writer to the Hebrews quoted Haggai 2:6 and emphasized that we have received "a kingdom [the kingdom of God] that cannot be shaken" (Heb. 12:28).

2:7. The phrase **the desired of all nations** may signify the "desirable things" of the nations that would be brought to **fill** this future temple or the "desirable One"—the Messiah—who would come. This latter view has been held by many people, including some ancient Jewish rabbis, early Christian leaders like Jerome and Martin Luther, and many modern commentators. Either view is possible, but the former seems more likely in the context of rebuilding the temple. The reference to "silver" and "gold" in the next verse would suggest that these are the kinds of "desirable things" that Haggai had in mind. Furthermore, when the "desired of all nations" comes, this future temple will be filled **with glory**. Verse 9 connects this "glory" with the "glory" and opulence of Solomon's temple. However, Jesus the Messiah will certainly be present and ruling from the future temple following the shaking of the heavens and the earth.

2:8–9. In verse 8 God reminded the little band of Judahites, possibly discouraged because their building was so inferior to Solomon's, that all the wealth (**silver, gold**) of the universe was at his disposal. He would ensure that his temple was properly adorned (cp. v. 7). Neither should they feel that their task was insignificant. Eventually, the grandeur (**glory**) of their temple would surpass that of **the former house**, the temple destroyed by the Babylonians. By the time it was completed, Herod's temple (not a third but a continuation of the second temple) was a larger complex and in many ways more grand than Solomon's (Mark 13:1). Moreover, the second temple was afforded more honor because it was graced by the presence of God incarnate, Jesus Christ.

In addition to the wonderful new building, God would **grant peace** to Jerusalem, a comforting promise to people surrounded by hostile neighbors. Probably the ultimate fulfillment of this passage is the reign of Messiah and the temple of the messianic age. Only then will the world have genuine peace.

Consequences of Judah's Past Lack of Commitment (2:10–19)

> **SUPPORTING IDEA:** *Haggai reminds the people that their previous lack of commitment has defiled the nation and prevented God's blessing.*

2:10. Haggai's third message is dated at December 18, 520 B.C. Between Haggai's second ("seventh month," 2:1) and third sermons (**ninth month**), the prophet Zechariah began his ministry ("eighth month," Zech. 1:1).

2:11–14. The Lord instructed Haggai to **ask the priests** for an official ruling from **the law** on two matters. First, can ceremonial holiness be transferred to **other food** when it comes into contact with **consecrated meat** (cp. Jer. 11:15), meat for sacrifice? Of course not! Second, can ceremonial defilement be transferred to others by **a person defiled by contact with a dead body**? They answered **yes** (Num. 19:11–13). In verse 14 Haggai applied these rulings to the people of Judah. While holiness cannot be transferred, sin among the people renders their worship and offerings unacceptable (defiled) to the Lord. The result is a lack of God's blessing. Association with the wrong crowd can also bring spiritual defilement. The apostle Paul warned, "Do not be misled: 'Bad company corrupts good character'" (1 Cor. 15:33).

2:15–19. Haggai took the illustration a step further and reminded his audience that before their obedience, they were defiled by sin and, thus, were not being blessed (cp. 1:5,9–11). Three of the five uses of the phrase, **give careful thought**, appear in these verses. Now that they had repented, God promised, **From this day on I will bless you.** An exciting new day was in store for God's people.

E The Future Hope of Those Committed to God (2:20–23)

> **SUPPORTING IDEA:** *Haggai concludes his prophecy by assuring the faithful that their God will triumph over the world.*

2:20–22. The prophet's fourth and final message came on the same day as the third, December 18, 520 B.C. Although the message was specifically addressed to Zerubbabel, the promise of the glorious future kingdom described here was for all believers. Zerubbabel's task of leading this tiny group of Jews on the outskirts of the vast Persian Empire was difficult, so God gave him a special word of encouragement. First, Zerubbabel was assured that his God would ultimately be victorious over all world powers. Once more, the Lord promised to **shake** nature and nations. Earth's mighty kingdoms (even the great Medo-Persian Empire) would fall before the Lord. As the apostle John exclaimed: "The kingdom of the world has become the kingdom of our Lord and of His Messiah, and He will reign forever and ever!" (Rev. 11:15 HCSB).

2:23. Second, Zerubbabel was assured that he was God's **chosen** servant whose rule (**signet ring**, the symbol of ruling authority) had divine blessing. However, the ultimate fulfillment of this verse goes far beyond anything that could be said of Zerubbabel. The destruction of the world powers in the previous verse is eschatological and prepares the way for a new kingdom. **On that day** refers to the future day of the Lord. (For a discussion of the day of the Lord, see the "Deeper Discoveries" section for the Book of Zephaniah.) **My servant** or "my righteous servant" is a phrase elsewhere applied to the Messiah (e.g., Isa. 42:1; 52:13; 53:11), and Zerubbabel, a descendant of David, here represents the messianic line.

Thus the verse means that the final Son of David, Jesus the Messiah, will rule the world in his glorious future kingdom. The power of the wicked will be broken, and peace will pervade the earth (vv. 21–22). God's promise of this new world would have encouraged Zerubbabel. It has been a source of hope for believers in all times.

MAIN IDEA REVIEW: *Individuals and nations committed to God will be blessed. God promises victory for them in this life and in the world to come.*

III. CONCLUSION

The Chicken and the Pig

A hen and a pig approached a church and read the posted sermon topic, "What can we do to help the poor?" Immediately the hen suggested they feed them bacon and eggs. The pig thought it sounded good, but he told the hen there was one thing wrong with feeding bacon and eggs to the poor. "For you it requires only a contribution, but for me it requires total commitment!"

Like the chicken, many modern Christians are willing to participate if it does not involve sacrifice. However, our Lord called for nothing less than total commitment: "Then Jesus said to his disciples, 'If anyone would come after me, he must deny himself and take up his cross and follow me'" (Matt.

16:24; cp. Luke 14:26). The prophet Haggai urged God's people to commit themselves unreservedly to God. Then they would receive his blessings.

PRINCIPLES

- God's kingdom (spiritual things) should be our priority rather than worldly possessions.
- From time to time, a careful examination of our spiritual condition is wise.
- A lack of commitment results in diminished blessing from God.
- Repentance will restore fellowship with God and bring divine blessing.
- Godly leadership is vital for a great nation.
- No work is insignificant if it is done for God's glory.
- The sin of disobedience renders our worship unacceptable to God.
- A healthy memory of sin's consequences is a deterrent to future sinful acts.
- Some day earth's evil kingdoms will be judged and Messiah will reign.

APPLICATIONS

- Recognize that excuses for lack of commitment are unacceptable to God.
- Determine that God and his kingdom will be your life's priority.
- If you have unconfessed sin in your life, confess it now and experience God's forgiveness and blessing.
- Rejoice in whatever task God has given you, whether small or great.
- Ask God to reveal any attitudes or actions that may hinder your worship.
- Take heart in knowing that Christ is coming to destroy evil and bring in a wonderful new world.

IV. LIFE APPLICATION

Martyr for Christ

Jim Elliot was an outstanding person. In 1949 he graduated with highest honors from Wheaton College (Illinois). He was a gifted public speaker and a college wrestling champion. His interests also included music, art, and literature. All the world was open to this young man, yet he chose to go as a missionary to people who had never heard the gospel of Jesus Christ. In 1952 Elliot arrived in Ecuador to minister among the Quechua Indians. The next year he married his college sweetheart, Elisabeth Howard, who joined him in the work.

Ecuador was also home to a primitive tribe called Aucas or "savages" by their neighbors. The Aucas had a reputation for violence, but Elliot and his fellow missionaries were determined to reach them with the gospel. For three months they flew over the area and lowered gifts in a bucket, hoping to assure the Aucas of their peaceful intentions. Then they landed their plane on a beach of the Curaray River and set up camp in a prefabricated tree house. On Sunday, January 8, 1956, Jim Elliot and four other missionaries were speared and hacked to death by the very people they had come to help. Five days later four bodies were found in the Curaray downstream. At the request of their wives, they were buried at the campsite where they were martyred for Christ. News of the five deaths shocked the world. What a tragedy! (A positive footnote to the story is that eventually many of the Aucas came to Christ as Lord and Savior.)

The world probably looked at the death of Jim Elliot as a waste. He had so much promise—the charisma, the talent! He could have accomplished so much in the world. He died so young (not even thirty). He was foolish to have thrown away his life like that. Yet Elliot himself answers such criticisms. In his diary Jim wrote these classic words: "He is no fool who gives what he cannot keep to gain what he cannot lose." The apostle John put it this way: "The world and its desires pass away, but the man who does the will of God lives forever" (1 John 2:17). Haggai calls on us to put God and his kingdom first at all costs. This is all that will endure. In C. T. Studd's words, "Only one life, 'twill soon be past; Only what's done for Christ will last."

V. PRAYER

O Lord, the world is so seductive and alluring. Please help us to remember what is really important in life. May our priority always be our relationship and commitment to you. Thank you for the victory you have promised your followers. In Christ's name we pray. Amen.

VI. DEEPER DISCOVERIES

A. King Darius I (1:1)

Darius I (522–486 B.C.), son of Hystaspes, was the third in the line of Medo-Persian rulers, following Cyrus and his son, Cambyses II. Hearing a report that a usurper had seized the throne in the eastern part of the empire, Cambyses committed suicide. Darius then claimed the throne and went about the business of putting down the insurrections that cropped up around the kingdom. By the end of 520 B.C., the time Haggai wrote his prophecy, Darius was firmly in control. Darius had the famous Behistun Inscription written on a high cliff in Behistun, Iran, as a testimony to his military successes. The Behistun Inscription (written in three languages: Old Persian, Babylonian, and Elamite) is three times the length of the Book of Deuteronomy. This famous inscription was the key to the decipherment of the Babylonian language (Akkadian), which opened up a world of historical and linguistic information for better understanding the Bible. Darius I was a successful ruler whose only serious defeat was at the hands of the Greeks at the famous battle of Marathon (490 B.C.).

B. Zerubbabel, Governor of Judah (1:1)

Zerubbabel probably is a Babylonian name meaning "seed of Babylon," apparently so named because he was born there. Haggai identified Shealtiel as Zerubbabel's father, whereas in 1 Chronicles 3:17–19 Shealtiel's brother, Pedaiah, is listed as his father. The difference is explained by Israel's practice of levirate marriage (Deut. 25:5–10). If a man died childless, his brother was obligated to marry his wife and raise up an heir to carry on his brother's name. Evidently, Shealtiel (the legal father) died, and his brother Pedaiah (the natural father) married his brother's widow. Zerubbabel was the offspring of that marriage. King Jehoiachin was Zerubbabel's grandfather, and thus Zerubbabel was of royal blood.

Zerubbabel returned to Judah with fifty thousand other Jewish exiles in 538/7 B.C. and laid the foundation of the second temple in 536 B.C. (Ezra 3:8–13). In Haggai 1:1 and again in 2:2, Zerubbabel is called governor of Judah. He would have been appointed by the Persian government to this post. Zerubbabel was an extremely important person in Bible history. His name appears twenty-five times in the NIV text of the Old Testament, including seven times in Haggai. As a matter of fact, being the grandson of King Jehoiachin probably meant that Zerubbabel was the heir to the throne of David. Although some scholars disagree, a comparison of Ezra 3:8 and 5:16 seems to confirm that Zerubbabel is the same person as Sheshbazzar (Ezra 1:8; 5:14). Zerubbabel was the last Davidic heir to serve in the role of governor of Judah.

C. Historical Background of Haggai's Prophecy

The following is a summary of the key historical events that form the background for the Book of Haggai:

586 B.C.	Solomon's temple destroyed by the Babylonians; about fifty thousand Jews taken into exile
539	Fall of Babylon to Cyrus, king of Medo-Persia
538	Cyrus's decree to allow the exiles to return and rebuild the temple (Ezra 1)
538/7	About fifty thousand Jews return to Judah (Neh. 7; Ezra 2)
536	Work on the temple stopped (Ezra 3)
530	Cyrus's death
530–522	Reign of Cambyses II, Cyrus's son
522–486	Reign of Darius I
520	Darius I confirms Cyrus's decree (Ezra 6)
520	Haggai's messages; Zechariah begins his ministry
516	Temple completed and dedicated (Ezra 6:15–16)

D. Cyrus the Great, Liberator of the Jewish Exiles

Ezra (1:1–4; 6:3–5) records that Haggai, Zerubbabel, Joshua, and their fellow Jews were allowed to return to their land in 538/7 B.C. by decree of the first ruler of the Medo-Persian Empire, Cyrus the Great (539–530 B.C.). Archaeology has confirmed the accuracy of Ezra's account. In 1879 archaeologist Hormuzd Rassam discovered a small clay cylinder in the ruins of ancient Babylon. Inscribed on the barrel was Cyrus's official decree permitting exiles to return to their lands and rebuild their temples, exactly what the Bible says took place. For this and other reasons, Cyrus was viewed positively by most of his subjects. Cyrus's actions were also a fulfillment of Scripture. One hundred and fifty years earlier, the prophet Isaiah had predicted, "I [the LORD] will raise up Cyrus in my righteousness: I will make all his ways straight. He will rebuild my city and set my exiles free, but not for a price or reward, says the LORD Almighty" (Isa. 45:13; cp. 44:28; 45:1). Isaiah's naming the liberator of the Jewish exiles by name over one hundred and fifty years in advance is an amazing prophecy and proof of the Bible's supernatural character.

E. The Second Temple (1:14)

The second temple had a humble beginning but eventually rivaled Solomon's magnificent structure. Ironically the second temple reached its greatest period of grandeur under the evil King Herod (37–4 B.C.). One of Herod's last atrocities was the massacre of the babies in Bethlehem in an attempt to kill the newborn king, Jesus (Matt. 2:16–18). Herod, an Idumean, was never accepted by the Jewish people. Yet his lavish improvements on the Jewish temple in Jerusalem made it one of the most beautiful structures of that time (see Mark 13:1).

Herod doubled the size of Solomon's temple mount by extending the eastern wall and adding walls on the other three sides. This resulted in a platform roughly 1,000 feet wide and 1,550 feet long. One stone on the Western Wall measures 40 feet in length, 10 feet in height, and weighs over 500 tons! Herod then constructed the Royal Stoa, the largest structure in the complex. This grand hall stretched across the southern end of the temple mount and contained 4 rows of 40 columns each. The temple complex had 4 courts, those of the Gentiles, the women, the men (Israel), and the priests. Improvements to the temple continued long after Herod's death.

The beautiful edifice of cream stone and gold was hardly finished (A.D. 64) before it was destroyed by the legions of the Roman general Titus (A.D. 70). The temple's golden candelabra and the table of showbread were carried to Rome and are depicted on the Arch of Titus. All that remains of Herod's temple complex today is the Western Wall (Kotel, in Hebrew), better known as the "Wailing Wall."

VII. TEACHING OUTLINE

A. INTRODUCTION

1. Lead Story: Hero of United Airlines Flight 93
2. Context: Haggai was the first of the postexilic prophets. He encouraged his fellow countrymen to finish the temple, begun about sixteen years earlier. The problem was a lack of commitment to God. The people had become complacent and consumed with their own lives rather than focusing on God's work. Immediately on hearing Haggai's message, his audience repented and quickly resumed the construction of God's house. Haggai called on the people to be courageous and promised that the work would be finished. He concluded his book with a wonderful prophecy of the future messianic kingdom.
3. Transition: In this book, Haggai reminds us that our priority should be God and his kingdom. Like ancient Judah, we suffer consequences for lack of commitment to the Lord. The solution is to repent and obey. Then we will experience the fullness of God's blessing in every area of our lives. We should be courageous because our omnipotent God will grant success in everything he directs us to do, and he has a great future in store for us after this life.

B. COMMENTARY

1. A Committed Prophet and an Uncommitted People (1:1–2)
2. A Rebuke for Lack of Commitment and the People's Repentance (1:3–15)
3. Commitment and Courage (2:1–9)
4. Consequences of Judah's Past Lack of Commitment (2:10–19)
5. The Future Hope of Those Committed to God (2:20–23)

C. CONCLUSION: THE CHICKEN AND THE PIG

VIII. ISSUES FOR DISCUSSION

1. How committed to Christ do you think the average church member is? Do you think they would make real sacrifices for God's work? How committed are you?

2. Take the following test and evaluate your life's priorities. What percentage of your financial resources do you give to support God's work? What percentage do you spend on yourself? How much of your time do you give to God?

3. Haggai teaches that God blesses his people economically for their faithfulness. How might this principle be misused?

4. Do you rejoice in whatever task God has given you to do, whether small or great?

Zechariah 1–2

God Cares for You!

I. **INTRODUCTION**
Angels Watching over You

II. **COMMENTARY**
A verse-by-verse explanation of these chapters.

III. **CONCLUSION**
She's My Hero!

An overview of the principles and applications from
these chapters.

IV. **LIFE APPLICATION**
God Is My Pilot

Melding these chapters to life.

V. **PRAYER**
Tying these chapters to life with God.

VI. **DEEPER DISCOVERIES**
Historical, geographical, and grammatical enrichment of the commentary.

VII. **TEACHING OUTLINE**
Suggested step-by-step group study of these chapters.

VIII. **ISSUES FOR DISCUSSION**
Zeroing these chapters in on daily life.

Quote

"*He* who counts the stars and calls them by their names, is in no danger of forgetting His own children."

Charles   Haddon   Spurgeon

PROPHECY PROFILE

- Zechariah's 211 verses make it the longest of all the minor prophets. Hosea is second with 207 verses.
- Zechariah contains more messianic references than any prophetic book except Isaiah.
- The historical background of the book is the same as that of the Book of Haggai.
- Zechariah is quoted or alluded to seventy-one times in the New Testament.
- The book consists of a wide variety of literary material. Chapters 1–8 are written in prose and include historical accounts and visions, whereas the burdens of the future in chapters 9–14 contain both prophetic poetry and prose. Most scholars also consider the book an example of apocalyptic literature. This genre (kind of literature) uses visions, symbolism, angelic messengers, and so forth to convey its message.
- Zechariah carefully dates the prophecies of chapters 1–8 from the second to the fourth year of Darius I (520–518 B.C.). Chapters 9–14 are undated because, unlike the earlier prophecies which were connected to historical events like rebuilding the temple, they concern the distant future. These latter chapters were probably written late in the prophet's career.
- Ezra records the historical background for this prophecy and specifically mentions Zechariah in Ezra 5:1–2 and 6:14.
- The Book of Zechariah contains a message of hope and encouragement for the struggling Jewish returnees. Their work of rebuilding the temple and the nation would succeed, and their

future as a nation was assured. Probably no other prophetic book is so dominated by hope and blessing for God's people as is Zechariah. The enduring message of the book is that the kingdom of God will triumph.

- Some scholars have separated chapters 9–14 from the first of the book, and they attribute these later chapters to another author(s), usually of the Greek period (332 B.C. and later). Evidence for such a view is quite subjective and often is based on a predisposition against the possibility of predictive prophecy (particularly the mention of Greece in 9:13). No manuscript support for such a division exists, even among the Dead Sea Scrolls discovered at Qumran.

AUTHOR PROFILE: ZECHARIAH THE PROPHET

- Zechariah ("the LORD remembers") is one of the most common names in the Bible. All of the approximately thirty individuals with this name lived in the Old Testament era except the father of John the Baptist (Luke 1:5). Most likely the name is a plea for God to remember his covenant with Israel and to extend divine aid.

- Zechariah's father was Berekiah, the son of a priest named Iddo who returned from the exile with Zerubbabel (Neh. 12:4). Evidently Zechariah was a young man (2:4), at least when he wrote chapters 1–8 of his book.

- Like Jeremiah and Ezekiel, Zechariah was a priest as well as a prophet (Neh. 12:4,16) and a contemporary of the prophet Haggai (Ezra 5:1; 6:14).

- Zechariah has been called the greatest of the postexilic prophets.

- Some manuscripts of the ancient Greek version of the Old Testament called the Septuagint attribute Psalms 137 and 145–148 to Haggai and/or Zechariah, whereas the Latin Vulgate assigns Psalms 125–126 and 145–147 to Haggai and/or Zechariah.

READER PROFILE: THE POSTEXILIC NATION OF JUDAH

- In 539 B.C. Babylon fell to the Medo-Persian armies of Cyrus the Great (Dan. 5). From this point until its defeat by Alexander the Great in a series of battles (334–331 B.C.), the Medo-Persian Empire dominated the world. Judah became a province of the empire and was ruled by a governor appointed by the Medo-Persians. Cyrus was a benevolent ruler who permitted the exiled Jews (and other peoples) to return to their homeland. Zechariah and his fellow countrymen had now returned to Judah and were in the process of rebuilding the country.

- Zechariah's prophecy is a message of hope for this postexilic group of Jewish believers who had been back in the land for almost twenty years. Like Haggai, Zechariah specifically names both Zerubbabel, the governor (4:6), and Joshua, the high priest (3:1; 6:11).

- Conditions were difficult for the returnees, yet they were filled with joy at being back in the land of Abraham, Isaac, and Jacob (Ps. 126:1–3).

I N   A   N U T S H E L L

In chapters 1–2, Zechariah calls on his countrymen to repent of sin and obey God. After this initial rebuke (which the people heed), the prophet shares three of his eight night visions. The vision of the horses and riders affirms God's concern for his people and assures them that the nation will be reestablished. The vision of the four horns and four craftsmen teaches that God will judge the enemies of his people. The vision of the man with the measuring line was a promise that Jerusalem (then in ruins) would be rebuilt.

God Cares for You!

I. INTRODUCTION

Angels Watching over You

Billy Graham includes the following amazing story of God's care for his people in his wonderful little book, *Angels: God's Secret Agents:*

> The Reverend John G. Paton, a missionary in the New Hebrides Islands, tells a thrilling story involving the protective care of angels. Hostile natives surrounded his mission headquarters one night, intent on burning the Patons out and killing them. John Paton and his wife prayed all during that terror-filled night that God would deliver them. When daylight came, they were amazed to see the attackers leave. They thanked God for delivering them.
>
> A year later the chief of the tribe was converted to Jesus Christ. Paton, remembering what had happened, asked the chief what had kept him and his men from burning down the house and killing them. The chief replied in surprise, "Who were all those men you had with you there?" The missionary answered, "There were no men there; just my wife and I." The chief argued that they had seen many men standing guard—hundreds of big men in shining garments with drawn swords in their hands. They seemed to circle the mission station so that the natives were afraid to attack. Only then did Paton realize that God had sent His angels to protect them" (Graham, *Angels: God's Secret Agents*, Garden City, N.Y.: Doubleday, 1975, p. 3).

God does not always act in such an unusual manner, but he is always concerned for the welfare of his children. This is the message of the first two chapters of the Book of Zechariah. In these chapters God expresses his concern for the helpless and oppressed people of ancient Judah. Zechariah begins with a call to repentance (which the people heed) and follows with three fascinating visions, each conveying in some manner God's care for his people. Zechariah's message of God's care was written not only for the Jews of twenty-five hundred years ago but for believers today.

II. COMMENTARY

God Cares for You!

MAIN IDEA: *God cares for his children and ensures their well-being and success in this life and beyond.*

A The Prophet and His Times (1:1)

SUPPORTING IDEA: *Zechariah preaches a message of hope in difficult days.*

1:1. This verse serves not only as an introduction to the first six verses (or first eight chapters) but to the entire prophecy. **The eighth month of the second year of Darius** I (522–486 B.C.) would be October/November 520 B.C. The eighth month began on October 27 in 520 B.C., so Zechariah probably began his work in November, two months after Haggai's first sermon ("sixth month," Hag. 1:1).

Zechariah dated his prophecy by a heathen king because there was no king in Israel. Dating the prophecy by a foreigner also indicates that the times of the Gentiles had begun. This period began with the destruction of Jerusalem by Nebuchadnezzar and would continue until the return of Christ (Luke 21:24). Darius I (the Great) was one of the most distinguished of eastern rulers. He put down widespread revolts and later conducted military campaigns in Armenia, east of the Caspian Sea, and in northwestern India. His army invaded Greece but was defeated at Marathon in 490 B.C. Darius I died while preparing for a new attack on Greece. His son, Xerxes (the Ahasuerus of the Book of Esther), succeeded him to the throne. (For more information on Darius I, see the "Deeper Discoveries" section for the Book of Haggai.)

In 520 B.C. Zechariah was a young man (2:3). When he returned to Judah from Babylon with Zerubbabel and about fifty thousand others in 538/7 B.C., he must have been a mere child. God sent the young prophet to preach to this small group of struggling Jews. The return was a time of great hope but also of great fear and uncertainty. They had begun the temple about sixteen years earlier in 536 B.C., but due to opposition from the Samaritans, the work had stopped. Now the people were concerned with other matters and had not shown an interest in completing God's house.

Like Haggai, Zechariah called on the nation to finish the project. Zechariah's mission also was to assure the people that God cared for them and would keep his covenant promises to Israel. The nation would be reestablished, prosper, and play a crucial role in events at the end of this present age. Four years after Zechariah began his ministry (March 516 B.C.), the people finished the temple in the sixth year of Darius I (Ezra 6:15).

Zechariah means "the LORD remembers." The name could signify that God had remembered the parents by giving them a son but more likely was a plea for God to remember his covenant with Israel and to extend divine aid. This seems to explain the popularity of the name during the exilic and postexilic periods.

The prophet's father was **Berekiah** ("the LORD blesses") who apparently died young, leaving Zechariah to be raised by his grandfather, **Iddo**. This would explain the absence of Berekiah's name in Ezra 5:1 and 6:14. "Son" in Hebrew may mean grandfather or descendant, and this would be the meaning in the Book of Ezra (NIV's "descendant"). According to Nehemiah 12:4, Iddo was a priest who returned from the exile with Zerubbabel. Like Jeremiah and Ezekiel, Zechariah was both a priest and a prophet.

The phrase, **the word of the LORD came**, appears six times in the book (1:1,7; 4:8; 6:9; 7:1,8) and over one hundred times in the Old Testament (twenty-four times in Jeremiah and fifty times in Ezekiel). Zechariah's words were not just his opinion but the words of the Lord himself. Here the prophet makes a strong claim for the divine inspiration of the book.

🅱 God's Caring Invitation (1:2–6)

SUPPORTING IDEA: *God cares for his people in spite of their sin and lovingly invites them to return to him.*

1:2. Zechariah's first message is recorded in verses 2–6, no doubt a synopsis of a much longer sermon. This call to repentance sets the tone for the whole book, which declares that repentance brings God's blessing.

In this verse Zechariah set forth an incentive to repent—a reminder of the fate of their rebellious, sinful ancestors. **Very angry** is emphatic in the Hebrew text. Jerusalem's sad condition was an object lesson. Zechariah could say to his countrymen, "Look around! Jerusalem is in ruins, and Solomon's magnificent temple is destroyed. This is the result of rebellion and sin. We must not rebel against the Lord like our ancestors (**forefathers**) did. We must repent!" Zechariah's lesson about the consequences of Judah's sin was even more compelling since some of his audience had seen the destruction of their beloved Jerusalem firsthand (only sixty-six years before in 586 B.C.), and virtually everyone had experienced exile.

1:3. Yet the Lord still loved his people. He pleaded with them to **return to me** and promised that if they did so, **I will return to you.** The divine title **the LORD Almighty** (traditionally, "the LORD of hosts") emphasizes God's power. He is the one who controls the forces (and armies) of heaven and earth and may use these to punish sin. Often this title is used in judgment contexts and implies a threat of divine punishment. The term is found five times in this brief call to repentance in verses 2–6 (three times in v. 3 alone). The LORD Almighty is the characteristic name for God in the postexilic prophets, occurring more than ninety times (Haggai, fourteen times; Zechariah, fifty-three times; and Malachi, twenty-four times).

This is what the LORD Almighty says is KJV's familiar "thus saith the LORD of hosts." This phrase, or the shorter "thus saith the LORD," occurs over four hundred times in the Old Testament and indicates the Bible's divine origin. Old Testament prophets were the faithful conveyors of God's message.

The word "return" is frequently used for repentance in the Old Testament. Both "turn" (v. 4) and "repented" (v. 6) are translations of this same Hebrew word. It picturesquely communicates the nature of repentance, which is a turning from sin and turning to God. Zechariah did not name the specific problem, but Ezra recorded that Zechariah, like Haggai, called on the people to resume work on the temple (Ezra 5:1–2; 6:14). Although the rebuilding of God's house had already begun (Hag. 1:14–15), there may still have been some resistance. Zechariah may also have had in mind other sinful practices that cropped up among the people.

God's promise, "I will return to you" (plural in Hebrew), promises fellowship with individuals after repentance but would have had national significance as well. Ezekiel watched as the glory of God departed from Jerusalem (Ezek. 11:22–23). Now that Judah had repented, the Lord was returning to his land (Isa. 40:3–11). Once more God's special presence, blessing, and protective power would rest on the nation. The rebuilding of God's house, the temple, symbolized God's return to his people.

1:4. Mercifully, before judgment came God had warned Judah to repent through his **prophets** (2 Chr. 36:15–21). These **earlier prophets** included Isaiah, Jeremiah, Ezekiel, Habakkuk, Zephaniah, and many others. Clearly, Zechariah and his fellow Jews already recognized these prophetic writings to be Scripture (canonical). Yet their **forefathers . . . would not listen or pay attention** to the Lord.

1:5–6. The point of Zechariah's questions in verses 5–6a is that the **prophets** (like Isaiah) died, but God's word lived on (Isa. 40:6–8) and eventually caught up with (**did . . . overtake**) their evil **forefathers**. Moses warned that if Israel were unfaithful to God's covenant, "All these curses will come upon you. They will pursue you and overtake you until you are destroyed, because you did not obey the LORD your God and observe the commands and decrees he gave you" (Deut. 28:45; cp. 28:15). Judgment was certain and inescapable. The proof was the present desolate condition of Jerusalem. Indirectly, Zechariah cautioned the people that just as the former prophets' words were true, so the words of God's current prophets, Zechariah and Haggai, were true and should be obeyed. **My servants the prophets** occurs nine times in the Old Testament (2 Kgs. 9:7; 17:13; Jer. 7:25; 26:5; 29:19; 35:15; 44:4; Ezek. 38:17; Zech. 1:6).

In captivity their forefathers **repented** and acknowledged that what had happened to them was the fulfillment of God's word. Before, they had denied that prophets like Jeremiah had spoken for God but later had no choice but to admit it. They also realized that they deserved God's judgment for their sins. When the Jewish people repented, God forgave them and blessed them by restoring them to the land.

Zechariah's message was twofold. Sin brings judgment, but repentance brings blessing. The prophet encouraged the people in his day to choose the latter option. Happily, they did so, as is demonstrated by their subsequent actions. They rebuilt the temple, completing it on March 12, 516 B.C. (Ezra 6:15). Most of the remainder of the book is a positive message of hope and blessing for the people of God.

Ⓒ God's Care Demonstrated by His Presence (1:7–17)

SUPPORTING IDEA: *God knows his people's plight and is present with them during their suffering.*

1:7. Now we encounter some of the most fascinating material in the Bible. Zechariah received eight visions from the Lord in which he saw angels, horses of various colors, horns and craftsmen, a flying scroll, and much more! Most scholars hold that all of the visions date from the same night (Feb. 15, 519 B.C.). The visions usually follow a similar pattern: introductory words, a depiction of what Zechariah saw, the prophet's request for an interpretation of the vision, and the angel's explanation. All the visions have historical relevance for the postexilic Jewish community, but at some points move beyond the prophet's day to the end times. Zechariah's visions were given three months after his call to repentance in 1:1–6 and after Haggai 2:10–23. These visions are prophecies of hope and comfort.

1:8. Although it was **night**, the **vision** came not in a dream but while the prophet was awake. Zechariah saw **a man riding a red horse**. The word **standing** may refer to the horse upon which the rider sat or to the rider who had now stepped down from the horse. The man among the myrtle trees is identified in verse 11 as "the angel of the LORD," yet he is no ordinary angel. Frequently in the Old Testament, the angel of the Lord is identified as God (Gen. 16:7–13; 22:11–12; Exod. 3:2–6; Judg. 6:14,22; 13:9–18,22). According to Lindsey, "That this 'Angel' (literally, 'Messenger') is a manifestation of the preincarnate Christ is established in chapter 3 where He is specifically called 'the LORD' who yet refers to 'the LORD' as another Person (3:2). Also He is seen exercising the divine prerogative of forgiving sins (3:4)" (Lindsey, 1550). Moreover, this person is plainly in command for the riders (angels) of the other horses report to him (v. 11). According to Feinberg, the Babylonian Talmud states: "This man is no other than the Holy One, blessed be He; for it is said, 'The Lord is a man of war'" (Feinberg, *Minor Prophets*, 275).

Myrtle trees are fragrant evergreens with white or pink flowers and dark berries. They reach a height of about thirty feet. Myrtle trees grew in the neighborhood of Jerusalem (Neh. 8:15) and were used for making booths during the Feast of Tabernacles. Esther's Hebrew name, Hadassah (Esth. 2:7), means "myrtle." This grove of myrtle trees was located **in a ravine**, literally, "a deep place." Presumably, the setting of the vision was a spot near Jerusalem familiar to the prophet, most likely the deep Kidron Valley that runs between the Mount of Olives and the temple mount. Behind the man standing among the myrtle trees were **red, brown, and white horses**. The word "brown" is a translation of a Hebrew adjective found only here in the Old Testament. It seems to be derived from a Hebrew root meaning "to intertwine" and so describes a mixed color, probably "sorrel" (NKJV, NASB, NRSV), which is a light reddish-brown.

Visions are intended to convey spiritual truth in symbolic fashion. Specific statements in verses 12–17 indicate that this vision was intended to express God's concern for Israel. With this in mind, the vision has usually been interpreted in the following manner. The sweet-smelling myrtle trees symbolize the people of God (Israel), pleasing and precious to him. The phrase "in a ravine" represents Israel's present lowly and degraded position among the nations of the earth. The angel of the Lord standing among the trees signifies God's presence with and watchful care over his oppressed people. We find a similar picture in Revelation 1:12–20. Christ's position in the middle of the seven lampstands, symbolic of the seven churches, affirms his presence with and concern for his suffering followers.

The colors of the horses represent the work each rider had to accomplish (cp. Zech. 6:2–8). Red (color of blood) symbolizes war as a judgment on the enemies of God's people (Rev. 6:4). A white horse is associated with conquest (Rev. 6:2; 19:11,14) and symbolizes the victory of God's people. The interpretation of the sorrel horse (a mixed color) is the most problematic. Various suggestions (e.g., a mixed mission of judgment and blessing) have been offered, but none are certain. Regardless of the exact meaning of the colors, the general mission of these horses with their riders is clear. They traveled about the earth and did the bidding of the Lord, to whom they reported (v. 11). Thus the vision is a wonderful message of God's care for his struggling people. God saw their plight and was present with them.

1:9. Zechariah was puzzled by the scene and asked **the angel who was talking** to him for an explanation. This was the interpreting angel, different from the angel of the Lord in the previous verse.

1:10. Verses 10–17 are the inspired commentary on the vision. **The man standing among the myrtle trees**, rather than the interpreting angel, explained the meaning. He informed the prophet that these horses and riders had been sent to patrol the earth, symbolic of the fact that God knew what was happening to his people and was concerned. Baldwin comments: "Like the Persian monarchs who used messengers on swift steeds to keep them informed on all matters concerning their empire, so the Lord knew all about the countries of the earth, including the great Persian state" (Baldwin, 95).

1:11. The rider on the horse among the myrtle trees is now specifically identified as the angel of the Lord (see "Commentary" discussion on 1:8). The riders reported to him that they had patrolled the earth and found all to be **at rest and in peace.** By this time Darius I was firmly in control, and no great wars were taking place. However, Israel was humiliated (in a low place) while the heathen of the earth dwelled safely and securely. Their oppressors seemed to have immunity from pain while God's people suffered.

1:12. The **angel of the LORD** interceded for **Jerusalem** and **Judah.** The phrase **How long**, a familiar cry occurring sixty-five times in the Bible, often expresses anguish over God's perceived delay in bringing justice (Pss. 6:3; 13:1–2; 35:17; 79:5; 94:3; Rev. 6:10). It includes the ideas of faith, expectation, and wholehearted sympathy and longing. Although fifty thousand Jewish captives had returned, the land was still in ruins. Jerusalem was not inhabited, and the temple was not yet rebuilt. Furthermore, the heathen nations were experiencing peace and rest rather than the judgment they deserved.

Jeremiah had predicted that the Babylonian captivity would last **seventy years** (Jer. 25:11–12; 29:10). This period began with the first conquest of Jerusalem by Nebuchadnezzar in 605 B.C. and ended with the return of the Jewish exiles in 537/6 B.C. What an amazing prophecy! Interestingly, the temple was destroyed in 586 B.C., and its rebuilding was completed in 516 B.C., also a span of seventy years.

In this verse one divine person ("the angel of the LORD" = preincarnate Christ) interceded to another, the LORD **Almighty**. Here we are afforded an Old Testament glimpse of the Trinity. This passage reminds us of Christ's great intercessory prayer in John 17.

1:13. **The LORD responded to the angel** with the **kind** (literally, "good") and **comforting** (or "compassionate"; see v. 17) **words** of verses 14–17. In these verses we discover at least six comforting words from God.

1:14–15. First, God cares for his people. **Very jealous** expresses the Lord's zealous watchcare over and deep concern for Israel. (For a discussion of God's jealousy, see the "Deeper Discoveries" section for Nahum 1.) He had seen their plight and was **very angry** with the **nations** who had mistreated them. The Hebrew term rendered **feel secure** ("at ease," KJV, NKJV, NASB, NRSV) suggests an attitude of indifference and arrogance (Amos 6:1; Isa. 32:9,11). The nations had oppressed God's people and did not care. To be sure, the Lord himself had been angry with his people for their sin and had even used Babylon as his rod to punish them (Hab. 1:6), but the nations' mistreatment of Israel went far beyond anything God condoned and **added to the calamity** (literally, "helped for evil"). Their intent was evil, and they even attempted to annihilate the covenant people. The phrase **a little angry** may mean "for only a little while."

1:16. Second, the angel's request for God's **mercy** on Israel was granted. Third, the temple would be completed. This was an encouraging promise for the Jewish returnees now engaged in the daunting task of rebuilding. Fourth, **Jerusalem**, still mainly in ruins, would be rebuilt. Just as a **line** was formerly stretched over the city to destroy it (2 Kgs. 21:13; Isa. 34:11), a **line** was now extended over Jerusalem before its rebuilding (see 2:1–5; Job 38:5).

1:17. Fifth, the nation would grow as **towns** in Judah would spring up and prosper. By the time of Jesus, the nation was thriving and overflowing with people. Sixth, **Jerusalem** would once again occupy a special place as the Lord's chosen city. **Zion** specifically was the hill on the southeastern part of the city on which the original city of David was built, but later it came to represent the whole capital, becoming synonymous with Jerusalem.

In conclusion, this first vision was an exciting message of hope to the poor exiles of Zechariah's day. Its promises of God's presence, concern, mercy, and blessing for his people also apply to us.

Ⓓ God's Care Demonstrated by the Punishment of Oppressors (1:18–21)

SUPPORTING IDEA: *God cares about the mistreatment of his people and will punish those responsible.*

1:18–19. In Zechariah's second vision, he saw **four horns** and asked the interpreting **angel** for an explanation. The angel replied, **These are the horns that scattered Judah, Israel and Jerusalem.** According to Barker, "The horns are presumably on the heads of animals, since they are capable of being terrified (v. 21)" (Barker, 615). Often in Scripture **horns** symbolize nations (Dan. 7:24; 8:3–4; Mic. 4:13), and in verse 21 they are referred to as "horns of the nations." The figure is taken from animals such as the bull whose strength is in their horns. These horns had **scattered** the Jewish people.

The three most common interpretations of these horns are as follows:

1. Past kingdoms that had oppressed the Jews. These are normally identified as Egypt, Assyria, Babylon, and Medo-Persia.
2. The four kingdoms prophesied by Daniel (Dan. 2; 7). This view has been popular with modern interpreters and was held by early Christian leaders like Jerome (A.D. 345–419). Evangelical scholars identify Daniel's four empires as Babylon, Medo-Persia, Greece, and Rome. No doubt, Zechariah was familiar with Daniel (who died less than twenty years before) and his prophecies of the four empires.
3. A symbolic description of all Israel's foes (the totality of Gentile powers). Four represents the four points of the compass or the four corners of the earth.

Any of the above views is possible, and all agree that the horns represent oppressors of the Jewish people. The Hebrew verb translated *scattered* is rendered in past tense in English versions, but this is not decisive. The verb form could be translated as a present or even a future tense in English. Nevertheless, the first view is most likely for several reasons. First, this vision is clearly an explanation (or expansion) of verse 15 where God declares his anger with past nations that have mistreated his people. Second, Israel and Judah seem to refer to the Northern and Southern Kingdoms, respectively, the two divisions of the Jewish tribes before the exile. If so, the oppressors of these kingdoms must be those of the past since no such division existed later. Third, specific nations would seem to be in the minds of Zechariah's audience rather than generic oppressors.

1:20–21. Zechariah observed **four craftsmen,** skilled workers in metal, wood, or stone. The phrase **so that no one could raise his head** is a graphic description of the severe oppression of God's people inflicted by these nations (**the horns**). **To terrify** and **throw down** indicates that the purpose of the craftsmen was to destroy the horns, apparently with hammers, the tools of their trade. Craftsmen also have a role of judgment in Ezekiel 21:31 where "men skilled in destruction" reads literally, "craftsmen of destruction."

Interpretation of the craftsmen is determined by one's view of the horns. If the horns are the past nations of Egypt, Assyria, Babylon, and Medo-Persia, the craftsmen symbolize the nations God used to overthrow each of them. Some of these nations may represent both a horn and a craftsman. For example, Persia was an oppressor (a horn) but also a craftsman whose mission had been to destroy the previous oppressor (horn), Babylon.

Regardless of the specific identification of the horns and craftsmen, the point is clear—nations that oppress God's people may "feel secure" (v. 15) now, but judgment will come.

🄴 God's Care Demonstrated by the Promise of a Glorious Future (2:1–13)

SUPPORTING IDEA: *God promises that his people will enjoy temporal success (Jerusalem rebuilt) and ultimate victory.*

2:1–2. Barker asserts that the "dominant emphasis of the book is encouragement to God's people because of the glorious future" (Barker, 600). Zechariah predicted both a prosperous future for the postexilic nation and Messiah's blessed reign at the end of the age. In this third vision we encounter **a man** [an angel in human form] **with a measuring line in his hand.** Just as in 1:16, the measuring line symbolizes the rebuilding of Jerusalem (see v. 4).

2:3–4. The interpreting **angel** was ordered by **another** (possibly the angel of the Lord) to hurry (**run**) and tell Zechariah the exciting news of Jerusalem's grand future. The city would be rebuilt and so filled with inhabitants that they would overflow the walls into the surrounding suburbs. Living **without walls** also suggests peace and safety. What wonderful promises for the struggling group of returnees in Palestine! Most scholars rightly understand the term **young man** (Heb. *na'ar*) to be a description of Zechariah rather than the angel. Such a designation would seem inappropriate for a heavenly being.

2:5. In this verse God assured Israel of his protection and presence with them. Jerusalem had no wall until Nehemiah built it about eighty years later. A wall was necessary for protection, and Israel was surrounded by hostile neighbors. Thus God's promise to **be a wall of fire around** the city was very reassuring. As God did during the exodus from Egypt, he would stand between Israel and her enemies (Exod. 14:19–20). The phrase **I will be its glory within** signifies that the Lord would dwell in the city—spiritually in Zechariah's day and physically (in the person of Jesus Christ) in the future.

According to Barker, "The scope of the restoration and blessing promised in this vision is such that its fulfillment must extend beyond the historical restoration period to the messianic kingdom era" (Barker, 616). Of course, the promises of God's blessing, protection, and spiritual presence with his people apply to God's children in every age.

2:6. Verses 6–13 include a warning to flee Babylon (vv. 6–9) and a promise of a blessed future for Jerusalem and Judah (vv. 10–13). The latter part of the chapter is not unrelated to the first but confirms that the rebuilt Jerusalem will be a secure home for the Jews (to which they may safely return) and has a glorious future.

In the Hebrew language, repetition indicates emphasis (**Come! Come!**). Jews still living in Babylon are urgently warned to return home and **flee from the land of the north**—Babylon (see v. 7; Jer. 6:22; 16:15). North was the direction from which the Babylonian army had invaded Judah.

2:7. So urgent was the warning that Zechariah repeated it a second time (**Escape** from Babylon!). The phrase **Daughter of Babylon** refers to Babylon as the mother of its inhabitants. Although fifty thousand exiles had returned in 538–537 B.C., most Jews had not. Babylon was still the grandest city in the world with all the amenities of a metropolis. Jews had a comfortable life there and were economically much better off than in their desolate homeland. No doubt, they felt more secure in Babylon behind its massive walls than in Jerusalem with no wall at all (2:5). However, such thinking was a mistake. (In Rev. 18:4, we find a warning for God's people to flee the doomed future Babylon.)

2:8. Babylon was under the curse of divine judgment (vv. 8–9). Babylon's approaching calamity is not identified. **After he has honored me and has sent me** is literally, "After glory he has sent me." The idea seems to be that God will bring glory (or "honor") to himself when the power of these nations is broken. "Sent me" has been taken to refer to the prophet (as in 4:9), but most evangelical scholars identify the sent one in this chapter (2:8–9,11; also 6:15) as the angel of the Lord (preincarnate Christ). The latter interpretation must be correct because this sent person brings judgment on Babylon and other nations (v. 9), a divine prerogative, and is equated with the Lord in verses 10–11. God will punish the offending nations because his people are precious to him—**the apple of his eye.** Apple (literally, "gate") is the pupil of the eye (Deut. 32:10; Ps. 17:8; Prov. 7:2), the most sensitive part. We protect it with the greatest care.

2:9. The sent one (Christ) of verse 8 will **raise** his **hand** to strike (or possibly "wave" his hand to dissipate) the nations who have mistreated God's people. The phrase **their slaves will plunder them** suggests that nations who served Babylon will now rule over their former master. Judgment of the nations (particularly Babylon) will demonstrate to Israel that **the LORD Almighty** had **sent** the angel of the Lord = Christ (**me**) to act on their behalf. Certainly, this verse is rooted in the historical situation of Zechariah's day, but the ultimate vindication of God's reality and Jesus' claims (and the final judgment of the nations) will be at Christ's return.

2:10–11. Israel should rejoice, for the Lord is **coming** to **live among** them. The Hebrew verb rendered **live** ("dwell," KJV, NKJV, NASB, NRSV) in this verse and the next is *shakan*, "connected with the *Shekinah* (hence, the verb *shakan*) glory of God and with the word for the tabernacle (*Mishkan*; Exod. 25:8)" (Kaiser, *Mastering the Old Testament*, 316). In this future age, Gentile **nations** will also join the celebration as part of God's family. Again, we see the divine character of the sent one. In verse 10 the Lord declares that he is coming to live among his people, whereas here the one **sent** by **the LORD Almighty** is coming to **live among** the people. He also calls God's people, **my people.** Thus two divine persons are clearly identified in this passage.

In light of later revelation, we understand that the Father sent the Son (Messiah = Christ) as the Savior and judge of the world. According to Barker, the promise of God's personal coming to his people is an indirect messianic prophecy because it can be literally fulfilled only through the Messiah (Barker, 619).

2:12. Judah (God's land) and **Jerusalem** (God's city) will have honored positions. Kaiser comments: "God certainly is not finished with the city He chose years ago in 1000 B.C. for the throne of David. It will be God's chosen center of worship and place of adjudication during the messianic rule and reign of Christ on earth during the Millennium" (Kaiser, *Mastering the Old Testament*, 317). Today we often speak of Israel as **the holy land,** yet surprisingly this is its only occurrence in the Bible. (Psalm 78:54 does not include the word "land" in the Hebrew text.) Perhaps Judah is called "holy" to contrast it with its former defilement (Jer. 2:7; 3:2,9).

2:13. Like a mighty warrior who awakes from sleep, God is about to exit **his holy dwelling** (his heavenly temple; cp. Hab. 2:20; Deut. 26:15) and act on behalf of his people. Let all the earth tremble in silence ("hush" or "be silent" is better than **be still**), for great will be the day of the Lord (Joel 2:31; Rev. 6:15–17)!

Verses 10–13 assure Zechariah's audience and present-day believers of God's presence with his people and his judgment of those who would harm them. However, the ultimate fulfillment of this passage must be eschatological. The physical presence of God with his people (vv. 10–11; cp. 14:4), Jesus' vindication as the Messiah (v. 11; cp. 12:10), the true holiness of Israel (v. 12; cp. 13:1–2), and the judgment of the world (v. 13) will not occur until the return of Jesus Christ. Moreover, "in that day" (v. 11) often denotes the eschatological "day of the LORD."

> **MAIN IDEA REVIEW:** *God cares for his children and ensures their well-being and success in this life and beyond.*

III. CONCLUSION

She's My Hero!

In August 2001, fourteen-year-old Edna Wilks and five friends were swimming about fifty yards off shore in Little Lake Conway in Orlando, Florida. Suddenly an alligator locked its powerful jaws around Edna and dragged her under water. When the alligator surfaced, Edna frantically began fighting to free herself. By the time the reptile let go, all her friends had fled except one. Best friend Amanda Valance stayed with Edna and pulled her to shore as the alligator followed. "She saw his tail whipping around in the water, and she told me she thought to herself she couldn't let me die," Edna said from her hospital bed. Edna underwent surgery, treatment for a broken arm, and received blood transfusions. The girl is sure that if her friend had not been brave enough to help, the alligator would have killed her. Two alligators, one over eleven feet in length and the other over six feet, were caught soon after the incident near the place where the attack occurred. Edna was quoted as saying of Amanda, "We've been best friends for about two and one-half years, and now she's more than my best friend; she's my hero."

Amanda's concern for her friend is heartwarming. Yet God cares for us far more than any earthly friend ever could. In the first two chapters of Zechariah, God expresses in visionary form his loving concern for his people. He sees our plight and is aware when his children are mistreated. God promises that in all circumstances he will be present with us. He will deal with those who mistreat us and will give his people success as we carry out his will. We should rejoice, for some day God in the person of his Son Jesus Christ is coming to live with us eternally.

PRINCIPLES

- God loves us even when we are out of his will.
- Past experiences teach valuable lessons for present living.
- Repentance results in God's blessings.
- God's people are precious to him like a sweet fragrance and the apple of his eye.
- God is always present with us.
- God ensures our success when we are obeying his will.
- God will punish those who mistreat his people.
- God will some day live among his people in the person of the Lord Jesus Christ.

APPLICATIONS

- Repent of any sin that could prevent you from receiving God's blessings.
- Learn from past failures.
- Remember that God cares for you and is always present with you. You are very precious to him.
- Do not take revenge. Allow God to deal with those who mistreat you.
- Be encouraged as you remember that God will grant success in everything he leads you to do.
- Rejoice! Jesus is coming!

IV. LIFE APPLICATION

God Is My Pilot

We have all heard the saying, "God is my copilot." For Bob Frayser of Hoisington, Kansas, God was not only the copilot but the pilot as well. In December 1997 the family physician took off in his small Piper Comanche

400 for a meeting in Topeka. After about thirty minutes, Frayser was overcome by carbon monoxide fumes and blacked out. His plane then flew two hundred and fifty miles on autopilot (about two hours) before running out of fuel. Miraculously, the plane glided into a snowy field, skidding on its belly for five hundred feet before crashing into a row of trees near Cairo, Missouri.

The forty-seven-year-old man said he woke up disoriented with a terrific headache. He began preparing for a landing by switching the fuel tanks and so forth. Finally, he realized he was already on the ground! "I saw the trees around me, so I opened the door and got out," Frayser said. Then he staggered about a quarter of a mile to a house where help was called. The amateur pilot walked away with only a broken wrist and a few cuts and bruises. Jim Wesley of the Federal Aviation Administration quipped, "The man won the lottery."

However, Frayser recognized that it wasn't luck but God's care that had protected him through the ordeal. He remarked, "Most credit I give to the Lord." Frayser's experience is an amazing demonstration of how God cares for his children. While he doesn't always deliver them from harm, he always loves and watches over them.

Sometimes we are tempted to become discouraged and to think that no one cares for us. This can never be true, for God is always there. He is "a friend who sticks closer than a brother" (Prov. 18:24). We are tempted to fear changes in the economy, but David exclaimed, "I was young and now I am old, yet I have never seen the righteous forsaken or their children begging bread" (Ps. 37:25). God will provide. Martin Luther, the German reformer, went through a period of great despair. One morning his wife appeared at the breakfast table wearing a black armband. Luther inquired who had died. His wife replied, "Well, with the way you've been carrying on around here, I thought God did."

Do we behave sometimes as if God has died—worrying, fretting, filled with fear? Let us remember that our omnipotent God is alive and well and watching over every facet of our lives. He cares for us more than we could ever imagine. The apostle Peter shares the following word of comfort: "Casting all your care upon Him, because He cares about you" (1 Pet. 5:7 HCSB). If God could raise the nation of Israel from the dead in Zechariah's day and land an airplane for a sleeping pilot, he certainly can take care of us.

V. PRAYER

O Lord, thank you that you care for us. Help us to remember that you are always with us and will see us through any challenge. When we are tempted to worry, feel alone, or be afraid, remind us that you are there and can solve our problems. Thank you also for your protection from those in the world who would harm your children. We rejoice in your spiritual presence in our hearts and in anticipation of the day when you will physically dwell with your people in the person of your Son, Jesus Christ. In his name we pray. Amen.

VI. DEEPER DISCOVERIES

A. Returns from Exile

The Babylonian exile came about in several waves. First, Daniel and his friends were taken to Babylon in 605 B.C. Second, King Jehoiachin and ten thousand of Judah's leading citizens (including the prophet Ezekiel) were deported in 597 B.C. Third, approximately fifty thousand of Judah's citizens were carried away in 586 B.C. when the city and temple were destroyed. In similar fashion the return from exile came about in three successive movements. A synopsis of these returns is as follows:

RETURN	FIRST	SECOND	THIRD
DATE	538 B.C.	458 B.C.	445 B.C.
LEADER	Zerubbabel	Ezra	Nehemiah
PERSIAN KING	Cyrus	Artaxerxes I	Artaxerxes I
REFERENCE	Ezra 1–6	Ezra 7–10	Nehemiah 1–13
FOCUS	Temple	Law	Rebuilding wall

The first group of about fifty thousand Jews was by far the largest. Approximately eighteen hundred made the journey with Ezra, but the number with Nehemiah is not specified. Zechariah and Haggai came with the first group.

B. Apocalyptic Literature

Portions of the Book of Zechariah are categorized as apocalyptic literature. The term *apocalyptic* is derived from the Greek word *apokalypsis,* "revelation, disclosure," and the verb *apokalypto,* "uncover, reveal." Thus literature of this kind may be expected to reveal what has been hidden. Key features of apocalyptic literature are as follows:

- It is a revelation from God.

- Often angels or even Christ himself mediates the message.

- A prophet receives the revelation.

- The message usually speaks of future events.

- The apocalypse was written during a time of persecution or historical crisis.

- Often the message is presented in visions or dreams.

- There is much use of symbolism and numerology.

- The major theme of apocalyptic is the triumph of the kingdom of God over the kingdoms of the earth.

The Book of Daniel is the first real apocalypse and the classic example of this literary genre in the Old Testament. Its counterpart in the New Testament is the Book of Revelation. Other biblical passages, such as Isaiah 24–27 and Joel 3, are usually classified as apocalyptic material.

During the intertestamental period over a dozen Jewish apocalypses (e.g., 1 Enoch) appeared. Following the New Testament era, Christian apocalypses (e.g., the Ascension of Isaiah) were penned as well. These writings were considered unworthy of inclusion in the biblical canon because of their pseudonymous nature (false name for the author), pseudo-predictions, and various doctrinal and ethical problems. Essentially, these later apocalyptic works seem to be second-rate and uninspired imitations of Daniel and Revelation.

How should the believer regard the apocalyptic literature of the Bible? Canonical apocalyptic should be viewed positively as a method (or genre) used by God to "unveil" wonderful truths to his people. First, apocalyptic grants the world a glimpse of God himself. In apocalyptic works God is portrayed as sovereign, just, and powerful. He is in control of the universe and the lives of individuals. Second, canonical apocalyptic works unveil the future, not in order to satisfy idle curiosity but as a source of comfort and encouragement to the saints during their time of need.

C. Dating of Zechariah's Prophecies (1:1)

Like Haggai, Zechariah carefully dated the first eight chapters of his book from the second to the fourth year of Darius I (520–518 B.C.). According to our modern calendar (the Gregorian), the dates are:

Oct./Nov. 520 B.C.	First prophetic message (1:1–6)
Feb. 15, 519 B.C.	Eight night visions and symbolic crowning of Joshua (1:7–6:15)
Dec. 7, 518 B.C.	Questions about fasts (chs. 7–8).

Some scholars have questioned Zechariah's authorship of the two burdens recorded in chapters 9–14 because, unlike chapters 1–8, they are left undated. However, the most reasonable explanation is that these chapters are undated because they were not connected to a specific historical event, such as the rebuilding of the temple. These latter prophecies concern the distant future, and in all probability Zechariah wrote them late in his career.

D. Zechariah's Influence on the New Testament

Zechariah is quoted at least six times (four different passages) by the New Testament writers—more frequently than any other prophetic book except Isaiah, Jeremiah, and Hosea. Quotations are: Zechariah 9:9 (in Matt. 21:5 and John 12:15); 11:12–13 (in Matt. 27:9–10); 12:10 (in John 19:37); and 13:7 (in Matt. 26:31 and Mark 14:27). The last quotation is attributed to Jesus and indicates the Lord's belief in predictive prophecy.

However, Zechariah's influence on the New Testament reaches far beyond these specific quotations. According to Kaiser:

> There are seventy-one quotations from or allusions to Zechariah in the New Testament. One third of these appear in the Gospels and thirty-one are found in the Book of Revelation (including twenty from chapters 1–8 and eight from chapters 9–14). Of all the Old Testament books, Zechariah is second only to Ezekiel in its influence on the Book of Revelation (Kaiser, *Mastering the Old Testament*, 285).

Thus, the inspired writers of the New Testament recognized the Book of Zechariah as God's Word and considered it edifying for believers.

VII. TEACHING OUTLINE

A. INTRODUCTION

1. Lead Story: Angels Watching over You
2. Context: In the first two chapters of the book, Zechariah shares a wonderful message of encouragement and hope for postexilic Israel. After the prophet's initial call to repentance, which the people immediately heeded, Zechariah shares three night visions that contain the following comforting messages for God's people: (1) God is present and concerned; (2) Jerusalem will be rebuilt; (3) Judah will prosper; (4) Israel's oppressors will be judged; and (5) believers have a glorious future with God.
3. Transition: As we study this section of Zechariah, we will discover God's promises for us—his presence, concern, success, protection from enemies, and a bright future in Messiah's kingdom. Like Zechariah's audience we may have joy even in the midst of difficult circumstances.

B. COMMENTARY

1. The Prophet and His Times (1:1)
2. God's Caring Invitation (1:2–6)
3. God's Care Demonstrated by His Presence (1:7–17)
4. God's Care Demonstrated by the Punishment of Oppressors (1:18–21)
5. God's Care Demonstrated by the Promise of a Glorious Future (2:1–13)

C. CONCLUSION: SHE'S MY HERO!

VIII. ISSUES FOR DISCUSSION

1. The Lord extends the following invitation to his people: "Return to me . . . and I will return to you." Specifically, what does it mean to return to the Lord? In what sense does God return to us?
2. What lessons can we learn from studying God's dealings with sinful practices in history? What happened to Israel in biblical times when

the nation turned from God? Name other nations that collapsed because of sin.

3. What can you say to people who feel that God has forgotten them or does not care what they are facing?

4. What does God mean when he speaks of his people as "the apple of his eye"?

5. In what sense does God dwell with us now, and how will he dwell with his people in the future?

Zechariah 3

God Forgives

I. INTRODUCTION
Japan's Hero of Pearl Harbor

II. COMMENTARY
A verse-by-verse explanation of the chapter.

III. CONCLUSION
Luther's Nightmare

An overview of the principles and applications from the chapter.

IV. LIFE APPLICATION
Missionary Forgives Peru

Melding the chapter to life.

V. PRAYER
Tying the chapter to life with God.

VI. DEEPER DISCOVERIES
Historical, geographical, and grammatical enrichment of the commentary.

VII. TEACHING OUTLINE
Suggested step-by-step group study of the chapter.

VIII. ISSUES FOR DISCUSSION
Zeroing the chapter in on daily life.

Zechariah 3

IN A NUTSHELL

In chapter 3 Zechariah records a dramatic vision of the cleansing of Joshua, the high priest. In this courtroom scene Joshua appears before the angel of the Lord with Satan accusing him. However, the angel of the Lord is both judge and defense attorney and pronounces Joshua forgiven of his sin. Joshua's forgiveness is possible because of the atoning work of the Messiah, described as God's servant, the Branch. The chapter concludes with a prophecy of the messianic kingdom.

God Forgives

I. INTRODUCTION

Japan's Hero of Pearl Harbor

*P*resident Franklin Roosevelt called December 7, 1941, "a day that shall live in infamy." On that beautiful Sunday morning in the Hawaiian island of Oahu, 360 Japanese fighters, bombers, and torpedo planes launched an attack on the unsuspecting U.S. Pacific Fleet. The leader of the assault was Commander Mitsuo Fuchida. After he gave the order for his squadrons to attack, he radioed back these famous words to the Japanese fleet: *"Tora, tora, tora!" Tora* means "tiger" and was the go-ahead signal for the attack on Pearl Harbor. More than 2,300 Americans were killed; 5 of the 8 battleships in the harbor were destroyed; and 14 other ships were either sunk or damaged. Fuchida boasted that this was "the most thrilling exploit of my career."

After the war Fuchida returned home, discouraged and bitter over Japan's humiliating defeat. His life was miserable. Though married he had a mistress in Tokyo and visited her frequently. While on one such trip in October 1948, he saw an American handing out leaflets entitled *I Was a Prisoner of Japan* in a Tokyo train station. The leaflet was based on a book by an American soldier, Jacob DeShazer, who had been part of Colonel Jimmy Doolittle's daring bombing raid over Japan on April 18, 1942. DeShazer's B-24 bomber ran out of fuel and went down over Japanese-held territory. He spent the next forty months of the war in a Japanese prison camp where he was routinely tortured. DeShazer's book told how he overcame his hatred for his captors through Christ. After the war DeShazer returned to Japan, not as a soldier but as a missionary. Fuchida was stunned by DeShazer's story.

A few days later at the same train station, Fuchida saw a Japanese man selling Bibles. He purchased one. As he began to read this strange book, he was struck by Jesus' words in Luke 23:34, "Father, forgive them, for they do not know what they are doing." Fuchida later wrote, "I was impressed that I was certainly one of those for whom Jesus had prayed. The many men I had killed had been slaughtered in the name of patriotism, for I did not understand the love of Christ." Fuchida received the Lord and went on to become an evangelist in Japan and Asia. He even became friends with his former enemy, Jacob DeShazer. Fuchida faithfully served the Lord until his death in 1976 at the age of seventy-four. Incredibly, God's grace and forgiveness had reached the leader of one of the most horrendous massacres in America's history. God's forgiveness knows no bounds.

In Zechariah's fourth vision, we find a captivating account of the cleansing of Joshua, symbolic of forgiveness of sin. As we study this chapter, we will better comprehend the seriousness of sin and the grace of God. We will learn timeless truths about forgiveness that apply to anyone, anywhere, and at any time. We are also afforded several glimpses of the Messiah, whose sacrifice on the cross makes our forgiveness possible.

II. COMMENTARY

God Forgives

MAIN IDEA: *God graciously forgives sin on the basis of Messiah's atoning work.*

A Joshua on Trial (3:1)

SUPPORTING IDEA: *Satan accuses sinners before the heavenly judge.*

3:1. The phrase **he showed me** may refer to the interpreting angel or God. The words **standing before the angel of the LORD** have been interpreted to denote service, and the verb "to stand" does appear with this meaning in the Old Testament. For example, in Daniel 1:19, "They [Daniel and his friends] entered the king's service" literally reads, "They stood before the king" (cp. KJV). "Standing" also represents priestly ministry in Deuteronomy 10:8 and 2 Chronicles 29:11. Certainly Joshua in his role as high priest ministered before the Lord.

Nevertheless, service is not the idea here. Rather, in this fourth vision we have a courtroom scene with **Joshua the high priest** on trial and standing before the heavenly judge, the angel of the Lord. We may observe the prominence of the angel of the Lord in this vision. He is plainly in charge. As in 1:11–12, the angel of the Lord is none other than the Lord himself. When the angel of the Lord speaks, verse 2 identifies him as "the LORD." In verse 4 the angel of the Lord forgives sins, a divine prerogative. We may understand this divine person to be a preincarnate appearance of Christ.

The name **Satan** is found only in Zechariah 3:1–2 in the prophets. This mighty angel (also referred to as the "devil" [*diabolos* = "slanderer"] over thirty times in the New Testament) is the leader of the evil angels, called demons in the Bible. In this heavenly court scene, Satan was standing at Joshua's **right side** (literally, "right hand") **to accuse him.** The right side was the place of accusation under the law. For example, in Psalm 109:6 we read, "Appoint an evil man to oppose him; let an accuser stand at his right hand." Satan may be compared to a prosecuting attorney who was accusing Joshua before the heavenly judge. In verse 4 we discover that Satan's charges were that Joshua was sinful and unworthy of divine favor. Similarly, this heavenly prosecutor appeared with the angels (literally, "the sons of God") and accused Job of serving God out of selfish motives rather than love (Job 1:6–11). Today Satan continues to accuse the saints, but some day God will put an end to his attacks (Rev. 12:9–10).

As we shall see, the high priest Joshua also represented Israel as a priestly nation (Exod. 19:6). Thus Satan was reminding the Lord of the nation's past wretchedness (1:2,4–6) and its unworthiness. Israel certainly did not deserve God's forgiveness or the divine promises of restoration set forth in the previous visions.

Satan's accusations are still the same. He argues that we are sinful and deserve judgment, not forgiveness. Nevertheless, the prophet Isaiah declared that God is merciful and forgives those who repent: "Let the wicked forsake his way and the evil man his thoughts. Let him turn to the LORD, and he will have mercy on him, and to our God, for he will freely pardon" (Isa. 55:7). Satan has no grounds for condemning believers (Rom. 8:1) since Christ took the punishment for our sins at the cross, thereby paying our sin debt (Col. 2:13–14).

B Joshua's Defense (3:2)

SUPPORTING IDEA: *The Lord is both the sinner's judge and defender.*

3:2. **Satan** was vehemently accusing Joshua when the Lord intervened. Joshua's defender was none other than the Lord himself—also the judge! No doubt existed about the outcome of this trial. Joshua was sure to win his case.

The phrase **the LORD rebuke you** is also directed against Satan in Jude 9: "But even the archangel Michael, when he was disputing with the devil about the body of Moses, did not dare to bring a slanderous accusation against him, but said, 'The Lord rebuke you!'" The word *rebuke* "indicates a check applied to a person or peoples through strong admonitions or actions. Jacob rebukes Joseph when he relates the dream of sun, moon, and eleven stars bowing to him (Gen 37:10). Aggressive nations flee before God when he checks their deed against his people (Isa 17:13)" (Harris, Archer, and Waltke, TWOT, 1:170).

As the vision unfolds, it becomes apparent that

Joshua was functioning in his high priestly capacity as representative of the nation Israel. God's choice of Jerusalem, not Joshua, was the basis of the rebuke. Later the sin was removed from the land, not just from Joshua (v. 9). Joshua and his priestly companions were said to be "men symbolic of things to come" (v. 8). Therefore, much as the high priest represented the entire nation on the Day of Atonement (cp. Lev. 16:1–10), so here Joshua the high priest was accused and acquitted on behalf of the nation Israel (Lindsey, 1554).

Satan's accusations of Israel's wrongdoing are not denied. Yet God had sovereignly **chosen Jerusalem** and graciously rescued the nation from destruction, like **a burning stick snatched from the fire** (cp. Amos 4:11). Barker adds, "This verse raises the problems of how a holy God can bless a filthy nation like Israel. The answer is that he can do so only by his grace through the work of the Messiah" (Barker, 624).

C Joshua's Crimes (3:3)

SUPPORTING IDEA: *Sin is unimaginably abhorrent to God.*

3:3. The basis for Satan's accusation is specified here, namely, Joshua's impurity—**dressed in filthy clothes.** We are told in verse 4 that the removal of these filthy clothes describes forgiveness from sin. The Hebrew term rendered "filthy" is found only here and in verse 4 in the Old Testament. However, other words from the same Hebrew root denote human excrement (Deut. 23:13; Ezek. 4:12) and the drunkard's vomit (Isa. 28:8). According to Feinberg, this is "the strongest expression in the Hebrew language for filth of the most vile and loathsome character" (Feinberg, *God Remembers,* 46). Joshua's garments were covered with this kind of filth.

Generally, human beings have quite a casual attitude toward sin. Most people would agree that no one is perfect, but they feel that sin really isn't all that bad. Yet here we are afforded a glimpse of God's view of sin. It is repulsive beyond measure. Could we fellowship with someone covered with such filth? Of course not! We would not want to be in the same room with such a person. So it is with the Lord. Our sin must be cleansed before we can enter into the presence of a holy God.

D Joshua's Pardon (3:4–5)

SUPPORTING IDEA: *By God's grace, sinners may be cleansed of sin.*

3:4. The Lord (the angel of the Lord) commanded angels in the vision to remove Joshua's **filthy clothes,** symbolic of his forgiveness of **sin** ("iniquity," KJV, NKJV, NASB; "guilt," NRSV). These filthy garments represent moral defilement rather than ritual defilement because by this act Joshua's sin was cleansed. The fact that the angel of the Lord had the power to forgive sins affirms his deity. Here Joshua's justification, the act whereby the judge declares a person righteous or pardoned, is depicted. Justification implies deliverance from the penalty of sin. It is noteworthy that this act of forgiveness was accomplished by the Lord alone. Salvation is a work of God.

Clothing Joshua with clean garments illustrates positional sanctification—our righteousness in Christ. **Rich garments** were worn on special occasions, such as festivals. Being clothed in righteousness is a figure found elsewhere in the Bible. For example, the psalmist declared, "May your priests be clothed with righteousness; may your saints sing for joy" (Ps. 132:9). Isaiah added: "I delight greatly in the LORD; my soul rejoices in my God. For he has clothed me with garments of salvation and arrayed me in a robe of righteousness, as a bridegroom adorns his head like a priest, and as a bride adorns herself with her jewels" (Isa. 61:10). Such picturesque language has made its way into many of our best loved hymns. In Edward Mote's "The Solid Rock," we find these words: "When He [Christ] shall come with trumpet sound, O may I then in Him be found, dressed in His righteousness alone, faultless to stand before the throne."

3:5. Apparently Zechariah was overcome with excitement and cried out for Joshua to be crowned with a **clean turban.** The turban was the finishing touch. On the high priest's turban was a plate of pure gold inscribed with the words: "HOLY TO THE LORD" (Exod. 28:36; 39:30). Now Joshua was clean and fit for service.

E Joshua's Responsibility (3:6–7)

SUPPORTING IDEA: *Forgiven sinners should live and serve faithfully.*

3:6–7. The angel of the LORD admonished Joshua to **walk in** God's **ways and keep** God's **requirements.** The first admonition was about Joshua's personal holiness, the second the faithful administration of his official duties as high priest. Both are very important. We may observe the divine order—personal holiness precedes effective service. Before a person can function as God's servant before others, the heart must be pure. As Feinberg puts it, "Service is to flow out of a godly life" (Feinberg, *Minor Prophets,* 286).

If Joshua were to keep these two conditions, he would have the following two privileges: (1) He would continue in his position as high priest. Duties of the high priest included settling matters of dispute (**govern my house**) and guarding the temple from defilement and idolatry (**have charge of my courts**). (2) Joshua would be granted special access to God. **Place** is literally "walks" or "journeys." NASB's "free access" and NRSV's "right of access" seem to capture the idea well. Those **standing here** were the angels in the vision. Thus Joshua would have special access to God like the angels of heaven. This special access to God may have included the high priest's privilege of entering into the temple's most holy place on the Day of Atonement.

In summary, God charged the forgiven to live a life of personal holiness and faithfulness. If we do so, God will honor us with privileged responsibility and unhindered fellowship with him. Nationally, Israel was admonished to be holy and faithful in order to retain its privileged position and access to God as a priestly nation.

⧉ Joshua's Savior (3:8–9)

SUPPORTING IDEA: *Forgiveness is made possible by the atoning work of the Messiah.*

3:8. Listen (literally, "listen now!") is an exhortation indicating an important message will follow. The phrase **men symbolic of things to come** reads literally "men of wonder" or "a sign [of future events]." The NIV's "symbolic of things to come" follows the latter idea and seems to capture the meaning well. **Joshua** and his priestly **associates** were symbolic of the person and work of the coming Messiah—the true high priest (Heb. 3:1; 4:14; 6:20; 9:11). Joshua's cleansing also foretold Messiah's future work of cleansing the priestly nation. Zechariah used three figures to describe the coming Messiah.

First, **my servant** is a popular name for the Messiah in Scripture (Isa. 42:1; 49:3; 50:10; 52:13; 53:11; Ezek. 34:23–24; Phil. 2:6–8). Christ was the obedient servant who came to do the will of God the Father.

Second, the Hebrew noun, *tsemach,* occurs a dozen times in the Old Testament, five of which are rendered **the Branch,** a messianic title (Isa. 4:2; Jer. 23:5; 33:15; Zech. 3:8; 6:12; cp. Isa. 11:1). Like a branch that sprouts from a tree, the Messiah will come from the line of David. The messianic view is also an ancient Jewish interpretation.

3:9. Third, **the stone** with its **seven eyes** (or "facets") and engraved **inscription** has been variously interpreted as the kingdom of God (or the church), a final stone for the temple, a jewel worn by Joshua, and the Messiah. Many evangelical scholars hold the messianic view, and this seems preferable. A messianic interpretation is supported by the context (unmistakable messianic titles in v. 8) and conforms to the many places in Scripture where the figure of a stone or rock refers to Christ (Gen. 49:24; Ps. 118:22; Isa. 28:16; Matt. 21:42; Acts 4:11; Eph. 2:19–20; 1 Pet. 2:6–8). Moreover, the stone appears to be associated with the removal of **sin**—a work of Messiah—spoken of in the latter part of the verse.

The stone was **in front of Joshua** in prophetic prospect. **One stone** means a unique stone and symbolizes the fact that Messiah is the unique one. No other is like him. Evangelicals who hold the messianic view generally take the **seven eyes on** (better than "over") the stone to symbolize Christ's intelligence and omniscience (cp. 4:10). Some evangelicals agree with early Christian interpreters that God's engraving **an inscription** on the stone depicts the marks on Messiah's body at the crucifixion—nail prints, crown of thorns, scourging, and so forth. Others understand the engraving to describe Messiah's beauty, gifts, graces, and preciousness—like a beautifully cut precious stone.

Messiah's atoning work is specified in the last part of the verse. The forgiveness of sin described in verse 4 is possible only because of the shed blood of Christ at the cross. Isaiah affirmed: "We all, like sheep, have gone astray, each of us has turned to his own way; and the LORD has laid on him the iniquity of us all" (Isa. 53:6). National as well as individual pardon is made possible by Christ's sacrifice. Israel as a nation rejected Jesus as their promised Messiah, but some day the nation (**this land**) will turn to him and receive forgiveness—**in a single day** (cp. Zech. 12:10; 13:1; Rom. 11:25–29).

Barker comments: "Prophetically, the one day is the once-for-all deliverance potentially provided at Calvary—to be actually and finally realized in Israel's experience at the second advent of her Messiah, when there will be cleansing and forgiveness for the nation as a whole" (Barker, 626). This act was symbolized by the removal of Joshua's filthy clothes in verse 4. The reference to the removal of the iniquity of the land anticipates the sixth and seventh visions (Barker, 626).

G Joshua's Future (3:10)

SUPPORTING IDEA: *Forgiven sinners will be part of Messiah's blessed future kingdom.*

3:10. When Messiah forgives Israel's sin, the messianic age will ensue. The phrase **in that day** refers to the eschatological day of the Lord. "In that day" or "on that day" (both are the same in the Hebrew) appears approximately twenty times in the Book of Zechariah. **Under his vine and fig tree** speaks of spiritual and physical blessings in Israel (1 Kgs. 4:24–25; 2 Kgs. 18:31; Mic. 4:4). According to Barker:

> The vine and the fig tree speak not only of spiritual blessing but also of the agricultural blessing of the land when the desert will blossom like the crocus and once again be fruitful (cp. Isa. 11:1–9; 35; 65:17). There can be no such prosperity and peace for Israel till the messianic kingdom has fully come on earth, no such kingdom till Israel is restored, and no true restoration of Israel till the Lord returns to the earth with his saints (cp. Dan. 7:13–14,27; Mic. 4:1–4) (Barker, 627).

Of course, Christ's rule will ensure safety, peace, and prosperity not only for Israel but for all the earth.

MAIN IDEA REVIEW: *God graciously forgives sin on the basis of Messiah's atoning work.*

III. CONCLUSION

Luther's Nightmare

Walter Kaiser shares the following account from the life of the great reformer, Martin Luther (A.D. 1483–1546).

> One of the most famous ink spots in the world is the one on the wall of Wartburg Castle, Germany, where, it is said, Martin Luther had it out with the Devil over the evil one's constant dredging up of Luther's past sins. . . . The story is that Luther dreamt that Satan appeared to him reading a long scroll with all his many sins from his birth on. As the reading of the list proceeded, Luther's terrors grew until finally he jumped up and cried, "It is all true, Satan, and many

more sins I have committed in my life which are known to God only; but write at the bottom of your list, 'the blood of Jesus Christ, God's Son, cleanses us from all sin.'" Then grasping the inkwell on his table, he threw it at the Devil, who immediately fled. The memorial of this incident is now the famous spot on the Wartburg Castle (Kaiser, *Mastering the Old Testament*, 320–321).

As in Luther's dream, Satan accused Joshua of sin and vehemently contended with God that Israel's high priest was unfit for blessing or service. Satan's accusations about Joshua's sinfulness were true. The question becomes, How then can a holy God (the judge) be just and still pardon sinful Joshua? God in his mercy has provided a way through Messiah's atoning work (Zech. 3:8–9). On the cross Jesus Christ "bore our sins in his body on the tree, so that we might die to sins and live for righteousness; by his wounds you have been healed" (1 Pet. 2:24; Isa. 53:4–6; Heb. 1:3; 9:14; 1 John 2:1–2). Messiah's work also makes possible the forgiveness of the nation Israel (represented by Joshua).

PRINCIPLES

- Satan is our adversary who accuses us of being sinful and unworthy of forgiveness.
- Christ is our advocate who defends us from Satan's attacks.
- Sin is unimaginably repulsive to God, like the worst filth.
- In salvation our sin is forgiven, and we are clothed with the righteousness of Christ.
- Those who are forgiven should live holy and faithful lives in order to be used of God and maintain unhindered fellowship with him.
- Forgiveness is possible because of Messiah's atoning work.
- When Messiah (Jesus Christ) comes, the world will experience true peace and prosperity.

APPLICATIONS

- If you have never accepted God's offer of pardon for your sin (based on Christ's sacrifice at the cross), do so now and experience forgiveness, new life in Christ, and the assurance of a future with God.

- When Satan attacks, claim God's promise of forgiveness given to all who are in Christ.
- Determine to live a holy and faithful life so that you may be used to do great things for God and have unhindered fellowship with him.
- Thank God for providing pardon for your sins and a wonderful future through the work of his Son, Jesus the Messiah.

IV. LIFE APPLICATION

Missionary Forgives Peru

Even while attending a Christian college in North Carolina, Jim and Roni (Veronica) Bowers knew that some day they wanted to be foreign missionaries and spread the gospel. In 1993 that dream came true when the Association of Baptists for World Evangelism appointed them to serve in Peru. Their job was to plant churches and train leaders in the small villages along the Amazon River. They could not have been happier as they lived on a houseboat with their son Cory and newly adopted baby girl, Charity.

On April 20, 2001, the Bowers were flying back from getting a new visa for Charity when suddenly their peaceful flight turned into a nightmare. Mistaking them for drug smugglers, a Peruvian Air Force pilot opened fire on the small craft. Thirty to forty bullets exploded through the cabin, killing Roni and baby Charity instantly and just missing Jim and Cory. Pilot Kevin Donaldson was seriously wounded but amazingly was able to land the pontoon plane on a river.

From the moment Jim realized his wife and daughter were dead, God gave him a peace "that they're with Him." Peru has promised to replace the plane and has expressed regret. "Yet," Jim says, "never once has anybody from the air force [Peruvian] said that 'We were wrong, we shouldn't have shot. We have no excuse.' No one's ever talked that way, never said they're sorry even." Nevertheless, in a new book about the tragedy, *If God Should Choose* by Kristen Stagg (Chicago: Moody Press, 2002), Bowers has expressed forgiveness to the Peruvian government for the deed.

Bowers's story grabbed headlines around the world, and the media has followed up with the account of Bowers's forgiveness. The headlines for the Associated Press story in my local newspaper read, "Slain missionary's husband forgives Peru for fatal attack." In the article Bowers is quoted as saying,

"Cory and I are experiencing inexplicable peace, and to me that's proof that God is in this. . . . Our attitude toward those responsible is one of forgiveness. Is that not amazing? It shouldn't be amazing to us Christians." What a marvelous testimony this is to an unbelieving world!

Even for Christians, forgiveness can be difficult. We might feel, "I can't forgive that person. He doesn't deserve it. He has hurt me too deeply." Yet we must consider what God has done in forgiving us. Joshua's filthy clothes offer a glimpse of how repulsive our sin is in the eyes of God. Our sins put Jesus on the cross (1 Pet. 2:24). Yet God still loves us and has forgiven us, unworthy as we may be.

Jesus told a story in Matthew 18:21–35 about a master who forgave his servant the equivalent of millions of dollars in today's money while that servant was unwilling to forgive a fellow servant a debt of a relatively small amount. The point of Jesus' story is that since God has forgiven us a debt of sin we could never pay, surely we should be willing to forgive others who wrong us. The apostle Paul expressed it this way: "Be kind and compassionate to one another, forgiving each other, just as in Christ God forgave you" (Eph. 4:32).

V. PRAYER

Lord, thank you for the forgiveness made possible by Christ's sacrifice for us on the cross. We realize that we can never pay you back, but help us to live in a way that will show our love and gratitude to you. May we be willing to forgive others as you have forgiven us. In Jesus' name we pray. Amen.

VI. DEEPER DISCOVERIES

A. Chronology of the Persian Period

In 539 B.C. Cyrus conquered Babylon and brought an end to the Babylonian Empire. From that time until Alexander the Great's forces caused the Persian Empire to crumble in 331 B.C., Persia was the dominant world ruler. Daniel ministered in the first few years of Persian rule, and the postexilic prophets—Haggai, Zechariah, and Malachi—all prophesied during this period. Ezra, Nehemiah, and Esther lived during this era as well, Esther and Nehemiah even holding prominent positions in the Persian court. Following is a chronology of Persian kings who served during the Old Testament era with their biblical connections.

PERSIAN KING	DATES	BIBLICAL CONNECTION
Cyrus	539–530 B.C.	First return—Zerubbabel, Joshua, Haggai, Zechariah (Ezra 1–3)
Cambyses	530–522 B.C.	Rebuilding at Jerusalem stopped (Ezra 4)
Darius I	522–486 B.C.	Haggai and Zechariah prophesy (520 B.C.); temple completed (516 B.C.) (Ezra 5–6)
Xerxes	486–465 B.C.	Story of Esther (Esth. 1–9)
Artaxerxes I	464–423 B.C.	Return of Ezra (458 B.C.) (Ezra 7–10); return of Nehemiah (445 B.C.) (Neh. 1–2); prophecy of Malachi (433 B.C.) (Mal. 1–4)

Persian kings who served after the Old Testament era are: Darius II (423–404), Artaxerxes II (404–359), Artaxerxes III (359–338), Arses (338–335), and Darius III (335 and 331). Darius III was defeated by Alexander the Great in a series of battles between 333 and 331 B.C. After the Medo-Persian Empire collapsed, the Greek Empire dominated the Mediterranean world until the Roman period.

B. The Angel of the LORD (3:1,5–6)

In the Book of Zechariah, the prophet frequently interacted with angels. Sometimes these were ordinary angels (1:19; 4:1,4,11; 5:5,10; 6:4–5), but in six cases "the angel of the LORD" designated God himself (1:11–12; 3:1,5–6; 12:8). "Angel" means "messenger," and in these instances the one who brought the message was deity. The rider of the red horse in 1:8 is identified as "the angel of the LORD" in 1:11. His preeminence is demonstrated by the fact that the other riders (angels) reported to him (1:11). In chapter 3 the angel of the Lord presided over the heavenly court. When he spoke in verse 2, he was identified as "the LORD." In verse 4 the angel of the Lord forgave sins, a divine prerogative. In 12:8 the angel of the Lord was identified with both names—"the LORD" and "God."

Elsewhere in the Old Testament the angel of the Lord is equated with deity. After Hagar, Sarah's maid, encountered the angel of the Lord (Gen. 16:7–12), she called him "the God who sees me" (Gen. 16:13). In speaking to Abraham, the angel of the Lord said, "I swear by myself, declares the LORD"

(Gen. 22:16). The angel of the Lord appeared to Moses in a burning bush (Exod. 3:2). When Moses investigated, God spoke to him from the bush (Exod. 3:4–6). In the angel of the Lord's conversation with Gideon, the text repeatedly identifies the speaker as "the LORD" (Judg. 6:11–24). Samson's parents recognized that in their visit with the angel of the Lord, they had "seen God" (Judg. 13:20–22).

Evangelical scholars usually identify the angel of the Lord as a preincarnate appearance of Christ—the second person of the Trinity. Paul Enns offers the following support for this interpretation:

> The theophanies prove His [Christ's] eternal existence. A theophany may be defined thus: "It is the Second Person of the Trinity who appears thus in human form." . . . The identification of Christ with the appearances of the angel of the Lord (the theophany) can be demonstrated in the following manner. The angel of the Lord is recognized as deity. He is referred to as God (Judg. 6:11,14; note in verse 11 He is called "angel of the LORD," while in v. 14 He is called "LORD"). The angel of the Lord in other instances is distinct from Yahweh because He talks to Yahweh (Zech. 1:12; 3:1–2; cp. Gen. 24:7). The angel of the Lord could not have been the Spirit or the Father, because neither the Spirit nor the Father [is] ever revealed in physical form (cp. John 1:18). The angel of the Lord no longer appears after the incarnation of Christ. There is no mention of the angel of the Lord in the New Testament; He ceases to appear after the birth of Christ (Enns, *The Moody Handbook of Theology,* Chicago: Moody Press, 1989, p. 216).

In the appearances of the angel of the Lord, we are granted a glimpse of Christ's glory before his incarnation. He is fully God with all the prerogatives of God at his disposal. For example, he forgives sin (3:4), makes descendants numerous (Gen. 22:17; see Gen. 16:10), brings Israel out of Egypt (Judg. 2:1; cp. Exod. 23:20–21), knows the future (Judg. 13:3), and performs miracles (Exod. 3:2; Judg. 13:20). These passages also preview the doctrine of the Trinity (three persons—Father, Son, and Holy Spirit—one God). Even in the Old Testament era, it was revealed that our one God exists as more than one person.

C. Satan (3:1–2)

The name *Satan* is found only in Zechariah 3 (vv. 1–2, three times) in the prophets. Hebrew *satan* occurs twenty-seven times in the Old Testament and means "adversary." As a proper name, it is used to designate the leader of the fallen angels or demons. In the NIV the Hebrew noun is translated as follows: "Satan" (eighteen times), "adversary" (four times), "oppose" (two times), "accuser" (one time), "adversaries" (one time), and as part of the phrase, "turn against" (one time). The verb is found six times and means "to be or act as an adversary" who opposes, slanders, or accuses. Examples of human adversaries are Hadad the Edomite (1 Kgs. 11:14) and King Rezon of Aram (1 Kgs. 11:23,25), who were enemies of Solomon during the last years of his reign.

Most references in the Old Testament to the Hebrew noun, *satan*, denote our angelic adversary, Satan. In this passage the following facts indicate that this accuser must be an angel. Zechariah's vision was a heavenly, not earthly, court scene, and this adversary who accused Joshua before the Lord was plainly not human. In Job 1:6 Satan appeared before God with the angels (literally, "the sons of God"), and Job named this angelic accuser as Satan fourteen times in his book.

In Zechariah 3:1–2 *satan* is preceded by the definite article *the*. For this reason, some scholars have argued that the text should not be translated as a proper name ("Satan") but rather as "the adversary" (who of course would still be Satan). The presence or absence of the article cannot settle the matter because on occasion proper names do appear with the article. The personal nature of the scene and the usage of the term *Satan* elsewhere in the Bible to designate our angelic adversary or accuser favor a proper name. For example, in Revelation 12:9–10 our heavenly accuser is specifically identified as Satan (cp. Job 1:6–12). However, no doubt exists that by the second century B.C. Satan had become a personal name.

In addition to the above, the Bible informs us that Satan committed the following evil acts: inspired David to take a census of Israel, an act suggesting sinful pride—a characteristic of Satan (1 Chr. 21:1), tempted Jesus (Matt. 4:10; Mark 1:13), crippled a woman (Luke 13:11,16), inspired Judas to betray the Lord (John 13:27), inspired Ananias to lie to the Holy Spirit (Acts 5:3), tempts (1 Cor. 7:5) and schemes against the saints (2 Cor. 2:11), hinders God's work (1 Thess. 2:18), and energizes the "lawless one" (2 Thess. 2:9). His power is great, but Christ has defeated him at the cross and soon will "crush Satan" completely (Rom. 16:20). Believers should respect Satan's might (Jude 8–9) but do not have to fear him because our God is infinitely more powerful and protects us (Matt. 6:13; John 17:15). When we resist Satan through faith in God's Word, he flees (Jas. 4:7). Eventually, Satan will be judged and consigned to the lake of fire for eternity (Matt. 25:41; Rev. 20:10).

Walter Elwell lists twenty-six other names for Satan found in the Bible. Some of these are: devil (the other most common name; Matt. 4:1), Abaddon (Rev. 9:11), Apollyon (Rev. 9:11), Beelzebub (Matt. 12:24), Belial (2 Cor. 6:15), dragon (Rev. 12:9), evil one (Matt. 6:13), god of this age (2 Cor. 4:4), murderer (John 8:44), and serpent (Rev. 12:9) (Elwell, *Topical Analysis of the Bible,* Grand Rapids, MI: Baker Book House, 1991, pp. 294–97).

D. The Branch (3:8)

The Hebrew noun *tsemach* occurs a dozen times in the Old Testament, five of which are rendered "the Branch," a messianic title (Isa. 4:2; Jer. 23:5; 33:15; Zech. 3:8; 6:12; see also Isa. 11:1). Like a branch that sprouts from a tree, the Messiah will come from the line of David. The messianic view is also an ancient Jewish interpretation.

Charles Feinberg shares the following helpful summary of the significance of this important messianic figure:

> The name Zemach (a proper noun in our text) conveys several truths. First, it brings out the lowliness and humiliation of the Messiah (Isa. 11:1). Second, it reveals His eminence (Isa. 53:2). He grows up before the Lord Himself. Third, it directs our attention to His humanity. He is connected with the earth, and more particularly the land of Palestine (Zech. 6:12). Fourth, it relates Him to the Davidic dynasty (Jer. 23:5,6). Fifth, it focuses our thought upon the deity of the Branch (Isa. 4:2). Sixth, it conveys the truth of His fruitfulness in comparison with the barrenness of all others (Isa. 11:1; 53:10). Seventh, it speaks of his priestly work and character; for being touched with the feeling of our infirmities, He is a becoming and fit High Priest for sinful men (Zech. 6:12). How unspeakably full are the designations of God for His only-begotten and much-beloved Son! (Feinberg, *God Remembers,* 51).

In Jesus of Nazareth, all the promises of the Branch figure are fulfilled.

VII. TEACHING OUTLINE

A. INTRODUCTION

1. Lead Story: Japan's Hero of Pearl Harbor

2. Context: In Zechariah's fourth vision, he sees Joshua the high priest standing before the angel of the Lord. Joshua's clothes are covered with the vilest filth, symbolic of his sin. Satan viciously charges Joshua, who represents the nation Israel, of being unworthy of forgiveness and blessing. However, God in his mercy sovereignly chooses to forgive Joshua based on Messiah's work described under three figures—"my servant," "the Branch," and "the stone" (vv. 8–9). This chapter illustrates justification (God's declaration of righteousness) and sanctification (clothed in righteousness).

3. Transition: Zechariah 3 helps us to understand the gravity of sin and the grace of God. Like Joshua, all of us are sinful and undeserving, yet God is merciful and willing to forgive. Our forgiveness is possible because of the atoning work of Jesus the Messiah who will some day bring in a world where peace and safety pervade.

B. COMMENTARY

1. Joshua on Trial (3:1)
2. Joshua's Defense (3:2)
3. Joshua's Crimes (3:3)
4. Joshua's Pardon (3:4–5)
5. Joshua's Responsibility (3:6–7)
6. Joshua's Savior (3:8–9)
7. Joshua's Future (3:10)

C. CONCLUSION: LUTHER'S NIGHTMARE

VIII. ISSUES FOR DISCUSSION

1. Do you think most people take sin seriously enough? Do you think many people believe their sin is really bad enough to keep them from going to heaven? How does such a casual attitude toward sin make it more difficult for people to appreciate the gospel ("good news" of salvation)?

2. Name ways that Satan accuses us today.

3. Explain how God can be a just judge and still pardon our sin.

4. What are some blessings of holy living and faithfulness?

5. What is the significance of the messianic titles "my servant" and "the Branch"? Name ways these titles were fulfilled in Jesus.

Zechariah 4

God Empowers

I. INTRODUCTION
Miracle of Dunkirk

II. COMMENTARY
A verse-by-verse explanation of the chapter.

III. CONCLUSION
Christian on Mission Trip Saves Plane

An overview of the principles and applications from the chapter.

IV. LIFE APPLICATION
Captive in a Church Attic

Melding the chapter to life.

V. PRAYER
Tying the chapter to life with God.

VI. DEEPER DISCOVERIES
Historical, geographical, and grammatical enrichment of the commentary.

VII. TEACHING OUTLINE
Suggested step-by-step group study of the chapter.

VIII. ISSUES FOR DISCUSSION
Zeroing the chapter in on daily life.

Quote

"Our spiritual power does not lie in money, genius, anointed plans, or dedicated work. Rather, power for spiritual conquest comes from the Holy Spirit."

Bill Bright

Zechariah 4

 **I N A N U T S H E L L**

In his fifth vision Zechariah sees a golden lampstand and two olive trees. Oil flows from the trees to the lamp, symbolizing the power of the Holy Spirit on the nation and its leaders—Joshua and Zerubbabel. The vision signifies that the work of rebuilding the temple (a daunting task from a human perspective) will be completed by the power of the Spirit of God.

God Empowers

I. INTRODUCTION

Miracle of Dunkirk

*A*dolph Hitler's German troops had stormed through Norway, Denmark, Holland, Luxemborg, Belgium, and France. By May 20, 1940, almost four hundred thousand British and French troops were trapped against the coast of Flanders near Dunkirk, France's third largest port. With Hitler's tanks just ten miles away, the situation seemed hopeless. Escape across the English Channel was the only possible option, but such a large force could never be evacuated in time.

Britain put out a call for all seaworthy vessels to help in what was dubbed Operation Dynamo. A flotilla of about seven hundred small craft of all kinds—including 45 passenger ships, 230 fishing boats, and more than 200 private launches—crossed the English Channel to join the destroyers and transport ships in the rescue effort. Between May 26 and June 4, 198,000 British and 140,000 French and Belgian troops were saved. British Prime Minister Winston Churchill called the rescue at Dunkirk "a miracle of deliverance."

Yet there is a more amazing story behind the so-called "miracle of Dunkirk." It is the miracle of prayer. On May 23, many British leaders, newspapers, and King George VI issued a call for a national day of prayer to be held on Sunday, May 26. According to an article in James Dobson's newsletter:

> Just 24 hours after the call for prayer, Adolf Hitler inexplicably ordered his armies to halt, to the surprise and dismay of even his own generals. Two days later, on May 26, the nation gathered to pray. Church attendance skyrocketed, including a large gathering at Westminster Abbey, during which people pleaded with the Almighty to spare their husbands, sons and fathers at Dunkirk.

Operation Dynamo began on the evening of the day of prayer, and the first troops were brought home that very night. General Sir Edmund Ironside, former chief of the British Imperial Staff, wrote, "I still cannot understand how it is that the [Germans] allowed us to get [our troops] off in this way. It is almost fantastic that we have been able to do it in the face of all the bombing and gunning." Without doubt, Dunkirk was a turning point in the war. Various explanations for Hitler's actions have been offered, but Dobson and many others believe that Hitler's armies were halted by the power of Almighty God.

We are amazed when we hear such stories, but we should not be. The God who can speak the universe into existence with its trillions of stars can just as easily turn the course of human history. In Zechariah 4 we are reminded of God's power in overcoming a hostile world. Zerubbabel had attempted to rebuild the temple about sixteen years before but was ordered to stop by the Persian government. He was surrounded by hostile neighbors whose goal was to prevent the resurgence of the Jewish nation. Could the work be completed? The answer was a resounding *yes*. In this fifth vision, God promised that no obstacle or earthly power can withstand the power of the Spirit of God.

II. COMMENTARY

God Empowers

MAIN IDEA: *God's purposes will be accomplished by the power of the Holy Spirit.*

A The Vision: A Lampstand and Two Olive Trees (4:1–3)

SUPPORTING IDEA: *Zechariah's fifth vision symbolically assures God's people of the Spirit's power for work and witness.*

Joshua, the Jewish religious leader, was encouraged by the vision in chapter 3. In this fifth vision God encouraged the civil leader, Zerubbabel. Haggai and Zechariah were calling on the nation and its governor, Zerubbabel, to resume work on the temple (Ezra 5:1–2). The foundation had been laid about sixteen years before (about 536 B.C.) under Zerubbabel's leadership (Ezra 3:8–11), but the Persian government ordered a halt to construction based on complaints from Israel's enemies, primarily the Samaritans (Ezra 4:1–5). Zerubbabel may have been fearful of Persia and his hostile neighbors. Later Nehemiah experienced a great deal of opposition from these same enemies, including threats of war (Neh. 4:7–23).

So this vision was given to instill courage in the heart of Zerubbabel. Moreover, some people may have reasoned that since the work had been stopped, God was not pleased with Zerubbabel or his efforts. Here God put any such notions to rest and vindicated Zerubbabel in the eyes of the people.

The vision was also a comforting word for Joshua who, though not specifically named, is referred to in symbol (vv. 3,12,14).

4:1. All eight of Zechariah's visions were received in one night (Zech. 1:7–8), but evidently there was a lapse of time between the fourth and fifth visions. Zechariah may have fallen asleep because of exhaustion or entered into a trancelike state from which the interpreting **angel** had to rouse him (cp. Dan. 10:9–11).

4:2–3. The angel directed the prophet's attention to the new vision with a question (cp. 5:2; Jer. 1:13). As Zechariah gazed at the vision, he saw **a solid gold lampstand** and **two olive trees**. We are not told the size of this lampstand, but the lampstand in the tabernacle was made of one talent of pure gold (Exod. 25:39). A talent weighed approximately seventy pounds, making a talent of gold worth several hundred thousand dollars today!

The lampstand (Heb. *menorah*) in Zechariah's vision was similar to that in the tabernacle (and later in the temple). Both had **seven** branches (or prongs) with small cuplike repositories at the end of each branch for oil. These were lit and provided the light in the tabernacle. Zechariah's lampstand was different from that in the tabernacle in three key features. (1) There was **a bowl** of oil above it (or **at the top**). (2) **Channels** (or pipes) ran to each of the **lights**. (3) Two olive trees stood beside it, **one** to its **right** and **the other** to **its left**. Thus the oil flowed by gravity from the bowl to the seven lights burning at the end of each branch of the lampstand. Priests would replenish the oil in the tabernacle daily, but no priest was needed here because the inexhaustible supply of oil flowed on its own from the bowl to the lamp.

The Hebrew text most likely means that **seven channels** ("pipes," KJV, NKJV; "spouts," NASB; "lips," NRSV) flowed to each of the seven lights, making a total of forty-nine channels, thereby indicating the great quantity of oil for the lights. This large supply of oil was derived from the two olive trees.

Although the text is not specific, the lampstand represents spiritual light or witness, most likely designating God's people (here the nation Israel) as bearers of that light. Light as a symbol of spiritual witness is clearly defined in the Bible. In Matthew 5:14, Christ called believers "the light of the world" (cp. Matt. 5:16; Luke 12:35; Phil. 2:15). In Revelation 1:20 Christ explicitly identified the "seven golden lampstands" in the opening vision of the Book of Revelation (1:12) as "the seven churches" (God's people). In Revelation 11:4 God's two future witnesses to the nations are symbolically called "the two lampstands" (light bearers). Often in the Gospel of John, Jesus is described as the light of the world (John 1:4–5,7–9; 3:19; 8:12; 9:5; 12:35–36,46).

Israel was to be a spiritual light to the nations, and effective witness is possible only by the power of God's Spirit (the oil). The many channels of oil suggest the inexhaustible supply of the Spirit's power. Oil flowing from the bowl with no human agency indicates that God's work will be accomplished by his sovereign power, not by human might (cp. v. 6). In the previous vision Israel (represented by Joshua the high priest) was cleansed. Now the priestly nation was prepared to be God's witness to the nations.

From ancient times the menorah (lampstand) has served as a national symbol for the Jewish people and is the emblem of the modern state of Israel. A large sixteen-foot-high bronze menorah stands in front of the Knesset, the Israeli parliament building.

Ⓑ Angelic Interpretation of the Vision: God's Power (4:4–7)

SUPPORTING IDEA: *God's will is accomplished not by human power but by the might of the Holy Spirit.*

4:4. In verses 4–7 we have the angel's interpretation of the vision. Zechariah politely (**my lord**) asked the interpreting angel the meaning of what he had seen. Probably Zechariah had in mind all the elements of the vision, not just the olive trees (as some scholars propose). The prophet asked for insight twice more in the vision (vv. 11–12).

4:5. The angel's question may be rhetorical (a question not expecting an answer). However, the angel may have genuinely been surprised that Zechariah did not comprehend some of the symbols in the vision, particularly the oil as representative of the Spirit's power. Oil is a clearly defined symbol in the Bible. According to Feinberg, "Everywhere in Scripture oil is seen as the type of the Holy Spirit. The oil of consecration for prophet, priest, and king was understood to symbolize the work and presence of the Holy Spirit" (Feinberg, *God Remembers*, 59). A passage that plainly illustrates the connection between anointing with oil and the Holy Spirit's power coming to rest on an individual is 1 Samuel 16:13, "So Samuel took the horn of oil and anointed him [David] in the presence of his brothers, and from that day on the Spirit of the LORD came upon David in power." There was nothing magical about olive oil being poured on a person's head. Rather, the power came from the Spirit of God, the one symbolized by the oil.

4:6. Zechariah was informed that the vision was a message from the Lord in symbolic form. **Zerubbabel** was specifically named because as the governor, he was responsible for taking the lead in the work of rebuilding. The angel now interpreted the abundance of oil described earlier as symbolic of the Spirit's power. The task of finishing the temple would be completed, "**Not by might nor by power, but by my Spirit**," says the LORD Almighty. This is truly one of the great verses in the Bible. Human beings are frail and weak, but God has all power, and nothing is impossible for him (Mark 10:27).

4:7. Before Almighty God, mountains can be leveled. Every obstacle would be removed from Zerubbabel's path by the Spirit of God. (For some of these obstacles, see Ezra 4–5.) Neither Israel's impoverished condition, her small numbers, the power of Israel's hostile neighbors, nor the might of Persia could prevent the temple's completion. Solomon took seven years and almost two hundred thousand men to build his temple with all of his wealth. For a poor group of fifty thousand to build the temple in the face of stiff opposition was a daunting task. Its **capstone**, the final touch, would be put in place with **shouts** of joy (cp. Ezra 3:11; 6:16–18).

The phrase **God bless it! God bless it!** reads literally, "Grace, grace to it!" Repetition suggests emphasis. These shouts at the end of the verse may be understood as an exclamation of the gracefulness or beauty of the finished temple or a prayerful desire for God's gracious blessing to rest upon it.

The principle of this passage applies with equal force to both individuals and churches in today's world. In our own strength we cannot meet the challenge. Only through God's power can God's work be done. Unless we are filled and empowered by the omnipotent, omniscient Spirit of Christ, we are doomed to failure and despair. As Jesus taught, "I am the vine; you are the branches. If a man remains in me and I in him, he will bear much fruit; apart from me you can do nothing" (John 15:5).

God's Power Ensures Success (4:8–10)

SUPPORTING IDEA: *God's irresistible power ensures that his work (rebuilding the temple) will be accomplished.*

4:8–9. Zechariah received a second promise of Zerubbabel's success. Sixteen years earlier, **Zerubbabel laid the foundation of this temple** (Ezra 3:8–13) but was forced by the Persian government to halt construction until the reign of Darius I (Ezra 4:1–5). Now God assured the governor that his present efforts would be successful. Ezra recorded that Darius ordered a search of Persia's royal archives and found King Cyrus's original decree permitting the Jews to rebuild their temple. Darius then commanded other governors in the area to permit the work to go on and even contributed financial support from the royal treasury (Ezra 6:1–12). The work was completed four years later, March 516 B.C. (Ezra 6:15). In earlier passages (Zech. 2:8–9,11), the person **sent** was identified as the Messiah. Here the prophet likely is in view because the context is the completion of the second temple. When Zechariah's words were fulfilled about the temple's construction, the people would know that God had sent him. However, some scholars continue to interpret the sent one as Messiah, contending that there is an immediate application to Zerubbabel and a distant reference to Messiah, who will build a future temple.

4:10. We know from Ezra 3:12–13 and Haggai 2:3 that some people despised the **small** beginnings of the restoration temple. In comparison to Solomon's magnificent structure, this little building made of inferior materials seemed insignificant. Yet in God's eyes it was a great work. Moreover, this tiny edifice would eventually become the grand Herod's temple that rivaled Solomon's building in glory, and in some ways even surpassed it. Herod's temple complex was certainly larger.

Yet most of the people rejoiced when Zerubbabel began the work. The **plumb line** (literally "stone of tin") was a heavy weight, originally of stone but now made of metal, at the end of a cord used to determine whether a wall was vertical. The numeral, **seven**, occurs almost four hundred times in the Bible and sometimes symbolizes completion or perfection. Here the **seven eyes of the LORD** (cp. 3:9) represent God's omniscience or perfect knowledge. (Some interpreters connect the seven eyes with the seven lights of v. 2.) All the **earth** is open before his watchful gaze (2 Chr. 16:9).

In context this was a message of comfort for Zerubbabel and the Jewish people. God saw their efforts and was pleased. In some English translations (e.g., NKJV, NASB), **these seven** eyes of God are construed as the subject of **will rejoice.** This is possible and may even be preferable. The idea would be that though some people despised Zerubbabel's seemingly small work, God was watching and rejoiced over it. Of course, pleasing God is all that really matters.

Ⓓ Angelic Explanation of the Two Olive Trees: Power to Serve (4:11–14)

SUPPORTING IDEA: *God anoints his servants (the two olive trees) with the Spirit's power to carry out his work.*

4:11–13. After the intervening oracle of verses 6–10, the prophet's questions (begun in v. 4) about the meaning of the vision resume. First, Zechariah asked for an explanation of the **two olive trees.** Before the angel had time to answer, he asked about the significance of the **two olive branches**. Apparently, the branches had clusters of olives from which flowed the **golden oil** (literally, "gold," referring to the color of the olive oil).

4:14. In the context of chapters 3–4, **the two who are anointed** (literally "sons of oil") **to serve the Lord** can only be Joshua, the high priest, and Zerubbabel, the civil ruler. Both priests and kings (civil rulers) were anointed with oil. Feinberg distinguishes the olive trees and the olive branches as follows: "The olive trees are the priestly and kingly offices in Israel; the two olive branches or twigs are their then incumbents, Joshua and Zerubbabel" (Feinberg, *God Remembers*, 64). On the other hand, the "branches" may (by extension) further signify the "trees." Human beings are often compared to trees in Scripture (cp. Ps. 1:3; Dan. 4:20–22). God's sovereignty is emphasized by the phrase, **the Lord of all the earth**.

Just as the oil flowed from the branches to the lamp, so Joshua and Zerubbabel (and the offices they represented—king and priest) were channels through which the Holy Spirit manifested His power and grace to the nation. Both the lampstand (Zech. 4:2) and the "two olive trees" (4:3,11,14) are used as symbols of God's two future witnesses (ones anointed to bear spiritual light) in Revelation 11:3–4 (cp. the very similar wording in this verse and Rev. 11:4).

Barker seems justified, particularly in light of Zechariah 6:9–15, in stating,

> This combination of ruler and priest is evidently intended to point ultimately to the messianic King-Priest (cp. 6:13; Ps. 110; Heb. 7). In keeping with one of the key ideas of the chapter (viz., bearing testimony), only the messianic King-Priest may be acknowledged as the perfectly "faithful and true witness" (Rev. 3:14) (Barker, 631).

MAIN IDEA REVIEW: *God's purposes will be accomplished by the power of the Holy Spirit.*

III. CONCLUSION

Christian on Mission Trip Saves Plane

Clarke Bynum was traveling to Uganda on a church mission trip when he was suddenly awakened by screams and the howl of engines. The British Airways jumbo jet had lapsed into a nosedive. As he peered out the window, he could tell the plane was plummeting straight down.

Though sure he was about to die, he leaped from his seat and rushed toward the cockpit. His mind raced. What would he encounter? Terrorists with knives or guns? What he found was a tall Kenyan man (later identified as a suspected mental patient) trying to crash the plane and the pilots struggling frantically to stop him. Bynum, a former Clemson University basketball player, was six feet seven inches tall and weighed over two hundred pounds. He was able to wrap his arms around the attacker and wrestle him to the floor. The plane had plummeted nineteen thousand feet, and pilots said that seconds more and the plane would have been unable to recover. When reporters asked the South Carolina native about his courage, Bynum explained, "There were literally hundreds of people back home praying for us, knowing we were going on this mission trip. There was this strength within that made me get up and go. It came from God."

Just as God's Spirit empowered Zerubbabel to build the temple, he gave a modern-day Christian strength to save an airplane filled with hundreds of people. That same Holy Spirit is present within every believer (John 14:17). Through his anointing power, we can be light in a spiritually darkened world and accomplish seemingly impossible tasks for God.

PRINCIPLES

- Nothing is impossible for our omnipotent God.
- God's spirit empowers his people to carry out his work.
- God's people are to be spiritual light in a dark world.
- No work is small if God is in it.
- Without the Spirit's power upon our lives, we are powerless.

APPLICATIONS

- Commit yourself to be a spiritual light in your community.
- Recognize that without the power of God's Holy Spirit on your life, you cannot accomplish spiritual work.
- Renounce any sins that may be quenching the Spirit of God and hindering you from serving the Lord effectively or are harming your witness for Christ.
- Rejoice in the tasks God has given you to do, knowing that whether they seem great or small, God is pleased.

IV. LIFE APPLICATION

Captive in a Church Attic

Leslie Marie Gattas was the daughter of a prominent Memphis businessman. She seemed to have a charmed life, but no one could imagine the incredible ordeal that this fifteen-year-old girl would endure. On November 19, 1981, Leslie was sound asleep in her parents' home when at 2:30 a.m. a man brazenly crawled through a laundry room window and stole the girl out of her bed. For four months, he held her captive in, of all places, a choir loft crawl space in one of the largest churches in Memphis. The kidnapper planned to collect a ransom for her release.

From November 1981 until March 1982, Leslie's kidnapping was a nationwide mystery. It was called the Memphis version of the Lindbergh baby kidnapping. Neither local police nor the FBI had a clue of her whereabouts, yet all the while Leslie was in the church. At night she and her captor would sneak down to the kitchen and get food. During these outings she left notes around the church asking for help. Thinking they were pranks, the pleas for help were discarded.

Eventually church employees became suspicious because of the great quantities of missing food. One night two maintenance men set a trap for the culprits. Around 11:30 they spotted the kidnapper and his young victim. During the struggle that ensued, one of the maintenance men hit the kidnapper with a club, whereupon he released the girl and fled (later apprehended by police). To their astonishment the girl they had rescued was Leslie Gattas!

Journalists, publishers, TV producers, and Hollywood screenwriters begged for Leslie's story, but she would not capitalize on it. Over ten years later, she finally granted an interview to a Memphis reporter as a way of saying thanks to all those who had prayed for her.

How could a fifteen-year-old girl survive such a horrifying experience? Leslie credited her faith. The night before her kidnapping she had been praying with friends. During the ordeal she prayed. Once her atheist kidnapper taunted her (while she was praying), "Your God ain't so good. He can't help you now." But God did help her. During her captivity, Leslie prayed up to eight hours a day and sensed God's power like never before. Ironically, she said that being captive in a church was comforting: "What better place to be than in God's house?"

Today Leslie is a lawyer with a wonderful family. Is she bitter about her experience? Absolutely not. She says, "If I had to do it all over again (just to be that close to God), I would." She adds, "Faith is a great thing. Most people go their whole lives wondering if there is a God. I'm one of the lucky ones. I know there is."

While we marvel at demonstrations of God's power at the dividing of the sea and the falling of fire on Mount Carmel (and rightly so), in some ways the power of God to sustain a young girl through four months of horror is even more remarkable. When our strength is not sufficient, God is there to see us through. Is there a task that seems impossible? God's Spirit can accomplish it. Is there a situation that seems hopeless? Nothing is impossible with God. Do you have a need? God can meet it. To paraphrase Zechariah 4:6: "Our strength and resources are not sufficient, but all things are possible by the power of the Spirit of God."

V. PRAYER

O Lord, we pray that our light will shine for you in a spiritually dark world. Thank you for the comfort and power of your indwelling Holy Spirit. May we always depend on your power and not our own. Help us to remember that you are pleased with us when we are faithful, whether the task is seemingly small or great. In the name of Jesus we pray. Amen.

VI. DEEPER DISCOVERIES

A. Zechariah's Lampstand (4:2)

Commentators are divided over the exact form of Zechariah's lampstand. If the lampstand was shaped like that in the tabernacle (and later the temple), it would have a base that divided into seven branches or prongs with repositories or bowls for oil at the end of each stem. The oil in these seven bowls would be lit and provide the light for the tabernacle. However, other scholars think the following description (with minor variations) by J. Baldwin is correct: "Lamp pedestals excavated from Palestine cities . . . were cylindrical in shape, hollow, and looked rather like a tree trunk. They were usually made of pottery. . . . Zechariah's lampstand (*menora*) was probably just a cylindrical column, tapering slightly towards the top, on which was *a bowl.* . . . Zechariah's large bowl . . . had *seven lamps on it, with seven lips on each of the lamps.*

The picture is of seven small bowls, each with a place for seven wicks, arranged round the rim of the main bowl" (Baldwin, 119–20).

While recognizing that the exact appearance of Zechariah's lampstand is subject to controversy, Lindsey maintains: "Appearing in a context of priestly temple ministry (cp. the previous vision), this lampstand was apparently similar to the lampstand placed in Israel's tabernacle (cp. Ex. 25:31–40), and the 10 lampstands of Solomon's temple (1 Kings 7:49)" (Lindsey, 1555). Lindsey seems to be correct.

Of course, the message conveyed by the lampstand symbol is more important than how it looked. In either case this light seems to signify light-bearing or witness.

B. The Number Seven in the Bible (4:2)

Four times in the Book of Zechariah, we encounter the number seven (3:9; 4:2[twice],10), and the number appears almost four hundred times in the Bible. In addition to its literal numerical value (e.g., Gen. 23:1; 1 Sam. 16:10), seven often has symbolic significance. According to G. G. Cohen:

> The Lord himself establishes and confirms the symbolic and sacred significance of seven. Hence in Ex 29:30 the garments of a new high priest were ordered by Moses speaking for the Lord to be consecrated for seven days. This was a ceremonial action and it could just as well have been accomplished in more or less days, yet the Lord prescribed exactly seven! In Ex 23:15 the unleavened bread was to be eaten seven days, and in Ex 25:37 the Menorah, or sacred lamp stand of the tabernacle, was to have one main stem with six lateral stems, making seven (Harris, Archer, and Waltke, TWOT, 2:898).

In an article in the *Holman Illustrated Bible Dictionary* J. F. Drinkard Jr. has the following helpful summary of the symbolic use of the number seven:

> In addition to their usage to designate specific numbers or quantities, many numbers in the Bible came to have a symbolic meaning. Thus seven came to symbolize completeness and perfection. God's work of creation was both complete and perfect—and it was completed in seven days. All of mankind's existence was related to God's creative activity. The seven-day week reflected God's first creative activity. . . . Major festivals such as Passover and Tabernacles lasted seven days as did wedding festivals (Judg. 14:12,17). In Pharaoh's

dream, the seven good years followed by seven years of famine (Gen. 41:1–36) represented a complete cycle of plenty and famine. . . .

A similar use of the number seven can be seen in the New Testament. The seven churches (Rev. 2–3) perhaps symbolized by their number all the churches. Jesus taught that forgiveness is not to be limited, even to a full number or complete number of instances. We are to forgive, not merely seven times (already a gracious number of forgivenesses), but seventy times seven (limitless forgiveness, beyond keeping count) (Matt. 18:21–22).

All four instances of seven in the Book of Zechariah seem to have symbolic significance. Particularly clear is its usage in 4:10: "These seven are the eyes of the LORD, which range throughout the earth." "Eyes," used for observation, are associated with knowledge, and "seven eyes" would suggest complete or perfect knowledge (cp. 3:9). Examples of the symbolic use of the number seven have been found in the literature of other ancient peoples.

C. Trees as a Figure for Human Beings (4:3,11–12,14)

In 4:14 the angel informed Zechariah that the two olive trees signified "the two who are anointed to serve the Lord." Scholars generally agree that these trees symbolize Joshua the high priest and Zerubbabel the civil ruler and/or the offices they represent—priest and king (see "Commentary" discussion on Zechariah 4:14). Human beings are often compared to trees in Scripture. In Psalm 1:3 the righteous person is compared to "a tree planted by streams of water, which yields its fruit in season and whose leaf does not wither." Believers are described as being like a fruitful "palm tree" and a strong "cedar of Lebanon" in Psalm 92:12–14. The Shulammite girl compares Solomon to a pleasant "apple tree" (Song 2:3). Nebuchadnezzar, king of Babylon, is symbolized by a great tree in his dream (Dan. 4:20–22). Jesus compared false prophets to trees that produce bad fruit (Matt. 7:15–20). Other passages where people are compared to trees are Judges 9:8–15; Psalms 37:35; 52:8; Isaiah 56:3; Jeremiah 11:19; Jude 12; and Revelation 11:4.

D. The Holy Spirit in the Old Testament (4:6)

Few subjects are as misunderstood by the average Christian and as hotly debated by scholars as the person and work of the Holy Spirit in the Old Testament era. In Zechariah 4:6 we are introduced to the Holy Spirit for the first time in the book. The Hebrew word rendered "Spirit" is *ruach*, and it occurs over 380 times in the Old Testament. According to Leon Wood, the range of meaning for *ruach* is as follows: (1) wind, 101 times; (2) breath, 18 times; (3) odor, 13 times; (4) space, 6 times; (5) human spirit, 84 times; (6) God's Spirit, 97 times; (7) life principle, 11 times; (8) emotional response, 28 times; (9) angels, 4 times; (10) evil spirits, 18 times; and (11) life force of an animal, 1 time (Wood, *The Holy Spirit in the Old Testament,* Wipf and Stock Publishers, 1998, pp. 16–17).

In Zechariah *ruach* clearly speaks of the Holy Spirit in 4:6; 6:8; and 7:12. "A spirit of grace and supplication" (12:10) may refer to an attitude of repentance but most likely speaks of God's Spirit as conveying grace, leading to the people's crying out to God for mercy. Elsewhere in Zechariah, *ruach* refers to angels (6:5), the spirit of man (12:1), and a disposition (13:2).

The Holy Spirit is mentioned from earliest times in the Bible (cp. Gen. 1:2; 6:3). He is directly referred to in twenty-three of the thirty-nine Old Testament books, and his work is implied in others.

The Person of the Holy Spirit. From the Spirit's name we know that he is a spirit and that he is holy. David was the first to call him the "Holy Spirit" (Ps. 51:11), and this exact title is found twice more in the Old Testament (Isa. 63:10–11). In the Old Testament the deity of the Holy Spirit is evident. He is specifically called the "Spirit of God" (Gen. 1:2; Exod. 31:3; Num. 24:2; 1 Sam. 10:10; Ps. 106:33), and characteristics of deity are attributed to him— ability to create (Job 33:4; Ps. 104:30), omniscience (Isa. 40:13), power (Judg. 14:6,19; Isa. 11:2; Zech. 4:6), and omnipresence (Ps. 139:7).

Some scholars have denied that Old Testament saints understood the Holy Spirit to be a person, yet there is abundant evidence to the contrary. A study of the Old Testament reveals that the Spirit exhibits traits of personality. He has emotions. In Isaiah 63:10 we read that Israel "grieved his [God's] Holy Spirit." Impersonal forces or powers are not grieved—only persons. He has a mind. Isaiah speaks of the Spirit's "wisdom," "understanding," and "knowledge" (Isa. 11:2). Nehemiah says that God gave his "good Spirit to instruct them" (Neh. 9:20), and the Spirit told Ezekiel what to say (Ezek. 11:5). The distinctive personality of the Spirit is readily apparent in Isaiah 48:16: "And now the Sovereign LORD has sent me, with [or "and"] his Spirit."

The Work of the Holy Spirit in the Old Testament. In Old Testament times, the Holy Spirit was extremely active. The Spirit was involved in the creation of the universe (Gen. 1:2) and continues his role in the creation of life (Job 33:4; Ps. 104:30). In Genesis 6:3 we discover that the Spirit convicts unbelievers of sin.

The Holy Spirit inspired the Scriptures. In 2 Samuel 23:2 David said, "The Spirit of the LORD spoke through me; his word was on my tongue."

Zechariah prophesied, "They made their hearts as hard as flint and would not listen to the law or to the words that the LORD Almighty had sent by his Spirit through the earlier prophets. So the LORD Almighty was very angry" (Zech. 7:12). In Nehemiah 9:30 we read, "By your Spirit you admonished them through your prophets."

Modern believers may be surprised to learn that the Spirit was quite active in the lives of individual Old Testament saints. We find that the Holy Spirit imparts wisdom (Neh. 9:20; Isa. 11:2); guides (1 Kgs. 18:12; Isa. 30:1); inspires prayer (Zech. 12:10); and empowers (Zech. 4:6).

In the Old Testament the empowering work of the Spirit is especially prominent and deserves further comment.

The Spirit came upon or filled the following persons with power for service: (1) *a craftsman:* Bezalel (Exod. 31:3; 35:30–31); (2) *leaders:* Moses (Num. 11:17); seventy elders (Num. 11:25); Othniel, judge (Judg. 3:10); Gideon, judge (Judg. 6:34); Jephthah, judge (Judg. 11:29); Samson, judge (Judg 14:6,19; 15:14); Saul, king (1 Sam. 10:10; 11:6; 19:23); David, king (1 Sam. 16:13); and (3) *prophets:* Balaam (Num. 24:2); Azariah (2 Chr. 15:1); Zechariah (2 Chr. 24:20); and Ezekiel (Ezek. 3:24; 11:5). Both priests and kings were anointed with oil, symbolic of the Spirit's power coming upon them to serve in these capacities (Exod. 29:7; 1 Sam. 10:1; 16:13; 1 Kgs. 1:39). The Spirit's anointing power on an individual could be removed (Saul, 1 Sam. 16:14) or remain for life (David, 1 Sam. 16:13).

The permanent indwelling of the Spirit is not unequivocally taught in the Old Testament except in the context of the new covenant passage of Ezekiel 36:27: "And I will put my Spirit in you and move you to follow my decrees and be careful to keep my laws." Thus, it is generally held that the Holy Spirit came upon Old Testament saints for specific purposes but did not permanently indwell them. Passages that speak of the Spirit coming upon and departing from individuals are usually cited to support this view (e.g., Judg. 3:10; 6:34; 1 Sam. 10:10; 16:13–14). However, such examples are best taken to refer to God's anointing power for a task and do not shed light on the question of permanent indwelling. Even David's plea that God not take his "Holy Spirit from me" (Ps. 51:11) seems best understood as reflecting David's fear that the Spirit's anointing power for kingly service would be taken from him as it had been from Saul (1 Sam. 16:13–14).

A number of evangelical scholars contend that the Holy Spirit did, in fact, regenerate and permanently indwell Old Testament believers. W. C. Kaiser Jr. presents a compelling case for this position and deals with difficulties associated with it in his excellent book, *Toward Rediscovering the Old Testament*

(Grand Rapids: Zondervan, 1991). No doubt exists that Christians today are blessed with the indwelling presence of the Holy Spirit (Rom. 8:9).

VII. TEACHING OUTLINE

A. INTRODUCTION

1. Lead Story: Miracle of Dunkirk

2. Context: In his fifth vision Zechariah sees a golden lamp stand and two olive trees. Oil flows from the trees to the lamp, symbolizing the power of the Holy Spirit upon the nation's leaders (the olive trees-branches), Joshua and Zerubbabel. These anointed ones, and the offices of king and priest that they represented, are channels through which the Holy Spirit manifests his power and grace to the nation. The vision signifies that the work of rebuilding the temple (a daunting task from a human perspective) would be completed by the power of the Spirit of God.

3. Transition: In this chapter we are reminded that all things are possible with God. There is no task, obstacle, or difficulty that can thwart God's plan. The Spirit of God (symbolically represented by the oil) empowers believers to carry out God's will and anoints us to be witnesses (lights) in a spiritually dark world. No matter how small our task may seem, the Lord is pleased when we are obedient.

B. COMMENTARY

1. The Vision: A Lampstand and Two Olive Trees (4:1–3)

2. Angelic Interpretation of the Vision: God's Power (4:4–7)

3. God's Power Ensures Success (4:8–10)

4. Angelic Explanation of the Two Olive Trees: Power to Serve (4:11–14)

C. CONCLUSION: CHRISTIAN ON MISSION TRIP SAVES PLANE

VIII. ISSUES FOR DISCUSSION

1. What aspect of the Holy Spirit's work in the Old Testament is emphasized in this chapter?

2. How may you be a light for Christ in your community, workplace (or school), family, and social circle? Name specific ways that you could minister in these settings. What are some actions or attitudes that could harm your witness?

3. Do you ever feel that the work God has given you to do for his kingdom is insignificant? What does Zechariah 4 say about such thoughts?

4. Do you think the average Christian depends on the power of the Holy Spirit for service and daily living? Why?

Zechariah 5–6

Sin's Devastation and Defeat

I. INTRODUCTION
Tragedy at Columbine High

II. COMMENTARY
A verse-by-verse explanation of these chapters.

III. CONCLUSION
Whatever Became of Sin?

An overview of the principles and applications from these chapters.

IV. LIFE APPLICATION
Amazing Grace

Melding these chapters to life.

V. PRAYER
Tying these chapters to life with God.

VI. DEEPER DISCOVERIES
Historical, geographical, and grammatical enrichment of the commentary.

VII. TEACHING OUTLINE
Suggested step-by-step group study of these chapters.

VIII. ISSUES FOR DISCUSSION
Zeroing these chapters in on daily life.

"*S*in wouldn't be so attractive if
the wages were paid immediately."

A u t h o r   U n k n o w n

Zechariah 5–6

 I N   A   N U T S H E L L

*I*n chapters 5 and 6 Zechariah has three more visions and symbolically crowns Joshua the high priest. In vision six the prophet sees a
large flying scroll upon which is written the punishment (curse) for sins.
Vision seven portrays a woman (symbolic of wickedness) in a basket
whisked away by angels to Babylonia. The eighth and final vision describes four war chariots pulled by different colored horses through a
valley outside Jerusalem. These war chariots symbolize God's judgment on the enemies of his people. Chapter 6 concludes with the
crowning of Joshua the high priest. A priest ruling on his throne symbolically represents the uniting of the offices of king and priest in the
person of the Messiah, the one who will defeat sin and bring its devastation to an end.

Sin's Devastation
and Defeat

I. INTRODUCTION

Tragedy at Columbine High

*A*pril 20, 1999, started out like just another day for the students at Columbine High School in peaceful Littleton, Colorado (a suburb of Denver), but it would end like no other day in American history. At approximately 11:20 a.m. (as the cafeteria was filling for lunch), two disturbed students heavily armed with semiautomatic handguns, shotguns, and explosives conducted a commando-like assault on Columbine High and the people inside. Eric Harris and Dylan Klebold, dressed in black trench coats, first opened fire in the parking lot, killing two. Stepping into the cafeteria, they began shooting as students dived for cover. Eventually, the two seniors made their way upstairs to the library, where four dozen students were studying through the lunch period.

The killers ordered athletes to stand up, threatening to kill them all. Some students were killed at their desks. The gunmen laughed and taunted their victims as they went about their grisly business. By 12:30 the lasts shots were heard as the two perpetrators turned their guns on themselves. When it was all over, 12 students, 1 teacher, and the 2 gunmen lay dead. Ten victims and the two shooters were found in the library. In addition to the fatalities, 24 students were transported to 6 local hospitals, and 160 students were treated at the scene. The incident at Columbine High was the deadliest high school shooting in U.S. history.

In the midst of the horror, stories of heroism have come to light. Dave Sanders, the only teacher fatality, was shot twice while directing students down a hallway to safety. Daniel Rohrbough, 15, was shot as he held an exit door for other students to escape. According to a fellow student, one of the killers pointed his gun at Cassie Bernall, a dynamic young Christian, and asked, "Do you believe in God?" She bravely replied, "Yes, I believe in God." These were the last words she ever spoke as the gunman fired at point-blank range. At her funeral the minister told the crowd of two thousand mourners: "Cassie died a martyr's death. She went to the martyr's hall of fame." Rachel Scott, who had witnessed to the gunmen a few weeks before the incident, was shot just outside the school doors as she sat reading her Bible. Some reports indicate that she also was asked if she believed in God before she was killed.

When such tragedies occur, the world cries out, How could this happen? What could lead two young people from an affluent community to commit these despicable acts? Secularists have suggested a plethora of explanations for the Columbine tragedy, but those with a biblical worldview, while shocked, understand. Though many factors were involved, the root cause of the massacre at Columbine and all other evils in our world is what the Bible calls *sin*. In chapters 5 and 6 of Zechariah, we are shown the devastating consequences of sin for individuals and nations. Yet the section ends on a note of triumph—a preview of the Messiah who will defeat sin and ultimately put an end to it altogether.

II. COMMENTARY

Sin's Devastation and Defeat

MAIN IDEA: *Sin has devastating consequences for individuals and nations, but the Messiah (the King-Priest) will win the victory over sin and end its reign of terror.*

A The Curse of Sin: The Flying Scroll (5:1–4)

SUPPORTING IDEA: *A flying scroll, with curses for sin written on its front and back, symbolizes the consequences of sin for those who break God's moral law.*

5:1. Zechariah was granted a sixth vision in which he saw a **flying scroll.** The Hebrew word translated "scroll" is *megillah*, which literally means "a roll." It was so named because books in ancient times were not in modern page form but were handwritten on sheets of papyrus (similar to our paper) or animal skins (parchment) and attached to one another in long rolls. Then they were rolled at each end. As they were read, they would be unrolled from one side to the other. Handwritten Torah scrolls are still read in Jewish synagogues today. Jews use the plural form of *megillah, Megilloth,* as a technical term for five Old Testament books—Song of Songs, Ruth, Lamentations, Ecclesiastes, and Esther—read on specific Jewish feast days. "Flying" may suggest the rapid and sudden approach of the things declared in the scroll. Perhaps the scroll flew overhead to draw more attention to it, like a plane flying over a sports stadium or a beach with an advertisement trailing behind it.

5:2. As in the fifth vision (4:2), the angel asked the prophet what he saw. The scroll was large, **thirty feet long and fifteen feet wide.** In the Hebrew text the scroll's proportions are given in cubits—twenty cubits long and ten cubits wide (cp. KJV, NKJV, NASB, NRSV). A cubit is approximately eighteen inches, and the NIV translators have converted the measurements for us. The dimensions of this scroll are the same as those of the Holy Place in the tabernacle (Exod. 26:15–25) and the porch of Solomon's temple (1 Kgs. 6:3). No significance for this correspondence is specified, but many commentators have inferred that the similar dimensions indicate that judgment must begin at the "house of God" (1 Pet. 4:17 KJV)—Israel, God's people. Another possibility is that God's judgment will be meted out based on his holy character.

Since the scroll could be measured, it must have been unrolled. It was unrolled so that its contents could be read and was large so that everyone could read its warning. The scroll may also have been large to symbolize the many violations of God's law.

5:3. Sin brings devastating consequences (**curse**) for perpetrators throughout **the whole land**. The immediate application was to the people in Zechariah's day, but all of the world will be judged according to God's moral law some day. When Israel was on the brink of entering the promised land, Moses offered this warning: "See, I am setting before you today a blessing and a curse—the blessing if you obey the commands of the LORD your God that I am giving you today; the curse if you disobey the commands of the LORD your God and turn from the way that I command you today by following other gods, which you have not known" (Deut. 11:26–28).

Specific blessings for Israel's faithfulness included national prosperity, fruitfulness, victory over enemies, a special relationship as God's people, and rain (Deut. 28:1–14). Curses included economic austerity, lack of fruitfulness, disease, drought, plagues on crops, defeat by enemies, and exile (Deut. 28:15–68).

Individuals and nations have the same two options today—a blessing or a curse. Obeying God's moral laws results in blessing (joy, peace, heaven, and more); disobeying them brings sin's curse with all its miseries. Humanity's problem is that no one except Jesus himself has ever been able to keep all the requirements of God's laws perfectly. Thus all are under the curse (judgment) of the law—spiritual death (Rom. 6:23). But we may rejoice to know that "Christ redeemed us from the curse of the law by becoming a curse for us" (Gal. 3:13). On the cross, Jesus the Messiah took our judgment (curse) for sin, so that we could be free from the penalty of sin and some day free from the very presence of sin.

Only two sins are specifically named here—stealing and swearing. But since the scroll was so large, it probably contained many more of the Pentateuch's 613 laws (common rabbinical number), surely all of the Ten

Commandments (Exod. 20:1–17). Stealing and swearing falsely by God's name apparently signify humankind's violation of the whole law. As James tells us, "For whoever keeps the whole law and yet stumbles at just one point is guilty of breaking all of it" (Jas. 2:10). Stealing (law eight of the Ten Commandments) is representative of sins against humanity (laws five–ten) and swearing (law three) for sins against God (laws one–four). Possibly, theft and swearing falsely were the two most common sins of the time, or they may have been singled out because they fall roughly in the middle of the two respective classes of laws in the Ten Commandments—sins against God and sins against humanity.

Lawbreakers will be **banished** from (literally, "cleansed" from or "purged" out of) the land. They will be found guilty when their actions are judged in light of what is written on the scroll (God's law). Similar scrolls with a judgment theme are found in Ezekiel 2:9–10; Revelation 5 and 10:2.

5:4. No escape from sin's curse of judgment is possible for those who break God's law. Divine judgment will pursue the lawbreakers (the **thief** and the one who **swears falsely by** God's **name**) even behind the stone walls of their homes. As a matter of fact, God's judgment will be so thorough that the house itself will be annihilated, even the **stones**. God's word is efficacious. Kaiser aptly comments: "Crime did not pay in Zechariah's time, nor will it ever pay—regardless of whether law enforcement agencies and the legal profession handle criminals adequately. Criminals will come under the judgment of God" (Kaiser, *Mastering the Old Testament*, 337).

Here Zechariah returns to the theme set forth at the beginning of his book (1:2–6). Before showers of blessing will fall, people must repent of sin. Israel did repent and received the blessing of God as evidenced by the restoration of the nation, the rebuilding of the temple, and national prosperity. Some commentators see here the removal of sin from the land as preparatory to the coming messianic kingdom (cp. 3:9–10).

B Wickedness and Its Removal: A Woman in a Basket (5:5–11)

> **SUPPORTING IDEA:** *Judah's wickedness (represented by a woman in a basket) had brought destruction on the nation and resulted in their exile. In the exile the people had repented and left their idolatrous practices in Babylon.*

5:5–6. The angel now directed Zechariah's attention to **a measuring basket** that appears in his seventh vision. The KJV's and NASB's "ephah" is a transliteration of the Hebrew word. An ephah was a dry measure of grain, equal to one-tenth of a homer and one bath of liquid (Ezek. 45:11). It was also equal to ten omers (Exod. 16:36). An ephah was approximately twenty-two liters or three-fourths of a bushel.

According to the angel, the basket symbolized the **iniquity** in Israel. The Hebrew has also been rendered "their resemblance" (KJV, NKJV) or "their appearance" (NASB). This translation is more difficult but could still mean that the basket Zechariah saw was a visionary symbol ("an appearance") of the people's sinfulness. A measuring basket would be an apt emblem for sin because unscrupulous merchants used dishonest measures to deceive the unwary buyer (Lev. 19:36; Deut. 25:14; Prov. 20:10; Ezek. 45:10; Amos 8:5).

5:7. The **cover of lead** may be rendered "talent of lead." If so, the cover weighed a talent which approximated seventy pounds. When the cover was **raised**, the prophet saw a **woman** sitting **in the basket**! Obviously, a woman could not sit in a bushel basket. Either the ephah was much larger than normal, or the woman was small enough to fit in the basket and be held captive by a seventy-pound lead cover.

5:8. Zechariah was informed that the woman was **wickedness**. Perhaps sin is represented as a woman here since the Hebrew word for "wickedness" is feminine. On the other hand, if idolatry is the specific or primary sin in view, the woman figure would be easily understandable. Harlotry is often used as a figure for idolatry (Jer. 2:20; Ezek. 16:15; 23:7; Hos. 9:1; Rev. 17:1), the sin being characterized as spiritual adultery. This interpretation would fit the woman's removal to Babylonia (v. 11) because Judah's idolatry was purged there. Apparently, the woman was struggling to free herself and wreak havoc on the nation once more since the angel had to push her **back into the basket**. Later Ezra, Nehemiah, and Malachi would face the problem of incipient idolatry among their Jewish countrymen (Ezra 9:1–2; Neh. 13:23–27; Mal. 2:11).

5:9. Now we are introduced to **two** other **women** who will dispose of the wicked one in the basket. With their powerful storklike wings, they swooped down swiftly (**the wind in their wings**) and carried **the basket** high into the sky. The two women are normally taken as nothing but drapery for the story, and the stork is a familiar bird in Palestine.

5:10–11. Sin had brought devastation on the entire nation—death, destruction of cities, leveling of the temple, and exile; but in Babylon the Jewish people had repented and had been forgiven (Zech. 3:4). In these verses we seem to have a striking depiction of their forgiveness, since wickedness was whisked away. Zechariah was told that the wicked woman was being flown to **the country of Babylonia** (literally Shinar), the place of Judah's recent captivity. Shinar is an archaic name for Babylonia (Gen. 11:2) and was the site of the tower of Babel (Gen. 11:9), a monument to human pride, rebellion, and likely idolatry. Probably Shinar was chosen because of the sinister overtones associated with it. Being **set there in its place** in **a house** in Babylon speaks of the permanent removal of wickedness from Israel.

"A house" may also refer to a temple (NASB), the house of a god. The phrase "set there in its place" could denote an idol's pedestal. If the latter is correct, it would further support the woman's identification as idolatry. Idolatry was purged from Israel during the Babylonian captivity. When the Jews returned to their homeland, idolatry was left in exile. Idolatry was still a threat to be guarded against in postexilic Judah, but for the most part it never reached its preexilic proportions. The idolatrous woman standing alone and immovable on a pedestal in faraway Babylon furnishes a striking portrait of the futility and powerlessness of false gods. Idolatry began in Shinar at the tower of Babel and was now consigned to remain there.

If the total and permanent removal of wickedness is in view, the prophecy must also have a future application, for a world without sin awaits the coming Messiah. Moreover, as Kaiser points out, "Given the part that Babylon plays in the eschatological drama of the closing days of this present age, the removal of wickedness to Babylon might have been in preparation for the final conflict between good and evil" (Kaiser, *Mastering the Old Testament*, 340).

Ⓒ Judgment of the Nations: The Four Chariots (6:1–8)

SUPPORTING IDEA: *Nations will reap judgment for their sin.*

6:1. In the eighth and final vision, God sent forth his judgment on nations that had oppressed his people (cp. 1:18–21; 2:8–9). Zechariah watched as **four chariots** (in succession) charged through the valley **between two mountains.** The Hebrew term for "chariot" here usually designates a war chariot, and so their mission of judgment is emphasized at the outset. **Four** signifies that the judgment is universal—to all four points of the compass (cp. 6:5–8).

The definite article is present in the Hebrew ("the two mountains"), indicating that two specific mountains are in view. Since Zechariah was located in Jerusalem, these mountains are associated with that city. Three mountains are possible, Mount Zion, the Mount of Olives, or Mount Moriah (the temple mount). Most commentators identify the mountains as the Mount of Olives and Mount Zion. The Kidron Valley is formed at their base.

Bronze ("brass," KJV) is often associated with judgment. For example, the large altar in the tabernacle courtyard on which sin offerings were made was overlaid with bronze (Exod. 27:2–6). These sacrifices represented God's judgment falling on the animal substitute rather than on the worshiper. Christ's feet of "bronze" (Rev. 1:15; cp. Rev. 2:18) were a visionary representation of the crushing (judgment) of the wicked. Therefore, judgment issued forth from these mountains, that is, from the God who resided in Jerusalem.

6:2–3. Each of the four chariots was pulled by **powerful** and distinctively colored horses. **The first chariot had red horses, the second black, the third white, and the fourth dappled** ("bay," KJV). A dappled animal is spotted. According to Genesis 31:10,12, some of Jacob's goats were this color.

We have encountered horses with symbolic colors before—red, brown, and white ones in Zechariah's first vision (1:8). An even more arresting parallel is found in the Book of Revelation where certain affinities are apparent between Zechariah's eighth vision and the white, red, black, and pale horses described in Revelation 6. Both passages mention four horses, and each group goes forth to carry out God's judgment on the world. Both passages describe white, red, and black horses. If Zechariah's dappled horse was a spotted light gray, it could possibly be connected to Revelation's pale horse.

Elements of a vision usually have symbolic meaning; therefore, the colors of the horses are probably significant. Red (the color of blood) would stand for war as a judgment on the enemies of God's people (cp. Rev. 6:4). White horses were associated with conquest (cp. Rev. 6:2; 19:11,14) and here represent God's victory over his foes. If the black horses have the same meaning as that of Revelation 6:5–6, they would signify famine (and possibly the death associated with it). Some commentators have suggested that the dappled horses denote pestilence and plagues. Regardless of the exact meaning of the colors, the mission of the horse-drawn war chariots is unmistakable—judgment of the nations.

6:4–5. Now the angel interpreted the vision for Zechariah. **Four spirits** could be rendered "four winds" (NRSV), but the former is correct because these **spirits** stood **in the presence of the Lord**, an obvious allusion to angels (cp. Luke 1:19; Rev. 8:2). Although not previously stated, the angels apparently were driving the chariots. They were sent forth from God to judge the earth. God's sovereignty is emphasized by the phrase, **the Lord of the whole world**.

6:6. At least three of these angels were assigned to specific areas. The chariot pulled by the **black horses** went to **the north country**—Babylonia. The **white horses** went **west** or possibly "after them" (KJV, NASB). If "after them" is correct, the **white horses** joined **the black** in their assault on Babylonia in **the north**, two chariots suggesting a more severe judgment on that country. **The dappled horses** hastened to judge Egypt in **the south**. Nothing is said of the east or the red horses, but conceivably the red horses judged nations toward the east. If so (and the NIV's translation, "toward the west" is followed), all four points of the compass are involved. On the other hand, the directions unquestionably identified in the text are north and south—the locations of Babylon and Egypt, Israel's principal foes. Babylon and Egypt were judged through the Medo-Persians and subsequent invaders. Neither country ever attained its former glory.

6:7–8. The phrase **throughout the earth** emphasizes their universal mission of judgment. When the chariot drawn by the black horses (and possibly the white as well) carried out their judgment on Babylon (**the land of the north**), God's anger against this sinful nation subsided (**given my Spirit rest**). According to Barker, "Since conquest is announced in the north, victory is assured over all enemies" (Barker, 637). This final vision set forth the judgment of Israel's enemies in Zechariah's day, but its universal overtones suggest an application to the eschatological judgment of the future Babylon at Christ's return (Rev. 14:8; 16:19; 18:2,10,21).

Ⓓ A Prophecy of the Messiah: The Crowning of Joshua (6:9–15)

SUPPORTING IDEA: *Messiah, the King-Priest, will defeat sin at the cross and some day will eradicate its very presence.*

6:9. Zechariah's visions have ended, and the chapter concludes with the record of an actual historical event—the crowning of Joshua. Once more we meet the familiar prophetic formula, **the word of the LORD came**. This exact phrase (in the NIV) appears over one hundred times in the Old Testament and six times in Zechariah (1:1,7; 4:8; 6:9; 7:1,8; cp. 7:4; 8:1,18). This message to Zechariah will include a dramatic element (cp. 11:4–17).

6:10. Heldai, Tobijah and Jedaiah arrived with gifts from the Jewish **exiles** still in **Babylon**. Although these Jews had chosen not to return, they were concerned about their homeland and desired to help in the rebuilding of their beloved temple (v. 15). Many modern Jews have elected not to reside in Israel, but they care deeply about what is going on there and support the Jewish state in various ways. The phrase **the same day** may refer to the day of the exiles' arrival or the day of the visions. God told Zechariah to meet these guests at Josiah's home. Josiah must have been a distinguished citizen since his ancestry is given and his home was selected as the meeting place. Some commentators have listed Josiah as a fourth exile, but the fact that he had a home in the city suggests that he already lived there.

6:11. Zechariah was now told to do a very strange thing. As a matter of fact, it could have been dangerous if viewed by the Persian government as an act of insurrection. God commanded the prophet to fashion a **crown** with **the silver and gold** that the exiles had delivered. Although the word rendered "crown" is a Hebrew plural ("crowns," KJV), only one crown is meant because it was placed on one **head** (Joshua's) and is used with a Hebrew singular verb form ("will be given") in verse 14. In the Hebrew language a plural may describe an item with multiple parts. For example, the Hebrew word for "face" is always plural, since the face is a combination of a variety of features. Thus Zechariah's was a composite crown made of two precious metals (silver and gold) and apparently consisted of several circles.

Crowns were worn by kings, but Joshua was a priest, not a king. As a matter fact, Joshua could never have been a legitimate king under Israelite law since kings had to be from the tribe of Judah and more specifically from the line of David. As a priest Joshua was from a different tribe altogether— that of Levi—and descended not from David but Aaron. Zechariah's associates probably were stunned because such actions made no sense. Moreover, if Zechariah was encouraging Joshua to declare himself as king of Israel, the wrath of the Persian government would certainly be unleashed against the nation. Of course, Zechariah had no such intention. As we shall see, the crowning of Joshua was strictly a symbolic act. Feinberg points out that verse 11 is one of the twenty-six verses in the Old Testament that contain all the letters of the Hebrew alphabet (Feinberg, *God Remembers,* 81).

6:12. As in 3:8 **the Branch** is a messianic title (Isa. 4:2; Jer. 23:5; 33:15; Zech. 3:8; 6:12; cp. Isa. 11:1). (For a discussion of the Branch, see the "Deeper Discoveries" section for Zechariah 3.) Thus Joshua's crowning is explained as symbolic of that of the coming Messiah. **Branch out from his place** means that the Messiah will grow up in his own land, Israel. Perhaps the prophecy of Messiah's coronation immediately following Zechariah's vision about the judgment of the nations is significant. Messiah will not be acknowledged by all earth's peoples as Lord until human rebellion is put down.

6:13. Three important facts about Messiah and his reign are outlined in this verse. First, Messiah **will build** a future **temple of the LORD.** Zechariah's hearty band of Jews were busy constructing the second temple, but another far greater edifice would be erected during Messiah's reign (cp. Ezek. 40–43; Mic. 4:1). That Messiah would construct a new temple (cp. v. 12) is repeated to emphasize its significance.

Second, he would **rule** the world. **Majesty** ("glory," KJV; "honor," NASB) may denote divine or royal "splendor" (1 Chr. 16:27; 29:25; Ps. 96:6), and both attributes apply to Messiah—the divine king. When Jesus came the first time, he was born in obscurity. His birth was announced only to a few shepherds and wise men. During his life he was maligned, rejected, and ultimately murdered. Only a handful of followers recognized him as God's Messiah. When he returns in glory, earth's peoples will finally give him the honor he deserves. As the apostle Paul proclaimed: "For this reason God also highly exalted Him and gave Him the name that is above every name, so that at the name of Jesus every knee should bow—of those who are in heaven and on earth and under the earth—and every tongue should confess that Jesus Christ is Lord, to the glory of God the Father" (Phil. 2:9–11 HCSB).

Messiah's **throne** will be in the new temple. In the future sanctuary described by Ezekiel, it is noteworthy that no ark (symbolic of the presence of God) will rest in the Most Holy Place (Ezek. 41:3–4). No ark will be needed in the messianic kingdom, because God himself in the person of the Messiah will be present with us and rule from the temple's inner sanctum.

Third, Messiah will be both **priest** and king ("rule on his throne"). Jewish kings had to be from the tribe of Judah, and priests had to come from the tribe of Levi. How then could a priest ever rule as a king? Jesus the Messiah could be a legitimate king because he was a member of the tribe of Judah and a descendant of the line of David. Though not from the tribe of Levi, the writer of Hebrews explained that Jesus could serve as our high priest because he was of a higher priestly order, the priesthood of Melchizedek (Heb. 7:1–17; cp. Gen. 14:18–20). No other individual in history could have united these two offices (**harmony between the two**). On the cross Jesus performed the work of high priest by offering himself as an atoning sacrifice (Heb. 9:11–14); as king he rules the universe. This amazing prophecy and Psalm 110 are the two key Old Testament passages that tell us the coming Davidic king will also be a priest.

6:14. Zechariah's audience understood that his actions were symbolic and that Joshua was not intended to sit on a literal throne in Jerusalem and rule the world. Thus **the crown** was removed from Joshua's head and placed in the **temple** as a reminder (**memorial**) that some day the Messiah—its rightful owner—would come. Historically, the crown may also have served as a testimony to the devotion of the exiles who made the long trek from Babylon with their gift. **Hen** ("gracious one") is another name for Josiah (both have the same father, v. 10), likely so called because of the gracious hospitality extended to his house guests.

6:15. Just as Jewish exiles had come from far-away Babylon to build Zerubbabel's temple, peoples from all over the globe (cp. 2:11; 8:22; Isa. 2:2–4; 56:6–7; 60:1–7) will help to provide for the future messianic **temple** (see v. 13). When Messiah comes and these prophecies are fulfilled, all will **know that the LORD Almighty has sent me** [Messiah] **to you.** In the context of the future temple and the messianic age, the one sent by the Lord can only be Messiah (as in 2:8–9,11) whose claims will be vindicated in the eyes of the world at his coming. Those who **diligently obey the LORD** will share in this wonderful new world. God will assure that true believers remain faithful by the enabling power of the Spirit.

> **MAIN IDEA REVIEW:** *Sin has devastating consequences for individuals and nations, but the Messiah (the King-Priest) will win the victory over sin and end its reign of terror.*

III. CONCLUSION

Whatever Became of Sin?

The idea of sin is becoming increasingly unpopular in our secular society. Behavior previously deemed wrong is now considered normal and acceptable. People act badly, it is often claimed, because they have been programmed to do so or have been deprived in some way. However, humanity's ills will never be understood and cured until sin is recognized for what it is. The late Karl Menninger even argued that sin really does exist in his book entitled *Whatever Became of Sin?*

> The famous psychiatrist was distressed that modern society tries to figure out its problems and talk about morality without mentioning the word *sin*. He was convinced that the only way to raise the moral tone of present-day civilization and deal with the depression and worries that plague clergy, psychiatrists, and ordinary folk is to revive an understanding of what "sin" is (Paul Lee Tan, *Encyclopedia of 7,700 Illustrations*, Rockville, MD: Assurance Publishers, 1979, pp. 1284-85).

Chapters 5 and 6 of Zechariah teach that sin is indeed real and has devastating consequences. In the vision of the flying scroll, we are reminded that sin brings a curse on individuals and nations. If there is no repentance, the consequences of sinful actions are inescapable. Judah had been sent into exile, and Jerusalem was turned into ruins because of the "wickedness" that had infected its population. The vision of the war chariots conveyed the truth that judgment will eventually fall on all earth's sinful nations. Yet this section climaxes with the glorious prophecy of the Messiah, who would defeat sin and free us from it. Messiah's priestly work (his sacrifice on the cross) would deliver us from sin's penalty (spiritual death), and as king he will banish the very presence of sin.

PRINCIPLES

- Sin is a reality.
- Sin has devastating consequences for individuals and nations.
- Without repentance and faith in Christ, sin's ultimate penalty— spiritual death—is inescapable.
- When we receive Jesus Christ as Lord and Savior, God removes our sin so far that it can never return.
- Sinful nations will be judged.
- Jesus the Messiah (Christ) is both our priest (Savior) and king.

APPLICATIONS

- We must be vigilant to guard our lives against sin's devastating consequences. Determine to avoid television programs, movies, Internet sites, or magazines that may tempt you to sin in thought or action.
- Warn your children about the dangers of sinful practices (drugs, immorality, worldliness, and so forth). You may desire to illustrate your warning by pointing to sin's harmful effects on an actor, music star, athlete, or other public figure with whom your child is familiar.
- If you have never repented of your sin, do so and receive the pardon made possible by Christ's (Messiah's) substitutionary death on the cross.
- Thank God that Jesus the Messiah is coming to put an end to the evils of sin.

IV. LIFE APPLICATION

Amazing Grace

Karla Faye Tucker was born on November 18, 1959. At age seven she began smoking marijuana and by age ten had progressed to heroin. During her teenage and young adult years, she was involved with drugs, gangs, and eventually prostitution. In June 1983 Karla passed from obscurity to infamy when she and a male friend, under the influence of drugs, broke into an apartment and committed one of the most gruesome double murders in Texas history. For her shocking crime, Karla was sentenced to death. She was reaping the wages for her incredibly sinful life.

Yet the story does not end there. Awaiting trial in the Harris County jail, Karla went to a Christian worship service—a puppet show. She was not a churchgoer but did not want to be left alone in her cell. While reading the Bible later that night, she came under conviction of sin, fell to her knees, and cried out to God for forgiveness. On October 29, 1983, this very wicked young woman became a new creation in Christ.

In the coming months and years, her life did indeed seem to demonstrate God's transforming power. For example, speaking to CNN's Larry King from death row less than a month before her execution date, King asked if she remained upbeat. When she replied yes, King said, "You have to explain that to me a little more. It can't just be God."

She explained: "Yes, it can. It's called the joy of the Lord. . . . I know what forgiveness is, even when I did something so horrible. I know that because God forgave me and I accepted what Jesus did on the cross. When I leave here, I am going to be with him."

Karla's case became a flash point in the death penalty debate and captured national and even international attention. Through her testimony people all over the world came to recognize the reality of Christ. In her final statement Karla expressed genuine remorse to the victims' families and confidence that she was about to see Jesus face-to-face. On February 3, 1998, Karla Faye Tucker's sentence was carried out at a Huntsville, Texas, prison.

Karla's story offers a graphic lesson about sin's devastation (to her victims and herself) but also a lesson of hope to all who will repent and believe in Christ. Her life was indeed a testimony to the "amazing grace" of our merciful God. Pardon from sin with a home in heaven is possible because of the priestly work of Messiah, who gave himself as an offering for sin on the cross.

Few people would ever commit the horrible acts that Karla did, but all of us have sinned in a myriad of ways and need God's forgiveness. What a joy to know that though sin is destructive, Christ has won the victory over sin and some day will deliver us from its very presence.

V. PRAYER

Dear heavenly Father, help us to remember how dangerous and destructive sin can be to our lives and to the lives of those around us. Help us to be alert and avoid situations where we could be tempted to sin against you. Thank you that we may be forgiven for sin because of the work of our great High Priest, Jesus the Messiah. In his name we pray. Amen.

VI. DEEPER DISCOVERIES

A. What's a Cubit? (5:2)

Zechariah saw a flying scroll that was thirty feet long and fifteen feet wide (NIV). In the Hebrew text the proportions are given in cubits (cp. KJV, NKJV, NASB, NRSV). A cubit was a standard measure in Israel and throughout the Ancient Near East (though varying somewhat at different times and places). The Hebrew word for cubit appears approximately 250 times in the Old Testament. It first occurs as a measurement for Noah's ark (Gen. 6:15); Zechariah's usage (only in this verse) is one of its latest.

A cubit was the average distance from the elbow to the tip of the middle finger of an adult, about eighteen inches. We find confirmation of this figure in the so-called "Siloam Inscription" (now on display in the Istanbul Museum). This inscription records the digging of a tunnel commissioned by King Hezekiah just before 701 B.C. An Assyrian attack was imminent, and a channel was carved out of the rock to allow water to flow from the Gihon Spring to the Siloam pool, near (or inside) Jerusalem's walls. According to the inscription (found in the tunnel), the length of this passageway was 1,200 cubits. Archaeologists have measured the tunnel and found it to be about 1,749 feet long, thus indicating that a cubit was about 17 ½ inches—rounded off, 18 inches.

B. Angels in the Old Testament (5:5,10; 6:4–5)

Angels are prominent in the Book of Zechariah, the word *angel* occurring twenty-one times (about one-fifth of its total usage in the Old Testament). The Hebrew word translated "angel" is *mal'ak* and basically means "messenger." *Mal'ak's* 213 appearances are split rather evenly between heavenly messengers or angels and human messengers (1 Sam. 11:3). The prophet Malachi's name means "my messenger." Angels are also called "sons of God" (Job 1:6; 2:1 KJV, NKJV, NASB); "mighty ones" (Ps. 29:1); "heavenly beings" (Ps. 89:6); and "holy one(s)" (Ps. 89:5,7; Dan. 4:13,17,23; 8:13). God created angels to serve and praise him (Pss. 103:20–21; 148:2). As spirits, they normally are not seen but may appear to humans and even take on bodily form (Gen. 19:1–22). Different orders of angels are mentioned in the Old Testament. Cherubs (Ezek. 1:4–14; 10:19–22) and seraphs (Isa. 6:2), possibly different titles for the same beings, seem to be the highest order of angels and stand before the very throne of God.

Angels are divided into holy angels and evil angels (demons). Two good angels are named in the Bible—Gabriel (Dan. 8:16; 9:21; Luke 1:19,26) and Michael (Dan. 10:13,21; 12:1; Jude 9; Rev. 12:7). Of the evil angels, only their leader, Satan, is identified. (For a discussion of Satan, see the "Deeper Discoveries" section for Zechariah 3.) Presumably, the spiritual condition of every angel was settled at the time of Satan's rebellion against God. Those who followed Satan are forever doomed, while those who remained true to God are forever blessed. The prophet Daniel pulled back the veil and permitted us a glimpse into the unseen world of angelic warfare (Dan. 10:12–11:1).

As their names indicate, angels are holy and mighty beings who serve as God's messengers to human beings (Dan. 9:21–23; Zech. 5:2,5,10–11). They also protect the saints (2 Kgs. 6:8–17) and carry out God's will (Ps. 103:20; Zech. 1:10–11). Angels are individual creations of God who have unlimited lifetimes and supernatural powers. Many times in the Old Testament, the phrase "the angel of the LORD" refers to a divine person (a preincarnate appearance of Christ) rather than an ordinary angel. (For a discussion of the angel of the Lord, see the "Deeper Discoveries" section for Zechariah 3.)

In conclusion, God's angels are mighty beings who should command our respect and appreciation as fellow servants of Christ. Though magnificent, angels should never be worshiped (Rev. 19:10; 22:9). Like human beings, they are still only creations of our sovereign God. Angels help human beings today just as they did in biblical times. We probably will never know all that angels do for us until the next life.

C. Words for Sin in the Book of Zechariah

Except for a few chapters in Aramaic, the Old Testament is written in the Hebrew language. English versions like the New International Version and King James Version are translations of the Hebrew text. Hebrew is a very picturesque language, and in it we find a number of words for sin. Each of these reflects a different nuance of meaning. An examination of these words will help us to understand the nature of sin more precisely. Zechariah uses several of these important terms.

First, Hebrew *ra'*, its feminine form *ra'ah,* and the related verb *ra'a'* occur a total of six times in the Book of Zechariah and about 750 times in the Old Testament. Essentially, they denote a bad thing or action, either in the physical or moral realm. Thus, the terms are rendered "evil" in Zechariah 1:4 (twice), 7:10, and 8:17 but "calamity" (a bad thing) in 1:15 and "bring disaster" (the verb) in 8:14. In Genesis 37:33 *ra'* is even used for a "ferocious" animal ("evil beast," KJV). Understanding that the term may speak of bad things in the physical world helps to explain God's declaration in Isaiah 45:7: "I form the light and create darkness, I bring prosperity and create disaster; I, the LORD, do all these things." The KJV translates "create disaster" as "create evil," giving the impression to some that God created moral evil or sin. In context the passage is better understood to mean that God may use "disaster" or physical judgments to punish sinful people.

Second, the Hebrew word *'awon* is translated in the NIV as "sin" in Zechariah 3:4,9 and "iniquity" (traditional rendering) in 5:6. The word occurs 232 times in the Old Testament. Probably *'awon* is derived from a verb meaning "bend, twist, distort." If so, the word would describe sin as "a deviation from or a twisting of the [God's] standard" (Richards, *Expository Dictionary of Bible Words,* 566).

Third, *rish'ah,* "wickedness," is found only once in Zechariah (5:8) and fifteen times in the Old Testament. Yet other words from the same Hebrew root occur over three hundred times. "Wickedness" is the opposite of righteousness (Prov. 12:3). Isaiah declared that the wicked have no rest or peace (Isa. 57:20–21).

Fourth, words derived from the Hebrew root *chata'* occur about 580 times in the Old Testament. Surprisingly, the verb form is never found in Zechariah, but the noun *chatta't* is translated "sin" in 13:1 and "punishment" (for sin) in 14:19 (twice). Like the Greek word *hamartano,* the basic meaning of *chata'* is "to miss the mark." Judges 20:16 offers a striking example of the word's fundamental sense. There we are told of seven hundred left-handed Benjamite soldiers who "could sling a stone at a hair and not miss [the mark]." Thus, sin is missing the standard of perfection that God has set for human beings, not accidentally but on purpose. As the apostle Paul reminds us, "For all have sinned and fall short of the glory of God" (Rom. 3:23).

Fifth, *pasha'* ("to rebel" or "transgress) does not appear in Zechariah but is another key word for sin in the Old Testament (forty-one times). Its noun form is found ninety-three times and means "rebellion" or "transgression."

From our examination of the above terms, we may conclude that sin is morally bad, a deviation from God's standard, the opposite of righteousness, a deliberate missing of God's mark [requirement] of perfection, and rebellion against God.

D. Babylonia or Shinar (5:11)

We pointed out in the "Commentary" section that the Hebrew word translated "Babylonia" in 5:11 is *Shinar*. This archaic name for Babylonia appears eight times in the Old Testament (see Gen. 10:10; 11:2; 14:1,9 NIV, KJV, NKJV, NASB, NRSV; Josh. 7:21 NASB, NRSV; Isa. 11:11; Dan. 1:2; Zech. 5:11 KJV, NKJV, NASB, NRSV). H. J. Austel provides the following helpful summary:

> Shinar is the Old Testament designation for southern Mesopotamia, the alluvial plain between the rivers Euphrates and Tigris. The area was known by the Sumerians as Sumer and Akkad. It later became known as Babylonia. In two of the eight passages Shinar is called Babylonia in the LXX (Isa 11:11 and Zech 5:11).
>
> In Gen 10:10 we are told that the great tyrant and empire builder Nimrod founded his kingdom in Babel, Erech (Sumerian Uruk), Akkad (Agade) and Calneh in the land of Shinar. From here he pushed north into Assyria. It was here also, in Shinar, that rebellious man built the well-known tower of Babel in direct defiance of God (Gen 11:2). In Daniel 1:2 it is the land of Shinar to which Nebuchadnezzar removes the vessels of the temple of God, and in Isa 11:11 we are told that Shinar is one of the lands from which regathered Israel will return when the Millennial age is established. In Zech 5:11 the woman in the ephah, representing a concentration of evil (v. 8), is removed to the land of Shinar where a temple is built for her.
>
> All of this points to a sinister significance for Shinar as being the major center for the development of a culture and civilization built on counterfeit religion, rebelliousness against the true God and his revealed word, the cradle of imperial tyranny and the enemy of God's

people, in short, the epitome of wickedness (Harris, Archer, and Waltke, TWOT, 2:943).

No doubt, Zechariah selected the term because of the dramatic effect its sinister overtones would have on his audience.

E. Bronze or Brass? (6:1)

In the KJV we have "mountains of brass," whereas the NIV reads "mountains of bronze." Most modern translations render the Hebrew word *nechoshet* as "bronze" rather than "brass" elsewhere in the Old Testament as well. The metals are similar, primarily consisting of copper. Bronze was an alloy of copper and tin, whereas brass was an alloy of copper and zinc. Bronze was developed very early, about 3500 B.C., by the ancient Sumerians in the Tigris-Euphrates Valley. Bronze-making spread to Persia around 3000 B.C. (ornaments, weapons, and the like) and to both Egypt and China by 2000 B.C. However, brass did not appear in Egypt until about 30 B.C., and the Romans were the first to use brass extensively, for example, for coins and ornaments. In fact, a Roman coin from about 20 B.C. is one of the earliest known samples of brass. For these reasons, most modern versions favor "bronze" (or in a few instances, "copper") rather than "brass" as the translation of the Hebrew word.

VII. TEACHING OUTLINE

A. INTRODUCTION

1. Lead Story: Tragedy at Columbine High
2. Context: In chapters 5–6 of Zechariah, the prophet receives the last three of his eight visions and crowns Joshua the high priest. The vision of the flying scroll warned of the inescapable consequences for all who break God's moral law. Vision seven described a woman trapped in a basket who was permanently banished to Babylon. The angel tells Zechariah that the woman symbolizes "wickedness." Judah's sin, particularly the sin of idolatry, had resulted in the Babylonian exile and destruction of the nation. During the exile the people repented, and their idolatrous ways were left in Babylon, making their present blessing possible. The eighth vision told of God's judgment on the world's sinful nations. Chapter 6 concludes with the

visit of a Jewish delegation from Babylon who came with gifts for the building of the temple. God commanded Zechariah to take silver and gold from these exiles and make a crown and place the crown on the high priest Joshua's head. This action symbolized the uniting of the offices of priest and king under the coming Messiah. Thus the prophet's action was a messianic prophecy in dramatic form.

3. Transition: These chapters emphasize sin's devastation for individuals and nations. Individuals who break God's law with no repentance cannot escape sin's consequences. Nations are ravaged by sin as well. Judah's wickedness brought destruction and exile, though repentance eventually led to national restoration. The war chariots charging across the earth warn that all sinful nations will some day be judged for their sin. This section concludes with a wonderful prophecy of hope. Messiah's priestly work on the cross would provide victory over sin's penalty. As King, Messiah will some day banish the very presence of sin.

B. COMMENTARY

1. The Curse of Sin: The Flying Scroll (5:1–4)
2. Wickedness and Its Removal: A Woman in a Basket (5:5–11)
3. Judgment of the Nations: The Four Chariots (6:1–8)
4. A Prophecy of the Messiah: The Crowning of Joshua (6:9–15)

C. CONCLUSION: WHATEVER BECAME OF SIN?

VIII. ISSUES FOR DISCUSSION

1. What is the curse of sin? Do you think most people believe their sin is serious enough to keep them from going to heaven? Name other consequences of sin.
2. God removed Judah's wickedness to Babylon. How may we apply this principle to the way God deals with the sin of believers today?
3. What is the fate of all sinful nations? Name some past nations that have experienced God's judgment.
4. How would Jesus of Nazareth fulfill the roles of both priest and king? How could Jesus be called a priest since he was not from the tribe of Levi or a descendant of Aaron?

Zechariah 7–8

Motivation Matters

I. INTRODUCTION
The Amazing Sergeant York

II. COMMENTARY
A verse-by-verse explanation of these chapters.

III. CONCLUSION
Win One for the Gipper!

An overview of the principles and applications from these chapters.

IV. LIFE APPLICATION
First Time My Dad Ever Saw Me Play

Melding these chapters to life.

V. PRAYER
Tying these chapters to life with God.

VI. DEEPER DISCOVERIES
Historical, geographical, and grammatical enrichment of the commentary.

VII. TEACHING OUTLINE
Suggested step-by-step group study of these chapters.

VIII. ISSUES FOR DISCUSSION
Zeroing these chapters in on daily life.

Quote

"*If* Christ be God and died for me, no sacrifice is too great for me to make for Him."

Nelson C. Hinkson

Zechariah 7–8

IN A NUTSHELL

Chapters 7 and 8 of Zechariah deal with questions about fasts. A Jewish delegation from Bethel inquired of the priests and prophets if it was necessary to continue certain fasts that commemorated the destruction of Jerusalem, the temple, and related events. No doubt, the present rebuilding of the temple was the impetus for this inquiry. The question implies that the people were weary of keeping these burdensome fasts and desired to end them. God replies that these fasts were not commanded by him in the first place and would be replaced by joyful festivals now that his blessing had returned to the nation.

Motivation Matters

I. INTRODUCTION

The Amazing Sergeant York

*A*lvin C. York was born on December 13, 1887, in tiny Pall Mall, Tennessee, about one hundred miles east of Nashville. Life was hard for the Yorks as they barely eked out a living in the Tennessee hills. Though he worked extremely hard during the week, on the weekends Alvin turned into a hard-drinking, gambling troublemaker. But on New Year's night 1915, Alvin attended a revival meeting and made a profession of faith in Jesus Christ as Lord. That night his life was forever changed.

York became a model citizen, even teaching Sunday school and leading the music in his church. York was making plans to marry his sweetheart, Gracie Williams, when in 1917 he received notice to register for the draft. On religious grounds, he adamantly opposed killing other human beings, and Pastor Pile urged him to seek an exemption as a conscientious objector. After all appeals were denied, York entered the armed forces to do his duty.

York did indeed do his duty and more. He was assigned to the 82nd Infantry Division at the Meuse-Argonne Offensive. On the morning of October 8, 1918, in France's Argonne Forest, York and sixteen other men were ordered to circle around a hill and attack the machine gun nests that were checking his regiment's advance. Nine of his patrol were either killed or wounded, leaving only eight. While the other seven were pinned down by heavy fire or stood guard over the few prisoners they had captured, Corporal York attacked the machine gun nests alone. Firing with deadly accuracy at the enemy, he killed 25, prompting the others to surrender. Capturing even more Germans on his way back to the American lines, he arrived with an astounding 132 prisoners, including 3 officers.

For his heroics, York was promoted to the rank of sergeant and received many honors, including the Distinguished Service Cross, the French Croix de Guerre, and the Congressional Medal of Honor. Marshal Ferdinand Foch of France declared York's feat "the greatest thing accomplished by any private soldier of all the armies of Europe."

York's life was immortalized in the 1941 film, *Sergeant York,* starring Gary Cooper. The movie was one of the top-grossing Warner Brothers films of the entire war era and earned Cooper the Academy Award for best actor. In a memorable scene from the film, York and several officers were surveying the battlefield where the incident took place. One officer asked York why he changed his mind about taking enemy lives. York replied that when he saw the machine guns slaughtering hundreds, maybe thousands, he knew he had to stop those guns at any cost. In other words, he took lives to save lives. The stunned officer shook his head in amazement and said, "York, what you've just told me is the most extraordinary thing of all." Alvin York had a proper motivation.

In chapters 7 and 8 of Zechariah, we learn the right and wrong motivations for serving God. We also discover God's motivation for acting on behalf of his people. As you study this section, think about your motivations for serving God.

II. COMMENTARY

Motivation Matters

MAIN IDEA: *A proper motive for service is necessary to please God. God's motivation for acting on our behalf is loving concern (divine jealousy).*

A A Lack of Motivation (7:1–3)

SUPPORTING IDEA: *We should not grow weary in serving God.*

7:1. Chapters 7 and 8 of Zechariah deal with questions about fasts, and they form a clearly defined unit in the book. Five different oracles may be identified in this section, each beginning with the familiar, **the word of the LORD** [or LORD Almighty] **came** (7:1,4,8; 8:1,18). **In the fourth year of King Darius . . . on the fourth day of the ninth month, the month Kislev** would be December 7, 518 B.C. Almost two years had passed since Zechariah had begun his recorded prophetic work.

7:2. **The people of Bethel had sent** a delegation led by **Sharezer** and **Regem-Melech** to Jerusalem to seek the favor of the Lord, probably for sacrifice. Bethel was a small town located about ten miles north of Jerusalem. Formerly, Bethel had been one of the centers of the cultlike worship established by Jeroboam I when the tribes of Israel were divided into Israel, the ten northern tribes, and Judah, the two tribes in the south (931 B.C.). Although he claimed to worship the Lord, Jeroboam radically changed the true religion

(1 Kgs. 12:25–33). He established new feast days, new qualifications for priests, and new temples for worship in Bethel and Dan, bypassing Jerusalem altogether. To make matters worse, he placed golden calves in these new temples as symbols of his new religion. No doubt these objects were influenced by his years in Egypt while in exile during Solomon's reign (1 Kgs. 11:40), since the sacred bull was a prominent religious symbol there.

Jeroboam's new religion was contrary to God's Word and severely condemned in Scripture as an abomination in the eyes of the Lord. Jeroboam himself was repeatedly labeled the man who "caused Israel to sin" or "commit" sin (cp. 1 Kgs. 15:30,34; 16:26; 22:52). Amos journeyed to Bethel and denounced its false religion (Amos 7:10–13; 4:4), and Hosea (10:5) nicknamed Bethel, "house of God," Beth Aven, "house of wickedness." By now the idolatrous worship centers had long been destroyed, and Bethel was inhabited by believers. Bethel had truly become a "house of God" once more.

Sharezer and **Regem-Melech** are foreign names, apparently indicating that they were born in Babylon. Likely, they had returned to their homeland with Zerubbabel twenty years before and had settled in Bethel. They came to Jerusalem to seek divine guidance (**entreat the LORD**).

7:3. These men sought a divine word from the **priests** and **prophets** about several fasts. In Old Testament times God's primary spokesmen were the **priests** and the **prophets**. Priests were the teachers of the law. They rendered decisions on points of the law (Deut. 17:8–9). The high priest received special divine guidance by means of the Urim and Thummim (Exod. 28:30; Num. 27:21). Even wicked King Herod followed the practice of consulting the priests for information on scriptural issues (Matt. 2:4). Prophets received direct revelations from God about his will. This council would have included the high priest Joshua and the prophets, Haggai and Zechariah. The delegation from Bethel wanted to know if they should continue to keep certain fasts.

Only the **fast** of **the fifth month** is mentioned in verse 3, but three others are specified later in the text. All of these fasts were associated with the fall of Jerusalem to Babylon.

First, the fast held on the tenth day of the fifth month (7:3,5; 8:19) commemorated the burning of Jerusalem in 586 B.C. (Jer. 52:12–13), including Solomon's beautiful temple (2 Kgs. 25:9). Today the Jews remember the destruction of both the first (586 B.C.) and second (A.D. 70) temples with a special day called the Ninth of Ab (or July/August). This is the saddest day on the Jewish calendar and the greatest fast of the year, apart from that of the Day of Atonement.

Second, in the seventh month (7:5; 8:19), Gedaliah, the Jewish governor of Judea, was killed and the remnant fled (2 Kgs. 25:23–26; Jer. 41:1–3). Feinberg notes, "The third day of the seventh month is still observed in orthodox Judaism as the Fast of Gedaliah" (Feinberg, *Minor Prophets*, 305).

Third, the fast of the fourth month (8:19) recalled the day when the Babylonians finally broke through the walls and entered Jerusalem (2 Kgs. 25:3–4; Jer. 39:2).

Fourth, on the tenth day of the tenth month (8:19), Nebuchadnezzar began the siege of Jerusalem (2 Kgs. 25:1–2; Jer. 39:1).

These fasts had been instituted by the nation and were not part of God's law, but the people still wanted a word from God about whether they should continue to keep them or not. No doubt, the present rebuilding of the temple was the impetus for this inquiry. Construction had resumed two years earlier and was at its halfway point. Apparently, many Jews questioned the need to continue the fasts since the nation had returned and the temple was being built.

The Jewish people had kept these fasts for **many years**, from 586 until 518 B.C. Four times a year for sixty-eight long years, they had mourned and fasted over these past events. Reading between the lines, we may fairly conclude their question implies that the people were weary of keeping these burdensome fasts and desired to end them. Whether the fasts were now needed or not, we sense little motivation on their part to keep them.

Many of God's saints today exhibit a low level of motivation for serving the Lord. Some church members are not faithful to the services, and others do not give or serve anywhere in the church. Pastors often become frustrated in their attempts to "pump" people up. Even those who are faithfully serving the Lord can become "weary in doing good" (Gal. 6:9). How can we stay motivated? The most important motivating factor for any believer is love for the Lord. As Jesus affirmed, "If you love me, you will obey what I command" (John 14:15).

B A Wrong Motivation (7:4–7)

SUPPORTING IDEA: *A proper motive for our service is necessary to please God.*

7:4–5. Another oracle is introduced by the phrase, **the word of the LORD Almighty came to me.** Here the second of four fasts mentioned in chapters 7 and 8 is named, that of the **seventh** month. As stated above, the fast of the seventh month (also 8:19) recalled the assassination of Gedaliah, the Jewish governor of Judea (2 Kgs. 25:23–26; Jer. 41:1–3). Jeremiah had predicted the Babylonian captivity would last **seventy years** (Jer. 25:11–12; 29:10), and it is noteworthy that seventy years also passed between the destruction of the temple in 586 B.C. and its completion in 516 B.C. Aware of Jeremiah's prophecy, the people may have reasoned that since the time of judgment was complete, these fasts were no longer necessary.

In verses 5–7 the Lord addressed three questions to **all the people of the land and the priests**—all those involved in keeping and administering the fasts. First, the Lord asked a very convicting question, **When you fasted and mourned** for these many years, **was it really for me that you fasted**? Yes, these Jews had denied themselves food and mourned four days a year for over half a century. However, the real issue was motive. Had they done this at God's command, or was it something they had established on their own? The answer was the latter. Only one fast was prescribed in the law—the Day of Atonement, Yom Kippur (Lev. 16:29; 23:27,29,32). On that day the Jewish people were to fast (as a sign of humility) and mourn over their sins. The high priest entered the most holy place with the blood of the sacrifice and sprinkled the blood over the top of the ark (traditionally called "the mercy seat," KJV, NASB, NRSV) to make atonement for Israel's sins.

Furthermore, had the people kept these fasts because of a love for God or for selfish reasons? This seems to lie at the heart of the matter, and the Lord's inquiry implies that the latter was the case. Selfishly, the Jewish people desired to see their homeland prosper once more. They longed to see Jerusalem return to its former glory and to worship in a magnificent temple again. Their fasts implored God to restore the nation. In itself, nothing was wrong with this wish, but dreams and hopes must focus on God's glory and God's kingdom, rather than our own. Our motivation must always be, What is best for the kingdom of God and will most glorify Christ?

Like ancient Israel we sometimes do things, even very good things, with a wrong motive. How would we have to answer the Lord's question, "Was it really for me?" about what we say and do? When you taught that Sunday school lesson, attended church last Sunday, sang a solo, or even preached a sermon, was it really for the Lord? When you prayed for finances or healing, was it for the glory of God? As Kaiser says, "All religious acts must flow out of a genuine response of faith and obedience to God, or they are merely self-serving, self-glorifying and, consequently, self-condemning" (Kaiser, *Mastering the Old Testament*, 355).

7:6. The Lord's second question is the flip side of the first. Not only had they fasted for selfish reasons; their motives for keeping the annual festivals were not pure. Festivals like Pentecost and Tabernacles were not fasts but feasts in which the people celebrated by **eating and drinking**. For many people, the occasions were just fun, not worship (the way some Americans regard Christmas!). Certainly Zechariah's words are not intended to be absolute. Many Jewish believers surely fasted and observed the festivals with a pure heart, but others did not. In light of the next verse, we may understand this attitude to have been particularly characteristic of those in preexilic Judah.

7:7. In question three the Lord reminded Zechariah's audience of the penalty for rituals without a devoted heart. When the nation was filled with people and **prosperous**, God warned **through the earlier prophets** that he desired reality, not ritual (Isa. 1:11–17; 58:3; Hos. 6:6; Amos 5:21–24). Zechariah's countrymen only had to look around to see the devastation such hypocrisy brought on their beloved city, temple, and nation. The fact that Jerusalem was destroyed for its sin may imply that fasting over its fall was unwarranted since its destruction was a result of God's righteous judgment (cp. Ezek. 24:15–27). **The Negev** (literally, "dry") was the arid region in southern Palestine beyond Beersheba down to the highlands of the Sinai Peninsula. The **western foothills** ("Shephelah") were between the Judean hills and the Mediterranean coastal plain. Even these least desirable areas, used for agriculture and grazing, were previously inhabited.

🄲 A Right Motivation (7:8–14)

SUPPORTING IDEA: *A proper motive for life and service is heartfelt obedience to the will of God.*

7:8. Like the others in chapters 7 and 8, God's third message to Zechariah is signaled by the phrase, **the word of the LORD came**. Rather than outward religious show or religious acts for selfish reasons, we should be motivated to live for God and serve him out of obedience to his word. Of course, our obedience must flow from a heart of love for God. To the saying, "God said it, I believe it, that settles it," we should add, "Now I will do it!" In verses 11–14 God reminded Zechariah's audience of the consequences of disobedience—the present desolation of the nation.

7:9–10. In these verses God summed up the kind of lives he expected his people to live in four simple commands. As the apostle John said, "This is love for God: to obey his commands. And his commands are not burdensome" (1 John 5:3). The injunctions are: **administer true justice** (in their courts, 8:16), **show mercy** [or "faithful love"] **and compassion to one** another, do not take advantage of the helpless, and **do not think evil of each other**. Widows, orphans, foreigners, and **the poor** were the four classes of vulnerable people protected in the Book of the Covenant (Exod. 21–24). Thinking **evil of each other** would include hatred, malice, revenge, and plotting to harm others (cp. 8:17). Obeying these four simple commands would solve most of society's problems then and now.

7:11–12. Zechariah reminded his countrymen of the wickedness and judgment of their ancestors, hoping to encourage his audience to obey the Lord. Their forefathers' hardened obstinacy is expressed in five ways: **refused to pay attention, turned their backs, stopped up their ears, made their hearts as hard as flint**, and **would not listen** to God's word through the **prophets**. What a picture! They turned their backs on God, covered their ears, and hardened their hearts. They would not listen to the written word (**the law**) or to God's message through the prophets, inspired by the Lord's **Spirit**. God is unimaginably patient, but such actions provoked his divine wrath.

7:13–14. Just as they refused to **listen** to God when he pleaded with them to repent, God **would not listen** to them when the Babylonian armies swept through the land. They were not expressing genuine repentance even then but like many people today simply wanted God to deliver them from calamity. The result of their rebellious hearts was exile and the desolation of **the pleasant** [or "desirable"] **land**, or Israel (elsewhere only in Jer. 3:19; Ps. 106:24).

Ⓓ Divine Motivation (8:1–17)

SUPPORTING IDEA: *God's motivation for acting on our behalf is a loving concern (jealousy) for his children.*

8:1. A new division in chapters 7 and 8 is signaled by the key phrase, **the word of the LORD Almighty came**. God had sternly warned the people about the dangers of disobedience, but now he offered a thrilling message of comfort and encouragement for the faithful returnees. In essence God said that judgment was over, and he planned to bless and rebuild their country. Zechariah 8:1–17 contains seven oracles (likely in summary form), each beginning with the phrase, "This is what the LORD Almighty [or "LORD"] says," traditionally, "thus says the LORD of hosts [or "LORD"]" (8:2–4,6–7,9,14). In the following verses we discover seven wonderful promises for Israel.

8:2. First, the promise of God's care. God promised to act on Judah's behalf, and his motivation for action is expressed most emphatically—**very**

jealous for Zion . . . burning with jealousy for her. God's jealousy speaks of his loving concern for his people, like a loving husband who watches over his bride to guard her from harm. (For a discussion of God's kind of jealousy, see the "Deeper Discoveries" section for Nahum 1.) Actually, the other promises are based on the first. God's loving concern for his people leads him to act on their behalf.

8:3. Second, the promise of God's presence. As in the days before the exile, God's special presence would rest upon **Jerusalem**, ensuring blessing, prosperity, and protection for the nation. The phrase **will return** is very emphatic in the Hebrew original (the so-called "prophetic perfect" form). **Jerusalem will be called the City of Truth** (or "the faithful city") because the Lord's truth will be propagated there, and the temple mount (**the mountain of the LORD Almighty**) **will be called the Holy Mountain** because the holy God will dwell there. Spiritually, this prophecy was fulfilled by the restoration of the nation and the rebuilding of the temple (God's house = dwelling place) but would be literally realized at Christ's return. Only then would Jerusalem be the "City of Truth" or the temple mount be "the Holy Mountain" in an absolute sense.

8:4–5. Third, the promise of peace and security. Material blessing follows spiritual blessing. People will live safely to an old age, and the land will be blessed with many children who play unafraid in the streets. According to Barker, "The weakest and most defenseless members of society will be able to live securely" (Barker, 650). Once more we may find a partial fulfillment of the passage in postexilic Israel, but perfect peace and security await Messiah. As we view the tragic events in Israel in our day, we can only pray that this prophecy will be fulfilled soon.

8:6. Fourth, the promise of God's power. The accomplishment of these amazing promises may seem impossible (**marvelous**) to human beings but not to **the LORD Almighty**, literally, "the LORD of hosts." For the one who creates and commands all the forces of heaven and earth (the "hosts"), nothing is too difficult. In Mark 10:27 Jesus proclaimed that "all things are possible with God."

8:7–8. Fifth, the promise of Israel's regathering. The Lord promises to regather his people from the nations where they had been scattered. The phrase **the countries of the east and the west** refers to Babylon and Egypt, respectively—the areas where most Jews had been exiled. These directions represent totality because the passage indicates that all God's scattered people will come home. If the text means that all Israel will become God's **people** in an absolute spiritual sense, a future application is required.

8:9–13. Sixth, the promise of God's blessing. By this time (518 B.C.) the people were in the middle of temple construction and needed encouragement. Contrasting their dismal past with their present improved conditions and bright future would be an incentive to keep up the good work. Commentators generally understand the reference to the laying of the temple **foundation** in verse 9 to the renewed effort to build the temple inspired by the **prophets** Haggai and Zechariah in 520 B.C. rather than its original beginning in 536 B.C.

We may note the key phrases, **before that time** and **but now.** Before the people were obedient to God, they were beset with problems (Hag. 1:3–11). Now God promised to reverse matters and bless the faithful nation with economic prosperity, safety from enemies, abundant crops, and honor (**a blessing**) among the nations. Previously foreigners had wished the appalling desolation of Israel on their enemies (**an object of cursing**); in the future they would wish Israel's prosperity (as **a blessing**) on friends. Both at the beginning and end of this oracle, the people are exhorted to be courageous (**let your hands be strong**).

8:14–17. Seventh, the promise of God's favor. Just as God had **determined to bring** judgment (exile) on their ancestors, now he had **determined to do good again to Jerusalem and Judah.** They need **not be afraid** because God was on their side (Rom. 8:31). For these good things to continue, however, the people must live holy lives. As in 7:9–10, God emphasized four specific commands. In the Hebrew text **courts** literally reads "gates" (KJV, NASB). Barker explains, "The gates of cities in ancient Palestine often had built-in stone benches, where people could sit with friends, transact business, make legal contracts, hold 'court,' make public proclamations, etc. (Ruth 4:1–2; 2 Sam 18:24)" (Barker, 653). God's attitude toward sin is succinctly put: **I hate all this.**

E A New Motivation (8:18–23)

> **SUPPORTING IDEA:** *God's people should serve the Lord with a renewed joy because of their glorious future.*

8:18–19. The fasts of the **fifth** and **seventh** months have already been mentioned (7:3,5); here we are introduced to those of the **fourth** and **tenth months.** As previously noted, all four had to do with the fall of Jerusalem to Babylon. The fast of the fourth month commemorated the day when the Babylonians broke through the walls and entered Jerusalem (2 Kgs. 25:3–4; Jer. 39:2) and that of the tenth month, the beginning of Babylon's siege of Jerusalem (2 Kgs. 25:1–2; Jer. 39:1). These somber, sad fasts would **become**

joyful and glad occasions and happy festivals for Judah. The fasts would become feasts. No longer were the people to dwell on their miserable past, but they were to look forward to a bright and joyous future with God. What a motivation for renewed zeal in the Lord's work! God's people have a great future ahead and should serve the Lord with excitement and joy. **Love truth and peace** is a warning. To preserve joyful festivals rather than sad fasts, the people must obey God.

8:20–23. In these verses we are told that people from all over the world would travel **to Jerusalem to seek the LORD Almighty and to entreat** his favor (cp. 2:11; Isa. 2:1–4; Mic. 4:1–5). Israel's God would be recognized by the world as the only true God. Though these verses could be applied spiritually to Gentiles coming to know God in this age, the primary focus is on the future messianic age when all the world's people will acknowledge Christ as Lord.

When we think of Christ's coming and the wonderful new world in store for us, we are motivated to serve the Lord with enthusiasm. Our opportunities to serve God in this life will soon be over. Jesus reminds us, "We must do the works of Him who sent Me while it is day. Night is coming when no one can work" (John 9:4 HCSB).

As we come to the close of these two chapters, we might wonder if Zechariah had lost sight of the original question posed by the Bethel delegation. Should they continue the fasts or not? Actually Zechariah answered the question several times throughout chapters 7 and 8, though indirectly. No, they did not need to continue the fasts for the following reasons: (1) The fasts were never commanded by the Lord (7:5). (2) They were held for selfish reasons (7:5). (3) The destruction of Jerusalem was God's righteous judgment for its wickedness (7:11–14). (4) God's blessing had returned to the nation, as evidenced by its restoration and the rebuilding of the temple (8:1–17). (5) The fasts of old would be replaced with joyous festivals in the future (8:18–23).

MAIN IDEA REVIEW: *A proper motive for service is necessary to please God. God's motivation for acting on our behalf is loving concern (divine jealousy).*

III. CONCLUSION

Win One for the Gipper!

Probably the most famous story in all of sports is that of "the Gipper." Yet few people know much about the Gipper or even know his real name. George

Gipp was recruited to play football at Notre Dame by the famed coach, Knute Rockne. Nicknamed "the Gipper," he became one of the greatest players in college football history, playing in thirty-two consecutive games and scoring eighty-three touchdowns. Sadly Gipp died in his senior year from pneumonia (December 14, 1920). Rockne visited Gipp at St. Joseph's Hospital in South Bend just a few hours before his death.

For eight years Rockne kept Gipp's last words to himself until halftime in a scoreless game with Army, Notre Dame's great rival. His 1928 team had been decimated by injuries, and they had already lost two of their first six games. It was then that George Gipp passed from greatness into legend. Rockne told the beleaguered players about a deathbed request that Gipp had made of him during that last visit. "I've got to go, Rock. It's all right. I'm not afraid. Some time, Rock, when the team is up against it, when things are wrong and the breaks are beating the boys, tell them to go in there with all they've got and win just one for the Gipper. I don't know where I'll be then, Rock, but I'll know about it, and I'll be happy."

Rockne continued: "Gipp asked me to wait until the situation seemed hopeless—then ask a Notre Dame team to go out and beat Army for him. This is the day, and you are the team." When Rockne finished speaking, the weeping players were electrified. They nearly tore the hinges off the door getting out of the room and back on the field. Needless to say, Notre Dame won. What made the difference? Motivation.

In this section of the Book of Zechariah, we have discovered that motivation really does matter. In fact, it is the key to pleasing God. In the prophet Zechariah's day, the Jewish people had lost their motivation for keeping several burdensome fasts. To make matters worse, their observance of these fasts had not pleased God because they had kept them for the wrong reasons. Zechariah shared with them an acceptable motive for serving God—loving obedience. The prophet also revealed that God's motivation for acting on our behalf is a jealous love for our well-being. Chapter 8 concludes with God's promise of a glorious future for his people, a comforting truth that should stir believers to be even more zealous in serving the Lord.

PRINCIPLES

- People can perform religious acts for wrong reasons.
- A proper motive for serving God is obedience to his word.
- Refusal to heed God's warnings to repent of sin will result in disaster.

- God acts on our behalf because of his loving concern (jealousy) for us.
- Nothing is impossible with God.
- God has a glorious future in store for believers.

APPLICATIONS

- If you have lost your zeal for serving the Lord, take a few moments and think of all the wonderful things he has done for you, especially the sacrifice of Jesus on the cross.
- Examine the motives for your religious service. Are they pleasing to the Savior?
- Determine to live a life of obedience to God.
- Thank God that he lovingly watches over your life, always ready to act on your behalf.
- Rejoice in the glorious future God has planned for his children.

IV. LIFE APPLICATION

First Time My Dad Ever Saw Me Play

When Lou Little coached football at Georgetown University, he had on his squad a player of average ability who rarely got into the game. Yet the coach was fond of him and especially liked the way he walked arm in arm with his dad on campus.

One day, shortly before the big contest with Fordham, the boy's mother called Little and said her husband had died that morning of a heart attack. "Will you break the news to my son?" she asked. "He'll take it better from you."

The student went home with a heavy heart that afternoon, but three days later he was back. "Coach," he pleaded, "will you start me in that game against Fordham? I think it's what my father would have liked most."

After a moment's hesitation, Little said, "OK, but only for a play or two." True to his word, he put the boy in—but he never took him out. For sixty action-packed minutes that inspired youngster ran, blocked, and passed like an all-American. After the game the coach praised him: "Son, you were terrific! You've never played like that before. What got into you?"

"Remember how my father and I used to go arm in arm?" he replied. "Well, few people knew it, but he was totally blind. I like to think that today was the first time he ever saw me play!"

That boy was motivated to play his best because he knew his father was watching. As we go about our lives, we should remember that our heavenly Father is watching us as well. Our greatest motivation for godly living and religious service should be to please him. When we stand before the Lord some day, let us determine to live in such a way that Jesus will be able to say, "Well done."

V. PRAYER

O Lord, we pray that our motives will always be pleasing to you. When we are tempted to grow weary in serving you, help us to remember all that you have done for us. May we also strive to be obedient to your revealed will. Thank you that you love us and are jealously watching over us, ready to help in time of need. Thank you also for the wonderful future that you have prepared for us. In Christ's name we pray. Amen.

VI. DEEPER DISCOVERIES

A. Bethel (7:2)

Readers may be puzzled to find that the NIV text reads, "The people of Bethel had sent" (similar in NASB, NRSV), whereas the KJV has, "When they had sent unto the house of God" (similar in NKJV). The difference in the translations arises because the name *Bethel* means "house of God" and thus may be taken as a town name or a reference to the temple. The KJV's "they" is literally a masculine singular ("he/it") in the Hebrew text. In certain cases the masculine singular may be taken as a collective plural, but the singular would more likely indicate that the subject is "Bethel." In the KJV's reading "they" leaves the identity of those who sent indefinite, and the statement, "sent unto the house of God," is less likely since the temple was still two years away from being completed. Although the KJV translation is certainly possible, taking Bethel as the subject is simpler grammatically and makes excellent sense in the context.

Bethel was a small town about ten miles north of Jerusalem. The name occurs about seventy times in the Old Testament. According to D. C. Fredericks in the *Holman Illustrated Bible Dictionary:*

Bethel was important in the Old Testament for both geographic and religious reasons. Because of its abundant springs, the area was fertile and attractive to settlements as early as 3200 B.C., and first supported a city around the time of Abraham. Today the village of Beitin rests on much of the ruins of Bethel. Located at the intersection of the main north-south road through the hill country and the main road from Jericho to the coastal plain, Bethel saw much domestic and international travel. Bethel became a prominent border town between tribes and the two kingdoms later. Religiously, Bethel served as a sanctuary during the times of the patriarchs, judges, and the divided kingdom, hence was second only to Jerusalem as a religious center.

Abraham visited the site (Gen. 12:8; 13:3), but it was Jacob who changed its name from Luz to Bethel after his encounter with God there (Gen. 28:10–22).

Jeroboam I selected Bethel and Dan as the centers of his apostate worship when the twelve tribes of Israel were divided into the kingdoms of Israel (north) and Judah (south) in 931 B.C. Amos denounced this false religious system at Bethel (Amos 7:10–13; 4:4), and Hosea (10:5) nicknamed Bethel ("house of God") the pejorative Beth Aven ("house of wickedness"). Bethel was destroyed by fire in the sixth century B.C. (presumably by the Babylonians).

After being freed by the Persians, some Jewish exiles returned to the town (Ezra 2:28; Neh. 7:32; 11:31) and resumed the worship of the Lord. Then Bethel truly became a "house of God" once more. It was a delegation from this group that visited the Jerusalem priests and prophets (including Zechariah). Bethel seems to have been a significant city in Christ's day and survived until the later Arab conquest.

B. Fasting in the Bible (7:3)

Zechariah 7–8 deals with questions about certain fasts. Fasting is a practice mentioned frequently throughout the Bible. Fasts were of three different types. (1) A normal fast involved total abstinence from food. (2) A total fast precluded food and drink (Esth. 4:16; Acts 9:9). (3) Daniel seems to have engaged in a partial fast (Dan. 10:2–3). Fasts varied in length. Though most lasted one day, the people of Jabesh Gilead (a town Saul had protected) fasted seven days over King Saul's death (1 Sam. 31:13). Esther and her fellow Jews in Susa fasted three days (Esth. 4:16). When Moses received the Ten Commandments on Mount Sinai, he fasted forty days and nights (Exod. 34:27–28).

Fasts were enjoined to seek God's help or favor. For example, Ezra and Esther fasted for divine protection (Ezra 8:23; Esth. 4:16), and Jehoshaphat called a fast when threatened by an invading army (2 Chr. 20:1–4). Fasting was practiced when mourning the dead (1 Sam. 31:13; 2 Sam. 1:12). Often fasting accompanied confession of sin (1 Sam. 7:6; Dan. 9:3–20), and fasts were called during times of national crisis (Judg. 20:26; Joel 1:14). Individuals might wear sackcloth (a rough material), tear their clothes, sit in ashes, or throw dust on their heads as additional signs of humility when fasting (1 Kgs. 21:27; Neh. 9:1; Ps. 35:13).

Sincere fasting moves the heart of God. Ezra said, "So we fasted and petitioned our God about this [protection for his journey], and he answered our prayer" (Ezra 8:23). God spared Nineveh when the people of that wicked city repented and humbled themselves before God with fasting (Jonah 3:5–10). Incredibly, the Lord even postponed an element of predicted judgment on Ahab because the wicked king humbled himself and fasted before the Lord (1 Kgs. 21:27–29).

The only required fast in the Old Testament was the annual Day of Atonement ("deny yourselves," Lev. 16:29,31; 23:27,29,32). On that day the high priest sprinkled the blood on the top of the ark, symbolically covering Israel's sin. Confession of sin accompanied the fast.

Fasting was also practiced during New Testament times. Jesus himself fasted for forty days at the beginning of his ministry (Luke 4:1–2). When his fast was over, Luke says that "Jesus returned to Galilee in the power of the Spirit" (Luke 4:14). In the Sermon on the Mount, Jesus implied that fasting is a normal practice for believers (Matt. 6:16). God's Spirit gave spiritual guidance to the church at Antioch during a time of fasting and prayer (Acts 13:1–3). Jesus severely condemned insincere fasting (Matt. 6:16; cp. Isa. 58:3–5).

In conclusion, fasting demonstrates humility to God and allows the worshiper to concentrate more fully on spiritual things. For Old Testament saints, fasting was required only once a year, on the Day of Atonement. For New Testament believers, fasting is always voluntary. Still Jesus himself fasted and seems to imply that believers would fast on occasion. Through fasting we are able to commune with God more deeply, receive guidance, protection, power, answers to prayer, and many other blessings. Calls for national days of fasting are biblical as well.

C. The Fast of the Fifth Month (7:3)

The delegation from Bethel asked if they should continue to keep the fast of the fifth month. The fast in question was held on the tenth day of the fifth month (7:3,5; 8:19) and commemorated the burning of Jerusalem (Jer. 52:12–13) and Solomon's beautiful temple (2 Kgs. 25:9) in 586 B.C. Today the Jews remember the destruction of Solomon's temple with a special day called the Ninth of Ab (or July/August). The Ninth of Ab (Tisha B'Ab in Hebrew) is preceded by a full three-week mourning period and is the saddest day on the Jewish calendar and the greatest fast of the year, apart from that of the Day of Atonement. The day not only memorializes the destruction of Solomon's temple but a number of other Jewish tragedies.

Kaiser explains:

> According to the Talmud, it was also the day when God decreed that the people in the wilderness should not enter the land because of their unbelief. Further, it was the day on which not only the first, or Solomonic, temple was destroyed, but the second temple was destroyed by the Romans [in A.D. 70]. Moreover, it was the day on which the city of Bethar was taken under Bar Kokbah (A.D. 135), only to fall in turn into Gentile hands who put everyone to death including Bar Kokbah, the messianic pretender in the second Christian century. Finally, on that day, August 9th, wicked Turnus Rufus ploughed up the hill of the sanctuary and thus fulfilled Micah's prophecy, "Zion shall be ploughed as a field" (Kaiser, *Mastering the Old Testament,* 354).

The prohibitions on the Ninth of Ab are similar to those of Yom Kippur (Day of Atonement). In addition to not eating or drinking, observant Jews are not allowed to wash or even wear leather shoes. Unlike Yom Kippur, they are only permitted to study certain portions of the Torah and Talmud on the Ninth of Ab. The Book of Lamentations is read at the evening service.

D. "Mercy" (7:9)

The NIV's "mercy" (also KJV, NKJV) is a translation of the Hebrew word *chesed,* a theologically significant term. NASB and NRSV read "kindness" in this verse. *Chesed* occurs 244 times in the Old Testament, and its most common translations in the NIV are: "love" (129 times), "kindness" (41 times), "unfailing love" (32 times), "great love" (6 times), and "mercy" (6 times). According to Richards:

Among people, *hesed* describes a bond of loyalty, such as is established between relatives, friends, or allies. An act of *hesed* is carried out by free choice in harmony with the relationship; thus *hesed* is an expression of love appropriate to a relationship.

The term is theologically significant because it is often used to express divine attitudes and actions. It is closely linked with covenant in the Old Testament, and many believe it should be translated "covenant faithfulness." But "covenant faithfulness" is not an adequate explanation for God's actions. It was God's deep love that moved him to establish covenants with man in the first place. His acts of *hesed* are generated from his own loving character. Thus, in revealing himself to Moses, the Lord associated *hesed* with a constancy and forgiveness that went beyond the obligations to which the Mosaic covenant might bind him. God is "the LORD, the LORD, the compassionate and gracious God, slow to anger, abounding in love [*hesed*] and faithfulness, maintaining love [*hesed*] to thousands, and forgiving wickedness, rebellion and sin" (Ex 34:6–7) (Richards, *Expository Dictionary of Bible Words*, 418–19).

Thus, *chesed* is a term filled with meaning and difficult to translate with just one English word. It expresses love, kindness, and loyalty. Perhaps "faithful loving-kindness" would best capture the idea in most instances.

Regularly in the New Testament (Acts 9:32; 26:10; 1 Cor. 14:33) and sometimes in the Old Testament (Pss. 16:3; 34:9; Dan. 7:18,21), terms rendered "saint(s)" mean "holy one(s)." Yet in the Old Testament the word most frequently translated "saints" (in NIV) is *chasid*, an expression related to *chesed*. God's people may have been called *chasid* because they were recipients of God's *chesed*, but most likely they were so called because they were to be characterized by *chesed*—love and kindness.

E. Festivals in the Bible (8:19)

As in modern societies ancient Israel had its festivals or holidays. Each week Israel observed the Sabbath, which was to be a joyous celebration of worship (Lev. 23:3). At the beginning of the month, they held the New Moon festival (Num. 10:10; Neh. 10:33). Seven annual religious festivals are named in the Mosaic law.

Festivals in the First Month (Nisan or March/April)
1. Passover (Exod. 12:2–20; Lev. 23:5)
2. Unleavened Bread (Lev. 23:6–8)

3. Firstfruits (Lev. 23:9–14)

Festival in the Third Month (Sivan or May/June)
4. Feast of Weeks or Pentecost (Exod. 23:16; 34:22; Lev. 23:15–21)

Festivals in the Seventh Month (Tishri or September/October)
5. Trumpets (Rosh Hashanah) (Lev. 23:23–25; Num. 29:1–6)
6. Day of Atonement (Yom Kippur) (Lev. 23:26–32; Exod. 30:10)
7. Tabernacles or Booths (Lev. 23:33–43; Num. 29:12–39; Deut. 16:13)

The first two festivals commemorated Israel's deliverance from Egypt; Firstfruits, the consecration of the harvest to God; Pentecost, a celebration of the harvest; Trumpets, the beginning of the civil new year; the Day of Atonement, the atonement for the nation's sin; and Tabernacles, the forty years of wilderness wandering. According to the New Testament, festivals such as Passover (1 Cor. 5:7) and the Day of Atonement (Heb. 2:17; 9:11–14) prophetically typified Messiah's person and work.

Two other annual festivals were added to the Jewish calendar later in biblical times. Hanukkah (Feast of Dedication or Festival of Lights) is held in the ninth month (Kislev or Nov./Dec.). It commemorates the rededication of the temple in 164 B.C. after it had been desecrated by the Greek tyrant, Antiochus IV. This festival is mentioned in John 10:22. Purim is observed in the twelfth month (Adar or Feb./Mar.). It recalls the deliverance of the Jews from Haman (Esth. 9). Purim is one of the most festive Jewish holidays.

VIII. TEACHING OUTLINE

A. INTRODUCTION

1. Lead Story: The Amazing Sergeant York
2. Context: Chapters 8 and 9 of Zechariah deal with questions about fasts. A Jewish delegation from Bethel inquired of the priests and prophets if it was necessary to continue four fasts that commemorated the destruction of Jerusalem, the temple, and related events. By this time (518 B.C.) temple construction was at its midpoint. No doubt, this rebuilding of the temple was the impetus for the inquiry. The question implies that the people were weary of keeping these burdensome fasts and desired to end them. God replies that these fasts were not commanded by him in the first place and would be replaced by joyful festivals, now that his blessing had returned to the nation.

3. Transition: These chapters have much to say to modern believers about our motivations for religious service. Are we serving the Lord out of mere duty, or are we truly excited about the things of God? Are our motives selfish or pure? Loving obedience to God should be our primary motivation. As the late Nelson C. Hinkson, missionary to Eastern Europe and the former Soviet Union, reminds us, "If Christ be God and died for me, no sacrifice is too great for me to make for Him" (quoted in J. D. Woodbridge, *Ambassadors for Christ,* Chicago: Moody Press, 1984, p. 263).

B. COMMENTARY

1. A Lack of Motivation (7:1–3)

2. A Wrong Motivation (7:4–7)

3. A Right Motivation (7:8–14)

4. Divine Motivation (8:1–17)

5. A New Motivation (8:18–23)

C. CONCLUSION: WIN ONE FOR THE GIPPER

VIII. ISSUES FOR DISCUSSION

1. Name some wrong motives for religious service. Do you think the problem of wrong motivation is widespread in churches today? Do you think that some people (particularly those in cults and non-Christian world religions) perform religious acts and other good deeds in an attempt to earn eternal life? What does the Bible say about this?

2. What are some proper motives for serving God? Which one do you think is the most important?

3. What is the best way to motivate true believers to serve God faithfully?

4. What is God's motivation for blessing his children?

5. How do you think God's promises about the future world can motivate us to live better today? If you believe that Christ's coming is near, what should this motivate you to do?

Zechariah 9–10

The King Is Coming!

I. INTRODUCTION

Herod the Great—the Great Reprobate!

II. COMMENTARY

A verse-by-verse explanation of these chapters.

III. CONCLUSION

I Shall Return!

An overview of the principles and applications from these chapters.

IV. LIFE APPLICATION

The Rest of the Story

Melding these chapters to life.

V. PRAYER

Tying these chapters to life with God.

VI. DEEPER DISCOVERIES

Historical, geographical, and grammatical enrichment of the commentary.

VII. TEACHING OUTLINE

Suggested step-by-step group study of these chapters.

VIII. ISSUES FOR DISCUSSION

Zeroing these chapters in on daily life.

"*A*lexander, Caesar, Charlemagne, and myself founded empires. . . . Jesus Christ alone founded His empire upon love; and at this hour, millions of men would die for Him."

Napoleon Bonaparte

Zechariah 9–10

 IN A NUTSHELL

*I*n chapters 9 and 10 Zechariah describes the coming of two kings. The first is Alexander the Great, who conquered the Medo-Persian Empire (the one ruling in the prophet's time). His sweep through Syria, Phoenicia, and Philistine territory is graphically related. Most importantly for the Jewish people, God promised to protect them during Alexander's invasion. By contrast, Zechariah assures God's people that some day a greater king is coming—the King of kings and Lord of lords, their Messiah. Both Messiah's first (entering Jerusalem on a donkey) and second (universal rule) advents are prophesied. The latter part of chapter 9 describes the deliverance of God's people from the Greeks. Blessings of Messiah's kingly reign are set forth in chapter 10.

The King Is Coming!

I. INTRODUCTION

Herod the Great—the Great Reprobate!

*H*istory is replete with evil kings. Ironically, one of the most diabolical was Herod the Great who ruled Judea at the time of Christ's birth. Herod was born about 73 B.C. and was confirmed by the Roman Senate as "king of Judea" in 40 B.C. The Jewish people resented him because he was an Idumean (an Edomite). Herod did accomplish some good for the country. In his extensive construction program, he rebuilt Judean cities and made palaces for himself, including his remarkable palace-fortress at Masada. His greatest achievement was the remodeling of the temple, begun in 19 B.C., which transformed the temple complex into one of the world's most glorious buildings.

Yet the good he did is far overshadowed by his wicked character. Executions were commonplace with Herod. He even murdered his favorite wife, Mariamne I, and her mother. Fearing that his two sons by Mariamne, Alexander and Aristobulus, would attempt a coup, Herod had them strangled. Herod also had Mariamne's brother, Aristobulus III, drowned at a celebration in Jericho. Certain Pharisaic teachers were executed when they incited their students to remove the imperial eagle from above a temple gate. Five days before his death, Herod had Antipater (another son) executed. Caesar Augustus made the grim joke, "It's better to be Herod's pig than his son." The king's pig was safe because Herod observed Judaism's prohibitions on eating pork, but his sons were not.

According to the Jewish historian Josephus, on his deathbed the king ordered many prominent Judeans locked up, commanding his sister to execute them when he died so that he could be mourned even if on other people's account. Thankfully his sister rescinded the order. Herod died in 4 B.C. at the age of seventy. His sons carried him on a golden bier adorned with precious stones to the Herodion (a fortress-palace near Bethlehem), where he was buried.

One of Herod's most dastardly deeds occurred near the end of his reign. The wise men (or "magi") informed him that the "king of the Jews" had been born in Judea (Matt. 2:1–2). According to the prophet Micah (Mic. 5:2), the messianic king would be born in Bethlehem. When the wise men did not return with specifics, Herod massacred all the babies under two years old in the tiny village. Although this account is not found outside the Bible, it conforms to what we know of Herod's fanatical jealousy of his position and his sinister character.

Herod the Great is only one example of an endless number of history's wicked tyrants. What the world needs is a righteous king who will rule justly and lovingly. We need a ruler who will bring peace and safety to a war-torn, terrorized earth. That is exactly what Zechariah prophesies in chapters 9 and 10. He begins with a prophecy of Alexander the Great (a very important and comforting message for God's people who lived at that time) and then predicts the advent of Israel's great Messiah king. Zechariah tells us of Christ's humble first coming and his triumphant second coming. He concludes in chapter 10 with a description of the world as it will be under Messiah's reign.

II. COMMENTARY

The King Is Coming!

MAIN IDEA: *Our Messiah is the King of kings, and all earthly rulers (no matter how impressive) pale into insignificance when compared to him. At his first coming, he provided salvation from sin, and at his second coming he will bring peace to the nations and blessings for his followers.*

At this point in the book, we encounter a radical change in subject matter. According to Feinberg:

> Chapters 1 to 8 [of Zechariah] referred in the main, though not exclusively as we have already repeatedly shown, to Zechariah's own time. The goal in view was encouragement for the rebuilding of the Temple. Chapters 9 to 14, which form the second part of the book, deal chiefly with the future and were probably written [by Zechariah] a long time after the first eight chapters. Chapters 1–8 deal with Israel when she was under Medo-Persian rule; chapters 9 and 10 when she was governed by Greece; chapter 11 when she was under Roman domination; and chapters 12 to 14 when she shall be in the last days of her national history (Feinberg, *Minor Prophets*, 314).

The future aspect of Zechariah's latter prophecies is highlighted by eighteen instances of the eschatological phrase, "on that day." Zechariah divides these final chapters into two parts, clearly delineated by the term *oracle* (or *burden*) at the beginning of each section. Unger observes: "The first oracle embraces the first advent and rejection of Messiah, the Shepherd-King (chapters 9–11), and the second oracle deals with the second advent and acceptance of Messiah, [the] Shepherd-King (chapters 12–14)" (Unger, 151).

The Coming of a Worldly King (9:1–8)

SUPPORTING IDEA: *The enemies of God's people will be swept away by the Lord's agent of judgment, Alexander the Great.*

The first oracle begins with a description of the Lord's judgment on Syria, Phoenicia, and Philistia—traditional enemies of Israel—and God's contrasting defense of his people. Although the passage has been interpreted eschatologically, most evangelical scholars consider the instrument of the judgment described here to be Alexander the Great. The parallels between what is described in verses 1–8 and Alexander's invasion seem unmistakable. After routing the Persians in October 333 B.C. at Issus, Alexander marched toward Egypt, conquering Syria, Phoenicia, and Philistia along the way (the very areas described in vv. 1–7).

Such a prophecy had great relevance for the Jewish people. First, God was showing the means whereby he would sweep away Israel's hostile neighbors—Syria, Phoenicia, and the Philistines. Even Egypt and the great Medo-Persian Empire of Zechariah's day would fall before Alexander. Second, this prophecy assured the Jewish people living at the time of Alexander's invasion that God would protect them. Certainly such a promise would be comforting to the Jews who may have feared the destruction of their tiny nation and their own deaths at the hands of the Greek king. Thus the passage is a glorious prophecy of deliverance and security for Israel, relevant to Zechariah's contemporaries and beyond.

9:1. The NIV's "oracle" is rendered "burden" in many translations (KJV, NASB). The idea would be a heavy message, that is, a prophecy of judgment. (For a discussion of the word *oracle,* see the "Deeper Discoveries" section for Nahum 1.) The superscription, **An Oracle,** reads the same in the Hebrew in Zechariah 12:1 and Malachi 1:1 and appears only in these three instances in the Old Testament. Once more the prophet emphasizes the divine origin of his message.

In verses 1–2a the conquest of Syria is described. **The land of Hadrach** (mentioned only here in the Bible) is usually identified with Hatarikka, named in the annals of Assyrian kings as an Aramean city-state near Damascus and Hamath (v. 2). Assyria campaigned against the area in 772, 755, and 733 B.C. God's judgment would also fall on **Damascus**, the leading city-state of the Arameans.

The phrase **the eyes of men and all the tribes of Israel are on the LORD** is difficult. Perhaps all men looked to God for deliverance from Alexander, yet why would pagans look to Israel's God for help? Some commentators contend that when the world observed Alexander's conquests, they were actually gazing at the Lord, who raised him up as an instrument of divine judgment. A better solution is to translate "and all the tribes of Israel" as "even [or "specifically"] all the tribes of Israel," explaining that the "eyes of men" are those of the "tribes of Israel" (cp. NASB). Such an interpretation is linguistically acceptable and makes good sense here. While the eyes of the world were on Alexander and his phenomenal conquests, Israel looked to their God for deliverance.

9:2. The region of **Hamath** (modern Hama) was located about 130 miles north of Damascus along the Orontes River. Thus another Aramean city-state would be included in this judgment (Amos 6:2).

In 9:2b–4 the judgment of Tyre and Sidon is graphically depicted. These cities were located on the coast of ancient Phoenicia, known as Lebanon today. After Alexander conquered Syria, he swept down the Mediterranean coast in order to take the ports where the Persian fleet had its bases. Though **Sidon** was to its north, **Tyre** (probable meaning "rock") was named first because by this time it had become the more important of the two cities. Tyre and Sidon were **skillful** or "wise" (KJV, NASB, NRSV) in business dealings, and these maritime powers became great centers of commerce and trade. The people of Tyre were also proverbially arrogant—wise in their own eyes (Ezek. 28:3–5).

9:3. Tyre's defenses (**built herself a stronghold**) were formidable, and the city felt it was invincible. Actually, Tyre comprised two harbors, the old port on the mainland and one on an island about one-half mile out to sea. A wall 150 feet high surrounded the island city. Nebuchadnezzar had besieged the city for thirteen years (585–573 B.C.) and succeeded in conquering the mainland city. However, the Tyrians were able to transport most of their wealth to the island city, which the frustrated Babylonian king could not take. Not only was Tyre well protected; it was rich. Zechariah picturesquely described Tyre's **silver** and **gold** as so abundant that they were piled up like the **dust** and **dirt** commonly found in the **streets** of Oriental cities.

9:4. In spite of her wealth and massive defenses, Tyre would crumble, because the sovereign **Lord** (Heb. *'Adonay*) had decreed it. Tyre's wealth would be carried away, her domination of sea trade would end (or "cast her wealth into the sea," NASB), and the city would be burned. All of this did indeed happen to Tyre.

In 332 B.C. Alexander besieged the island city for seven months. Determined to conquer Tyre, Alexander took the ruins of the mainland city and threw them into the sea, building a causeway to the island some twenty-six hundred feet long and six hundred to nine hundred feet wide. His soldiers walked across the causeway with their siege engines, and the city fell. Alexander's conquest of Tyre has been called his greatest military achievement.

Tyre experienced the full fury of the Greek king's wrath. Ten thousand citizens were executed, thirty thousand were sold into slavery, and the city was burned. Alexander's causeway was never removed, and it turned the island into a peninsula.

Incredibly, Ezekiel prophesied, "I will scrape away her rubble and make her a bare rock" (Ezek. 26:4), an apt description of the city after Alexander's soldiers removed the rubble of the mainland city and threw it into the sea to build the walkway. God's word is truly amazing! Zechariah's prophecy was penned about two hundred years before this event and Ezekiel's about two hundred and fifty, yet both prophecies were fulfilled to the letter.

9:5. In these verses Zechariah described the conquest of Philistia, Alexander's next stop on his march to Egypt. As in Zephaniah 2:4, Goliath's hometown of Gath (1 Sam. 17:4,23) is the only one of the five main Philistine cities unmentioned. Various suggestions have been offered to explain this omission—too far inland, incorporated into Judah, or the town had been destroyed (see "Commentary" discussion on Zephaniah 2:4–7).

Ashkelon, a prosperous port city, observed the fate of Tyre and was terrified. If mighty Tyre could not withstand this Greek invader, what hope did they have? Alexander's last serious threat before reaching Egypt was **Gaza**, a fortress perched atop a mound sixty feet high. Persia used Gaza as its base for military operations against Egypt. Gaza was the only Philistine city specifically named in the records of Alexander's advance, and its siege and capture are well attested. After two months of bitter resistance, the city was taken. Once more Alexander dealt ruthlessly with the citizens for failing to surrender. Ten thousand of its inhabitants were slaughtered and the remainder sold into slavery. King Batis was tied to a chariot with thongs and dragged to death through the streets of Gaza.

However, the phrase **will lose her king** refers to Alexander's policy of abolishing monarchial governments, not merely the execution of Gaza's then-reigning king. **Ekron**, the city farthest north and nearest Tyre, expected Tyre to survive Alexander's onslaught but lost **hope** when the great city fell. The phrase **Ashkelon will be deserted** means that it would lose its population.

9:6. The NIV's **foreigners** has also been rendered "mixed race" (NKJV), "mongrel race" (NASB), or "mongrel people" (NRSV). Apparently, this refers to Alexander's policy of intermingling different conquered peoples. According to Feinberg, "The loss of political independence, the splendor of their cities, and the glory of their temples would mean the crushing blow to Philistine pride" (Feinberg, *Minor Prophets*, 316). Alexander's conquest was in reality the end of the Philistines. These cities were occupied in New Testament times, but they were distinctly Hellenistic with a mixed population.

9:7. This verse contains an absolutely shocking prophecy. One of Israel's most bitter foes, the Philistines, would some day be incorporated into God's family of believers. No longer would they eat their idolatrous sacrifices with **blood**, prohibited in the law (Lev. 7:26; 17:10,12). The phrase **forbidden food** ("abominations," KJV, NKJV, NRSV) refers to idolatrous sacrifices or ceremonially unclean foods. The Philistines would be like **leaders** (or "a clan") **in Judah** or **Jebusites**, early inhabitants of Jerusalem. In spite of the severe prophecy of judgment on the Philistines in verses 5–6, God loved these people and welcomed them into his family, once their sinful pride was broken.

9:8. When Alexander stormed through the area, the Jewish people were, no doubt, very concerned. No one had been able to stand against the mighty king. How would Alexander treat them? Could this be the end of their fragile nation? In this verse we find a reassuring promise of God's protection (**I will defend my house**) during this trying time. "Defend" is more literally, "camp around" (NKJV, NASB), and in this context "house" refers to the nation rather than the temple. Thus God promised to protect his people, and the Jewish nation was spared Alexander's wrath.

Josephus, a first-century Jewish historian, recorded a fascinating story of Alexander's visit to Jerusalem and the city's deliverance. Although Josephus's account may be clothed in legendary dress, a visit to Jerusalem by Alexander is not implausible, and the city was indeed spared, in spite of the fact that Alexander punished the Samaritans to the north.

Zechariah concluded verse 8 with a prophecy of Israel's final deliverance. The absolute nature of the promise, **never again will an oppressor overrun my people**, "must anticipate the second advent of the Messiah for the final, complete fulfillment" (Barker, 661).

B The Coming of the King of Kings (9:9–10)

SUPPORTING IDEA: *Our king, Jesus the Messiah, provided salvation at his first coming and will rule the world and bring peace to the nations at his second coming.*

9:9. In verse 9 we have a marvelous prophecy of Christ's first coming, while in verse 10 we find an equally glorious prediction of his return. Zechariah had described the coming of a great earthly king, but now he exhorted **Jerusalem** (Zion) to **rejoice greatly** and **shout** for joy because something wonderful would happen—Israel's king was about to enter Jerusalem. Of course, this king was none other than Jesus the Messiah—the greatest king in all of history. The New Testament writers make abundantly clear that this prophecy was fulfilled by Christ's triumphal entry into Jerusalem on Palm Sunday (Matt. 21:1–10; Mark 11:1–11; Luke 19:28–38; John 12:12–15). Matthew (21:5) and John (12:15) specifically quote portions of this verse. Throughout the centuries many Jewish rabbis have interpreted this passage to speak of the Messiah as well.

Israel's Messiah would be **righteous** or "just" (KJV, NASB). Alexander could be capricious and ruthless, but Christ was personally righteous and would rule justly. Messiah would bring spiritual, and ultimately physical, **salvation** to the human race. Unlike the arrogant Alexander (who even required the provinces to revere him as a god), Christ (truly God) would be **gentle** (or "humble," NASB, NRSV). He would not enter Jerusalem on a war horse (like Alexander), but rather **on a donkey**, specifically **on a colt**.

9:10. Between verses 9 and 10, there is a gulf of at least two thousand years. As the prophet informs us in chapter 11, this wonderful Messiah was rejected when he came the first time. He died, rose again, and ascended to heaven where he now reigns. Some day he will come to earth again, and this time it will not be as before. He will not enter Jerusalem on a donkey but as earth's conquering king with all his mighty angels (Rev. 19:11). Before, he was rejected by Israel as a nation; when he returns, Israel will receive him as their Messiah (Zech. 12:10). At his return Christ will put an end to war (**take away the chariots . . . and the war-horses**) and usher in world **peace**. Efforts to bring peace on earth are commendable, but true and lasting peace will only be achieved by the arrival of the Prince of Peace.

Messiah's universal reign is couched in language reminiscent of Psalm 72:8—**from sea to sea and from the River** (Euphrates), the eastern boundary of the promised land (Gen. 15:18; Exod. 23:31), **to the ends of the earth.**

Alexander actually ruled only a tiny fraction of the world; Messiah will rule it all.

Seven wonderful truths are set forth about Messiah and his coming in these verses. First, Messiah's first advent was accurately predicted. Jesus entered Jerusalem in the exact manner Zechariah foretold over five hundred years before. That the prophecy was understood as messianic is clearly indicated by the response of the Jewish people on Palm Sunday. Prophecies of Christ's second coming will be fulfilled just as specifically. Second, Messiah will reign as king. Jesus now reigns from heaven and some day will rule earth in direct fashion. Third, Messiah will be personally righteous and a just ruler. Fourth, he will bring spiritual salvation and ultimately physical deliverance for his followers. Fifth, Messiah will be humble and gentle. Sixth, his rule will be universal. Seventh, he will bring an end to war and establish world peace. Jesus of Nazareth perfectly fulfilled the prophecy of verse 9 and will fulfill verse 10 at his second coming.

Ⓒ Triumph of the King (9:11–16)

SUPPORTING IDEA: *Like a mighty warrior, Israel's king will lead his people to victory over their enemies.*

9:11–12. In 9:11–16 Israel's God is presented as a great warrior king leading his people to victory. Battle terminology permeates the passage: prisoners (v. 11), fortress (v. 12), bow (v. 13), sword (v. 13), arrow (v. 14), trumpet (v. 14), march (v. 14), shield (v. 15), and slingstones (v. 15).

In 9:11–12 God promised to deliver his people based on his covenant with them, and he encouraged their **return** to Jerusalem (**your fortress**). If these verses are connected to Christ's return in verse 10, they describe the deliverance, regathering, and blessing of his people at that time. Yet the prophet's words are reminiscent of earlier promises of deliverance for exiles in Babylon, and they call for Zechariah's contemporaries to return to their homeland (2:6–12). Likely the prophecy has application to both persons living in the prophet's day (rescued by the heavenly king) and at Christ's return (rescued by the messianic king).

The phrase **the blood of my covenant with you** may allude to the sacrifices of the Mosaic covenant since only in Exodus 24:8 is the similar phrase "blood of the covenant" found in the Old Testament. However, God's covenant with Abraham was also ratified with blood sacrifice (Gen. 15:9–11). In the Abrahamic covenant God promised that the patriarch's descendants would receive a land, would become a great nation, and would be blessed

(Gen. 12:1–2; 13:14–17; 15:18; 18:18), promises in view here. **Prisoners** had **hope** because their king was about to free them. A **waterless pit** was a dry cistern, often used as a prison. Both Joseph (Gen. 37:24) and Jeremiah (Jer. 38:6) were imprisoned in such cisterns. The phrase **restore twice as much to you** assures a full measure of blessing to Israel (Isa. 61:7) and may encompass the double portion of blessing bestowed on the firstborn (Deut. 21:17) as well.

9:13. In 9:13–17 the victory of the Jewish people over the Greeks is in view, with allusions to Messiah's eschatological triumph at points in the text. Various scenarios have been suggested, but historically the only known major conflicts between Judah and the Greeks were the Maccabean wars of the second century B.C. According to Lindsey:

> At least this verse, and perhaps the rest of the chapter, refer to the conflict of the Maccabees (169–135 B.C.) with Antiochus IV Epiphanes (cp. Dan. 11:32), Antiochus V Eupator, Antiochus VI, and Antiochus VII Sidetes, Greek rulers of Syria. This Jewish victory foreshadowed Israel's final conflict and victory when God will bring them into millennial blessing (Lindsey, 1563).

The role of Israel's God as a divine warrior is especially prominent in verses 13–16.

Judah is likened to the Lord's **bow**, **Ephraim** to his arrow, and **Zion** to his **sword**. With these weapons the Lord will destroy the enemy. Zechariah has already introduced us to **Greece** by way of Alexander the Great's invasion of the area (9:1–8). After Alexander's death in 323 B.C., his vast empire was carved up by his generals, eventually into four major divisions. Palestine was first controlled by the Ptolemaic Greeks who ruled Egypt but was later acquired by the Seleucid (Syrian) Greek kings. War broke out during the reign of the tyrannical Antiochus IV (175–163 B.C.) and continued for more than two decades after his death. A family known as the Maccabees led the Jewish resistance and eventually succeeded in gaining Judea's independence.

9:14. This verse figuratively depicts **the Lord** as a great warrior king doing battle for Israel. In conjunction with **storms of the south** (the most violent), the Lord's **trumpet** probably is thunder.

9:15. The phrase **the Lord Almighty** is literally "the Lord of hosts," the "hosts" being the armies of heaven at God's disposal. None can resist such force. Their victory will be decisive. **They will destroy** (literally, "devour") the enemy. The phrase **overcome with slingstones** may also mean that they would walk across the slingstones that had missed their mark (cp. NASB). Slingstones were catapulted at the opposing army, but no weapon is effective against God's people. Reliefs of the Assyrian King Sennacherib (704–681 B.C.) depict such stones, and slingstones from the Roman period are still piled up at Masada. The last part of the verse refers to the abundant provisions (**will drink, be full**) of the victory banquet and the exuberance (**roar as with wine**) of God's people as they celebrate the Lord's triumph on their behalf. **A bowl used for sprinkling the corners of the altar** emphasizes fullness, since it was filled to the brim. The NRSV's "they shall drink their blood like wine," is a mistranslation of the Hebrew text.

9:16. Israel will be saved (delivered) from her enemies, but the eschatological phrase **on that day** (the day of the Lord) suggests that this salvation also involves the spiritual change at Christ's return described in Zechariah 12:10–13:1. Then Israel will become **the flock of his people** in an absolute sense. Israel will dwell in God's **land** and be prized by the Lord like **jewels in a crown**. The Hebrew word for "crown" sometimes designates the "diadem" worn by the high priest (Exod. 29:6; 39:30). Perhaps the idea is that now Israel is restored as a priestly nation (cp. Zech. 3; Exod. 19:6). Commentators have pointed out the contrast between the precious jewels mentioned here and the worthless slingstones of the previous verse.

Ⓓ Blessings of the King (9:17–10:12)

SUPPORTING IDEA: *Messiah's reign will mean blessing for his people.*

9:17–10:1. From 9:17 through chapter 10, we witness the blessings bestowed on God's people, particularly during the messianic kingdom. *First, economic prosperity (9:17–10:1).* After Israel's deliverance there would be agricultural prosperity and physical health for believers. When rain is needed, all God's people have to do is **ask the LORD**. In a dry land like Israel, rain came to represent the epitome of blessing ("showers of blessing," Ezek. 34:26), and some commentators have understood the rain to symbolize spiritual refreshment here. Perhaps both literal rain and spiritual blessing are in view. **Rain in the springtime** (or "in the time of the latter rain," KJV) came in March/April and was important for strengthening and maturing crops. We must never fail to remember that all blessings come from God (Jas. 1:17).

10:2. *Second, a caring ruler (10:2–4).* In Israel and throughout the Ancient Near East, the word **shepherd** designated a variety of leadership positions: teachers, prophets, priests, judges, rulers, kings, and governors.

Here the primary focus is on civil rulers or kings (Isa. 44:28; Jer. 23:2–4). In verses 2–4 we have contrasting shepherds, wicked (10:2–3a) and caring (10:3b–4).

The wicked shepherds were idolaters who led the people astray because they followed the lies of their false gods. **Diviners** claimed to be able to foretell the future. Three methods of revelation are named here: direct divine communication (**speak**), **visions**, and **dreams**. In Old Testament times all were proper forms of revelation when received from the true God. Promises of success and well-being from the false prophets gave **comfort in vain**. As Jeremiah warned, "They dress the wound of my people as though it were not serious. 'Peace, peace,' they say, when there is no peace" (Jer. 8:11).

Zechariah had already stated in verse 1 that the source of true blessing was the Lord (not false gods). Without a shepherd who knew the way, **the people** wandered **like sheep**. These references do not suggest that idolatry was a present problem but are a reminder to Zechariah's audience of the past sins that had brought about the exile (1:4–6; 7:11–14). A preexilic focus is also indicated by the fact that after the exile Judah had no king (shepherd), only a governor appointed by the Persian government. Israel suffered because it had no godly Davidic king to guide them. The Messiah would fulfill that void.

10:3. For their wickedness the Lord would **punish** these unfaithful **leaders** (literally, "male goats"). Like male goats these rulers had bullied and oppressed the flock of God. Since Israel had no king at the time, apparently foreign oppressors bore the brunt of this condemnation. The verse contains a strong warning for political and religious leaders today that violation of the leadership trust will not go unpunished. When God removed these wicked leaders, he would personally **care for his flock**. He would change **Judah** from a flock of scattered and haggard sheep into **a proud horse**, a war horse fit for a king. Persian kings placed elaborate headdresses on their horses (Esth. 6:8).

10:4. God's Messiah would make possible Judah's deliverance described in the previous verse. **From Judah** is literally "from him," but the NIV correctly captures the sense. Messiah will come from the nation of Judah. Four titles for the Messiah are presented here: **cornerstone, tent peg, battle bow,** and **ruler**. Elsewhere in the Old Testament, the Hebrew term rendered "cornerstone" designates "leaders" (Judg. 20:2; 1 Sam. 14:38) and is specifically a messianic symbol in Isaiah 28:16 and Psalm 118:22. Jesus Messiah ("Christ") is the foundation of our faith. Upon him all power and ruling authority rests (Isa. 9:6). Moreover, as in Psalm 118:22 he is the crowning glory ("capstone") of the church. The expression is also a well-known symbol for Messiah in the New Testament (1 Cor. 3:11; 1 Pet. 2:6).

The tent peg figure may indicate the peg driven into the ground to hold up a tent (Judg. 4:21) or the large peg in an Oriental tent on which valuables were hung (Ezek. 15:3). A similar usage in Isaiah 22:22–24 favors the latter view. There God placed "honor" and "glory" on Eliakim, a government official, just as valuables were hung on a "peg" driven "into a firm place." Upon Christ honor and glory will rest.

Battle bow (symbol of strength for military conquest; 2 Kgs. 13:15–17; Rev. 6:2) depicts Christ as the conquering king who will subdue all the enemies of his people. The last part of verse 4 may mean that the Messiah would drive out all oppressors (KJV) at his coming or that from Judah **every** divinely approved king would come, the greatest being the Messiah. In this messianic context the latter view seems preferable.

What a magnificent description of the coming Messiah! Finally, the world will have a king who really loves and cares for its people, a glorious king with the power to ensure universal peace and security.

10:5–7. *Third, victory (10:5–7).* Now God's sheep are portrayed as **mighty warriors** who in the power of the Messiah will defeat their enemies. Various settings have been proposed for this victorious conflict. Following the messianic passage of verse 4, the primary focus would appear to be the future deliverance at the end of the age, with possible allusions to the Maccabean victories (9:13). Once more the nation would be reunited—**Judah,** the Southern Kingdom, and **Joseph** (from which two northern tribes came—Ephraim and Manasseh), the Northern Kingdom. While the context is future, no doubt Jews from all tribes returned to their homeland in the postexilic period. The nation would be fully restored to God's favor, as though they had not been **rejected.** God's pardon is full and complete (Ps. 103:12). The phrase **I will answer them** implies that they would cry out to God in repentance and faith for divine help (Zech. 12:10; Joel 2:32). Like Judah (v. 6), **the Ephraimites** (Northern Kingdom) would be victorious over the enemy and would **rejoice** when the Lord rescued them.

10:8. *Fourth, national regathering (10:8–12).* Due to the messianic context, these verses are best taken to refer to the regathering in the last days. The word **signal** is literally "hiss" or "whistle." According to Feinberg, "As beekeepers call their bees together by a whistle, so the Lord is represented as signaling for His ancient people. (See Is 5:26 and 7:18.)" (Feinberg, *Minor Prophets,* 322). More likely, "signal" describes the shepherd's call to the sheep by the sound of his pipe or his whistle. The Hebrew for **redeem** speaks of ransoming from slavery, captivity (Deut. 13:5; 2 Sam. 7:23; Mic. 6:4), and death (Job 5:20; Hos. 13:14). Israel's population would become **as numerous as before** her dispersion.

10:9–11. This future scattering would be that perpetrated by the Romans. When the Jewish people repented and called on the Lord (**remember me**), he would **return** them to their land. **Egypt** and **Assyria**, places where the Jews had been enslaved in the past, are representative of all countries where Israel would be dispersed. Israel's population would overflow into **Lebanon** and **Gilead** (in modern Jordan), but still there would not be **room enough for them**. All obstacles (like the **sea** dried up at the exodus) would be removed to allow Israel's return, and all evil world powers (again typified by Assyria and Egypt) would be vanquished.

10:12. Here the promise of divine strength is repeated (v. 6) and probably applies to all Israel, not just the Ephraimites (v. 7). Their return to the land was accomplished by the power of God, not by their own ingenuity. More-over, God's strength would also enable them to **walk** in the LORD's **name**, either as representatives or in accordance with his holy character. Micah had already prophesied that Israel would walk in the name of the Lord in Messiah's kingdom (Mic. 4:5), supporting a future interpretation for this passage.

> **MAIN IDEA REVIEW:** *Our Messiah is the King of kings, and all earthly rulers (no matter how impressive) pale into insignificance when compared to him. At his first coming, he provided salvation from sin, and at his second coming he will bring peace to the nations and blessings for his followers.*

III. CONCLUSION

I Shall Return!

With war raging around the world, President Franklin Roosevelt summoned Douglas MacArthur out of retirement in 1941 to command the American forces in the Philippines. After the Japanese attack on Pearl Harbor, the situation rapidly deteriorated, and in March 1942 the president ordered MacArthur to escape by submarine to Australia. Reluctantly MacArthur obeyed the president's order and left his men. Hopelessly outnumbered by the Japanese invaders, the American and Filipino troops were captured and endured the infamous Bataan Death March in which up to ten thousand of the seventy thousand prisoners died on the journey to the concentration camp.

Shortly after arriving in Australia, MacArthur made one of the most famous statements in American history, known even to those who know nothing else about him. Speaking to reporters, MacArthur declared, "The President of the United States ordered me to break through the Japanese lines and proceed from Corregidor to Australia for the purpose, as I understand it, of organizing the American offensive against Japan, a primary objective of which is the relief of the Philippines. I came through and *I shall return*."

On October 20, 1944, General MacArthur waded ashore at Red Beach, during the height of the fiercely contested Leyte invasion. Moments later he uttered these words in an emotional radio address, "To the people of the Philippines: *I have returned*. By the grace of Almighty God our forces stand again on Philippine soil." MacArthur had kept his promise.

Two thousand years ago someone else made a promise to return when he went away. His name was Jesus Christ, and more surely than the fact that MacArthur returned to the Philippines is the fact that Jesus Christ will come again to rescue his people. Zechariah prophesied that Messiah would come the first time to save from sin, the second time to rule the world and forever banish sin. He is coming again, and it may be soon!

PRINCIPLES

- God will sweep away the enemies of his people, often through providential means.
- The Lord defends his people from harm.
- Jesus Messiah (Christ) is both a gentle Savior and a conquering king.
- Messiah's future coming should bring joy and encouragement to believers.
- Blessing comes from the true God, not the false gods of this world.
- False religion deceives and destroys.
- God will judge leaders who mistreat his people.
- Christ is the cornerstone of our faith and a glorious, mighty king.
- Messiah will gather his people to himself at the end of the age.

APPLICATIONS

- Rather than seeking revenge, allow God to deal with those who mistreat you.
- Determine to be more like Jesus—righteous, gentle, and humble.
- Thank God for sending Jesus at his first coming to be your Savior.
- Rejoice in the fact that Jesus is coming again to bring in a wonderful new world of peace and joy.
- Guard yourself against the deceit of false religion.
- Be a faithful and loving leader, remembering that leaders will give an account to God. Study the life of Jesus in the Gospels to develop leadership principles for your life and ministry.
- Lean on the Lord for strength for living.

IV. LIFE APPLICATION

The Rest of the Story

As we look about our world, sometimes it appears that the forces of evil are winning. Evil is strong, crime is rampant, Christians are dying for their faith every day throughout the world, and the majority of our world's people still reject Jesus as Lord. Yet we are not seeing the whole picture. As radio personality Paul Harvey says, we need to hear "the rest of the story."

During the Battle of Waterloo, on June 18, 1815, the French, under the command of Napoleon, were fighting the Allies (British, Dutch, and Germans), under the command of Wellington. The people of England depended on a system of signals to find out how the battle was going. One of these signal stations was on the tower of Winchester Cathedral.

Late in the day the tower flashed the signal: "W-E-L-L-I-N-G-T-O-N- - -D-E-F-E-A-T-E-D." Just at that moment one of those sudden English fog clouds made it impossible to read the message. The news of defeat quickly spread throughout the city. The whole countryside was sad and gloomy when they heard the news that their country had lost the war. Suddenly the fog lifted, and the remainder of the message could be read. The message had four words, not two. The complete message was: "W-E-L-L-I-N-G-T-O-N- - -D-E-F-E-A-T-E-D- - T-H-E- - -E-N-E-M-Y!" It took only a few minutes for the good news to spread. Sorrow was turned into joy; defeat was turned into victory!

When it seems that the kingdom of God is losing, remember that the battle is not over. In his wonderful hymn, "I Heard the Bells on Christmas Day," Henry Longfellow expressed it this way:

> Yet pealed the bells more loud and deep:
> "God is not dead, nor doth He sleep;
> The wrong shall fail, the right prevail,
> With peace on earth, good will to men."

Our king is coming, and when he does, all the forces of evil will be defeated, and God's people will be delivered. Can Jesus win? All the power of heaven and earth is at his disposal. He cannot lose!

V. PRAYER

Dear God, when we are tempted to look about our world and fear, remind us that our King in heaven is able to take care of us and will see us through any situation. Thank you that you loved the world so much that you sent your Son Jesus to die on a cross as our Savior. We rejoice that Jesus is coming again to rule the world in righteousness and love. "Come, Lord Jesus." Amen.

VI. DEEPER DISCOVERIES

A. The Authorship of Chapters 9–14

Some scholars separate chapters 9–14 of Zechariah from the first of the book and attribute them to another author or authors, usually of the Greek period (about 332–200 B.C.). All of the latter chapters may be designated Second [Deutero] Zechariah, but often Second Zechariah is limited to chapters 9–11 with chapters 12–14 being labeled Third [Trito] Zechariah.

A number of arguments are raised against the unity of the book. First, since the prophet is not named in chapters 9–14, he must not have written them. However, Zechariah's declaration of authorship in 1:1 is intended to apply to the entire composition, as is the case with other prophetic books (Nah. 1:1; Hab. 1:1; Zeph. 1:1; Hag. 1:1).

Second, allusions to historical events or situations beyond Zechariah's lifetime demonstrate that later author(s) must have penned the prophecies. For example, since Greece is named in 9:13, this section must have been written in the Greek period (after Alexander's conquest in 332 B.C.). Often such reasoning reveals a preconceived philosophical bias against the possibility of the supernatural, in this case, predictive prophecy. For those who believe that God is omniscient (all-knowing) and have no problem with the miraculous, such an argument has no force.

Under the inspiration of the Holy Spirit, Zechariah was able to predict events of the Greek period, Alexander's coming, and the Maccabean wars. Obviously, if Zechariah could not have predicted events in the Greek period (two hundred years after his time), he certainly could not have predicted Christ's first coming (five hundred years later) or his second coming (at least two millennia later). Moreover, Jesus himself confirmed that the Old Testament did indeed contain miraculous predictions of his life and work: "You pore over the Scriptures because you think you have eternal life in them, yet they testify about Me" (John 5:39 HCSB), and "Then He told them, 'These are My words that I spoke to you while I was still with you, that everything written about Me in the Law of Moses, the Prophets, and the Psalms must be fulfilled'" (Luke 24:44 HCSB).

Third, literary and stylistic variations suggest different authors to some scholars—certain words or phrases absent or found more frequently in chapters 1–8 than in chapters 9–14 and the like. In reply, we would point out that these variations are usually the result of changes in subject matter. For example, in chapters 9–14 the expression "on/in that day" appears eighteen times, whereas it occurs three times in the earlier chapters. Yet "on that day" is an eschatological phrase, a major emphasis in the latter chapters. Moreover, there are marked stylistic similarities throughout the book (e.g., "LORD Almighty" [traditionally, "LORD of hosts"]).

On the other hand, Jewish and Christian tradition supports the unity of the book. For example, the apocryphal Ecclesiasticus (180 B.C.) refers to the minor prophets as the twelve books. If the author of Ecclesiasticus had divided Zechariah into two or three books, the number would have been more than twelve. Thus the author of Ecclesiasticus at this very early date evidences the Jewish belief that Zechariah was one composition. Furthermore, the Hebrew of the book is early, not late. Finally, the divisive view is subjective and without tangible, objective evidence to support it.

As Kaiser points out:

> The truth of the matter is that all talk about a lack of unity in the book is really hypothetical, for no Hebrew manuscript showing such a break between chapters 8 and 9 has ever been discovered. In fact, the Greek manuscript found in the Dead Sea Scrolls containing the

end of Zechariah 8 and the beginning of Zechariah 9 shows no gap or space between the two chapters (Kaiser, *Mastering the Old Testament*, 287–88).

When the evidence is considered, we must conclude that Zechariah penned the entire composition.

B. Alexander the Great (9:1–8)

Without question Alexander the Great was one of the great military strategists of history. The charismatic Alexander was born in 356 B.C., the son of a great conqueror in his own right—Philip II of Macedon. Philip had united Greece with Macedonia and was planning to attack Persia when he was assassinated in 336 B.C. Alexander, educated under the famed Athenian philosopher Aristotle, was only nineteen when he succeeded his father as king. One and one-half years later (334 B.C.), he launched his attack against the Persians. Hatred for the Persians had been brewing since the time of Cyrus because of constant quarreling and fighting between Persia and Greece, and the Greeks were especially bitter over the invasions of Darius I (490 B.C.) and his son, Xerxes I (480 B.C.). Alexander's attacks were intended to avenge these assaults upon his homeland.

In 334 B.C. Alexander crushed the Persian army at the Battle of Granicus (River) in Asia Minor, thereby bringing to an end the dominance of the Medo-Persian Empire. With his subsequent victories at Issus in October 333 B.C. and Arbela (also called the Battle of Gaugamela) in October 331 B.C., the conquest of Medo-Persia was complete. Incredibly within only three years Alexander had conquered the entire Near and Middle East. It was after his victory at Issus that Alexander turned south toward Egypt and invaded Syria, Phoenicia, and the Philistine cities mentioned in Zechariah 9:1–7.

Alexander conquered most of the known world of that day, his campaigns even reaching into India before his tired troops rebelled and insisted on returning home. Because of his incredible success the Greek king became arrogant. Achilles (the mightiest warrior on the Greek side in the Trojan War) was Alexander's hero, and he believed that Achilles and the god, Hercules, were his ancestors. Either out of pride or for political reasons, Alexander compelled the provinces to worship him as a god. Naturally, his Greek troops resented such an order.

The great conqueror succeeded in forging the largest Western empire of the ancient world—one and one-half million square miles. But at the pinnacle of his career, having conquered much of the known world, Alexander died. On returning to Babylon from the east, he came down with a severe fever (possibly malaria). On June 13, 323 B.C. he died at the age of thirty-two. (Some people have suggested that Alexander may have been poisoned.) His death in Babylon, in the palace of the great Nebuchadnezzar (also where the blasphemous Belshazzar saw the handwriting on the wall, Dan. 5:5), is ironic. Alexander had planned to make Babylon his imperial capital and restore its glory, but God had decreed that Babylon would never rise to its former grandeur (Isa. 13:19–22).

Alexander left two sons, Alexander IV and Herakles, both of whom were murdered. After a period of infighting and struggle, the empire came to be partitioned among four Greek military leaders, commonly designated as the Diadochi ("successors"). Alexander spread the Greek language and culture all over the world, an act that prepared the world for the gospel by giving it a common speech, Koine Greek, the language of the New Testament.

C. Tyre and Sidon (9:2–3)

Tyre and Sidon were located along the coastal plain of Phoenicia (modern Lebanon) between the mountains of Lebanon and the Mediterranean Sea. Both cities were ancient. Sidon was named in extrabiblical sources before 2000 B.C. and Tyre just after 2000 B.C. In the beginning Sidon was the most important, but eventually Tyre assumed the dominant role. Both cities were great maritime powers and centers of trade. Purple dye was one of Tyre's most popular exports.

Israel interacted with both cities but particularly with Tyre. David hired carpenters and stonemasons from Tyre and used cedars from that area to build his palace (2 Sam. 5:11; 1 Chr. 14:1). King Hiram of Tyre supplied materials and craftsmen for the construction of the temple in Jerusalem during the reign of Solomon (1 Kgs. 5:1–18). Later Tyre and Sidon supplied materials for the second temple built in Zechariah's day (Ezra 3:7). Ahab (874–853 B.C.) married Jezebel, the daughter of Ethbaal, king of Sidon (1 Kgs. 16:31), with disastrous results. She brought her Baal worship to Israel's court and promoted this abomination within the nation, brutally killing the Lord's prophets (1 Kgs. 18:13). The prophets often denounced Tyre and Sidon (Isa. 23:1–5; Amos 1:9–10), none more severely than Ezekiel, who characterized Tyre's king as the personification of pride (Ezek. 28:1–6). Judgment on Tyre was partially fulfilled by Alexander's destruction of the city in 332 B.C. (Zech. 9:2–4).

Under Roman rule Tyre was known for its textiles and for a purple dye extracted from sea snails, a dye said to be worth more than its weight in gold. Purple cloth became synonymous with wealth and royalty. Jesus visited Tyre and Sidon (Matt. 15:21), and Paul spent a week in Tyre after his third missionary journey (Acts 21:3–4). Today the population of Tyre has been estimated at seventy thousand and that of Sidon at eighty thousand.

D. "I Will Defend My House" (9:8)

When Alexander's seemingly invincible troops stormed through the area, the Jewish people were anxious. God's promise, given two hundred years before through the prophet Zechariah, to protect his people ("I will defend my house") must have been a great comfort to them. Josephus, a first-century A.D. Jewish historian, recorded a fascinating story of Alexander's visit to Jerusalem and the city's deliverance. The following is a summary of Josephus's lengthy account.

Alexander sent a letter from Tyre to the high priest in Jerusalem demanding assistance, supplies for his army, and the tribute money formerly sent to Darius, the Persian king. The high priest refused, asserting that he had given his oath to Darius not to take up arms against him. Alexander was livid and after Gaza's defeat decided the time was right to punish Jerusalem. Jaddus (or Jaddua), the Jewish high priest, called on the people to pray to the Lord for deliverance. In a dream God instructed the high priest to meet Alexander dressed in his high priestly garments while the priests and other citizens were to don white robes. Learning that Alexander was near the city, the delegation bravely marched out to meet the Greek king.

When Alexander saw the procession, he approached alone and fell prostrate before the high priest. The soldiers with Alexander were dumbfounded and asked the meaning of his actions. Alexander replied that he was not bowing before the high priest but before the high priest's God. He explained that while still in Macedonia, he had a dream in which he saw this very person, dressed in these exact clothes, who assured him of victory over the Persians. The Jews welcomed Alexander into the city of Jerusalem. There he was shown the amazing prophecies in the Book of Daniel that predicted one of the Greeks would defeat the Persian Empire. Alexander then granted favors to the Jews.

While Josephus's account seems to have legendary elements, it may have a historical basis. A visit to Jerusalem by Alexander certainly would not be out of the question, and the Jewish nation was indeed spared by the Greek king. Even Josephus's statement that Alexander was shown Daniel's predictions of Persia's fall to Greece (Dan. 8:5–8,21) is not unreasonable. Regardless of how God did it, he definitely kept his promise to "defend" his people.

E. The Maccabean Wars (9:13)

In 9:13 Zechariah referred to a conflict between Zion and Greece. The reference to Greece has been taken eschatologically to represent distant, unknown peoples who opposed Zion (God's people). Others have applied the text to the activities of Alexander the Great, but, as we have previously observed, Alexander did not attack the Jewish nation. The text has also been interpreted to describe the conflict between the church and the Gentile world. Historically, the only known major conflicts between Judah and the Greeks were during the Maccabean wars of the second century B.C.

Zechariah had already introduced Greece to us by his description of Alexander the Great's invasion of the area (9:1–8). After Alexander's death in Babylon at only thirty-two years of age, his vast empire was partitioned among his generals, eventually resulting in four major divisions. Originally, Palestine was controlled by Egypt's Ptolemaic Greek rulers, but during the reign of the Seleucid (Syrian) Greek king, Antiochus III (the Great; 223–187 B.C.), Palestine fell to the Seleucids. Severe conflict broke out between the Jewish people and their Greek overlords during the reign of the infamous Antiochus IV (175–163 B.C.). Antiochus designated himself Epiphanes, "god manifest," indicative of his arrogant character.

The hostility between Antiochus and the Jews reached fever pitch in 169 B.C., when the Greek tyrant plundered the temple in Jerusalem and slaughtered eighty thousand Jewish men, women, and children. In December 167 B.C. Antiochus even erected an altar to Zeus in the temple and offered pigs on it. These atrocities are recorded in the apocryphal books of 1 and 2 Maccabees (1 Macc. 1:20–63; 2 Macc. 5:11–21; 6:2–5).

Then God raised up a family known as the Maccabees, who led Israel's revolt against the Greeks. Originally the name *Maccabee* (or *Maccabeus,* meaning "hammer") was a title of honor given to Judas, a son of Mattathias. Later the name *Maccabees* was extended to include his whole family, specifically his father and four brothers—John, Simon, Eleazar, and Jonathan. Judas successfully defeated the Syrians in a series of battles and rededicated (Hanukkah) the temple to the Lord on December 14, 164 B.C. (1 Macc. 4:52).

These wars continued with later Greek rulers until Judea's independence was conceded by the Seleucid king Demetrius II in May 142 B.C. during the leadership of Simon. The Seleucid king Antiochus VII attempted to reassert his authority over Judea but died in battle with the Parthians in 128 B.C., bringing Seleucid control over Judea to a permanent end. At last the Jews were free. However, the cost was high for the Maccabean family. Eleazar and Judas were killed in battle, and Jonathan and Simon were assassinated. Although God used these courageous leaders to overthrow the Syrian yoke, Zechariah reminds us that their victories against overwhelming odds were made possible only by the power of "the Sovereign LORD" (9:14).

F. Shepherd as Leader (10:2–3)

In Israel and throughout the Ancient Near East, the word *shepherd* designated a variety of leadership positions: teachers, prophets, priests, judges, rulers, kings, and governors. In Zechariah 10:2–3 the primary focus is on civil rulers or kings. Shepherd was a common figure in Israel for kings. For example, King David was chosen by the Lord to "shepherd" the people of Israel (2 Sam. 5:2; cp. Isa. 44:28; Jer. 23:2–4). Elsewhere in the Ancient Near East, we find many examples of the figure. A king of Sumer (around 2450 B.C.) was called the shepherd of his people, and the Babylonian king, Hammurabi (about 1700 B.C.), described himself as a shepherd. King Ashurbanipal of Assyria (seventh century B.C.) and King Nebuchadnezzar (sixth century B.C.) were also represented as shepherds. "Shepherd" was sometimes applied to God as the divine king (Pss 23:1; 100:3).

VII. TEACHING OUTLINE

A. INTRODUCTION

1. Lead Story: Herod the Great—the Great Reprobate!
2. Context: In chapters 9–10, Zechariah describes the coming of one of history's greatest earthly kings, Alexander the Great. His conquests in Syria, Phoenicia, and Philistia are amazingly foretold two hundred years before they happened. Yet this mighty Greek king pales into insignificance when compared to Israel's messianic king, whose first and second advents are prophesied in 9:9–10. We are told that Messiah will bring salvation to the human race and ultimately world peace. Unlike Alexander, this king will be loving and humble, and his reign will be universal. Chapter 9 concludes with a prophecy of

conflict and victory for God's people over Greece, likely a reference to the Maccabean wars of the second century B.C. interspersed with allusions to Messiah's eschatological victory over all nations. In 9:17–10:12 we are shown the blessings provided by our messianic king—economic prosperity, a caring ruler, victory, and the regathering of God's people.

3. Transition: As we look into these chapters, we will better understand the wonder of our great coming king, Jesus the Messiah. At his first advent, he provided salvation for all who would receive it by dying on the cross for our sins. At his second advent he will bring peace to a war-torn world. We also discover God's providential working in history on behalf of his people. Alexander the Great was God's instrument of judgment on Israel's enemies, and the Lord delivered the Jewish people from the Syrian Greeks by raising up the Maccabees. Messiah's future deliverance of his people at the end of the age will bring in a wonderful world of prosperity, peace, and love.

B. COMMENTARY

1. The Coming of a Worldly King (9:1–8)
2. The Coming of the King of Kings (9:9–10)
3. Triumph of the King (9:11–16)
4. Blessings of the King (9:17–10:12)

C. CONCLUSION: I SHALL RETURN

VIII. ISSUES FOR DISCUSSION

1. In what ways do we see the providential working of God on behalf of his people in Zechariah 9–10?
2. How does the character of our messianic king differ from that of earthly kings like Alexander the Great?
3. How does it make you feel to know that Jesus is coming? How will conditions in Messiah's future kingdom differ from those in our present world?
4. Name ways that false religions (idols) are deceptive and dangerous.
5. What is the significance of the messianic designations, *cornerstone, tent peg,* and *battle bow*? What are some other names applied to the Messiah in these chapters?

Zechariah 11

Prophecy of the Rejected Shepherd

I. **INTRODUCTION**
Wrong Again!

II. **COMMENTARY**
A verse-by-verse explanation of the chapter.

III. **CONCLUSION**
Jonestown Massacre

An overview of the principles and applications from the chapter.

IV. **LIFE APPLICATION**
Where Is Jesus?

Melding the chapter to life.

V. **PRAYER**
Tying the chapter to life with God.

VI. **DEEPER DISCOVERIES**
Historical, geographical, and grammatical enrichment of the commentary.

VII. **TEACHING OUTLINE**
Suggested step-by-step group study of the chapter.

VIII. **ISSUES FOR DISCUSSION**
Zeroing the chapter in on daily life.

"*A*s a prophet, there were only two possible grades he could make on a test—100 or zero."

C h a r l e s   R .   S w i n d o l l

Zechariah 11

IN A NUTSHELL

*Z*echariah opens chapter 11 with a description of an invasion from the north. Then the Lord instructs the prophet to convey a message to the people of Israel by means of drama. Zechariah acts out the part of a caring shepherd, the Messiah, who is rejected by the sheep—the citizens of the nation. The people estimate the worth of this shepherd's loving leadership as a mere thirty pieces of silver, the price of a slave. Therefore, the Lord resigns as their shepherd, leaving the people at the mercy of uncaring shepherd-leaders who abuse and destroy.

Prophecy of the Rejected Shepherd

I. INTRODUCTION

Wrong Again!

*P*sychics profess the ability to foretell the future, but how accurate are they? In an Associated Press article dated January 1998, psychic predictions for 1997 were examined. The newspaper headline, "Psychic Predictions Way Off the Mark in '97," tells the story.

Had the psychics been right, 1997 would have gone down in history as the year Mick Jagger became a Parliament member and Walter Cronkite a critically acclaimed lounge singer. Princess Diana would be alive, too, though either 215 pounds because of a thyroid ailment or living in Africa while training as an Olympic long-distance runner, depending on which psychic you believed.

There was nothing that the psychics got right in their predictions for the *National Enquirer, National Examiner,* and other tabloids. So says the *Skeptical Inquirer.*

The magazine said it applies scientific method to claims of the paranormal. The psychics' collective strikeout came as no surprise to Gene Emery, who has been checking the forecasts for the magazine since 1979. "They are consistent," he said. Since 1979, Emery has found only one prediction that came half true. That was in 1993, when a *National Enquirer* psychic said Florida would be hit hard by an earthquake weeks after being devastated by the worst hurricane in state history. The timing of the forecast was right for Hurricane Andrew, but there was no tremor.

Among other predictions for 1997:

- Barbra Streisand was to convert Rush Limbaugh into a liberal Democrat.

- Pamela Anderson Lee was either to become a Washington lobbyist or star with Howard Stern in a rock musical version of *Gone with the Wind.*

- Sarah Ferguson was to join the cast of *Melrose Place* and marry Calvin Klein.

- Madonna, concerned about the quality of children's television shows, was to revive *The Mickey Mouse Club* and cast herself as its star.

The failures of 1997 weren't just a fluke. Other headlines from past years reflect the psychics' dismal record: "Crystal Balls Broken: Psychics Predicted 1990 That Wasn't" and "Year's [1991] Psychic Busts Inspire Annual Gloat." Moreover, in February 1998 the Psychic Friends Network folded because its parent company went bankrupt. Evidently, they went under because of "unforeseen expenses"! Shouldn't one of PFN's staff of two thousand fortune tellers have seen this coming?

It is abundantly clear that psychics and other false prophets cannot foresee the future. However, our God knows everything—the end from the beginning—and has revealed certain future events to his servants. In chapter 11 of Zechariah, we find one of the most amazing prophecies in all the Word of God. Over five hundred years in advance, Zechariah predicted Christ's rejection by the Jewish nation and even his betrayal for thirty pieces of silver. As we study the life of Jesus Christ, we find that this prophecy was precisely fulfilled in him. Feinberg has labeled this chapter about Messiah's rejection as "the darkest of Israel's history" (Feinberg, *Minor Prophets*, 324).

II. COMMENTARY

Prophecy of the Rejected Shepherd

MAIN IDEA: *Messiah is the Good Shepherd who truly cares for the sheep—the world's people. Sadly, many reject his offer of loving leadership and suffer the consequences.*

A The Result of Rejection (11:1–3)

SUPPORTING IDEA: *Rejection of the divine Shepherd brings devastating results.*

11:1–3. In this little poem (the poetic structure easily observed in the stanza format of the NIV), the prophet depicts the destruction of **Lebanon** to the north and **Bashan** to the east. The language is very picturesque—**trees** personified as wailing over their plight, **fire** devouring the cedars, **shepherds** weeping, and **lions** roaring. Often the passage is understood as a continuation of Messiah's victory over the nations described in chapter 10. The Lord's judgment, like a fire, will destroy the proud nations, symbolized by the **stately trees** of Lebanon and Bashan. Kings of these powers are represented as shepherds and lions.

Other commentators hold that verses 1–3 are not a conclusion to chapter 10 but an introduction to the account of the rejected shepherd in 11:4–14. When Israel rejected her Good Shepherd, the Lord consigned her to judgment (vv. 8–9). Thus the destruction of the land depicted so graphically here was a direct result of Israel's rejection of her messianic Shepherd-King. According to Laetsch, "Since the context refers to the days of the Messiah (v. 12ff.), the reference is to the siege and destruction of Jerusalem and the devastation of the entire land by the armies of Rome A.D. 70 and 71" (Laetsch, 467). Armies usually invaded the land of Israel from the north, Lebanon, and devastation extended to all the land including Bashan and areas around the Jordan River.

Resistance was futile, so Lebanon should **open** her **doors** (like the gates of a fortified city) to the fire of the divine judgment awaiting her. If Lebanon's magnificent **cedars** could not withstand the onslaught, what hope was there for the **pine** ("fir," KJV; "cypress," NASB, NRSV)? In the Talmud the Jewish rabbis interpreted Lebanon as representative of the temple because Lebanon furnished the cedars for its construction. Bashan was located to the north and east of the Sea of Galilee and was famous for large cattle that grazed in its plush pastures (Ezek. 39:18; Amos 4:1) and for its great oak trees (Isa. 2:13; Ezek. 27:6). The devastation would be so complete that what the fire did not destroy would be **cut down**. Shepherds would **wail** because their pastures were **destroyed** and the hungry lions had lost their lairs along the **Jordan** River.

The phrase **rich pastures** is literally "glory," and **lush thicket** is literally "pride" or "majesty." The NIV's translation seems to capture the idea well, however, for the "glory" of the shepherd would be plush grazing lands, and the "pride" of the Jordan River would likely be the trees that lined its banks where lions found refuge (Jer. 12:5). This passage has figurative elements; nevertheless, it graphically describes the devastation and horror inflicted on the land by an enemy army as it swept through, burning the fields and razing the trees (2 Kgs. 3:25).

Ⓑ The Wicked Shepherds (11:4–6)

SUPPORTING IDEA: *Ungodly shepherd-leaders wreak havoc on individuals and nations.*

11:4. According to Barker:

> The reason for the calamity in vv. 1–3 is now given, namely, the people's rejection of the messianic Shepherd-King (vv. 4–14). Just as the Servant in the Servant Songs (found basically in Isa 42; 49; 50;

53) is rejected, so here the Good Shepherd (a royal figure) is rejected. The same messianic King is in view in both instances (Barker, 675).

The Lord commanded Zechariah to do some creative preaching. He was to act the part of a good shepherd (**pasture**) and offer his services to **the flock**. Of course, "the flock" is the nation of Israel, and the shepherd's offer to pasture them is his presentation of himself as their leader. As the passage progresses, it becomes clear that Zechariah's good shepherd is the Messiah, an identification confirmed in the New Testament. In verse 11 we are informed that the people understood that the prophet's drama was a message from God. The phrase **marked for slaughter** suggests their cruel treatment under the buyers and shepherds described in verses 5–6. These sheep were being raised for their meat and would be sent to the slaughterhouse. Perhaps the destruction of countless lives at the hands of the Romans in A.D. 70 was specifically in view.

11:5. Zechariah compared the people to sheep bought and sold in the marketplace. The **buyers** and sellers were Israel's foreign rulers who slaughtered and exploited the people with no tinge of guilt, even boasting, **Praise the LORD, I am rich!** Foreign powers like Rome ruled nations for profit— taxes and other wealth. Worse still, Israel's own Jewish rulers (**their own shepherds**) cared nothing for the people. In Jesus' day, Jewish civil rulers and leaders like the Sadducees and Pharisees often seemed more interested in maintaining their position and riches than in the well-being of the populace. Thus we find that Israel had shepherds, but they were the wrong kind.

11:6. For its sin (specifically, for its rejection of the Messiah), the Lord would permit the land to fall to neighboring nations and foreign kings. The word **oppress** (literally, "beat" or "crush by beating") may describe the tyrannical Roman rule generally or Rome's attack and devastation of the Jewish nation in A.D. 70.

Ⓒ The Good Shepherd Rejected (11:7–14)

SUPPORTING IDEA: *Messiah is the Good Shepherd, rejected by ancient Israel and many people in our world today.*

11:7. Israel was beset with shepherds who abused and even slaughtered the people, so the Lord in his mercy sent them a Good Shepherd, who loved them and desired to protect them. Incredibly, they wanted nothing to do with him and even detested him (v. 8)!

Zechariah obeyed the Lord's command to act out the part of this Good Shepherd, the Messiah. The Hebrew word rendered **oppressed** means "poor, afflicted, or humble." The word here probably denotes the godly remnant of believers at Messiah's first advent. Messiah would shower special attention on these **oppressed of the flock**. A shepherd carried **two staffs** (Ps. 23:4)—a club to protect the sheep from wild animals and another staff for support and to retrieve the sheep from precarious places. Lindsey explains: "The staffs were given the symbolic names of Favor (or beauty, grace, pleasantness) and Union (literally, bands or 'ties'). They depicted God's gracious benefits toward His people (cp. 9:14-17) and the internal union of Israel and Judah as a nation (cp. Hosea 1:11)" (Lindsey, 1565). Messiah would bring God's favor and unity to the nation.

11:8. Scholars have puzzled over the first part of this verse for centuries. As many as forty different identifications for **the three shepherds** have been proposed. If the messianic view is maintained, the shepherds could not be historical leaders of Israel's past (e.g., high priests or Seleucid kings) because the Messiah would remove (**I got rid of**) them. Most likely the three shepherds were not three individuals but rather represented the three classes of leadership in Israel—prophet, priest, and king (civil leaders) that would be wiped away (Exod. 9:15; 23:23) in the Roman destruction. **One month** is best understood as signifying the short period of time in which the shepherds would be removed. The word **detested** (Hebrew word used only here in the Old Testament) means "to feel loathing to the point of nausea." The phrase **grew weary** (literally, "be short") seems to mean that Christ lost his patience with them.

11:9. After all his miracles, wonderful teaching, and kind deeds, the Messiah was still rejected by the nation. Christ then acquiesced to their wishes and relinquished his position as their shepherd, leaving the nation without proper guidance and protection. The result was death and destruction. Josephus, the Jewish historian, recorded a shocking instance of cannibalism (**eat one another's flesh**) that took place in Jerusalem during the Roman siege of A.D. 70.

11:10-11. Zechariah broke the **staff called Favor**, symbolizing that divine blessing and protection no longer rested on the nation. God's protective **covenant** that prevented **the nations** from harming or destroying Israel would be lifted. Messiah's deity is clearly seen in verse 10, since only God controls the world's nations. **Afflicted** is a translation of the same Hebrew word rendered "oppressed" in verse 7. As in that case it represents believers in Israel who perceived that Zechariah's actions were indeed a message from the Lord. First-century believers also would have recognized the Roman destruction of Israel as the fulfillment of God's promise (Matt. 23:34–39).

11:12. Verses 12–13 contain one of the most amazing prophecies in all the Bible. The Messiah had been rejected as the nation's shepherd, so he asked for his severance **pay** but added that if they did not wish to pay him, they should **keep it.** Messiah's pay, his worth in the eyes of the nation, was **thirty pieces of silver,** the price for a slave gored by an ox (Exod. 21:32), an insulting sum.

11:13. The Lord instructed Zechariah to **throw it to the potter,** contemptuously calling the thirty pieces of silver **the handsome price at which they priced me!** Zechariah threw the money **into the house of the LORD to the potter.** The connection between the temple and the potter sounds strange and has been variously explained. Since potters were needed to make vessels for the temple rituals (Lev. 6:28), some interpreters have surmised that a guild of potters served there (Jer. 18:6; 19:1). The phrase "throw it to the potter" may also have been a proverb for discarding something worthless or contemptible like our "throw it to the dogs." As we shall see, the New Testament unraveled the mystery of the temple-potter link.

Zechariah's prophecy was marvelously fulfilled in the life of Jesus. First, Judas betrayed our Lord for thirty pieces of silver (Matt. 26:15; 27:3,9). Second, filled with remorse, Judas threw the money into the temple when he returned it to the Jewish leaders (Matt. 27:3–5). Third, the chief priests used the money to buy a potter's field for a burial place for foreigners (Matt. 27:6–10).

11:14. Breaking the **second staff called Union** has been interpreted to signify internal strife (particularly during the Roman siege of Jerusalem) or disunity within the nation. **Judah** in the south and **Israel** in the north were the two divisions of the twelve tribes during the divided monarchy period.

Ⓓ The Worthless Shepherd (11:15–17)

SUPPORTING IDEA: *The alternative to the Good Shepherd (Messiah) is a foolish and worthless shepherd-leader.*

11:15. Zechariah has played the part of the messianic Good Shepherd, and now the LORD instructed him to act the part of another kind of **shepherd,** an evil one. People must have leaders. If the loving Messiah is rejected, other leaders who are not so kind will fill the void. The word **again** evidently refers back to verse 7 where the prophet put on the attire and gear, including two staffs, of a shepherd to act out his drama. In addition to staffs, the **equipment** of a shepherd (whether good or bad) included such items as a bag for food, a pipe for calling the sheep, and a knife. The word **foolish** speaks of one who is morally evil and despises "wisdom and discipline" (Prov. 1:7).

11:16. God himself would **raise up** this leader as a judgment on the nation for rejecting its Messiah. The foolish shepherd cares not for the sheep but only for himself. If they lose their way, even the little ones, he does not seek them out and bring them home. The **injured** are left to die and the **healthy** are not fed. Rather than feeding them, he feeds on them, even **tearing off their hoofs** to devour the last edible morsel. Barker points out that when "not" is removed from the verse, we discover elements of an effective pastoral ministry—care for the lost (or "perishing," NASB), seek the young (or "scattered," NASB), heal the injured, and feed the healthy (Barker, 679).

11:17. This substitute for the Messiah is not only foolish; he is a **worthless** leader who **deserts the flock** in time of need. He is unable to deliver the nation from its ills and certainly cannot save from sin. According to Barker:

> While this counterfeit shepherd may have found a partial, historical fulfillment in such leaders as Bar Kokhba, who led the Jewish revolt against the Romans in A.D. 132–135 and was hailed as the Messiah by Rabbi Akiba, it seems that the final stage of the progressive fulfillment of the complete prophecy awaits the rise of the final Antichrist (cp. Ezek. 34:2–4; Dan. 11:36–39; John 5:43; 2 Thess. 2:3–10; Rev. 13:1–8) (Barker, 679–80).

Judgment will fall on this sinister ruler. If a warrior's **arm** was struck, he could not wield his weapons; and if his **right eye** was **blinded**, he could not peer around the shield without exposing his whole face. He was powerless. (For a description of Antichrist's doom, see Dan. 7:8–11,26; 2 Thess. 2:8; Rev. 19:19–21; 20:10.)

MAIN IDEA REVIEW: *Messiah is the Good Shepherd who truly cares for the sheep—the world's people. Sadly many reject his offer of loving leadership and suffer the consequences.*

III. CONCLUSION

Jonestown Massacre

Jim (James Warren) Jones founded his People's Temple in Indianapolis in 1955 His emphasis on human freedom, racial equality, and love was popular, and during the 1950s he gathered a large following of over nine hundred members. (Later his message became explicitly socialistic or even communistic.) Jones professed to be a prophet of God, then Christ himself; as proof, he claimed to perform miracles such as curing cancer. Jones preached that the end of the world would arrive on July 15, 1967, and he moved his group to Ukiah, California (a place he believed to be safe), to wait for the imminent nuclear war. When the end did not come, he moved his church to San Francisco and Los Angeles.

After a magazine exposé raised suspicions of illegal activities within the organization, Jones left with some of the membership for the jungles of Guyana and founded a supposedly "utopian community" dubbed Jonestown. Rumors of human rights abuses prompted Leo Ryan, a California congressman, to visit Jonestown in November 1978 to investigate. As Ryan's group and fourteen defectors from the cult prepared to leave from a nearby airstrip, heavily armed members of the temple's security guards (acting on Jones's orders) arrived and opened fire, killing Ryan and four others. Fearing retribution, Jones forced his followers to commit suicide by drinking a cyanide-laced drink on November 18. Guards were ordered to shoot anyone who refused or tried to escape. The death toll was 913, including 276 children. Jones was found shot through the head.

We could mention countless other "foolish-worthless shepherds" like Jim Jones. David Koresh convinced the Branch Davidians that he was the messiah, and most of them perished in flames as their compound in Waco, Texas, burned to the ground in April 1993. Marshall Applewhite of the Heaven's Gate cult led thirty-nine people to commit suicide in March 1997 by promising they would be transported to a spaceship of aliens supposedly hidden behind the Hale-Bopp Comet! James Dobson reported in his January 2002 newsletter that the Indian guru Maharishi Yogi's latest project is to have forty thousand yogis in India hop while assuming the lotus position. Supposedly, this will create a force field that will repel hatred and spread happiness throughout the world!

What we see in our world today reinforces Zechariah's 2,500-year-old message. Foolish, worthless shepherds abound and lead their followers to ruin, eternally and often temporally. Jesus the Messiah is the Good Shepherd who loves us and proved it by giving his life on the cross for our sins. If we accept him, we will receive an abundant life of peace and joy now and heaven some day. How could anyone pass up an offer like that?

PRINCIPLES

- Rejection of the Good Shepherd (Messiah) leads to ruin.
- God will judge unfaithful leaders (shepherds).
- Following Christ brings divine blessing ("Favor") and unity ("Union") to a family, community, church, or nation.
- Divine protection rests upon nations that follow the Lord.
- Believers will discern the truth of God's Word.
- Christ's worth is not appreciated by the majority.
- God's patience with sinners will some day come to an end.
- When individuals and nations reject the Good Shepherd (Messiah) as their leader, foolish and worthless shepherds (leaders) step in to fill the void.

APPLICATIONS

- If you have been rejecting Christ as your Lord, surrender your life to him now.
- Think of a personal experience in which Christ has especially blessed or cared for you.
- Share with a friend how wonderful it is to have Christ as a loving shepherd. Point out reasons for Christ's greatness.
- Pray that your nation will choose leaders who honor Christ.
- List the services that a good shepherd performs for the sheep and apply these to your personal leadership responsibilities in church, family, and community.
- Read Psalm 23 and note the blessings of being the Lord's sheep set forth in this great passage.

IV. LIFE APPLICATION

Where Is Jesus?

After terrorists attacked the World Trade Center and the Pentagon on September 11, 2001, President Bush gathered a number of religious leaders in the National Cathedral in Washington to give comfort to the nation. Various faiths were represented, including Muslims, Jews, and Christians. One of the speakers was Billy Graham, who delivered an outstanding message in which he spoke of our hope in Christ. My local newspaper printed the text of

Graham's address in the next morning's edition. As I read his words, I was a bit puzzled because there was no mention of Jesus. "God" appeared often and "Christian" once, but the words *Jesus, Christ,* and *cross* were nowhere to be found. I wondered, "Where is Jesus?"

A day or two later, the mystery was solved when the newspaper printed another version of Graham's sermon, apparently after people had voiced complaints. Comparing the two, I found that in the first printing all references to Jesus and the cross had been edited out! Evidently, the name of Jesus was too offensive to be included.

Charles Colson tells of similar experiences with the press in his book *Kingdoms in Conflict* (Grand Rapids. MI: Zondervan, 1987):

> Over the years since I became a Christian, I have always deliberately explained that I have "accepted Jesus Christ." These words are invariably translated into "Colson's professed religious experience." I discovered that one major U.S. daily, as a matter of policy, will not print the two words *Jesus Christ* together; when combined, the editor says, it represents an editorial judgment.

Talking about God is rather fashionable today (especially after September 11), but Jesus the Messiah is still rejected by, and even offensive to, the majority of the world, just as he was two thousand years ago.

Why does the name of Jesus Christ (Messiah) make people uncomfortable? First, as the sinless Son of God, Jesus exposes sin, and people don't like that. Long before Jesus' birth, Plato (428–348 B.C.), the Greek philosopher, predicted: "If ever the truly good man were to appear, a man who would tell the truth, he would have his eyes gouged out and in the end be crucified." Second, Jesus claimed to be the only way to heaven: "I am the way and the truth and the life. No one comes to the Father except through me" (John 14:6). That is particularly distasteful to our politically correct, ecumenical world. Third, Jesus claimed to be God himself (John 5:18; 8:58; 10:30). "How audacious!" the world cries. "Jesus was a nice fellow and a good teacher, but God? No way!"

Rather than taking offense, the world should rejoice that God became a man and provided a way for the human race to receive eternal life through Jesus the Messiah. As Christ proclaimed, "I am the good shepherd. The good shepherd lays down his life for the sheep" (John 10:11). Jesus died on the cross so people may have their sins forgiven and inherit a home in heaven.

Let us entreat those in our world to accept, not reject, this wonderful Good Shepherd as their Lord and Savior.

V. PRAYER

Lord, thank you for being our Good Shepherd who cares for us and always watches over our lives. May the people of our world turn from following shepherds who oppress and lead them astray and receive you as their Lord. In the name of Jesus Christ we pray. Amen.

VI. DEEPER DISCOVERIES

A. Hebrew Poetry (11:1–3,17)

Zechariah penned verses 1–3,17 and other portions of chapters 9–14 in poetical form (9:1–10:12; 13:7–9). Hebrew poetry may seem strange to those in the Western world because it is not characterized by rhyme but is more analogous to English free verse. This is one reason that until relatively modern times scholars did not adequately comprehend the scope of Hebrew poetry in the Old Testament. The majority of the so-called books of Poetry (Job, Psalms, Proverbs, Ecclesiastes, and Song of Solomon) are written in poetical form, but as we discover in Zechariah, Hebrew poetry is not limited to these books. As a matter of fact, one-third of the Old Testament is written in poetry, and it is especially common in the prophetic books.

Modern translations like the NIV arrange poetic material in stanza form so the English reader may easily identify it. Yet how do translators distinguish poetry from prose in the Old Testament? In A.D. 1753 Bishop Robert Lowth published an epoch-making work identifying parallelism as the key characteristic of Hebrew poetry. Lowth set forth three types of Hebrew parallelism: synonymous, antithetic, and synthetic. Following is a description of these basic categories with a very clear example of each from the Book of Proverbs.

Synonymous parallelism repeats the same idea in the second line with different wording.

> Pride goes before destruction,
>
> a haughty spirit before a fall (Prov. 16:18).

"Pride" and "a haughty spirit" are synonyms, as are "destruction" and "a fall." Repeating essentially the same thought with different words was done to emphasize the writer's point.

Antithetic parallelism contrasts the second line with the first.

> For lack of guidance a nation falls,
> but many advisers make victory sure (Prov. 11:14).

Proverbs is filled with examples of this kind of parallelism.

Synthetic parallelism completes or supplements the thought of the first line in the second line.

> Wine is a mocker and beer a brawler;
> whoever is led astray by them is not wise (Prov. 20:1).

Zechariah 11:1 seems best to fit the synthetic category and 11:2 the synonymous ("Wail, O pine tree" = "Wail, oaks of Bashan"). Other categories have been proposed, such as emblematic, climactic, or inverted (chiastic), but these might best be viewed as variations of the three basic types identified by Lowth.

Hebrew poetry was used for prophetic speech as well as for music (particularly the Psalms). The writer's choice of poetry to convey the message was intended to provide emphasis and power to the message. For example, the destruction of the land is driven home forcefully by Zechariah's repetition in verse 2:

> Wail, O pine tree, for the cedar has fallen;
> the stately trees are ruined!
> Wail, oaks of Bashan;
> the dense forest has been cut down!

We can feel the emotion as we read the text.

Hebrew poetry, in particular, makes use of many literary devices (some only perceptible in the original language) such as simile, metaphor, word plays on the sound and meaning of words (paronomasia), and acrostic (verses beginning with subsequent letters of the Hebrew alphabet). Even from a literary standpoint, the Bible is the most magnificent book ever written.

B. Destruction of Trees and Pastures (11:1–3)

In verses 1–3 Zechariah depicted the destruction of trees, forests, and pastures. Walton, Matthews, and Chavalas comment:

Forestation and pasturage are valuable resources in this land that offers so little of them. Vast stretches of potentially productive land become trackless waste land when the greenery is destroyed. The modern state of Israel is reclaiming the land's productivity by reintroducing forestation into desolate areas. Ancient invaders strategically destroyed farmland, pasturage and forestation when seeking to cripple a nation long-term (Walton, Matthews, and Chavalas, BBCOT, 806).

Whether one takes the passage figuratively (e.g., as a poetic description of the arrogant nations' destruction) or as the description of a literal invading army, the imagery is drawn from the practice of burning the fields and razing the trees carried out by invading troops.

C. Shepherds in the Bible (11:3,5,8–9,15–17)

In the Bible shepherds are referred to over one hundred times and the word *sheep* appears over two hundred times. The word *shepherd* is derived from a verb that means "to feed, pasture, tend," reflecting that one of the shepherd's primary duties was to lead the sheep to food and water. The shepherd theme (or motif) is frequent in the Book of Zechariah, with "shepherd" or "shepherds" occurring eleven times.

Shepherding was an honored profession in ancient Israel. Sheep provided food, clothing, and leather. Sheep were also a key offering in Israel's sacrificial system (Exod. 20:24). Owning a large flock of sheep was a sign of wealth. Adam's son Abel (Gen. 4:2) was the first shepherd in the Bible, and shepherding was the primary occupation of the patriarchs: Abraham, Isaac, and Jacob. Even females served in this capacity, since Jacob's wife Rachel was specifically called a "shepherdess" (Gen. 29:9).

William Barclay describes the shepherd's challenging profession:

The life of the Palestinian shepherd was very hard. In Palestine no flock ever grazes without a shepherd, and the shepherd is never off duty. There is little grass, and the sheep are bound to wander far afield. There are no protecting walls, and the sheep have ever to be watched. On either side of the narrow plateau the ground dips sharply down to the craggy deserts and the sheep are always liable to wander away and to get lost. The shepherd's task was constant and dangerous, for, in addition, he had to guard the flock against wild animals, especially against wolves, and there were ever thieves and robbers ready to steal the sheep. . . . Constant vigilance, fearless courage, patient love for his flock, were the necessary characteristics of the shepherd (Barclay, *The Gospel of John*, Westminster John Knox Press, 1975, 2:61–62).

Little wonder that David felt it appropriate to apply the shepherd figure to the tender leadership of the Lord himself in Psalm 23.

In Israel and throughout the Ancient Near East, "shepherd" came to designate a variety of leadership positions: prophets, priests, kings, and other civil rulers. "Shepherd" was a common figure for Israel's kings (2 Sam. 5:2; cp. Isa. 44:28; Jer. 23:2–4), and civil rulers or kings were the focus of Zechariah's references to the "shepherd(s)" in 11:5,9,15–17.

Messiah is often designated as "shepherd" in both the Old and New Testaments. Israel's rejection of the Good Shepherd in Zechariah 11 speaks of their refusal to receive the Messiah as king (cp. Ezek. 34:23; Mic. 5:4). In the New Testament, Jesus is identified as Israel's Shepherd-King in Matthew 2:6 ("a ruler who will be the shepherd of my people Israel"). Christ's self-sacrifice and love for his followers explains his claim to be the Good Shepherd who "lays down his life for the sheep" in John 10:11. Unlike the "worthless shepherd" (Zech. 11:17), Jesus will never desert the flock!

D. Prophecies of Messiah's First Coming (11:8,12–13)

In chapter 11 the prophet shared four amazing prophecies that were fulfilled at Christ's first advent. First, he accurately predicted that the Messiah would be rejected. To be sure, many people received Jesus as Savior and Lord, but the Jewish nation as a whole spurned his offer to be their Shepherd-King. Jesus declared, "But first he [the Son of Man] must suffer many things and be rejected by this generation" (Luke 17:25). Second, Judas betrayed Jesus for thirty pieces of silver (Matt. 26:15; 27:3,9), exactly the sum Zechariah prophesied. Third, filled with remorse, Judas threw the money into the temple when he returned it to the Jewish leaders (Matt. 27:3–5). Fourth, the chief priests used the money to buy a potter's field for a burial place for foreigners (Matt. 27:6–10). Thus the money went to the potter. All of these prophecies were fulfilled literally and precisely in the life of Jesus Christ, just as the prophet had foretold five hundred years earlier. Are these merely coincidences? Of course not.

These four cases should be proof enough that Jesus is the promised Messiah, but there are many more. In his excellent book *Evidence That Demands a Verdict* (Nashville: Thomas Nelson, 1992 [orig. 1972]), Josh McDowell discusses sixty-one specific Old Testament prophecies fulfilled in Jesus. A sampling of these may be found below. Each listing contains the messianic prophecy, Old Testament reference, and New Testament fulfillment in Jesus. (McDowell includes prophecies from Zechariah 11, but these were discussed above and are not cited again.)

1. Born of a virgin (Isa. 7:14; Matt. 1:18,24–25)
2. From David's line (Jer. 23:5; Luke 3:23,31 and many others)
3. Born at Bethlehem (Mic. 5:2; Matt. 2:1)
4. Will be a prophet (Deut. 18:18; Matt. 21:11)
5. Will be a priest (Ps. 110:4; Heb. 3:1; 5:5–6)
6. Will be a king (Ps. 2:6; Zech. 9:9; Matt. 21:5; 27:37)
7. Preceded by a messenger (Isa. 40:3; Matt. 3:1–2)
8. Will enter Jerusalem on a donkey (Zech. 9:9; Luke 19:35–37; also as king)
9. "Stone of stumbling" to Jews (Ps. 118:22; 1 Pet. 2:7)
10. Resurrection (Ps. 16:10; Acts 2:31)
11. Forsaken by his disciples (Zech. 13:7; Mark 14:50)
12. Silent before accusers (Isa. 53:7; Matt. 27:12)
13. Wounded and bruised (Isa. 53:5; Matt. 27:26)
14. Struck and spit upon (Isa. 50:6; Matt. 26:67)
15. Mocked (Ps. 22:7–8; Matt. 27:31)
16. Hands and feet pierced (Ps. 22:16; Luke 23:33)
17. Crucified with thieves (Isa. 53:12; Matt. 27:38)
18. Rejected by his own people (Isa. 53:3; John 7:5,48)
19. Stared upon (Ps. 22:17; Luke 23:35)
20. Clothes divided and lots cast (Ps. 22:18; John 19:23–24)
21. His forsaken cry (Ps. 22:1; Matt. 27:46)
22. Bones not broken (Ps. 34:20; John 19:33)
23. Side pierced (Zech. 12:10; John 19:34)
24. Buried in a rich man's tomb (Isa. 53:9; Matt. 27:57–60).

What are the odds that all of these prophecies could be fulfilled coincidentally in one person? McDowell cites an analysis by Peter Stoner in *Science Speaks,* which demonstrates that coincidence is ruled out by the science of probability. Stoner concluded that the odds of just eight of these prophecies being fulfilled in one man would be one chance in more than one trillion, an inconceivable number.

It has even been suggested that Jesus and his disciples set out to fulfill prophecy in an attempt to deceive. Such a plan could never have succeeded because many of these predictions were beyond human control—place of birth, manner of birth, betrayal, manner of death, casting lots for clothing, piercing, and his burial place.

The only reasonable explanation is that these were supernatural prophecies revealed to the Old Testament writers by the Spirit of God. Their fulfillment is one of many confirmations that the Bible is the Word of God and that Jesus of Nazareth is the Messiah. Prophecies of Jesus' second advent will be fulfilled just as literally and precisely.

E. Matthew 27:9–10 and Zechariah 11:12–13

Matthew understood the purchase of the potter's field with Judas Iscariot's blood money to be a fulfillment of Old Testament prophecy: "Then what was spoken by Jeremiah the prophet was fulfilled: 'They took the thirty silver coins, the price set on him by the people of Israel, and they used them to buy the potter's field, as the Lord commanded me'" (Matt. 27:9–10). The apostle attributed the prophecy to Jeremiah, yet the greater portion is clearly from Zechariah 11:12–13: "I told them, 'If you think it best, give me my pay; but if not, keep it.' So they paid me thirty pieces of silver. And the LORD said to me, 'Throw it to the potter'—the handsome price at which they priced me! So I took the thirty pieces of silver and threw them into the house of the LORD to the potter."

Two problems confront us here—Matthew attributed the prophecy to Jeremiah rather than Zechariah, and Zechariah's prophecy says nothing about buying a field. How may we understand Matthew's quotation? Many explanations have been offered, but the following are the most plausible.

1. Matthew combined prophecies from both Zechariah and Jeremiah. Usually Matthew's allusion is connected to Jeremiah 18:1–6 (Jeremiah's visit to a potter's house) and 32:6–9,25 (a field purchased by the prophet in Anathoth for seventeen shekels of silver). Some scholars believe Matthew had Jeremiah 19:1–13 in mind. Jeremiah's name was mentioned because he was the better known and more prominent of the two prophets. This view is possible, but the difficulty is that none of these Jeremiah passages speak directly of purchasing a potter's field.

2. Feinberg provides a helpful summary of the second alternative:

> The Talmudic tradition shows that the prophetic writings in the order of their place in the sacred books were Jeremiah, Ezekiel, Isaiah, etc. This order is found in many Hebrew MSS [manuscripts]. . . . Matthew, then, quoted the passage as from the roll of the prophets,

which roll is cited by the first book. Compare the use of "psalms" in Luke 24:44 where the entire third division of the Hebrew canon is meant (Feinberg, *God Remembers*, 169).

This latter view is reasonable and avoids the difficulties associated with the first explanation. Therefore, it seems preferable.

As for the purchase of the potter's field, Zechariah simply said that the money went to the potter. He did not specify for what purpose, but later revelation shows that it was given to the potter as the purchase price for a field to bury foreigners (Matt. 27:7). What a marvelous prophecy!

VII. TEACHING OUTLINE

A. INTRODUCTION

1. Lead Story: Wrong Again!
2. Context: Chapter 11 of Zechariah opens with an account of the destruction of the land (vv. 1–3). This was probably perpetrated by the Roman armies on Palestine in A.D. 70 as a result of the rejection of their messianic shepherd. The Messiah's offer to shepherd the nation and its refusal are set forth in verses 4–14. In this remarkable prophecy, Zechariah predicts the rejection of Jesus Christ by the nation and his betrayal for thirty pieces of silver. Having rejected the Messiah, the people are left to worthless shepherds, who oppress them and lead them astray (vv. 15–17).
3. Transition: As we look into this chapter, we discover several spiritual truths: (1) The rejection of God's Messiah brings ruin, both individually and nationally. (2) Christ loves all people and nations and desires to be their loving Shepherd-King. Then he will care for and protect them from harm. (3) When Christ is rejected, foolish and worthless leaders fill the void and lead people astray. (4) Zechariah predicted events in Christ's life over five hundred years before they occurred, confirming that Jesus is the Messiah and the Bible is a supernatural book.

B. COMMENTARY

1. The Result of Rejection (11:1–3)
2. The Wicked Shepherds (11:4–6)

3. The Good Shepherd Rejected (11:7–14)
4. The Worthless Shepherd (11:15–17)

C. CONCLUSION: JONESBORO MASSACRE

VIII. ISSUES FOR DISCUSSION

1. Name some ways that Jesus, your Good Shepherd, has taken care of you.
2. What are some differences between Jesus Christ (the Good Shepherd) and other religious leaders? In what ways is Christ greater?
3. How do you think the Good Shepherd felt when his offer of love and care was rejected by Israel two thousand years ago? How do you think he feels when people reject him today?
4. What are some blessings for individuals when they follow Jesus as their shepherd (Lord)? For nations? What are some consequences of rejection—for individuals and nations?
5. How does fulfilled prophecy confirm the messianic claims of Jesus and the supernatural character of the Bible?
6. Give examples of some foolish and worthless shepherd-leaders in our world today. In what ways do they parallel the wicked shepherds referred to in Zechariah 11?

Zechariah 12–14

Israel's Future

I. **INTRODUCTION**
"Dead" Woman Wakes Up!

II. **COMMENTARY**
A verse-by-verse explanation of these chapters.

III. **CONCLUSION**
When Is Jesus Coming?

An overview of the principles and applications from these chapters.

IV. **LIFE APPLICATION**
The Way Things Ought to Be

Melding these chapters to life.

V. **PRAYER**
Tying these chapters to life with God.

VI. **DEEPER DISCOVERIES**
Historical, geographical, and grammatical enrichment of the commentary.

VII. **TEACHING OUTLINE**
Suggested step-by-step group study of these chapters.

VIII. **ISSUES FOR DISCUSSION**
Zeroing these chapters in on daily life.

Quote

"*The* future is as bright as the promises of God."

A d o n i r a m   J u d s o n

Zechariah 12–14

IN A NUTSHELL

In chapters 12–14 Zechariah presents a panoramic overview of Israel's future. In chapter 12 we find Israel settled in her land in the last days. God delivers the nation from her enemies, and Israel finally receives her promised Messiah with true repentance. God forgives the nation and cleanses the land from sinful practices. In 13:7–14:2 the prophet describes a time of trouble for Israel, presumably the result of striking her shepherd (13:7). The Lord's coming to earth to rescue his people and the wonderful new world under his reign are depicted in 14:3–21.

Israel's Future

I. INTRODUCTION

"Dead" Woman Wakes Up!

*I*n February 2002 seventy-seven-year-old Frances Foster of Brooklyn was found unconscious on her bathroom floor and mistakenly declared dead by paramedics. For hours the error went undetected until she was being placed in a body bag. According to the woman's daughter, a medical examiner's official said her mother "suddenly moved and opened her eyes and he jumped back, startled." His shock is understandable! The woman had suffered a stroke and was immediately hospitalized when the mistake was discovered.

Of course, this woman did not actually die and come back to life, but the nation of Israel has died twice and been resurrected each time. From the destruction of Jerusalem in 586 B.C. until Zerubbabel, Joshua, Zechariah, and the group of about fifty thousand Jews returned soon after 539 B.C., the nation of Israel was dead and buried. Then God supernaturally raised this lifeless nation back to life just as he had promised through the prophet Ezekiel (Ezek. 37:1–14). After the Roman destruction, Israel was once more dispersed among the nations, and for almost two thousand years the nation did not exist. But on May 14, 1948, Israel declared itself an independent state and incredibly came back to life once more. Historically, dead nations usually stay that way, and no record of any other nation's revival after such a long period is known. Yet everywhere in Scripture Israel is presented as dwelling in their land when Christ returns. As in Zechariah's day, Israel's reestablishment in modern times is a result of God's incredible power.

Israel is in a very precarious position today. It is beset by internal and external threats of titanic proportions. We might wonder if this tiny nation can possibly survive. In chapters 12–14 Zechariah provides a panoramic overview of Israel's future. So read and be amazed as God's prophet of twenty-five hundred years ago answers the question, What will happen to Israel?

II. COMMENTARY

Israel's Future

MAIN IDEA: *God will deliver Israel from an onslaught of the world's powers, and at that time the nation will repent and receive her rejected Messiah. Then Israel will share in Messiah's glorious kingdom, a kingdom characterized by peace, blessing, and righteousness.*

A A Problem for the Nations (12:1–3)

SUPPORTING IDEA: *Jerusalem will be a problem ("a cup" and "an immovable rock") for the world's nations.*

12:1. Now we come to the second oracle (or "burden") **concerning Israel.** Chapters 12–14 form a unit with one overriding theme: Israel's future. Zechariah's audience would have been keenly interested in this subject. They had reestablished the nation, but it was fragile and its fate was uncertain. What would happen to their beloved Israel? Would it survive? In this final oracle, Zechariah assured his fellow Jews that their nation would be in existence at the end of the present age and by God's grace would be delivered from her enemies and enter into its messianic golden age. Even though difficulties lay ahead for Israel, the best was yet to come.

The fulfillment of chapters 12–14 is yet future, since no coalition of nations or battles to compare with the following have ever occurred. Certainly the Messiah has not appeared on the Mount of Olives as chapter 14 describes. Another indication of the oracle's future setting is the repetition (sixteen times) of the eschatological phrase, "on that day." According to Feinberg, "From the angle of the light these chapters throw on the consummation of Israel's history, they are among the most important to be found in the prophetic Scriptures" (Feinberg, *Minor Prophets*, 330).

What follows is astounding, and the authority for Zechariah's message is crucial. Who dared to make such audacious pronouncements? The speaker was none other than the sovereign Lord of the universe, the Creator of the **heavens** and **earth.** With such power at his disposal, the Lord can certainly defeat the world's nations and rescue his people. The phrase **the spirit of man within him** shows that human beings consist of more than the physical. Within our bodies is a spirit that lives on eternally after death, a concept understood in Old Testament times (Eccl. 12:7).

12:2. In verses 2–3 the siege of **Jerusalem** is described (cp. 14:1–5). Two images are used to describe the fate of the armies who come against the city—**a cup** and "an immovable rock" (v. 3). Like those drunk on strong wine (cup), they will stagger and fall (**reeling**). The *cup* is a well-known symbol of God's wrath. In Isaiah 51:22–23a we read, "This is what your Sovereign LORD says, your God, who defends his people: 'See, I have taken out of your [Jerusalem's] hand the cup that made you stagger; from that cup, the goblet of my wrath, you will never drink again. I will put it into the hands of your tormentors,'" and in Revelation 16:19, "The great city split into three parts, and the cities of the nations collapsed. God remembered Babylon the Great and gave her the cup filled with the wine of the fury of his wrath" (see also Jer. 25:15,17; Rev. 14:10). Not only Jerusalem but the whole country (**Judah**) will be under attack.

12:3. On that day appears six times in chapter 12. This invasion is part of the "day of the LORD" judgment on the nations and immediately precedes Messiah's second advent with his "holy ones" (14:4–5; 2 Thess. 1:7; Rev. 19:11–14). The phrase **all the nations of the earth** points to the universal scope of this war which should be associated with the future battle (or campaign) of Armageddon (Rev. 16:13–16; 19:19). **Jerusalem** will be like an **immovable rock** (literally, "stone of burden") that injures anyone who tries to lift it. Israel will not be destroyed. Rather, God will use this assault on Israel to bring judgment on sinful nations (Joel 3:1–2).

B Deliverance from Invaders (12:4–9)

SUPPORTING IDEA: *The Lord will deliver Israel from an assault of the world's nations.*

12:4–9. Now Israel's God-given victory is detailed. (1) Divine immobilization of enemy armies. Lindsey remarks, "The characteristic chaos of a cavalry defeat is here ascribed to divine intervention" (Lindsey, 1566). War horses will **panic** in fear, and the bravest warrior will be struck with uncontrollable terror, **madness**. The three Hebrew terms rendered "panic" ("confusion"), "madness," and **blind** appear together once more in Deuteronomy 28:28. (2) Recognition of the Lord as the source of victory. Judah's **leaders** (less likely, "clans") will recognize that Jerusalem's deliverance was (or "will be") accomplished by divine intervention. (3) Empowerment of Judah's defenders. The Lord (**I**) will empower Judah's forces so that they can cut through the enemy like fire devouring dry wood or **sheaves** of grain, delivering the outlying areas of the country **first** so that **Jerusalem's inhabitants** will have no cause for feeling superior to the rest of the people. God will protect (shield) Jerusalem and so empower its soldiers that the weakest of them will fight like David, the slayer of Goliath the giant. The nations will not merely be fighting Israel; they will be doing battle with God—the Angel of the LORD. (4) Destruction of the invading nations. Israel's amazing deliverance from the nations is repeatedly attributed to divine intervention throughout the passage. The Lord's personal involvement is described in more detail in 14:3–5.

ℂ Deliverance from Sin (12:10–13:6)

SUPPORTING IDEA: *When Israel repents and receives her rejected Messiah as King, the Lord will forgive her sin and remove wickedness from the land.*

12:10. In the earlier verses of chapter 12, Israel is delivered from physical harm, but in 12:10–13:6 something far more wonderful is described—Israel's spiritual deliverance from sin. By God's **grace** the Jewish people will finally recognize their Messiah as Lord and Savior. **Spirit** could refer to a change of attitude (**a spirit of**, NIV), but here the word more likely denotes the Holy Spirit who by God's grace convicts Israel of its sin of rejecting the Messiah (11:4–14) and leads the people to pray (**supplication**) to God in repentance. The phrase **house of David** apparently designates the nation's leaders and **the inhabitants of Jerusalem**, the common people—thus excluding no Israelites (cp. 13:1). In this context "look on" means to look with favor or to regard with esteem. Israel's eyes will be opened to understand the true worth of this "pierced one."

Who is this person—**the one they have pierced**? First, he is the Lord God—**I will pour out . . . look on me**. Except for verses 7–8, God speaks in the first person throughout chapter 12. Yet how could God be pierced? Some contend that we must take this piercing as figurative for causing pain or sorrow, but there is a better explanation, as we shall see.

Second, he is someone "pierced" by the Jewish people. Historically, Jesus was crucified and literally pierced (John 19:34) by the Romans upon the request of the Jewish leaders. Pointing out this fact is not intended as an anti-Semitic barb. Many Jews in Jesus' day followed him, and most had no direct part in his death. In truth, all of us are responsible for Christ's crucifixion since he died for the sins of the world, and all of us have sinned. Nevertheless, the fact remains that the Jewish leaders pressured Pilate to crucify Jesus.

Third, he is the Messiah. According to Feinberg, "It is not some unknown martyr of whom Zechariah is speaking but of the coming Messiah Himself. The oldest interpreters of the passage, both Jewish and Christian, so understood it" (Feinberg, *Minor Prophets*, 333).

Fourth, he is Jesus. Commenting on Jesus' piercing by the Roman soldier, the apostle John quoted this verse: "And, as another scripture says, 'They will look on the one they have pierced'" (John 19:37). Thus John identified Jesus as this pierced one. Now Zechariah's prophecy becomes clear. God could be pierced because Jesus the Messiah was God in the flesh.

In this verse the first and second advents of our Lord are connected. At his first coming, Messiah was pierced for the sins of the world; at his second coming, Israel will recognize ("look on") Jesus as their promised Messiah and place their faith in him. According to God's covenant promises, the nation will be forgiven (Jer. 31:31–34; Ezek. 36:22–32; Rom. 11:25–27). Jesus predicted that upon his future return to Jerusalem, the people would proclaim, "Blessed is he who comes in the name of the Lord" (Matt. 23:39). Israel's sincerity is demonstrated by deep, heartfelt repentance. **They will mourn** ("wail" or "lament" with loud cries) over their sinful rejection of the Messiah **as one mourns for an only child, and grieve bitterly for him as one grieves for a firstborn son.**

12:11. The phrase **like the weeping of Hadad Rimmon in the plain of Megiddo** refers to the heartbreak over the death of Judah's beloved and godly King Josiah, who was killed in battle with Pharaoh Neco in 609 B.C. (2 Kgs. 23:29–30; 2 Chr. 35:22–27). Hadad Rimmon, a site near Megiddo, is a compound of two names of Syrian gods, Hadad and Rimmon (2 Kgs. 5:18).

12:12–14. The whole nation will mourn over their sin of unbelief from the citizens (**each clan by itself, with their wives by themselves**) to the leadership—civil rulers (**the house of David**), prophets (**Nathan** the prophet, or possibly the son of David, 2 Sam. 5:14), and priests (**Levi** and **Shimei** of the family of Gershon, son of Levi, Num. 3:17–18,21). Levi and Shimei apparently represent different classes of priests. According to Barker, "Individually and corporately, this is the experience of Leviticus 16 (the Day of Atonement) and Psalm 51 (a penitential psalm) on a national scale" (Barker, 685).

13:1. The phrase **on that day** denotes the same time as the events of chapter 12 (cp. 12:3). Israel's repentance and faith were set forth in chapter 12; now the nation's forgiveness is picturesquely described. As the gushing waters of a **fountain** wash away physical pollution, God will open a supernatural stream to cleanse Israel's **sin** and moral **impurity** (literally, something abhorred or shunned).

Cleansing sins with water is a not-infrequent figure in the Bible. In Ezekiel 36:25 the Lord promised Israel, "I will sprinkle clean water on you, and you will be clean; I will cleanse you from all your impurities and from all your idols." In Ephesians 5:25–26 we read, "Husbands, love your wives, just as Christ loved the church and gave himself up for her to make her holy, cleansing her by the washing with water through the word" (cp. Titus 3:5). In light of Zechariah 13:1 and Ezekiel 36:25, no wonder Jesus chided Nicodemus for not understanding what he meant by his declaration, "No one can enter the kingdom of God unless he is born of water and the Spirit" (John 3:5). Nicodemus, "Israel's teacher," should have known from Old Testament Scriptures that water symbolized cleansing from sin (John 3:10). Jesus was saying that in order to become part of God's family, persons must have their sins forgiven (by Christ's atonement) and be regenerated by the Holy Spirit.

In this verse we see the apostle Paul's words fulfilled:

> So that you will not be conceited, brothers, I do not want you to be unaware of this secret: a partial hardening has come to Israel until the full number of the Gentiles has come in. And in this way all Israel will be saved, as it is written: The Liberator will come from Zion; He will turn away godlessness from Jacob. And this will be My covenant with them, when I take away their sins (Rom. 11:25–27 HCSB).

At Calvary this cleansing fountain was opened potentially for the nation; now it becomes an actuality. What a wonderful promise for Israel!

However, the truth of this text reaches far beyond the scope of one nation. All who place their faith in Jesus the Messiah and repent—Jew or Gentile—will be forgiven. God will wipe the slate of our lives clean and carry our sins so far away that they can never be found again—"as far as the east is from the west" (Ps. 103:12). In the words of William Cowper's great hymn (based on this verse):

> There is a fountain filled with blood
> Drawn from Immanuel's veins;
> And sinners plunged beneath that flood
> Lose all their guilty stains.

What a wonderful Savior!

13:2. In verse 1 Zechariah described the internal cleansing of individuals from sin; now we see the external manifestations of wickedness removed from the land. Not only will **idols** (all forms of false religion) be banished; Israel will so completely forsake them that the names of these false gods will be erased from their memory. As verses 3–6 make clear, these **prophets** are false religious leaders. Moreover, true prophets will no longer be needed after Christ's return for two reasons: divine revelation will be complete, and the Lord will communicate directly with his people during the messianic age (Isa.

2:3). **The spirit of impurity,** probably better "unclean spirit" (KJV, NASB, NRSV), appears only here in the Old Testament. The phrase may denote an impure disposition or demonic spirits who inspire false religion (1 Cor. 10:20; 1 Tim. 4:1). "Unclean spirit" appears often in the New Testament for demon (Matt. 12:43; Mark 1:23; 5:8; in KJV, NASB, NRSV). Jesus warned that false prophets would continue to deceive throughout this present age (Matt. 24:4–5,11,23–24).

13:3. False religion will be so abhorrent that if anyone dares to prophesy **lies,** his own parents will take the lead in executing him, according to the procedure outlined in Deuteronomy 13:6–10. Presumably, this is a hypothetical case since Zechariah 12:10–13:1 indicates that the entire nation will be believers (at least at the beginning of Messiah's reign).

13:4. Obviously, in the face of such a severe penalty, false prophets will fear to identify themselves. Elijah wore a **garment of hair** (2 Kgs. 1:8), and this type of clothing came to be identified with the prophetic office. Later, John the Baptist wore clothes of camel's hair (Matt. 3:4). A false prophet might wear this garment to pass himself off as a true prophet (**to deceive**), like a wolf in sheep's clothing (Matt. 7:15).

13:5–6. When questioned, the false prophet will deny the allegation and claim to be engaged in the honorable occupation of farming. False prophets sometimes mutilated themselves, hoping to gain the attention and favor of their gods (1 Kgs. 18:28). If asked about these **wounds,** they contend that they were inflicted in friendly wrestling with **friends** or by parents ("friends" = literally, "my loved ones"). The NIV's **on your body** is literally, "between your hands." A few commentators entertain the messianic view here, understanding these wounds to be those inflicted on the hands of Jesus at Calvary. As inviting as this interpretation may be, false prophets are plainly the subject of verses 3–6. "Between your hands" most naturally would suggest the area between the arms—the chest or back. The wounds would be visible when the man stripped for work.

ⅅ A Time of Trouble (13:7–14:2)

SUPPORTING IDEA: *Israel will endure a time of trouble, precipitated by her rejection of the Good Shepherd.*

13:7. Zechariah returned to his familiar shepherd theme (10:2; 11:9,15–17). In chapter 11 the Messiah, Israel's Good Shepherd, was rejected; here he is struck by the **sword**—a figure for a violent death (Ezek. 5:2; 21:14). Jesus verified the messianic interpretation and specifically identified himself as this slain **shepherd** in Matthew 26:31: "Then Jesus told them, 'This very night you will all fall away on account of me, for it is written: "I will strike the shepherd, and the sheep of the flock will be scattered""" (cp. Mark 14:27).

At first glance verse 7 may seem out of place. In 12:10–13:6, Zechariah described Israel's future faith in the Messiah, the nation's forgiveness, and the wonderful new age. Suddenly, we are introduced once more to Israel's rejection of the Messiah (11:4–14) and even his death. Then there follows from verse 8 through chapter 14 a second account of Israel under attack, her miraculous deliverance by the Lord, and the messianic age. Actually, the verse is not out of place at all, but it explains Israel's predicament in 13:8–14:2 and the need for God's intervention. Israel's troubles described in 12:2–9 and 13:7–14:2 will come upon her for rejecting the Messiah (11:8–10), and these trials will continue until the end when she repents and is forgiven.

Zechariah 13:8–14:21 is a further description of the same invasion, divine rescue, and new world depicted in 12:1–13:6. We may observe a similar pattern in both accounts: (1) Messiah's rejection (11:4–14; 13:7); (2) Israel under attack (12:2–3; 13:8; 14:1–2); (3) Israel's deliverance by the Lord (12:4–9; 14:3–5); (4) Israel's faith in Messiah and forgiveness (12:10–13:1; 13:9; also implied in 14:9–11, 21); and (5) the glorious messianic age (13:2–6; 14:6–21).

In verse 7 we find three descriptive titles for the Messiah—"shepherd," "man," and the one "who is close to me." The Messiah is called **my shepherd**, emphasizing that he was chosen by **the LORD Almighty**. The word **man** (*gever,* "strong man") indicates Messiah's humanity, whereas **who is close to me** (literally, "my associate, fellow, or relation") suggests his deity. Elsewhere, the Hebrew term for "who is close to me" appears only in Leviticus (twelve times) for a neighbor or fellow countryman (Lev. 6:2; 19:15; 25:15). Thus, the Lord declared that the Messiah is his equal. Feinberg remarks: "It would not be possible to state in stronger terms the unimpeachable deity of the Messiah of Israel" (Feinberg, *Minor Prophets,* 339).

When the Messiah is struck, the disciples scattered and ultimately the entire nation was dispersed by the Roman legions. The words **turn my hand against the little ones** may denote judgment (strike with the hand) or protection (covering with the hand). Certainly, many citizens died in the Roman destruction of Jerusalem, but the expression, "the little ones," probably characterizes the remnant of believers who will be protected during this perilous time. Forty years before A.D. 70, Jesus warned his followers to flee the city when the invasion came (Luke 21:21).

13:8–9. Now we return from the rejection of the Messiah and dispersion of Israel in the first century to a regathered nation restored to her land in the last days. The text from verse 8 through chapter 14 is unmistakably eschatological, since the Lord's coming (14:4) ends the invasion and the messianic age immediately follows. As explained previously, verse 7 is necessary to explain the reason for Israel's crisis. The devastation on the nation will be horrific—only **one-third** of the people will survive. Nevertheless, their painful ordeal **will refine them** like fire purifies **silver** or **gold**. It is this group of survivors (this one-third) who will turn to the Lord and become the true spiritual **people** of God (cp. 12:10–13:1). At last, the new covenant promise to Israel will be fulfilled (Jer. 31:33).

14:1–2. Here the description of war and devastation continues from the previous chapter. Invading armies will have initial success and divide Jerusalem's **plunder** in the midst of (better than NIV's **among you**) the city. Once more, the Lord declared that all the nations would gather at **Jerusalem** to fight against it (12:2–3). The phrase **I [the Lord] will gather** indicates that these events are within God's sovereign plan—the judgment of the wicked nations (Joel 3:2,14). **Houses ransacked, women raped,** and prisoners taken (**go into exile**) were routine atrocities committed by the victors on a captured city.

E A Glorious Future (14:3–21)

SUPPORTING IDEA: *The Lord will come, deliver his people, and establish a glorious kingdom characterized by peace, blessing, and righteousness.*

14:3. All looked bleak for Jerusalem and Judah, but the tide was about to turn. Like a mighty warrior roused from his sleep, the Lord would **go out and fight against those nations.**

14:4. Often the Lord defended his people in indirect ways, but this passage describes the direct, personal intervention of God into history. Suddenly, and no doubt to the astonishment and absolute horror of Israel's enemies, the Lord will appear in physical form. He will descend from the sky and **his feet will stand on the Mount of Olives.** The Mount of Olives (2 Sam. 15:30) is part of a two-and-one-half-mile-long mountain ridge that towers over the eastern side of Jerusalem. The mountain receives its name from the fact that it is heavily covered with olive trees. Its top rises to about twenty-seven hundred feet or two hundred to three hundred feet above Mount Moriah—the temple mount. Between the Mount of Olives and Mount Moriah is the Kidron

Valley. The verse describes the second advent of our God incarnate—Jesus the Messiah. The angels promised he would return to this very spot.

In Acts 1:9–12 we read:

> After he said this, he was taken up before their very eyes, and a cloud hid him from their sight. They were looking intently up into the sky as he was going, when suddenly two men dressed in white stood beside them. "Men of Galilee," they said, "why do you stand here looking into the sky? This same Jesus, who has been taken from you into heaven, will come back in the same way you have seen him go into heaven." Then they returned to Jerusalem from the hill called the Mount of Olives, a Sabbath day's walk from the city.

Christ will arrive at the Mount of Olives and enter the city through the eastern gate (now blocked) that leads directly into the temple. There all the earth's people will worship him.

Perhaps due to an earthquake, the effects of warfare, or by supernatural means, the **Mount of Olives will be split in two from east to west, forming a great valley.** All attempts to identify this invasion of Jerusalem with that of Nebuchadnezzar in 586 B.C. or the Roman General Titus in A.D. 70 are fruitless. No other war has been halted by the personal return of the Lord, and the Mount of Olives is still intact.

14:5. Through this large **valley** God's people will be able to escape the city in an easterly direction. **Azel** is an unknown site, but evidently it was near the east side of the city. **The earthquake in the days of Uzziah king of Judah** (792–740 B.C.) must have been of unusual magnitude to have been remembered over two centuries later by Zechariah. Both the prophet Amos (1:1) and the Jewish historian Josephus mention this earthquake. Archaeologists have suggested it destroyed the city of Hazor about 760 B.C.

Now we reach the climax of the Book of Zechariah—**then the LORD my God will come!** After all Israel and the world have endured, finally God will arrive in the person of the Messiah and bring order, peace, security, joy, and the utopian age that human beings have long dreamed of. As previously noted, this coming Lord is Jesus the Messiah, the second person of the Trinity. **All the holy ones with him** would include the saints as well as the holy angels (1 Thess. 1:7; 3:13; Rev. 19:14).

14:6–7. The NIV's **no cold or frost** follows the ancient versions, but the Hebrew text more literally reads, "The splendid ones [heavenly bodies] will congeal." The NASB's "the luminaries will dwindle" (cp. NKJV) seems to capture the idea of the Hebrew well and explains why **there will be no light**. Verse 7 adds that this **day** will be **without daytime or nighttime**, that is, light from neither the sun, moon, nor stars will appear. Jesus predicted such conditions on earth when he returns: "Immediately after the tribulation of those days, the sun will be darkened, and the moon will not shed her light; the stars will fall from the sky, and the celestial powers will be shaken" (Matt. 24:29 HCSB).

Apparently, the sky will be clouded with smoke and debris from the war that will occur at Christ's second advent (12:3–9; 13:8–14:2; Rev. 16:12–16). **Unique day** is literally "one day," a day unlike any other in history. Evidently, Christ will supernaturally restore **light** on the **evening** of that incredible day.

14:8. Living water is life-giving water that flows **from Jerusalem** to the Dead Sea (**the eastern sea**) and to the Mediterranean Sea (**the western sea**). Christ will supernaturally restore life to the seas after the devastation of the last days (Rev. 8:8–9; 16:3). Other Old Testament texts speak of this supernatural stream in the messianic age (Ezek. 47:1–12; Joel 3:18), and Ezekiel declared that it would originate from the temple (Ezek. 47:1).

14:9. In the new world, **the LORD** in the person of Jesus the Messiah **will be king over the whole earth**. Finally, the world will have a perfect ruler. **His name** will be **the only name** worshiped on earth (cp. 13:2). Jesus instructed us to pray, " Our Father in heaven, Your name be honored as holy. Your kingdom come. Your will be done on earth as it is in heaven" (Matt. 6:9–10 HCSB). That prayer will now be answered.

14:10–11. Geba was located six miles north of Jerusalem, and **Rimmon** was usually identified with En Rimmon, thirty-five miles southwest of Jerusalem. This area will become a plain like that of the Jordan Valley, **the Arabah**, yet **Jerusalem will be raised up**. Certainly Jerusalem will be elevated in prominence because the Messiah will rule there (Isa. 2:2–4; Mic. 4:1–3). Perhaps Zechariah indicated a topographical change as well. Locations in different parts of the city are named to show that Jerusalem has survived and remained intact (**remain in its place**), in spite of the attacks against it. The city will be filled with people and **never again will it be destroyed**.

14:12–15. These verses provide further details about the Lord's victory over Israel's enemies in the conflict of 12:2–9 and 14:1–5. The **plague** on the attacking **nations** and their animals will be horrific: **Their flesh will rot while they are still standing on their feet, their eyes will rot in their sockets, and their tongues will rot in their mouths**. In other words, the flesh will melt away before the skeleton falls to the ground. Understandably, such a plague will strike **great panic** in the hearts of the attackers. **Wealth** will flow to **Judah** from the vanquished nations.

14:16–19. Each year all nations will go up (presumably their representatives) to Jerusalem **to worship the King, the LORD Almighty.** Failure to appear would be an act of rebellion against Christ, and these countries will be punished with drought, a punishment for disobedience named in Deuteronomy 28:22–24. During the millennium, disobedience will be possible but not in the eternal state. **The Feast of Tabernacles** was observed during the seventh month of the Hebrew religious calendar (our September/October). It commemorated the time in the wilderness when the Israelites lived in booths (Lev. 23:41–43). Also called the Feast of Ingathering (Exod. 23:16; 34:22), it celebrated the final harvest of the year's crops.

According to Feinberg:

> There are many views as to why choice was made of the Feast of Tabernacles, but the most probable is that, speaking of the joys of the ingathering, it will celebrate the gathering of the nations to the Lord and especially His tabernacling among them. The millennial feast is the Feast of Tabernacles, because then God will tabernacle with men more fully than ever before in man's long history (Feinberg, *God Remembers*, 203).

During the messianic age, all the earth will worship Jesus Christ, the king. He will finally receive the honor and glory that he was denied during his first advent. Perhaps **Egypt** is singled out to emphasize that this former enemy of Israel now worships the true God.

14:20–21. The messianic kingdom will be characterized by holiness. HOLY TO THE LORD were the words engraved on the sacred turban worn by the high priest (Exod. 28:36), but now these words will be written **on the bells of the horses.** Pots in the temple for cooking the sacrifices will be just as holy as the **sacred bowls in front of the altar** that caught the blood of the sacrifices for sprinkling before the Lord. The phrase **every pot in Jerusalem and Judah will be holy** signifies that holiness will pervade the private life of the people as well. The word **Canaanite** represents an unclean person (Lev. 18:3; not "merchant"), showing that all who worship at Jerusalem will be true believers.

Characteristics of the messianic kingdom outlined in this chapter are as follows: (1) the personal presence of the Lord-Messiah (14:4–5), (2) supernatural provision (14:6–8), (3) Messiah's universal rule (14:9–11), (4) worship (14:16–19), and (5) holiness (14:20–21). Cheer up, God has a great future in store for all his children.

> **MAIN IDEA REVIEW:** *God will deliver Israel from an onslaught of the world's powers, and at that time the nation will repent and receive her rejected Messiah. Then Israel will share in Messiah's glorious kingdom, a kingdom characterized by peace, blessing, and righteousness.*

III. CONCLUSION

When Is Jesus Coming?

In this final chapter of the Book of Zechariah, we see the grand finale of history, the return of Jesus the Messiah. The question is, When will he arrive? Throughout the years people have attempted to predict the exact date. The Millerites (followers of a minister named William Miller) predicted the Lord would return on October 22, 1844. Some of these "Adventists" did not plant crops that spring, and others closed their stores in anticipation of the event. Of course, the time came and went, and the Lord did not show, causing no small embarrassment for those involved and the church generally. Charles Taze Russell, founder of the Jehovah's Witnesses cult, erroneously predicted Armageddon and Christ's coming in 1914. Edgar Whisenant sold over two million copies of his little book, *88 Reasons Why the Rapture Will Be in 1988* (Nashville: World Bible Society, 1988). Whisenant set the rapture between September 11 and 13 of that year. Obviously, we are still here.

Anyone who is tempted to set an exact date for Christ's return should heed the Lord's words: "No one knows about that day or hour, not even the angels in heaven, nor the Son, but only the Father" (Matt. 24:36). Though no one can know the exact date, God has given us some clues, or signs, in the Bible about the general time of Christ's return. In this section of the Book of Zechariah, we find at least two. First, Israel will be reestablished in her land when Christ returns, rendering May 1948 a key date on the prophetic calendar. The fact that Israel has been miraculously restored as a nation suggests that we are in the final stage of earth's history. Second, Christ will return at a time of world conflict in which Israel will be the focus of an attack. World events today, especially in the Middle East, may be setting the stage for this future clash of nations. (For signs that Jesus gave about his return, see Matt. 24–25.)

Regardless of the exact day, the fact remains that Christ is definitely coming back to rescue his people, whether Jews or Gentiles. At the time of his return, Israel will recognize Jesus as their Messiah and be forgiven for their sin. All opposition to God's people will be vanquished, and a glorious new world will begin. Come Lord Jesus!

PRINCIPLES

- Israel as a nation will survive.
- Christ will deliver Israel, and all his people, from their enemies at his second coming.
- Forgiveness for sin is offered to all people (Jew or Gentile) who place their faith in Christ and repent.
- Sometimes suffering precedes blessing.
- Christ will keep his promise to return.
- Some day all the world will acknowledge Jesus as Lord and king.
- In the messianic kingdom, holy people will engage in true worship.
- The victory is the Lord's.

APPLICATIONS

- Pray that the present conflict in Israel will be resolved peacefully.
- Thank the Lord that Christ is coming to deliver all his persecuted people some day.
- Ask God to open an opportunity for you to share the good news of forgiveness through faith in Christ with someone this week.
- If possible, share with a Jewish friend why you believe Jesus is the Messiah.
- Determine that holiness and true worship will characterize your life in this age as well as the age to come.
- Write out a chronology of events in Israel's future from Zechariah 12–14.

IV. LIFE APPLICATION

The Way Things Ought to Be

According to a March 2002 Associated Press release, a Fort Worth nurse's aide was charged with murder for allegedly hitting a homeless man with her car. Both the man's legs were broken, and he was hurled headfirst through the windshield. Rather than call for help, the woman drove home with the man stuck in her windshield and ignored his pleas for help as he died in her garage. Police said the woman had been drinking and taking drugs the night of the incident. Apparently, she knew that if she acquired medical aid for the man, she would be arrested.

Such a story is astonishing, yet the outrageous is becoming more and more commonplace today. On April 20, 1999, two teenage boys shot and killed twelve of their fellow students and a teacher before killing themselves at Columbine High School in Littleton, Colorado. A year earlier two boys, aged thirteen and eleven, massacred four girls and a teacher at their elementary school in Jonesboro, Arkansas. Then there is the infamous case of Andrea Yates of Houston, Texas, who drowned her five children in the family bathtub. Recently, several cases of children being abducted from their homes have been reported in the media.

According to the FBI Uniform Crime Report, in the year 2000 the United States had 15,517 murders, 90,186 rapes, 407,842 robberies, 910,744 assaults, 2,049,946 burglaries, 6,965,957 larceny-thefts, and 1,165,559 vehicles stolen. This means that on an average day in America there are 43 murders, 247 rapes, 1,117 robberies, 2,495 assaults, 5,616 burglaries, and 3,193 vehicles stolen. In the year 2000 the number of adults behind bars, on parole, or on probation reached a record 6.47 million—one in thirty-two Americans!

On the international front, the world is in a state of turmoil. At the end of the last millennium, one-third of the world's 193 nations were embroiled in conflict, and this was before the war on terrorism began. News reports remind us daily of troubles in the Middle East.

Is this the way God intended our world to be? Absolutely not! The problem is that sin has pervaded the human heart and permeated the world. Happily, Zechariah assured God's people that a new world awaits us—"a day of the LORD is coming" (Zech. 14:1). Now is the day of the human—a time of sin, destruction, and death. Some day there will be a new day. The Lord's day will come. In this new era Christ will rule the world justly and lovingly. We will be able to leave our doors unlocked and go anywhere without fear. Actually, this new era is often described in the Bible as a return to garden of Eden conditions—peace with nature, absence of malice, prosperity, security, and fellowship with God. That is the way things ought to be!

V. PRAYER

Heavenly Father, thank you for forgiving all who repent of their sins and look in faith to your Son, Jesus the Messiah. We pray for all the nations of the world that they may experience the joy of knowing you. Thank you that Jesus is coming back and will make this world what you always intended it to be—a paradise of peace, joy, security, and love. In the name of Jesus the Messiah we pray. Amen.

VI. DEEPER DISCOVERIES

A. Key Dates in Israel's History

Israel is the national focus of the Book of Zechariah and the Bible as a whole. At the beginning of these latter chapters of Zechariah, we find a restored Israel residing in her ancient land. Where did Israel originate, and how did the Jewish people come to be in the land today? A survey of the following key dates in the history of Israel will be helpful for the reader.

KEY DATES IN THE HISTORY OF ISRAEL

The Old Testament Period

2166 B.C.	Birth of Abraham (following the early date for the exodus from Egypt and a 430-year stay in Egypt)
1876 B.C.	Jacob and family move to Egypt
1446 B.C.	Exodus from Egypt (thirteenth century, according to late-date view of the exodus)
1446–1406 B.C.	Wilderness wandering
1406–1050 B.C.	Conquest of Canaan and judges
1050–931 B.C.	United kingdom (Saul, David, Solomon)
931 B.C.	The division of the twelve tribes into two nations—Israel (Northern Kingdom) and Judah (Southern Kingdom)
931–722 B.C.	Divided kingdom period
722 B.C.	Destruction of the Northern Kingdom (Israel) by the Assyrians
722–586 B.C.	The surviving kingdom of Judah
586 B.C.	Destruction of Jerusalem and the Babylonian exile

KEY DATES IN THE HISTORY OF ISRAEL

539 B.C.	Babylon falls to Medo-Persia
538 B.C.	First return of exiles under Zerubbabel and Joshua
458 B.C.	Second return of exiles under Ezra
445 B.C.	Third return of exiles under Nehemiah
400 B.C.	End of the Old Testament era (approximate)

The Intertestamental Period

175–163 B.C.	Reign of the tyrant Antiochus IV Epiphanes, who attempted to eradicate the Jewish religion
164 B.C.	Rededication of the temple (Hanukkah) by Judas Maccabeus
63 B.C.	Pompey conquers Palestine for Rome
40–4 B.C.	Reign of Herod the Great

The New Testament Period

6–4 B.C.	Birth of Jesus Christ
A.D. 26	Baptism and beginning of Christ's public ministry
A.D. 30	Crucifixion of Christ
A.D. 35	Paul's conversion to Christianity
A.D. 60s	Execution of Peter and Paul
A.D. 70	Destruction of Jerusalem by the Romans
A.D. 95–100	Death of John, the last apostle

Intermediate History

A.D. 132–135	Revolt under Bar Kokhba. Jerusalem rebuilt by Hadrian as a Roman city, and no Jew could approach the city under penalty of death. Jerusalem's name changed to *Aelia Capitolina* and the name of the country from Judea to Syria Palestina—"Syria of the Philistines"—hence the name, Palestine
A.D. 330–634	Byzantine period (Roman)
A.D. 634–1099	Arab period (Muslim control begins)
A.D. 1099–1263	Crusader period

KEY DATES IN THE HISTORY OF ISRAEL	
A.D. 1263–1516	Mamluk period (Muslim control restored by Mamluk Sultan Baybars of Egypt)
A.D. 1517–1917	Turkish period
Modern Period	
1917	Jerusalem taken by Allies in World War I. British control
1930s–1940s	Jewish Holocaust. Six million Jews executed by Hitler's Nazis
1947	Partition of Palestine into separate Jewish and Arab states approved by the United Nations
1948, May 14	Israel declares itself an independent state. Israel-Arab War (with Egypt, Iraq, Lebanon, Syria, and Jordan). About half of the land designated for the Arabs gained by Israel. Palestinian land controlled by Jordan called the West Bank because it was located on the west side of the Jordan River. 700,000 Arabs displaced and go to neighboring Arab countries
1964	Creation of the Palestine Liberation Organization (PLO). In 1969, Mohammed Yasir Arafat becomes its leader.
1967	Israel-Arab War ("Six-Day War" with Egypt, Jordan, Syria). Much territory and all of Jerusalem comes under Jewish control. More Arabs become refugees.
1973	Israel-Arab War ("Yom Kippur War" with Egypt and Syria). More territorial gains by Israel.

Today about two million Palestinians live in the Gaza Strip and the West Bank, for the most part, in very poor conditions. Hatred between Arabs and Jews in Palestine continues to grow as violence escalates in the land. In claiming credit for a recent bombing of a cafeteria at Hebrew University, Hamas said that the Jews must leave the country. Since Israel is not about to leave, the problem seems to be insoluble. Certainly, we should pray for peace in the Middle East, but only Christ will be able to bring a permanent solution to this dilemma.

B. The One They Have Pierced (12:10)

In the "Commentary" discussion on 12:10, this "pierced one" was identified as Jesus the Messiah. Other views have been offered. Historical figures such as Onias III (Jewish high priest), assassinated in 170 B.C., or Simon the Maccabee (Jewish leader), assassinated in 134 B.C., have been suggested. Aside from the difficulty of dating the passage so late, no historical individual satisfies the requirements of the text. Others have argued for a symbolic meaning of "pierced" and applied the passage to God but not specifically to the Messiah.

An ancient Jewish view is that the "pierced" one is Messiah, but how could such a powerful world ruler be pierced? To solve the problem, this Messiah was identified as Messiah ben ["son of"] Joseph, a separate individual from Messiah ben David. Yet the Bible says nothing of a second Messiah. In the modern Jewish translation of the Hebrew Bible (the Old Testament) called the *Tanakh*, Zechariah 12:10 is rendered: "But I will fill the House of David and the inhabitants of Jerusalem with a spirit of pity and compassion; *and they shall lament to Me about those who are slain,* wailing over them as over a favorite son and showing bitter grief as over a first-born." Italics are added to emphasize key differences between the literal, "And they will look to me, whom they have pierced."

According to Kaiser:

> The problem with this translation is that it breaks the rules of Hebrew grammar to avoid the obvious implications of the Hebrew verse. It turns the active form of "pierce" ["have pierced"] into passive [*Tanakh's* "are slain"], and the subjects ["*they* have pierced"] into objects ["*those who* are slain"]; and this the Hebrew will not allow! It is a heroic effort to bypass the logical implication that the one who speaks is the one who was pierced by those who now stare in amazement in the eschatological, or future, day (Kaiser, *More Hard Sayings of the Old Testament,* 264; bracketed material added for clarity).

In summary, the view that this passage applies in literal fashion to Jesus the Messiah is sound grammatically, theologically, and historically, and conforms to the teaching of the New Testament. Jesus is deity, was pierced by the Jewish people at his first advent, and will be recognized by Israel as her Messiah at his second advent. Zechariah 12:10 is one of the most magnificent verses in all of the Bible.

C. Messiah and the Book of Zechariah (12:10; 13:7; 14:3–5,9)

Messiah (Heb. *mashiach*) means "anointed one" and is derived from a verb meaning to "anoint (with oil)." In the Bible, priests (Exod. 28:41; 29:7), kings (1 Sam. 10:1; 1 Kgs. 1:34), and apparently prophets (1 Kgs. 19:16) were anointed for service. The anointing symbolized the Holy Spirit's power coming to rest upon these individuals to accomplish their tasks, a truth beautifully illustrated in the account of David's anointing (1 Sam. 16:12–13; cp. Zech. 4:6).

From the very outset, God revealed that he would send someone to deliver the human race from the ravages of sin—pain, suffering, sorrow, death (Gen. 3:15). This individual came to be called the Messiah, particularly appropriate in light of the fact that he would come from the line of Davidic kings, an anointed class. However, he would not be anointed with oil (the symbol) but with the Spirit of God. In his role as king, Messiah would defeat the forces of evil, take away the curse of sin, and rule the world (Ps. 110:1–3,5–7; Isa. 2:2–4). In addition, the Messiah would fulfill the role of priest, another anointed class. As God's anointed high priest, he would offer the sacrifice that would truly take away sins (Ps. 110:4; Isa. 52:13–53:12).

First-century Jews were eager to receive a Messiah who would crush Rome, but most overlooked the necessity of Messiah's priestly work. A Messiah who would suffer and die for sins was not nearly as appealing as a universal king. Moreover, how could the Messiah suffer? An ancient Jewish interpretation (Babylonian Talmud) explained the dilemma by proposing two Messiahs—Messiah ben ["son of"] Joseph who would suffer and Messiah ben David who would reign as universal king. The two-Messiah theory also explained how Messiah could perform both roles of priest and king. According to R. Martin in the *Holman Illustrated Bible Dictionary,* "The people in the Dead Sea scrolls were evidently able to combine a dual hope of two Messiahs, one priestly and the second a royal figure." Such mysteries were solved by the later revelation of Messiah's two comings. He would come the first time to suffer and die for sins, the second to rule the world.

Christians have identified Jesus as this promised Messiah for a number of reasons. First, Jesus fulfilled Old Testament prophecies about Messiah's life and work. (For messianic prophecy fulfilled in Jesus, see the "Deeper Discoveries" section for Zechariah 11.) Second, his miraculous works, his prerogative to forgive sins, and his resurrection vindicated his claims. Third, Jesus explicitly claimed to be the Messiah. For example, in Jesus' encounter with the Samaritan woman, we read: "The woman said, 'I know that Messiah (called Christ) is coming. When he comes, he will explain everything to us.' Then Jesus declared, 'I who speak to you am he'" (John 4:25–26; cp. Luke 24:25–27). Fourth, messianic titles like Christ, Son of David, and Son of Man were attributed to him. Jesus is called Christ (Gr. form of Heb. *Messiah*) approximately five hundred times in the New Testament. Of course, Jesus' messianic claims will never be accepted without the inner witness of the Holy Spirit about their truthfulness.

Zechariah is the most messianic of the minor prophets and contains more references to the Messiah than any prophetic book except Isaiah. Key references to the Messiah in the Book of Zechariah follow:

KEY REFERENCES TO THE MESSIAH IN ZECHARIAH

Direct References

3:8–10	Messiah's work as high priest
6:9–15	Messiah as king-priest over the nations
9:9–10	Messiah as coming king
10:4	Messiah as Judah's promised ruler
11:4–14	Messiah as the rejected good shepherd
12:10	Messiah as the pierced one
13:7	Messiah as the slain shepherd

Indirect References

1:8–17	Man among the myrtle trees (angel of the Lord)
2:10–13	Messiah (God incarnate) living among his people
14:4	Messiah's (God incarnate) return to the Mount of Olives
14:9,16–17	Messiah (God incarnate) as king of the earth

Titles

3:8	My servant
3:8; 6:12	Branch
3:8	Stone
9:9; 14:9,16–17	King
10:4	Cornerstone, tent peg, battle bow, ruler
11:9; 13:7	Shepherd
12:10	The pierced one
13:7	Man who is close to me (my associate)

The Old Testament is not just the history of an ancient people, but a thrilling account of God's plan of redemption for the human race. Messiah is the key to that redemption. Zechariah predicted that Messiah would save from sin and ultimately deliver the human race from sin's devastating effects. That Messiah is Jesus of Nazareth.

D. No Canaanite in the House of the Lord Almighty (14:21)

Merchant is placed in the NIV margin as a possible reading for the Hebrew word *kena'aniy*, usually rendered "Canaanite." Other versions (NRSV, NLT) place "traders" in the text itself. Canaanites were well-known throughout the ancient world as mariners and merchants, thus the connection. In two instances the Hebrew term seems clearly to refer to "merchants" (Job 41:6; Prov. 31:24). If Zechariah was saying that no "merchants" would be allowed in the future temple, the meaning would be as follows: since everything will be holy, merchants (often dishonest) will not be needed in the temple precincts to sell animals and goods acceptable for sacred purposes (cp. Matt. 21:12; John 2:15).

On the other hand, the Hebrew term is translated in its usual sense, "Canaanite" or "Canaanites," about seventy times in the NIV, and this meaning suits the context of this passage perfectly. The inhabitants of Canaan (name of Israel's land before the conquest) came to be virtually synonymous with immoral, wicked, and idolatrous people. The Lord told Moses, "You must not do as they do in Egypt, where you used to live, and you must not do as they do in the land of Canaan, where I am bringing you. Do not follow their practices" (Lev. 18:3). In Leviticus 18:6–23 a list of some of the most vile and disgusting acts imaginable, including child sacrifice (18:21), are named as being carried on in Canaan. Archaeological evidence from the period has confirmed the biblical description of the Canaanites' moral degradation. Zechariah's point is that only holy people will enter the presence of the Lord in the messianic age.

VII. TEACHING OUTLINE

A. INTRODUCTION

1. Lead Story: "Dead" Woman Wakes Up!

2. Context: In chapters 12–14, Zechariah presents a panoramic over-view of Israel's future. Dispersed by the Romans, Israel will be reset-tled in its land in the last days. After a time of trial, the nation will recognize Jesus as their Messiah and turn to him in repentance and faith. He will forgive their sins and rescue them from their enemies. Upon Messiah's return to earth, he will establish the wonderful new world depicted in 14:3–21.

3. Transition: From this section we learn that God is truly in control of history. As a nation, Israel has "died" twice and miraculously come back to life both times. Israel's story also reminds us that God's love knows no limits. Though rejected as their Messiah at his first advent, Jesus still loves Israel and will forgive the nation when it repents. What is true of nations is true of individuals. God loves us and is willing to forgive. We are encouraged to read that Christ will deliver his people, Jew and Gentile, from their foes and will bring in the most glorious era in human history. Hope to see you there!

B. COMMENTARY

1. A Problem for the Nations (12:1–3)
2. Deliverance from Invaders (12:4–9)
3. Deliverance from Sin (12:10–13:6)
4. A Time of Trouble (13:7–14:2)
5. A Glorious Future (14:3–21)

C. CONCLUSION: WHEN IS JESUS COMING?

VIII. ISSUES FOR DISCUSSION

1. Why do you think that anti-Semitism has been such a problem throughout history? Name some examples of anti-Semitic acts com-mitted in the past. In the present.
2. What does the Bible say about Israel's future? Will the nation survive the present crisis?
3. What lessons do chapters 12–14 of Zechariah teach about salvation? How may we be saved? In whom do we place our faith? What dem-onstrates our sincerity?
4. Name some truths about the Messiah found in these chapters.
5. What are some characteristics of Messiah's reign?

Malachi 1

God's Love and Our Response

I. **INTRODUCTION**
Our Heavenly Father Knows Best:
The Lauren Chapin Story

II. **COMMENTARY**
A verse-by-verse explanation of the chapter.

III. **CONCLUSION**
Foolish Questions
An overview of the principles and applications from
the chapter.

IV. **LIFE APPLICATION**
Money Was No Object
Melding the chapter to life.

V. **PRAYER**
Tying the chapter to life with God.

VI. **DEEPER DISCOVERIES**
Historical, geographical, and grammatical enrichment of the commentary.

VII. **TEACHING OUTLINE**
Suggested step-by-step group study of the chapter.

VIII. **ISSUES FOR DISCUSSION**
Zeroing the chapter in on daily life.

"God proved his love on the cross. When Christ hung, and bled, and died it was God saying to the world—I love you."

Billy Graham

PROPHECY PROFILE

- Malachi is the sixth shortest book in the Old Testament (only fifty-five verses) and the twelfth shortest book in the Bible.
- Malachi uses the dialectical, or question and answer, method to convey his message. No less than twenty-seven questions appear in the book (NIV).
- Ezra and Nehemiah record the historical background for this prophecy.
- Malachi was written after the Babylonian exile during the time of Persian control of Judah. His ministry best fits the period between Nehemiah's two terms as governor of Judah.
- Malachi's status as a book of Scripture has never been questioned. It is listed as Scripture in Jewish writings at least two centuries before the time of Christ and was venerated as Scripture by the authors of the Dead Sea Scrolls.
- The book is repeatedly alluded to in the New Testament as an inspired prophecy (Matt. 11:10; 17:12; Mark 1:2; 9:11–12; Luke 1:17; and Rom. 9:13).
- Malachi's theme is stated clearly in the opening of the book (1:2–5), namely, God's love for his people Israel.
- Scholars disagree over whether Malachi contains poetic material. None is indicated in the NIV.
- At least three messianic references are found in the Book of Malachi (3:1; 4:2–3,5–6).

AUTHOR PROFILE: MALACHI THE PROPHET

- Malachi's name is unique to this biblical individual and means "my [the Lord's] messenger." Some interpreters have suggested that this is not a personal name but a designation for the prophet as the Lord's spokesman (messenger). However, every other prophetic book bears the name of its author, even the short prophecy of Obadiah; and it would be strange if this one were left anonymous.
- Nothing is known about the prophet's personal life except what is revealed in his book. It is clear that Malachi was a man of great courage and zeal for the truth. He preached pointed sermons on some very sensitive subjects.
- Malachi spoke with clarity, simplicity, directness, and power.
- Malachi was the last prophet of the Old Testament era. When his ministry ceased, no prophetic voice was heard until John the Baptist arrived on the scene 450 years later.

READER PROFILE: THE POSTEXILIC NATION OF JUDAH

- In 539 B.C. Babylon fell to the Medo-Persian armies of Cyrus the Great (Dan. 5). From this point until its defeat by Alexander the Great in a series of battles (334–331 B.C.), the Medo-Persian Empire dominated the world. Judah became a province of the empire and was ruled by a governor appointed by the Medo-Persians. Cyrus was a benevolent ruler who permitted the Jewish exiles to return to their homeland (538 B.C.). By Malachi's day the Jews had been in the land about a hundred years.
- Malachi ministered in the time of Ezra and Nehemiah—458 B.C. until at least about 430 B.C. Discouragement and spiritual lethargy seem to have set in upon the tiny nation, even among the priests. The temple had been rebuilt, but much of the city of Jerusalem was still in ruins. Even with the spiritual renewal brought about by Ezra and the rebuilding of the wall by Nehemiah, the people were discouraged by hard economic realities and Persian dominance. Some of the people felt that the Lord did not love them because of these factors (1:2–5). Many Israelite showing their dissatisfaction with the Lord by bringing

animals for sacrifices. Some even went so far as to assert that worshiping the Lord was drudgery (1:13) and serving God was a waste of time (3:13–15).

- The people blamed God when in reality their plight was in great part the result of their own sinfulness—corrupt priests, marriage to pagans, failure to tithe, not keeping the Sabbath, marital unfaithfulness, mistreatment of the weak, and perjury.
- Malachi's prophecy includes a rebuke for the people's sinful actions and attitudes while at the same time assuring Israel of God's love.

Malachi 1

 I N   A   N U T S H E L L

In chapter 1, Malachi deals with the first two of six key issues that form the framework of the book—God's love for Israel and Israel's heartbreaking response to God's love. In 1:2–5 God assures the people that in spite of the nation's difficult circumstances, he did indeed love them and had proved it by choosing Israel to be his covenant people. Malachi then chides the nation for failing to appreciate God's great love. Instead, the Israelites showed blatant disrespect for the Lord by offering blemished animals and complaining that serving God was drudgery.

God's Love and Our Response

I. INTRODUCTION

Our Heavenly Father Knows Best: The Lauren Chapin Story

Father Knows Best was one of the most popular television series of the 1950s and early 1960s. The program won six Emmy Awards and finished sixth in ratings during its final year of production. *Father Knows Best* continued to be shown in prime time for three years after production ended and then for another five years on ABC's daytime lineup. *Father Knows Best* may still be seen in reruns today.

The showstopper on the program was Lauren Chapin, the adorable little Kathy (nicknamed "Kitten"). Lauren appeared in many TV and radio programs as well as movies and commercials. Five times she was awarded Junior Emmy awards for best child actress. Elvis Presley, probably the most popular singer in the world at the time, was brought in by the studio to entertain at her private birthday party. Recently *E! True Hollywood Stories* aired a two-hour television special on Lauren's life that won ratings higher than any of the shows produced to date.

To all outward appearances Lauren had the perfect life—fame, money, and professional accolades. However, looks can be deceiving and that was certainly true of this little girl. Lauren's home life was totally dysfunctional. Secretly, her father was abusing her, and her mother was cold, unloving, and even cruel. When *Father Knows Best* was suddenly canceled, Lauren was devastated. With no direction she went from bad to worse. For years she lived a life of incredible misery—drugs, fast company, casual lovers, eight miscarriages, welfare, a mental hospital, and even prison!

Lauren had never been a religious person, but her son began going to church with relatives. When he threatened to quit if she did not attend with him, Lauren agreed. After visiting several churches, she found one where the pastor clearly shared the gospel. As the pastor preached, she felt he was speaking directly to her. For the first time, she heard that she had a father who loved her with an unconditional love, in spite of her many sins. With tears she received Christ as her Lord and Savior, and her life was changed forever. Today she has found personal and professional success. She shares her testimony in churches and with all who will listen. During the interview for her biography on the *E! True Hollywood Stories*, Lauren gave a bold gospel presentation of how Jesus Christ changed her life. Lauren was touched by the love of God.

In this chapter of Malachi, the prophet tells us that God loves us. Just as God acted on behalf of ancient Israel to demonstrate his love to them, he shows his love to people today in many ways. Of course, the greatest proof of God's love is the sacrifice of his dear Son Jesus on the cross for our sins. Since God has done so much for us, we should love him in return and treat him with honor (unlike many in Malachi's audience). This wonderful little prophecy, often neglected, has a timely message for our world. Now, as then, people need to know that God loves them.

II. COMMENTARY

God's Love and Our Response

MAIN IDEA: *God loves the world and has proven his love by his actions. We should respond by honoring God, offering him our best, and worshiping him with joy.*

A Introducing the Prophecy of Malachi (1:1)

SUPPORTING IDEA: *Malachi faithfully proclaims God's message of love and warning to his people.*

1:1. Malachi introduced his book with the familiar prophetic designation, **an oracle** (NIV, NASB, NRSV) or "burden" (KJV, NKJV). "Burden" would suggest the idea of a heavy message—one containing stern warnings or judgment. Malachi's prophecy does indeed contain a severe rebuke for his fellow countrymen who were engaged in sinful practices. (For a further discussion of the word *oracle,* see the "Deeper Discoveries" section for Nahum 1.)

From the outset the prophet made clear that his message was not just personal opinion but **the word of the LORD**. We should always keep in mind as we study the Bible that this is no ordinary book; it is God's word to the human race. The phrase, **an oracle: the word of the LORD,** is used exclusively after the Babylonian exile and occurs elsewhere only in Zechariah 9:1 and 12:1 (exact wording in Hebrew text).

Malachi apparently preached his message orally to the people of **Israel,** possibly during a festal gathering. Without question, the setting was in the postexilic period, although scholars debate the specific time of Malachi's ministry. The flagrant disrespect for God's worship and other conditions described in the book could never have occurred while Nehemiah was present in Jerusalem. Either Nehemiah had not yet arrived, or more likely, Malachi delivered these sermons between Nehemiah's two terms as governor (about 433 B.C.).

During the postexilic period, the nation experienced economic hardships and chafed under the rule of foreign domination. A century after the first return to the land under Zerubbabel, Israel was still just a tiny, struggling country on the outskirts of the vast Persian Empire. Clearly, many people had become discouraged because of the economic difficulties and other hardships. They even questioned whether God loved them. However, they were a sinful people, and Malachi pointed out in his book that one reason for their difficulties (even some of their economic woes) was unfaithfulness to the Lord.

Unlike most prophets **Malachi** shared virtually no personal information—no ancestry or hometown—only his name. Usually the prophet's name is understood to mean, "my [the LORD's] messenger." *Mal'ak* is the Hebrew word for "messenger" and may refer to a human messenger (like the prophet Malachi) or a heavenly messenger, an angel. Some scholars have suggested that the ending on the name is a shortened form of "the Lord" and signifies, "messenger of the Lord." Probably the former view is correct, but in either case Malachi was the Lord's messenger sent to declare the word of the Lord to Israel. Today's ministers are also entrusted by the Lord to communicate his word in loving and clear terms to a needy world.

As noted in the introduction, some scholars have proposed that Malachi was not a personal name at all, but a description of an unnamed prophet as the Lord's spokesman (messenger). Though possible, every other prophetic book bears the name of its author, even the short prophecy of Obadiah; and it would be strange if this one were left anonymous.

B God's Love (1:2–5)

SUPPORTING IDEA: *God loves the world and has proven it by his actions.*

1:2. Malachi's prophecy consists of six major sections, each identified by key questions. In each division the general pattern is as follows: a brief assertion of a truth, an objection, and the substantiation of the truth. The first section deals with the issue of God's love for Israel (1:2–5). God's declaration of his love for Israel is followed by the first key question (the objection), "How have you loved us?" Then the verification of the truth is set forth in verses 2c–5.

The force of the Hebrew verb form rendered **I have loved** is, "I have loved you and still do." God had repeatedly stated his love for his people throughout their history (Jer. 31:33; Hos. 11:1). Apparently, harsh conditions had led some people in Israel to question God's love, and they responded, **How have you loved us?** Malachi's questions were rhetorical but no doubt reflected the actual sentiment of and statements being expressed by his audience. In effect, people were saying, "God, you say you love us, but what have you ever done to prove it?"

Malachi moved quickly to provide the requested proof. He could have pointed out many acts of love that God had performed for Israel over the centuries (e.g., deliverance from Babylon). Instead he chose to remind them of God's greatest kindness—the selection of Israel as his covenant people. Of all the earth's nations, they were his "chosen" people. God could have opted for **Esau** and his descendants for this great honor, but he chose **Jacob**. From Jacob's sons came the twelve tribes of Israel and the Jewish nation. Of course, the choice of Israel did not mean that the Lord did not love other peoples. He did. As a matter of fact, Israel's mission was to share the love of God with the world—a whole nation of missionaries. Nevertheless, Israel was highly privileged as the custodian of the Scriptures, the beneficiaries of covenant promises, and the recipient of many other special blessings from the God of the universe. What a great act of love!

1:3. Verse 2 ends with God's wonderful affirmation, "I have loved Jacob," whereas verse 3 begins with one of the most hotly debated and misunderstood statements in the Bible, **Esau I have hated.** Here "Jacob" and **Esau** are spoken of as progenitors of nations (Israel and Edom) and the love-hate contrast (as elsewhere in Scripture; Gen. 29:30–31; Luke 14:26) is comparative. Thus God's gracious choice of Jacob's descendants, Israel, as his covenant people rather than Esau's descendants, Edom (v. 4), demonstrates his unfathomable love for Israel. God's passing over Esau and his descendants for this honor was almost like hate in comparison. In Romans 9:13 the apostle Paul cited Malachi 1:2c–3a to emphasize God's sovereignty.

God's love was also demonstrated by his continued protection of Israel from Esau's descendants, the Edomites. Edom (part of modern Jordan) became the archenemy of Israel. This was surprising since the two nations were relatives—fathered by twins born to Isaac and Rebekah (Gen. 25:21–26). Because of Edom's mistreatment of Israel and for other wicked acts, God judged the nation (**turned his mountains into a wasteland**). Probably this destruction was that carried out by the Nabatean Arabs in the fifth century B.C. If so, the illustration would have been contemporary and relevant to Malachi's audience. The reference to mountains is noteworthy, since Edom was a rugged, mountainous region with peaks that reached almost four thousand feet. **Desert jackals** (literally, "howlers") prowled Edom's desolate land.

1:4. In response to Edom's defiant boast (**we will rebuild the ruins**), **the LORD Almighty** ("the LORD of hosts"; twenty-four times in this short book) promised to **demolish** anything they attempted to rebuild. The pronouns **they** [may build] and **I** [will demolish] are emphatic, contrasting the power of weak humans with that of almighty God, who commands all the forces of heaven and earth. The word *demolish* literally means "to break down" or "tear down." If Edom attempted to rebuild, God would knock their buildings down like a house of cards. Edom was epitomized as **the Wicked Land** (contrast Israel's designation as "the holy land" in Zech. 2:12) upon whom God's **wrath** would forever rest, signifying that the nation would come to a permanent end. Malachi's prophecy has been literally fulfilled in history, since neither the nation of Edom nor the Edomites as a people exist today. The desolate ruins of Petra, located in the ancient territory of Edom, testify to the truthfulness of God's word.

1:5. What is the lesson for Israel? When Edom (this hostile foreign nation) is judged, Israel **will see it** and know that God loves them and that his power extends **even beyond the borders of Israel**. The LORD is no local deity, but the **great** God of the whole earth (cp. 1:11,14). Thus, the Lord proved his love by choosing Israel as his covenant people and protecting them from their enemies.

How may people today be sure that God loves them? The apostle John shared the greatest proof of all: "For God loved the world in this way: He gave His only Son, so that everyone who believes in Him will not perish but have eternal life" (John 3:16 HCSB).

Response to God's Love (1:6–14)

SUPPORTING IDEA: *We should respond to God's love by honoring him, offering him our best, and worshiping him with joy.*

1:6. Now we come to the second major section of Malachi. Here Malachi dealt with the people's heartbreaking response to God's love. God had done so much for them, but did they appreciate it? No! **Priests** and people alike were showing flagrant disrespect (**contempt**) for the God who loved them. Malachi's accusation prepares us for the key question in the passage, **How have we shown contempt for your name?**

Malachi began with a proposition. As a general rule children honor their parents and servants honor their masters. Then he followed with an application to the people in the form of two questions. Contrary to nature, God's **son** Israel (Exod. 4:22; Jer. 31:9; Hos. 11:1) did not **honor** his **father**, and unlike in a normal servant-master relationship, he showed no **respect** to the heavenly **master**.

Who in Israel would dare treat God so? Sadly, it was the very ones entrusted with teaching the Scriptures (2:7) and privileged to serve in God's holy temple—the **priests**. They had shown **contempt** (great disrespect) for God's **name**—God himself. In verse 14 Malachi made clear that laypeople were not blameless. Nevertheless, the priests were singled out because with privilege goes responsibility. For this reason their rebuke which continues into chapter 2 (v. 9) is the longest section in the book and one of the most severe (Jas. 3:1).

Years earlier Hosea had quipped, "Like people, like priests" (Hos. 4:9). How true! Seldom will the spirituality and commitment level of the people rise above that of their spiritual leaders. As the great English poet Chaucer (about A.D. 1342–1400) wrote in his *Canterbury Tales:*

> If gold can rust, then what will iron do?
> For if a priest be rotten, whom we trust,
> No wonder if a layman comes to rust.

A major problem in our nation today is that many spiritual leaders have been corrupted.

The priests couldn't believe their ears. "Who? Us? What have we ever done?" **How have we shown contempt for your name?** They claimed to be as innocent as newborn babies.

1:7. Malachi was quick to substantiate the allegation. He did so by pointing out that the priests had shown disrespect toward God by their wrong actions (vv. 7–10) and by their poor attitude (vv. 12–13). They had placed **defiled food** (literally, "bread" or sacrifices of bread, grain, and animals) on God's temple **altar**. In the Hebrew text, "altar" is placed before "food" in order to emphasize the gravity of the sin. "Defiled food" refers to sacrificial offerings that were ceremonially unacceptable—blemished or forbidden animals.

Once more the priests protested, **How have we defiled you?** The question seems redundant; perhaps the priests were attempting to make a distinction between the altar and God himself. As we shall see in verse 8, these priests were offering sacrifices that were strictly forbidden in the law, but they also complained that **the LORD's table** itself was **contemptible**. There is no reason to doubt that some disgruntled priests actually spoke these words. Their actions certainly demonstrated that this was what they thought. Here "the Lord's table" is the altar of sacrifice, not the table for "the bread of the Presence" (Exod. 25:30; "showbread," KJV), since animal sacrifices are offered upon it.

By showing disrespect for God's altar where the sacrifices were offered in worship, they actually demonstrated a lack of respect for God himself. Thus, when we do not respect the proper worship of God (or fail to worship altogether), we show that we really do not respect God.

1:8. What is wrong with bringing blemished animals for sacrificial offerings? First, to offer **blind, crippled,** or **diseased animals** was sin (**wrong**) because it violated the law of God (Exod. 12:5; 29:1; Lev. 1:3,10). God commanded the people to offer animals without defect because these Old Testament sacrifices were a type of the sinless Lord Jesus Christ, who would offer himself as the perfect sacrifice for our sins (cp. Exod. 12:5 with 1 Cor. 5:7). Second, to offer such animals showed a lack of respect for the greatness of God. Certainly, Malachi's friends would not have offered such animals to the **governor** (appointed by the Persian government) as payment of taxes or as a voluntary personal gift. What an insult! **Would he be pleased?** Absolutely not! **Accept you** is literally, "lift up your face." H. Wolf explains, "One who 'lifts up your face' shows a high regard for you and is willing to grant your request" (Wolf, 70).

Nehemiah served two terms as governor (Neh. 12:26), but this Persian ruler could not have been Nehemiah, since Nehemiah refused to accept the food allotted to the governor (Neh. 5:14–15,18). Apparently, this governor accepted these amenities, indicating Nehemiah's absence. Moreover, the abuses that Malachi addressed in the book could never have occurred if Nehemiah were present. Most likely Malachi delivered his message between Nehemiah's two terms as governor (Neh. 13:6–7).

1:9. God ironically called on the priests to pray on behalf of the people. Actually, these wicked priests had no power with God or right to ask God for anything. They were personally and ceremonially unfit to fulfill their role as mediators between God and the people. The word **implore** means literally "to make the face of one sweet or pleasant." The phrase **from your hands** emphasizes that these deplorable sacrifices were offered by the priests' own hands—those who knew better. We cannot expect God's blessings when our lives are filled with sin.

1:10. God was so repulsed by this disgraceful worship that he pleaded for at least **one** priest to have the decency to **shut the temple doors** and stop this disgraceful worship! The phrase **light useless fires on my altar** refers to the

fires that consumed the sacrifices. Such fires were useless because the offerings burned by them were unacceptable to God. The Lord was not just
unhappy with the sacrifices but with the priests personally—**not pleased
with you**. No offering, with or without defect, would be accepted from their
guilty **hands**. How shocking! God actually declared that he would rather have
no worship at all than this debacle. Would the Lord say the same of some
churches in our world today?

1:11. God might not be receiving the honor due him from these ingrates,
but some day all the world would acknowledge his great **name** and worship
him with **pure offerings**—acceptable offerings (ceremonially clean) presented by those pleasing to God. No longer would God receive the leftovers
but every person's best.

Most translations agree with the NIV that this universal worship was yet
future (**in every place incense and pure offerings will be brought to my
name**), but the NRSV and a few other translations render it in the present
tense ("in every place incense is offered to my name, and a pure offering").

Three primary interpretations of this worship are: (1) Pagans who worship their pagan gods are actually worshiping the Lord. Such a view may be
appealing in our politically correct world, but for Malachi the idea would
have been preposterous. Later he reprimanded those who married pagans by
saying they had married wives who served a different god ("the daughter of a
foreign god," 2:11). (2) Either dispersed Jews or Jews and their Gentile pros-
elytes were those living throughout the world who worshiped the Lord.
(3) The Lord will be worshiped universally in the future messianic age.

Undoubtedly, the last view is correct. Certainly, God has followers
throughout the earth today, but Jesus the Messiah will never be honored by
the majority of this world until he returns in power and glory (Isa. 2:2–4;
66:23; Zech. 14:9,16). Here is a great promise of hope and encouragement for
the faithful in Malachi's time and for us. Some day our Lord will receive the
respect and honor due his name.

1:12. The words **but you** strongly contrast the disrespectful Jewish
priests with the Gentile nations of verse 11 who would one day honor the
Lord. The priests were profaning (verb form indicates ongoing action)
God's name. The word **profane** means to treat as common (insignificant)
something that is holy. Their lack of respect for God was demonstrated by
the priests' willingness to offer blemished (**contemptible**) animals (**food**)
on the temple altar (**the Lord's table**). The general meaning of the text is
clear, but the precise import of the priests' words is a bit puzzling. They
seemed to be complaining about the **defiled** altar and the contemptible sac-

rifices when they were the very ones responsible for this outrage. Perhaps the priests were even hinting that the sacrificial system itself was the problem. After all, they may have reasoned, the Jews made it fine during the Babylonian exile without this outmoded worship system.

1:13. Not only had the priests acted wrongfully; they had a wrong attitude toward God's worship and ultimately toward God himself. To them worship services were not joyous celebrations of God's goodness, but **a burden** (something that makes a person weary or tired). They turned their noses up (**sniff at it contemptuously**) at God's worship services. God repeated the charge of verse 8 that the priests were offering blemished animals. **Injured** may speak of something "torn" by wild animals or "torn away" by force (stolen). Probably the former idea is intended here. In Exodus 22:31 the Israelites were instructed not to "eat the meat of an animal torn by wild beasts; throw it to the dogs"; thus to offer such an animal to God was an appalling insult. With spiritual leaders like these, no wonder the nation was in such a degraded condition! This passage is a warning to spiritual leaders and church members today who offer God the leftovers and despise worship as mere drudgery.

1:14. The attitude of the priests was also that of the people, and here we find the case of a deceitful vow. The worshiper made a vow (strictly voluntary) **to give** an unblemished **male** (Lev. 22:19) as a sacrifice if God would grant deliverance or favor in some matter (Num 30:2; Jonah 2:9). Yet after God granted the favor, the one who made the vow reneged and offered **a blemished** (ruined) **animal** instead. Did he really think he could con God? Such treatment of Israel's **great king** was inexcusable and would result in a frightful curse (Deut. 27:14–26; 28:15–19,45) upon this **cheat** ("the deceiver," KJV).

The chapter concludes on a positive note. Ironically, *Israel's* wayward priests and cheats had not honored the Lord, but *foreigners* (**the nations**) would. Many foreigners **feared** the Lord in Old Testament times, like Ruth the Moabite woman (Ruth 1:16). Yet Baldwin seems correct in understanding the fulfillment of this text as future: "By contrast Malachi was referring here, as in verse 11, to the imminent conversion of the nations, who would come, perhaps in a procession of homage, to the great King" (Baldwin, 232).

MAIN IDEA REVIEW: *God loves the world and has proven his love by his actions. We should respond by honoring God, offering him our best, and worshiping him with joy.*

III. CONCLUSION

Foolish Questions

Some questions are foolish, aren't they? For example, have you ever said something like, "I am going to Joe's funeral this afternoon," and had someone reply, "Oh, did Joe die?" You are tempted to say, "No. We just thought we would go ahead and have his funeral just in case!" And what is the first thing that someone says when you remark, "I have lost my car keys"? Usually, it is something like, "Where did you lose them?" "If I knew that, they wouldn't be lost!"

People ask foolish questions all the time. As a matter of fact, the Book of Malachi seems to be arranged around six key questions—foolish questions—asked by Malachi's audience (1:2,6; 2:14,17; 3:8,13). Actually, they are not just foolish; some of them border on blasphemy. In the first chapter of Malachi, we encounter two of these questions. In verse 2 the people responded to God's declaration of love for them by retorting, "How have you loved us?" How foolish! God's grace upon Israel was obvious, yet they wanted to know: "God, what have you ever done for us?" Patiently, God responded by sharing his great act of love in choosing them to be his covenant nation.

We find the second foolish question in verse 6. God stated that Israel did not honor or respect him but rather showed contempt for his name. In feigned innocence they pleaded, "How have we shown contempt for your name?" In other words, "What have we ever done?" Again, what a foolish question. Their disrespect for God was apparent—offering sick and worthless animals for sacrifice, the leftovers! They wouldn't treat their governor that way. God also heard their complaints about serving him—"What a burden!" Reading between the lines, we sense God's genuine heartbreak at their actions. After all the Lord had done for them, they treated their great King with utter disrespect.

It is easy to criticize Malachi's countrymen, but what about us? Do we ever question God's love when he has obviously done so much for us, particularly Christ's sacrifice on the cross? Do we show disrespect to God by offering him the leftovers of our time, talents, and resources? Do we ever view serving God as a burden? Let us remember who God is (the great King of the universe) and what he has done for us. Then we will appreciate and treat our heavenly Father as he deserves.

PRINCIPLES

- God loves us.
- God proves his love for us by his actions.
- We should respond to God's love with respect and gratitude.
- Insincere and loveless worship displeases God.
- Without a proper love for God, worship will be a burden.
- God is the great King of the universe and deserves our best.

APPLICATIONS

- Thank God that he loves you.
- Since God loves you, realize that you are very significant.
- Reflect on the many ways God has shown his love for you.
- Show your respect and gratitude to God by offering him your best.
- If your worship life has lost its joy, remember God's loving acts for you, especially the sacrifice of Christ on the cross.
- Keep your promises (vows) to God.

IV. LIFE APPLICATION

Money Was No Object

I was sitting at the lunch table with some colleagues a few years ago when a lovely lady walked over and said, "Hello. Do you remember me? I am one of your old girlfriends." Of course, I remembered her. We "went together" for a while in elementary school. I still remember going to a drugstore in our little town to buy her one of those heart-shaped boxes of candy for Valentine's Day. I had a paper route after school and made a little spending money. When the clerk asked how big a box I wanted, I told her a big one. Money was no object because I was in love!

While in college, another girlfriend (now my wife) went home for school break. I couldn't stand the thought of not seeing her for a few days, so I decided to make the one-and-one-half-hour drive to her home. The problem was that I worked nights at a motel. After working all night, I drove to see her, stayed all day, drove back just in time to get to work at 11:00 p.m., and then worked all night. If someone told me today, "I want you to stay awake for thirty-six hours straight," I would think, "You've got to be kidding." But I did it. Why? Again, because I was in love (and still am)! When we are in love, we don't mind spending money on someone. When we are in love, we don't mind making sacrifices. We don't mind spending time with those we love.

What was wrong with Malachi's audience? Their root problem was that they didn't love the Lord like they should have. This is *the* problem today. People have no time for God because they don't love him. Even believers can let their love grow cold. When we come to the place where we no longer desire to spend time with God, to serve God, or to give our financial resources for his kingdom's work, we have a love problem. As Jesus cautioned the church at Ephesus, "Yet I hold this against you: You have forsaken your first love" (Rev. 2:4). How is that love restored? Jesus counseled, "Remember the height from which you have fallen!" (Rev. 2:5). The key word is "remember." When we remember how Christ bled and died on the cross for our sins, and all the other wonderful things he has done for us, we will appreciate and love him like we should.

V. PRAYER

Dear Lord, how amazing and wonderful it is that you, the God of all the universe, love us! Thank you for demonstrating your love in so many ways—most of all by sending your Son, Jesus Christ, to die on the cross for our sins. May our lives and worship always show our respect and appreciation for all you have done. In Jesus' name we pray. Amen.

VI. DEEPER DISCOVERIES

A. Date of Malachi's Ministry (1:1)

There is no doubt that the Book of Malachi was written some time in the postexilic period. The Jews had returned to their land and were under the rule of a Persian governor (1:8). Temple services were being observed, so the book cannot be dated earlier than 516 B.C., the time when the second temple was finished.

Information contained in the prophecy leads most interpreters to agree that Malachi ministered in the same general time period as Ezra and Nehemiah. Malachi preached against many of the same sins named in the Book of Nehemiah: priestly negligence (1:6; Neh. 13:4–9,30), failure to tithe

(3:8–12; Neh. 13:10–13,31), and intermarriage with foreigners (2:10–16; Neh. 13:23–28).

Scholars differ, however, over whether Malachi preached in the period just before the coming of Nehemiah to Jerusalem, in the time between Nehemiah's two terms as governor of Palestine, during Nehemiah's second term, or after Nehemiah's rule. Any suggestion that Malachi delivered these oracles during Nehemiah's two terms as governor must be rejected because the conditions described by Malachi could never have occurred if Nehemiah had been present. Furthermore, Malachi 1:8 implies a governor who accepted gifts from the citizens, while Nehemiah distinctly said that he did not take advantage of this privilege (Neh. 5:14–16). Most likely Malachi preached these messages in the period (probably a number of years) between Nehemiah's two terms as governor (Neh. 1:1; 13:6–7). If so, the wrongs were quickly corrected upon Nehemiah's return.

The historical allusion to the defeat of the Edomites by a foreign power (Mal. 1:2–5) could refer to that of Nebuchadnezzar in 586 B.C. (Jer. 49:7–10; 25:9,21) or, more likely, to the one accomplished by the Nabatean Arabs in the fifth century B.C. (and following). Neither view would contradict the setting for Malachi's ministry suggested above.

B. Malachi as Scripture (1:1)

Malachi's place in the canon of Scripture has never been questioned. It is listed as part of the Twelve (the minor prophets) by the Jewish writer ben Sirach (Sir. 49:10) about 180 B.C. A fragment containing Malachi 1:13–14 has also been found among the Dead Sea Scrolls at Qumran. Although Malachi is not mentioned by name, the book is repeatedly referred to in the New Testament as an inspired prophecy (e.g., Matt. 11:10; 17:12; Mark 1:2; 9:11–12; Luke 1:17; Rom. 9:13).

C. Malachi's Question-and-Answer Style (1:2)

Malachi used a dialectical style, or a question-and-answer method of preaching. No fewer than twenty-seven questions appear in the book. According to R. Alden, "Even a casual reading shows Malachi's use of rhetorical questions. Seven times he put them into the mouths of his audience (1:2,6–7; 2:17; 3:7–8,13, and perhaps 2:14). In addition he asked the people several rhetorical questions (e.g., 1:6,8–9; 2:10,15; 3:2)" (Alden, "Malachi," 704). We may observe the following general pattern in Malachi's method: (1) statement of the truth, (2) objection in the form of a question, and (3) the prophet's substantiation of the truth. These rhetorical questions probably reflected Malachi's actual public debates with some of the priests and people.

The question-and-answer method of teaching became very popular in later Judaism and, in fact, became the usual format for the scribes and rabbis. Rhetorical questions are also quite common in the New Testament.

D. "I Have Loved Jacob, But Esau I Have Hated" (1:2b–3a)

This phrase is one of the most hotly debated and misunderstood statements in the Bible. How may God's hatred possibly be explained? After all, God is love (1 John 4:8). First, the context of the passage is national rather than personal. In other words, Jacob was chosen ("loved") as the ancestor of the privileged nation of Israel; Esau (father of the nation of Edom, v. 4) was passed over ("hated") for this honor.

Second, love-hate may be used in a comparative sense in the Bible. For example, in Genesis 29:30–31 we read, "Jacob lay with Rachel also, and he *loved Rachel more* than Leah. And he worked for Laban another seven years. When the LORD saw that *Leah was not loved,* he opened her womb, but Rachel was barren" (emphasis added).

The NIV's "not loved" in Genesis 29:31 is literally "hated," the exact word (in the Hebrew text) found in Malachi 1:3. The previous verse in Genesis (29:30) explains that Jacob's hatred for Leah simply means that he loved Rachel "more than" Leah. Certainly, Jacob did not hate Leah in the sense that he had a mean or vindictive spirit toward her. He fathered at least seven children by Leah! The Genesis passage means that Jacob's choice and the more favored wife was Rachel, not Leah. Here in Malachi we have the same idea. God's choice and the more favored of the two brothers was Jacob. (Jesus also used the word *hate* in a comparative sense of "to love less" in Luke 14:26.) Thus, God's gracious choice of Jacob's descendants, Israel, rather than Esau's descendants, Edom (v. 4), demonstrated his great love for Israel.

E. The Nation of Edom (1:3–5)

Edom played a key role in Israel's history and was a bitter antagonist of God's people. This is all the more ironic since Jacob, the father of Israel, and Esau, the father of Edom (Gen. 36:1), were brothers (Gen. 25:24–26). Esau was named Edom (from a Semitic root that means "red") when he sold his birthright to Jacob for a serving of "red stew" (Gen. 25:30). He eventually settled in the "land of Seir," which became "the country of Edom" (Gen. 32:3; 36:8).

Edom's territory (part of modern Jordan) extended from south of the Dead Sea to the Gulf of Aqaba, approximately one hundred miles long and up to forty miles wide. The rugged, mountainous terrain is forbidding, with peaks rising to about four thousand feet. Largely a semi-desert region, its sparse rainfall is not conducive to agriculture. For this reason, nomadic groups mainly inhabited the area in its early history; later the Edomites adopted a more settled life. Sela ("rock") was the capital (2 Kgs. 14:7) with other important towns being Bozrah and Teman (Amos 1:12).

Israel's relationship with Edom was rocky from the start. The Edomites refused Israel permission to travel through their territory after the exodus (Num. 20:14–21; 21:4). King Saul fought the Edomites (1 Sam. 14:47), and David put garrisons throughout the land (2 Sam. 8:14). For much of the pre-exilic period, Edom was subjugated by Judah and Israel but rebelled on occasion (2 Kgs. 8:20–22; 2 Chr. 21:8–10). Later Edom became a vassal state of Assyria, then of Babylon.

Edom's bitterness toward the Israelites was deep and exhibited itself whenever the opportunity arose. For example, when Judah was being attacked by Pekah, king of Israel, the Edomites took advantage of the situation and carried away Judean captives (2 Chr. 28:17). The psalmist recalled Edom's vengeful cries, "Tear it down . . . tear it down to its foundations!" when Jerusalem fell to the Babylonians (Ps. 137:7). Because of its bitter hatred and cruel acts toward Israel, Edom came to symbolize all the enemies of God and his people (e.g., Isa. 34:1–17).

Because of Edom's sins, the prophets predicted judgment on the land and its people (Jer. 49:7–22; Ezek. 25:12–14; 35:15; Joel 3:19; Amos 9:12; Obad. 10–21). Nebuchadnezzar ravaged many nations, including Edom (Jer. 49:7–9; 25:9,21). During the exile many Edomites migrated to southern Judah around Hebron, an area that came to be known as Idumea (Gr. for Edom). Edomites still living in Edom were pushed out of their land by the Nabatean Arabs from the fifth to third centuries B.C., bringing more to southern Judah. Petra, the awe-inspiring fortress city in the cliffs, was built by the Nabateans (about 300 B.C.). Judas Maccabeus subdued the Edomites in Judah (1 Macc. 5:65), and eventually they were incorporated into the Jewish people. Herod the Great was an Idumean.

In the New Testament period, Idumea was part of Palestine and joined the Jews in their ill-fated revolt against Rome. Consequently, the Romans destroyed the Idumeans in the war of A.D. 70. At that time the people known as the Edomites disappeared from history, a fulfillment of prophecy (e.g., Obad. 10,18).

VII. TEACHING OUTLINE

A. INTRODUCTION

1. Lead Story: Our Heavenly Father Knows Best: The Lauren Chapin Story

2. Context: Although Malachi does not provide a precise date for his prophecies (as Zechariah usually did), the setting is some time in the postexilic period. The Jewish people had returned to the land, and the temple had been rebuilt. Considerable time must have elapsed since the initial return from the Babylonian captivity and the ministries of Haggai and Zechariah. The initial exuberance at being back in the land was replaced by discouragement at the harsh realities confronting the tiny nation. The joy experienced soon after the temple services were reinstated now seems to have vanished, and disrespectful and joyless worship was common. Difficult circumstances had even caused some people to doubt that God really loved them. Both priests and people were showing disrespect toward God by offering blemished sacrifices and engaging in joyless worship. Malachi and Nehemiah dealt with similar problems (e.g., failure to tithe), thus we may place the prophet more precisely in the same general time as Ezra and Nehemiah (latter part of the fifth century B.C.).

3. Transition: Malachi addresses issues that are relevant for our modern world. Today's people also ask, "Does God love me and what has he done to prove his love for me?" God's Word answers that question affirmatively and provides abundant proof of God's love. The greatest evidence of God's love is the incredible sacrifice of Jesus Christ on the cross for our sins. His sacrifice makes possible heaven some day and an abundant life now. Like Malachi's audience, we can show disrespect toward God by offering him second best (of our time, talents, and resources) and by joyless worship that does not glorify Christ.

B. COMMENTARY

1. Introducing the Prophecy of Malachi (1:1)

2. God's Love (1:2–5)
3. Response to God's Love (1:6–14)

C. CONCLUSION: FOOLISH QUESTIONS

VIII. ISSUES FOR DISCUSSION

1. What are some ways that God reveals his love for us? What is the greatest demonstration of God's love?
2. How may we explain the statement, "I have loved Jacob, but Esau I have hated"? What are some other references in Scripture to things God is said to "hate"?
3. Name actions that show disrespect toward God. Do you think most people treat human dignitaries and movie stars with more honor than the God of the universe?
4. Discuss attitudes toward worship that displease God. Do you believe that many people today regard worship as a "burden"? Do you think that most people in our society view worship as relevant and vital?
5. In your opinion, do most people give God their best or just the left-overs? What does God think of this?

Malachi 2:1–16

Always Faithful

I. INTRODUCTION
Still Faithful

II. COMMENTARY
A verse-by-verse explanation of these verses.

III. CONCLUSION
No Sick Days in Sixty-Two Years

An overview of the principles and applications from these verses.

IV. LIFE APPLICATION
How to Have a Happy and Lasting Marriage

Melding these verses to life.

V. PRAYER
Tying these verses to life with God.

VI. DEEPER DISCOVERIES
Historical, geographical, and grammatical enrichment of the commentary.

VII. TEACHING OUTLINE
Suggested step-by-step group study of these verses.

VIII. ISSUES FOR DISCUSSION
Zeroing these verses in on daily life.

Quote

"*Semper Fidelis* (Always Faithful)"

Motto   of   the   United   States

Marine   Corps

Malachi 2:1–16

 IN A NUTSHELL

Malachi 2:1–16 is a call to faithfulness. In this section the prophet rebukes unfaithfulness: on the part of religious leaders, in community relations (dishonesty), to God (by marrying pagans), and to family (divorce).

Always Faithful

I. INTRODUCTION

Still Faithful

*E*very year several million people flock to Yellowstone National Park in Wyoming to view its wonders. Tourists come from all over the world to see the buffalo (bison) that roam about the two-million-acre park and hopefully to catch a glimpse of a grizzly bear lumbering along the side of a mountain. However, the main attraction at Yellowstone is the famous geyser called Old Faithful. Explorers dubbed the geyser Old Faithful in 1870 because it seemed to spout "faithfully" every sixty-three to seventy minutes; now it erupts about every eighty minutes. Geologists estimate that the geyser has been active for two hundred to three hundred years.

A few years ago I made the trek to Yellowstone and remember the excitement of seeing Old Faithful for the first time. It was June but quite cold. A schedule was posted with the times when Old Faithful was to come alive, and a crowd of us gathered around the geyser shivering as we waited for the next "show." Finally, the scheduled time arrived. Suddenly, the water began to boil up out of the ground, and we watched awestruck as several thousand gallons of hot water and billowing steam blew about 170 feet into the air. Old Faithful is *still* faithful.

Faithfulness is an important Christian virtue, and like Old Faithful we need to be faithful as well. In Malachi 2:1–16 we see the importance of faithfulness to God and our fellow human beings. Specifically, Malachi dealt with the need for faithfulness on the part of religious leaders, faithfulness to others in the community, faithfulness to God, and faithfulness to family. If people were faithful in these areas, most of society's problems today would be solved. Let us see how the message of a prophet who lived over twenty-four hundred years ago could make our modern world a better place.

II. COMMENTARY

Always Faithful

MAIN IDEA: *God demands faithfulness among religious leaders, to others in the community, to himself, and to our families.*

Ⓐ Faithfulness of Religious Leaders (2:1–9)

SUPPORTING IDEA: *Religious leaders are to be faithful to their God-given responsibilities.*

2:1–2. Malachi had already spoken of the priests' disrespectful behavior. In verses 1–9 he warned these religious leaders to **listen** to (and obey) his **admonition** (literally, "commandment," not a suggestion) to them. They must determine **to honor** God's **name**, rather than disgracing it as they had been doing (1:6,12). Ten times in this brief prophecy Malachi referred to the "name" of God (1:6[two times],11[three times],14; 2:2,5; 3:16; 4:2), seven of these in the first sixteen verses of the book. God's name represents God himself and is to be honored, not disgraced. If the people did not repent, **the LORD Almighty** would **send a curse** on them (Mal. 1:14). Deuteronomy 28:20–29 tells us that the **curse** included ruin, disease, drought, crop failure, famine, defeat by enemies, and ultimately destruction—manifestations of God's displeasure.

Priestly **blessings** refer to the material support of the priests primarily through the people's tithes and offerings. It was obvious that God had **already cursed** these blessings because the people's failure to tithe is specified (3:8). Perhaps one reason the people did not tithe was their lack of respect for these unfaithful priests.

2:3. The NIV's **descendants** is literally "seed," which may denote "offspring" ("seed of Abraham," Isa. 41:8 KJV) but more likely refers to "crops" here. The fact that God promised to reverse the present dismal economic conditions and bless their crops (3:11) indicates that crop failure was a serious problem. Moreover, the terminology is similar to that of the curse passage in Deuteronomy 28:20–24 (the Lord's "rebuke" of their agricultural endeavors). Righteousness and economic blessing are connected here and elsewhere in Malachi (3:10–12; cp. Matt. 6:33).

Offal refers to the intestines of the **sacrifices** and their contents (which would include literal dung). After the priests burned the sacrifices, the offal remained and was taken outside the camp and disposed of (Exod. 29:14; Lev.

8:17; 16:27). Because of the unfaithfulness of the priests, this disgusting filth would be spread on their **faces**! This figure for abject humiliation before the people could hardly be more graphic. Contact with this waste would also render them ceremonially unclean and unfit to serve. Like the offal, the priests would **be carried off**, that is, removed from office. Sex scandals, unbelief, and other unfaithful acts among some members of the clergy in our time have led to their public disgrace.

2:4. When judgment fell upon the priests, they would know that Malachi's **admonition** was the word of the Lord. God would purify the priesthood (by removing the unfaithful), so that the institution of the priesthood (**my covenant with Levi**) might **continue**. "Levi" represents the priesthood, since priests were appointed from the tribe of Levi, specifically from the line of Moses' brother Aaron. Even in the judgment of these unfaithful priests, we see God's grace in that the dross was to be removed for the good of the nation. God would preserve a godly priesthood (like Ezra, Ezra 1:1–5) that would teach the Word of God and lead the people in the right way.

2:5. Life and peace were gifts of God's **covenant** with Levi—the Levitical priesthood. In return, the priests were to honor (**reverence**) the Lord. Earlier priests did revere and respect their God (**stood in awe of my name**), unlike many in Malachi's day. Repeatedly, the Bible emphasizes that both spiritual and physical **life** and well-being (peace) are blessings of obedience (Deut. 4:40; 6:2; 30:15–20; Prov. 3:1–2; 4:10,22; 6:23). The phrase "covenant of life and peace" appears only here in the Bible, but the similar "covenant of peace" is found in Numbers 25:12 as a promise to Phinehas, the priest, for his faithfulness. Phinehas was also assured that his descendants would have a covenant of a lasting priesthood, "because he was zealous for the honor of his God and made atonement for the Israelites" (Num. 25:13).

Phinehas's example seems to be in the background of Malachi 2. The faithfulness of this ancient priest and his resulting blessings are intended as an encouragement to faithfulness on the part of the priests in Malachi's day. Probably "life and peace" for the Levitical priesthood as a whole meant that it would continue in existence and be blessed.

2:6. These earlier priests (Levi) also taught the truth (**true instruction**; literally, "the law of truth"), spoke righteous words (**nothing false**), lived righteous lives, **and turned many from sin** ("iniquity," KJV, NASB, NRSV) by example as well as by right teaching. Unlike many priests in Malachi's days, these earlier priests not only knew the law; they practiced it themselves.

2:7–8. Malachi contrasted the faithful earlier priests with those of his day. A **priest** was God's **messenger**, who should **preserve knowledge** and teach the truth. Yet many priests in Malachi's time were living ungodly lives (**turned from the way**) and were **teaching** falsehood. As a result of their ungodly example and misinterpreting the Word of God, they had **caused many to stumble**. Baldwin points out: "This terrible possibility of causing others to miss the way called forth from Jesus one of His sternest warnings (Mt. 18:5,6), and it is those with positions of leadership who are in greatest danger of misleading others" (Baldwin, 236). By their unfaithfulness, these priests had **violated the covenant with Levi** and were in danger of judgment and losing their positions. No dispute about the charges is possible because the one who brings them is **the LORD Almighty**, the omniscient heavenly judge.

2:9. For their unfaithfulness (**not followed my ways**), God **caused** these priests **to be despised and humiliated before all the people** (see 2:3). People had lost respect for these spiritual leaders and the priestly office generally. The priests despised God ("show/shown contempt" in 1:6; same Hebrew word as "despise" in this verse), so God caused the people to despise them— a fitting punishment.

Malachi's description of the spiritual leaders in his time sounds like some in our world today. In recent months newspapers have been filled with stories of priests accused of molesting children, and the escapades of certain well-known television evangelists are public knowledge. Some people have become disillusioned with the church because of such disappointments. However, we should remember two important facts. First, countless faithful ministers of the gospel serve selflessly and tirelessly throughout our world. Let us not condemn all because of some. Second, human beings (even spiritual leaders) may disappoint us, but Jesus never will. He is always faithful, and he is the object of our faith.

Malachi concluded this section by adding another charge to the list of the priests' sins. They had **shown partiality in matters of the law.** Priests also functioned as justices in legal matters (Deut. 17:9; 19:17), and apparently they were rendering favorable decisions to ingratiate themselves to the rich and powerful or for bribes (Deut. 16:19).

In summary, the priests in Malachi's day were being judged because they were unfaithful to God in both their personal and professional lives. May spiritual leaders today heed the warning set forth by God's faithful prophet twenty-four hundred years ago.

𝔅 Faithfulness to Others (2:10)

SUPPORTING IDEA: *We should deal faithfully and honestly with others in our society.*

2:10. In this verse Malachi addressed the problem of unfaithful behavior toward others in Judah. Earlier we saw spiritual leaders and laypersons ("the cheat," 1:14) who treated God shamefully. If they would treat God so, we should not be surprised to find them mistreating one another. George Horne states, "When men cease to be faithful to their God, he who expects to find them faithful to each other will be much disappointed" (Water, 351).

Malachi begins with two questions, each expecting an affirmative answer. They did in fact have **one Father**, and **one God** did **create** them. Israel's father in the flesh was Abraham, but most commentators agree with NIV that this reference is to God their spiritual Father. Moreover, "one God" in the next line seems to parallel "one Father," and previously in the book God is called Israel's father (1:6; cp. Isa. 43:1).

Thus, all Israel had God as their Father and Creator. Why then, Malachi asked, were they dealing dishonestly and sinfully with one another? Committing sinful acts prohibited in the law (e.g., the Ten Commandments) violated **the covenant** Israel made with God at Sinai. **Breaking faith** ("deal treacherously," KJV, NASB) in this context is not limited to unfaithfulness in marriage (2:11–16) but includes unfaithful dealings (dishonesty, deceit) among Judah's citizens generally—in business, marriage, and the like.

Mistreatment of others is a serious problem in our modern society. Dishonest dealings and selfish behavior are rampant. Examples of unscrupulous corporate executives who have become wealthy at the expense of company stockholders have been in the news lately. In July 1996 a woman from Albany, Georgia, was killed and her daughter was injured when a bomb exploded in Atlanta's Centennial Olympic Park during the summer Olympics. Some heartless person, learning from the media coverage that the woman had been killed and the family was out of town, burglarized the home! How we treat others reveals much about our character and our relationship with God.

ℂ Faithfulness to God (2:11–12)

SUPPORTING IDEA: *We should not compromise in our faithfulness to God.*

2:11. **Judah** had acted faithlessly toward God **by marrying the daughter of a foreign god**. During the divided kingdom period, Judah had been the name of the Southern Kingdom (two tribes) and **Israel** the name of the Northern Kingdom (ten tribes). After the exile both names were used to designate the country. Perhaps Malachi mentioned Judah, Israel, and **Jerusalem** (even the holy city!) to highlight the scope of the problem as countrywide. Israel, the ancient name for the nation, may also have been cited separately to call attention to the people's covenant relationship with the Lord.

The phrase **detestable thing** (traditionally, "abomination," KJV, NASB, NRSV) speaks of various abhorrent and repulsive acts. Frequently, the term is applied to idolatrous practices and objects (Deut. 7:25–26; 13:14; 20:18), and that is probably the idea here. Malachi was not condemning cross-cultural marriages but the marriage of Jews to idolaters. Israelites were permitted to wed foreigners if they were believers in the Lord. For example, Boaz married a woman from Moab named Ruth who became King David's ancestor (Ruth 4:13–22). Nevertheless, marrying pagans was strictly forbidden in the Mosaic Law because of the danger of infecting the person and nation with false religion (Exod. 34:11–16; Deut. 7:3; 1 Kgs. 11:1–2; cp. 1 Cor. 7:39; 2 Cor. 6:14–15). Nehemiah, Malachi's contemporary, described the seriousness of the problem (Neh. 13:23–28).

The phrase **daughter of a foreign god** designates these new wives as followers (spiritual children) of pagan deities, just as the Lord is deemed the Father of believers (Mal. 1:6; 2:10). Certainly these Israelites had violated God's law by marrying unbelievers, and the act itself was a compromise of their faith. Yet the use of "detestable thing" with its idolatrous connotations may suggest that these men were flirting with their wives' false religions.

Sanctuary (also NASB, NRSV) is literally "holiness," but here it designates the Lord's holy place, the temple. That the temple is in view is also implied by references to the temple "offerings" in verses 12–13. How did marrying pagans desecrate the **sanctuary**? Three explanations are: (1) The temple was defiled by the presence of pagans. (2) The nation as God's temple was defiled by this practice. (3) Priests had married unbelievers and were desecrating the temple because they were unfit to serve. Both Ezra (9:1–3) and Nehemiah (13:28) inform us that even some priests had married pagan wives. Perhaps elements of all three views were involved.

2:12. The NIV's **whoever he may be** is fairly literally rendered in the NASB as *"everyone* who awakes and answers." Apparently, the KJV translators by their "the master and the scholar" had in mind the teacher as one who awakes, rouses, or incites and the students who answer. "Awake" is a figure for resurrection (coming to life) in Scripture (Isa. 26:19; Dan. 12:2), and one who answers or responds is alive. Thus, the NIV's translation seems correctly to capture the sense of the Hebrew idiom as any living person. Wolf suggests, "The English expression of being 'alive and kicking' may not be far from the thrust of this Hebrew idiom" (Wolf, 89).

Those who defied their God by marrying pagan wives would be **cut off from the tents of Jacob**. The phrase "cut off" may mean excommunication, the death penalty (Exod. 31:14; Isa. 53:8), or the disappearance of one's family line from Israel. Nehemiah, the prophet's contemporary, did excommunicate a priest from the community who was guilty of marrying a pagan (Neh. 13:28). As governor, he had the authority to do so. Nevertheless, the sentence pronounced by Malachi on the culprit was that his line would cease. He did not take matters into his own hands but left the person to the Lord for punishment. Hopefully, the individual would repent and be forgiven.

The one who **brings offerings** could be the priests, but more likely these words refer to anyone who defied the Lord's command against marrying pagans and then brazenly offered a sacrifice to the Lord while at the same time desecrating his sanctuary (v. 11). Malachi and Nehemiah exhibited an uncompromising attitude toward the sin of marrying idolaters because they realized its dangers to fragile Judah. Baldwin explains, "Since apostasy had been responsible for the exile it was unthinkable that the whole community should be put at risk again" (Baldwin, 238).

Ⅾ Faithfulness to Family (2:13–16)

SUPPORTING IDEA: *We should be faithful to our marriage partners.*

2:13. Malachi now addressed the need for faithfulness to one's marriage partner. The people were flooding **the LORD's altar with tears** and weeping and wailing because God **no longer pays attention to your offerings or accepts them with pleasure from your hands**. How did they know that God did not accept their offerings? God did not answer their prayers for blessing. They prayed for God to bless their crops, but the harvest was dismal (3:11). Why was God not blessing them? They were not being blessed because they were not "blessable." For all the unfaithful acts mentioned in verses 10–16 (and other sins named elsewhere in the book), God refused to pay attention to them and pour out his blessing on the nation. They wept but had not repented.

The Lord's altar was the place of sacrifice, indicating that the people were still worshiping the Lord, although their worship involved unacceptable sacrifices and a wrong attitude (1:6–8,12–13). Only the priests had access to the altar, but the people brought the sacrifices. Clearly all were involved in this national sorrow.

2:14. Their crocodile tears were getting them nowhere with God, and they wondered, **Why?** What had they done now? Not only had they been unfaithful to God and others within the community; Malachi now charged that they had **broken faith** with their wives. The phrase **wife of your youth** reflects the fact that "in the ancient Near East the marriage was contracted at an early age. According to the Talmud a young man was cursed if he was not married by the age of twenty" (Verhoef, 274).

Years before, these husbands had entered into a **marriage covenant** with God as **witness** in which they made solemn vows to their wives and to God. Now they had reneged on those sacred promises and discarded their wives like yesterday's newspaper. When the husband had promised to remain true for life, he had lied to his wife (**partner**) and to God. The sin against the wife is emphasized by the three phrases: "wife of your youth," "your partner," and "wife of your marriage covenant." Wives could be divorced for many reasons in ancient Israel. In this case it seems that these husbands were divorcing their Jewish wives and marrying the pagans mentioned in verse 11.

2:15. This is the most difficult verse in the book and one of the most difficult in the Bible, evidenced by the plethora of different translations in the English versions. A literal rendering of the Hebrew is: "And did he not make one? And he had a remnant of the Spirit [or "spirit"]. And what purpose was the one? He was seeking a godly seed [offspring]." The first part may also be translated: "And one does not do so [divorce] who has a remnant of the spirit [intelligence, sound judgment]."

Three popular interpretations are: (1) A sensible person does not divorce a godly wife and marry another. He wants to raise up children who are godly. (2) Jewish interpreters and a few others favor Abraham as the "one" who married a second wife, Hagar, to produce a godly offspring. Yet this interpretation seems weak for a number of reasons. For example, Abraham did not divorce Sarah—the problem here in Malachi. (3) God gave Adam only one wife even though he had enough of the Spirit's power to make many wives. God's purpose in this one husband-one wife union ("one flesh," Gen. 2:24) was to raise up godly children. This latter view seems preferable. Divorce would be contrary to the one husband-one wife model established by God at the beginning (Gen. 2:18–25), and marriage to a pagan would hinder the rearing of children who would follow the Lord.

Since divorce is so dangerous, Malachi warned, **Guard yourself in your spirit**. After all, the lustful thoughts that may lead us to be unfaithful to our marriage partners originate in the spirit or heart. As Jesus reminded us, "For out of the heart come evil thoughts, murder, adultery, sexual immorality, theft, false testimony, slander" (Matt. 15:19).

2:16. **"I hate divorce"** [literally, "sending away"], **says the LORD God of Israel** is the most forceful denunciation of divorce in the Old Testament. We may emphasize that the text does not say that God hates divorced people. Certainly, he does not. He loves them, and this is precisely why God hates divorce. God sees the heartache of the rejected spouse, the wounded children, and the destruction to society that divorce brings. All this breaks the heart of God.

God's statement about divorce here does not contradict the provision for divorce in the Mosaic Law (Deut. 24:1–3). Divorce happens in society, and guidelines to regulate its practice are necessary. Jesus informed the Pharisees, "Moses permitted you to divorce your wives because your hearts were hard. But it was not this way from the beginning" (Matt. 19:8). In other words, God intended from the beginning that marriage be permanent, but he was fully aware that divorce would occur in a sinful world.

God also hates **a man's covering himself with violence as well as with his garment.** Spreading a garment over a woman expressed an intention to marry her (Ruth 3:9). Thus, some interpreters feel this garment covered with **violence** continues the thought of acting unfaithfully and unjustly toward one's spouse in divorce. However, Malachi began this section (2:10–16) with a rebuke of general unfaithfulness, and it would be fitting to close in a similar vein. If so, God was repeating his displeasure toward all kinds of unfaithful acts. The picture seems to be of a person whose clothes are covered with violence. The section closes with the admonition of verse 15, **So guard yourself in your spirit, and do not break faith.**

MAIN IDEA REVIEW: *God demands faithfulness among religious leaders, to others in the community, to himself, and to our families.*

III. CONCLUSION

No Sick Days in Sixty-Two Years

Mildred Parsons worked as a secretary for the Federal Bureau of Investigation in Washington, D.C., for sixty-two years, nine months, and two days. In all that time she never once missed a day of work due to sickness. Ms. Parsons retired in June 2002 at age 88, the longest-serving employee in FBI history. Surely, there were days when she didn't feel like going to work, but she went anyway. She was faithful to the task.

In this section of the prophecy, Malachi reminded us that God wants people to be faithful. In 2:1–9 he warned those who serve in positions of spiritual leadership in local congregations, denominations, and other areas to take seriously their responsibilities. Some of the most severe denunciations in the Book of Malachi and in the Bible are directed toward unfaithful and hypocritical spiritual leaders. Malachi also reprimanded those who are unfaithful in dealing with others in the community (2:10,16). Dishonest business dealings and other deceit destroy the very fabric of a society. Faithfulness to others begins with faithfulness to a holy God (2:11–12). Some people in Malachi's day were unfaithful to God because they married (and possibly worshiped with) pagans who venerated false gods. Finally, the prophet dealt with unfaithful spouses who were sending their wives packing and marrying others (2:13–16). Such actions break the heart of God because of the heartache and devastation they bring to his children.

PRINCIPLES

- God expects us to be faithful.
- Religious leaders should be faithful to their God-given responsibilities.
- If religious leaders are not faithful, they will be disgraced and lose the respect of the people.
- We should deal faithfully and honestly with those in our community.
- Christians should not be "unequally yoked" with unbelievers.
- God wants us to be faithful to our marriage partners.
- God will reward us for our faithfulness.

APPLICATIONS

- Resolve to be faithful to God and his kingdom's work.
- If you are a religious leader, determine to be faithful to God's calling on your life.
- We should respect, honor, and support religious leaders who are faithful to God.
- Are you honest in your dealings with others? Are there wrongs against others that you need to make right?

- If you are unmarried, determine to marry a believer who can help you to grow in your Christian faith. If you are already married to an unbeliever, live such a Christlike life that he or she will want to know your Savior.

- Renew your marriage vows to your spouse, pledging once more to be faithful until death do you part.

IV. LIFE APPLICATION

How to Have a Happy and Lasting Marriage

James Dobson has a Ph.D. from the University of Southern California and is one of the foremost authorities in the world on marriage and the family. In his best-selling book *Life on the Edge* (W Publishing, 2000), Dobson offers the following seven recommendations for having a marriage that will stand the test of time.

1. A Sunday school teacher gave me some advice when I was thirteen years of age that I never forgot. He said, "Don't marry the person you think you can live with. Marry the one you can't live without." There's great truth in this advice. Marriage can be difficult even when two people are passionately in love with one another. It is murder when they don't have that foundation to build on.

2. Don't marry someone who has characteristics that you feel are intolerable. You may plan to change him or her in the future, but that probably won't happen. Behavior runs in deep channels that were cut during early childhood, and it is very difficult to alter them. In order to change a deeply ingrained pattern, you have to build a sturdy dam, dig another canal, and reroute the river in the new direction. That effort is rarely successful over the long haul.

3. Do not marry impulsively! I can think of no better way to mess up your life than to leap into this critical decision without careful thought and prayer. It takes time to get acquainted and to walk through the first eight steps of the bonding process. . . . I suggest that you take at least a year to get beyond the facade and into the inner character of the person.

4. If you are a deeply committed Christian, do not allow yourself to become "unequally yoked" with an unbeliever. You may expect to win your spouse to the Lord at some future date, and that does hap-

pen on occasion. But to count on it is risky at best, foolhardy at worst. Again, this is the question that must be answered: "Just how critical is it that my husband (or wife) shares my faith?" If it is essential and nonnegotiable, as the Scripture tells us it should be for believers, then that matter should be given the highest priority in one's decision to marry.

5. Do not move in with a person before marriage. To do so is a bad idea for many reasons. First, it is immoral and a violation of God's law. Second, it undermines a relationship and leads often to divorce. Studies show that couples who live together before marriage have a 50 percent greater chance of divorce than those who don't, based on fifty years of data.

6. Don't get married too young. Those who wed between fourteen and seventeen are twice as likely to divorce as couples that wait until their twenties. Making it as a family requires some characteristics that come with maturity, such as selflessness, stability, and self-control. It's best to wait for their arrival.

7. Finally, I'll conclude with the ultimate secret of lifelong love. Simply put, the stability of marriage is a by-product of an iron-willed determination to make it work. If you choose to marry, enter into that covenant with the resolve to remain committed to each other for life. Never threaten to leave your mate during angry moments. Don't allow yourself to consider even the possibility of divorce. Calling it quits must not become an option for those who want to go the distance!

Most of Dobson's recommendations are for those contemplating marriage. For those already married we would add: faithfully attend church, have a daily devotional time, forgive, be kind to each other, love your partner sacrificially, never belittle your spouse, communicate (but do not argue), spend time together, avoid financial pressures, and tell your spouse "I love you" every day.

V. PRAYER

O Lord, thank you that you are always faithful to us, and we pray that we will always be faithful to you. May we fulfill our spiritual leadership roles in a way that pleases you. May we also be honest and circumspect in our dealings with others in our communities. Help us to be faithful to our marriage vows for a lifetime. When we appear before you some day, our hearts' desire is that you will be able to say, "Well done, my good and faithful servant." In Jesus' name we pray. Amen.

VI. DEEPER DISCOVERIES

A. Covenant (2:4–5,8,10,14)

The word *covenant* (Heb. *berit*), is one of the most significant terms in the Bible. *Berit* appears 284 times in the Hebrew text of the Old Testament. In the NIV the most common translations of *berit* are: "covenant" (246 times), "treaty" (26 times), "agreement" (3 times), and "compact" (3 times). Scholarly opinion varies, but most likely *berit* is related to the Akkadian (Babylonian) word *biritu,* "fetter," which comes from a verb meaning "to bind." Thus, a covenant is a binding agreement between parties.

"Make/made a covenant" is found approximately thirty times in the Old Testament (e.g., Gen. 15:18; 31:44; Exod. 23:32). The phrase is interesting because it is literally, "cut a covenant," the Hebrew idiom being derived from the practice of cutting animals in two as part of the covenant ritual (e.g., Gen. 15:9–11). According to Richards, "Perhaps . . . the most binding covenants were enacted in a ceremony that involved the offering of a sacrifice" (Richards, *Expository Dictionary of Bible Words,* 194).

Berit is used in a number of ways in the Old Testament. First, the term may describe a treaty or alliance between human beings. Individuals (Gen. 31:44), nations (Ezek. 17:13–18), a king and his subjects (Jer. 34:8–11), or married couples (Mal. 2:14) may make a covenant with each other. Second, a covenant may be established between human beings and God—either between God and individuals (Num. 25:10–13) or God and nations (Exod. 19:5).

Five important covenants are found in the Old Testament: the Noahic (Gen. 9:1–17); the Abrahamic (Gen. 12:1–3; 15:18; 17:1–21); the Mosaic (Exod. 19–24); the Davidic (2 Sam. 7:11–16; Ps. 89:3–4); and the new covenant (Jer. 31:27–40; Ezek. 36:22–38). In each of these covenants, God initiated and entered into a relationship with certain people. In the Mosaic covenant, the people of Israel were responsible to meet the obligations set forth by God so that they might enjoy its blessings. In the other four covenants, God promised blessings upon the recipients without any prior conditions to meet on their part.

The word *covenant* appears six times in the Book of Malachi, and five of these are in chapter 2. The first three instances (2:4–5,8) refer to God's covenant with Levi, that is, God's selection of the tribe of Levi as the priestly tribe. Nowhere in the Old Testament is a formal covenant between God and the tribe of Levi mentioned, but it is prescribed in the Mosaic Law (Deut. 18:1; 21:5) that Levi was to be the tribe of priests and temple servants. Profaning the "covenant of our fathers" (2:10) speaks of violating the laws of the Mosaic covenant made with Israel at Sinai. "The wife of your marriage covenant" (literally, "of your covenant") in 2:14 speaks of the binding nature of the marriage relationship. Covenant promises of lifelong faithfulness made during the marriage ceremony are not only directed to the wife but to God. The last reference to "covenant" in Malachi is "the messenger of the covenant" in 3:1.

By his atoning sacrifice Christ established a new covenant (Matt. 26:28; Heb. 9:15). When we receive Jesus Christ as Lord and Savior, we enter into this wonderful covenant relationship with God and are the recipients of all its blessings—forgiveness of sins, eternal life, joy, peace, and many others.

B. Break Faith (2:10–11,14–16)

The phrase "break faith" ("deal treacherously," KJV, NASB) is a translation of the Hebrew word *bagad*. *Bagad* is related to the Hebrew word *beged*, "garment." The idea of *bagad* is to cover or cloak [*beged*] things over, and so to act falsely, deceitfully, or faithlessly. Malachi's contemporaries attempted a "cover-up" job. The term appears only five times in the book (all in 2:10–16) and denotes unfaithful acts generally (vv. 10,16), unfaithfulness to God by marrying pagans (v. 11), and unfaithfulness to marriage partners (vv. 14–15). "Break faith" at the end of verse 16 has been limited to the marriage relationship (2:11–16) but like verse 10 probably refers to unfaithful dealings among Judah's citizens generally—in business, marriage, and the like. If so, we have a general admonition against faithless behavior at the beginning and end of the unit with specific acts mentioned within it.

C. Divorce in the Old Testament (2:13–16)

The discussion of divorce in the Old Testament is not limited to the Book of Malachi. In the NIV the words *divorce, divorced,* and *divorces* occur a total of fifteen times. Divorce seems to have been common in ancient societies and instruction relating to divorce is included in the Mosaic Law. In the first use of the word *divorced* in the Bible, priests are prohibited from marrying divorced women (Lev. 21:7,14; cp. Ezek. 44:22).

Malachi's candid discussion is one of three key passages on divorce in the Old Testament. The first is Genesis 2:24: "For this reason a man will leave his father and mother and be united to his wife, and they will become one flesh."

Although the word *divorce* is not mentioned, the fact that the couple are "united" and "become one flesh" indicates that God intended the marriage relationship to be permanent.

Deuteronomy 24:1–4 is the second key Old Testament passage on divorce. Here we are told that a husband may write "a certificate of divorce" and send his wife away if "he finds something indecent about her" (Deut. 24:1). Since according to the Mosaic Law adulterous spouses were executed (Lev. 20:10; Deut. 22:22), the indecent act would seem to be something repugnant but short of adultery. In the time of Jesus, the followers of Rabbi Shammai interpreted this passage to allow divorce only in the case of adultery, whereas the followers of Rabbi Hillel permitted divorce even for trivial matters. We must emphasize that Deuteronomy 24 in no way commands divorce but merely permits a legal divorce in certain circumstances. Then as now divorce was a fact of life, and civil laws were needed to regulate its practice.

Malachi's denunciation of the apparent epidemic of divorce among his countrymen took courage because divorce is an emotional and painful topic, probably no less so in the fifth century B.C. than today. We may summarize the prophet's message on divorce in six points. First, one reason God was not blessing the people was because they were wrongfully divorcing their wives (2:13). Second, God himself was a witness about the sinfulness of their breaking faith with "the wife of your youth" (2:14). Third, the marriage relationship is a "covenant" between the wife and husband (2:14). Covenant promises should be kept. Fourth, God made the husband and wife to be "one" for the purpose of raising up godly children (2:15). To break the marriage by divorce can endanger this plan. Fifth, God warns marital partners to "guard" their hearts so they will not be tempted to leave their spouse for another (2:15). Sixth, God's feelings about the matter are expressed in the strongest terms: "I hate divorce" (2:16).

Such strong words about divorce may seem harsh, but three facts should be kept in mind when considering this passage. First, this stern admonition was directed toward husbands who were divorcing their wives, not toward the innocent partners who were being sent away. Second, we may safely assume that these husbands had no justifiable cause for divorcing their partners. Apparently, they were divorcing their older wives ("the wife of your youth") for younger brides. Third, God says that he hates divorce, not divorced persons. God loves both the so-called "guilty" and "innocent" parties in a divorce and is willing to forgive the guilty.

Jesus specifically commented on Genesis 2:24 and Deuteronomy 24:1–4. In Matthew 19:3–6 we read: "Some Pharisees came to him to test him. They asked, 'Is it lawful for a man to divorce his wife for any and every reason?' 'Haven't you read,' he replied, 'that at the beginning the Creator "made them male and female," and said, "For this reason a man will leave his father and mother and be united to his wife, and the two will become one flesh"? So they are no longer two, but one. Therefore what God has joined together, let man not separate.'"

Jesus pointed the Pharisees to the Genesis account, specifically quoting Genesis 2:24 as evidence of the permanency of marriage. Yet these Pharisees persisted and cited Deuteronomy 24:1-4: "'Why then,' they asked, 'did Moses command that a man give his wife a certificate of divorce and send her away?' Jesus replied, 'Moses permitted you to divorce your wives because your hearts were hard. But it was not this way from the beginning'" (Matt. 19:7-8).

In other words, God intended from the beginning that marriage be permanent but was fully aware that divorce would occur in a sinful world. Thus provision was made in the Mosaic Law to regulate the practice. Jesus concluded his discussion on marriage with the statement, "I tell you that anyone who divorces his wife, except for marital unfaithfulness, and marries another woman commits adultery" (Matt. 19:9). Jesus' firm stance on divorce seemed even to astonish his disciples (Matt. 19:10). We may conclude from the Old Testament teaching and Jesus' interpretation of it that God's intent for marriage is one man-one woman "till death do we part."

VII. TEACHING OUTLINE

A. INTRODUCTION

1. Lead Story: Still Faithful
2. Context: In Malachi 2:1-16 the prophet deals with the important virtue of faithfulness. He begins by rebuking the priests for being unfaithful spiritual leaders and warns them of the severe consequences of continuing in their sinful ways (2:1-9). Then Malachi speaks of faithfulness to others in the community (2:10). Marriage to pagans is denounced as unfaithfulness to God himself, a compromise of faith (2:11-12). Marrying unbelieving foreigners was a particularly serious problem at this point in Judah's history (cp. Neh. 13:23-28). If believers intermarried with pagans, devotion to the true God could be jeopardized. In Malachi 2:13-16 we find the most severe condemnation of divorce in the Old Testament.

3. Transition: Malachi has much to say to our modern world about faithfulness. Unfaithfulness among religious leaders (immorality, unbelief, and so forth) has resulted in a loss of respect for ministers and the church. We should be faithful (honest) in our dealings with others in our community. Any compromise with false religion is dangerous. Finally, Malachi deals with the issue of divorce which is at epidemic proportions in our society.

B. COMMENTARY

1. Faithfulness of Religious Leaders (2:1–9)
2. Faithfulness to Others (2:10)
3. Faithfulness to God (2:11–12)
4. Faithfulness to Family (2:13–16)

C. CONCLUSION: NO SICK DAYS IN SIXTY-TWO YEARS

VIII. ISSUES FOR DISCUSSION

1. Do you believe that ministers and other spiritual leaders are as respected today as they were in the past? If not, why?
2. In your opinion, has society changed for the better or worse in matters such as honesty, personal integrity, and civility? Explain your answer.
3. What are some dangers of a believer marrying a nonbeliever?
4. Why would God say, "I hate divorce"? What advice would you offer for maintaining a happy and lasting marriage?

Malachi 2:17–4:6

How Are You Treating God?

I. INTRODUCTION
A Tale of Two Atheists

II. COMMENTARY
A verse-by-verse explanation of these verses.

III. CONCLUSION
Famous Last Words

An overview of the principles and applications from these verses.

IV. LIFE APPLICATION
You're Not Home Yet!

Melding these verses to life.

V. PRAYER
Tying these verses to life with God.

VI. DEEPER DISCOVERIES
Historical, geographical, and grammatical enrichment of the commentary.

VII. TEACHING OUTLINE
Suggested step-by-step group study of these verses.

VIII. ISSUES FOR DISCUSSION
Zeroing these verses in on daily life.

Quote

"*I*t pays to serve Jesus."

F r a n k   C .   H u s t o n

Malachi 2:17–4:6

IN A NUTSHELL

*I*n this final section of the Book of Malachi, the prophet contrasts the right and wrong treatment of God in his day. Malachi names three wrong ways to treat God: charging God with injustice (2:17–3:6), robbing God (3:7–12), and complaining that serving God is a waste of time (3:13–15). Malachi's preaching had not fallen on deaf ears, and the prophet concludes his book with the account of those who repented and honored the Lord—the right way to treat God (3:16–4:6). These true believers will be spared the coming judgment and will have a joyous future in Messiah's kingdom.

How Are You
Treating God?

I. INTRODUCTION

A Tale of Two Atheists

*M*adalyn Murray O'Hair was perhaps the most famous atheist in American history. Her outlandish antics are legendary. One night Ms. O'Hair stood on the lawn of her Baltimore, Maryland, home in a torrential rainstorm and shook her fists at God. With streaks of lightning flashing across the sky, she screamed obscenities at God and dared him to strike her dead. When lightning did not reduce her to a cinder, she turned to her family who had witnessed the spectacle and gloated at having "proven" that God does not exist.

Her life was consumed with attacks on God, spreading atheism (and communism), and attempts to remove all vestiges of God from American life. She fought vigorously to have the slogan "In God We Trust" removed from U.S. currency and even complained when our astronauts radioed a prayer to Earth as they circled the moon, arguing that this should not be permitted since their trip was funded by federal money! O'Hair's greatest triumph came in 1963 when the Supreme Court banned mandatory prayer from public schools. Her atheist teenage son, William (Bill) Murray, was the plaintiff of record in that landmark case.

Bill's mother told him that she didn't care if he became a drug addict, bank robber, or worse—just never become a Christian. For years Bill lived as if God did not exist. Alcohol, drugs, and sexual pleasures (including an extramarital affair and addiction to pornography) dominated his life. Finally, Bill realized his life was empty and without meaning. When Bill was thirty-three years old, his mother's worst nightmare came true. William Murray, the son of America's leading atheist, became a Christian! Murray's life was radically changed, and now he shares the gospel of Jesus Christ and the futility of atheism across the nation. He recounts his experiences as an atheist and his salvation in his candid autobiography, *My Life Without God* (Nashville: Thomas Nelson, 1982). Murray has also publicly stated, "The part I played as a teenager in removing prayer from public schools was criminal."

O'Hair disowned Bill and rebuffed all his attempts to share the love of Jesus Christ with her. She continued her blasphemous ways until her untimely death a few years ago. How remarkable that in the same family the mother treated God so shamefully while her son came to honor him.

In this final section of the Book of Malachi, the prophet contrasted the right and wrong treatment of God in his day. Malachi named three wrong ways to treat God—wearying God by calling him unjust (2:17–3:6), robbing God by stealing what rightfully belongs to the Creator (3:7–12), and insulting God by claiming that serving him is a waste of time (3:13–15). Malachi's preaching had not fallen on deaf ears, and the prophet concluded his book with the account of those who repented and honored the Lord—the right way to treat God (3:16–4:6). These true believers have a joyous future and will be spared the coming judgment. In our modern world we still find those who mistreat God (like Ms. O'Hair) but millions who love and honor him (like her son William). After Malachi, no prophetic voice was heard for four hundred years, so read carefully God's final message of the Old Testament era.

II. COMMENTARY

How Are You Treating God?

> **MAIN IDEA:** *People may mistreat their Creator in various ways, but God desires that we treat him with reverence and honor. Following God pays eternal dividends.*

Wearying God (2:17–3:6)

> **SUPPORTING IDEA:** *People may weary God by accusing him of being unjust. God will bring justice in his time.*

2:17. God is patient and kind, but here Malachi charged that the people (possibly unbelieving Jews; cp. 3:5) had actually **wearied the LORD**. As before, they feigned innocence and asked the fourth key question of the book, **How have we wearied him?** They had exhausted God's patience by brazenly accusing him (wrongly) of being unjust. Specifically, they alleged: (1) **All who do evil are good in the eyes of the LORD.** (2) As a matter of fact, God appears to be **pleased with** ["delight in"] **them**. (3) God seemed to be oblivious to the world's injustices—**Where is the God of justice?** These Judahites observed wicked individuals and nations prospering while they were having problems. They thought, "God, we have tried to serve you, but look what it has gotten us. Nothing! You must think evil people are really good because they are rich while we are poor. You must take special delight in them since you seem to bless them so greatly. God, if you are just, where are you? Why don't you step in and right the wrongs, punish the wicked, and bless us?"

We must point out that the same people who were claiming to be so righteous and deserving were the very ones offering God blemished animals, complaining about how burdensome it was to worship God, marrying pagans, and divorcing their wives! They were hardly paragons of virtue, deserving of God's blessing. Much of their suffering was self-inflicted.

Still, injustices were being done against godly individuals (e.g., 2:14) and the nation collectively. Their Defender was indeed just and was not asleep. He had seen these injustices and would certainly act. God simply had not acted on their timetable. We should remember von Logau's often repeated truism, "Though the mills of God grind slowly, yet they grind exceeding small; Though with patience He stands waiting, with exactness grinds He all."

3:1. The description of the coming judgment in 3:1–6 is the divine response to the people's outlandish accusations in 2:17. Malachi's audience had cried, "Where is the God of justice?" Here the nation was warned to prepare to meet "the God of justice" because the Lord himself, the heavenly judge, was coming! For the wicked, including the insolent in Judah, it would be as Amos foretold: "Woe to you who long for the day of the LORD! Why do you long for the day of the LORD? That day will be darkness, not light" (Amos 5:18).

Verses 1–6 contain amazing predictions of both Christ's first and second advents and of the one who would prepare the way for his arrival. Only in Malachi 3:1; 4:5–6; and Isaiah 40:3 does the Old Testament inform us that Messiah's coming will be preceded by a forerunner. **My messenger** (Heb., *mal'aki*; Malachi, the meaning of the prophet's name) would arrive to **prepare the way before me—the LORD Almighty.** Jesus himself quoted this verse and specifically identified John the Baptist as the messenger whose ministry prepared the way for his coming (Matt. 11:10). Mark (1:2) and Luke (1:76) also cited Malachi's prophecy as foretelling John as Messiah's forerunner. According to Wolf, "A messenger is normally a prophet, and none appeared from the time of Malachi until John arrived on the scene some 450 years later" (Wolf, 98). Since the messenger prepared the way for the coming of the Lord Almighty = me = Jesus, Jesus the Messiah is here equated with God.

Suddenly (unexpectedly), Jesus (the Lord) would appear at **his temple.** The Hebrew word *'adon,* Lord, with the definite article (the Lord) always denotes God (e.g., Exod. 23:17; 34:23; Isa. 1:24; 3:1), and "his temple" is, of course, God's temple. Thus, we have two further attestations of Jesus' deity in this verse. Jesus was taken to the Jerusalem temple when only eight days old (Luke 2:21–38), and he spent much time worshiping and teaching there during his ministry. Malachi's revelation that the Lord would come to his temple would surely have frightened the priests who had committed flagrant acts of disrespect in the temple worship. The phrase **are seeking** probably harks back to the question, "Where is the God of justice?" (2:17). Messiah was **the messenger of a new covenant** (Matt. 26:28; Heb. 8:8–13; 12:24) and would establish a new, faithful priesthood.

3:2. Verse 1 describes events at the time of Christ's first coming, whereas verses 2–6 depict Christ's judgment on the world at his second advent. According to Alden, "Like most of the Old Testament prophets, Malachi, in his picture of the coming Christ, mingled the two advents" (Alden, *Expositor's Bible Commentary,* 719; cp. Zech. 9:9–10). Malachi's countrymen complained that injustice was rampant and the wicked seemed to go free. Messiah would remedy this situation. As **a refiner's fire** purges dross from the silver (v. 3) and **a launderer's soap** cleanses impurities from clothing, all wickedness would be eradicated from the earth at Christ's return. **Who can endure the day of his coming? Who can stand when he appears?** The answer is, only those who have repented and believed in the Messiah. "The day of his coming" is the day of the Lord.

3:3–5. Unfaithful priests will be removed as Malachi has already prophesied, and only righteous priests **who will bring offerings . . . acceptable to the** LORD will remain, like the faithful priests of **former years** (2:4–6). Judgment will begin at the house of God and then fall on **sorcerers, adulterers and perjurers . . . those who defraud laborers of their wages, who oppress the widows and the fatherless, and deprive aliens of justice**—sins condemned in the Mosaic Law.

Sorcery (witchcraft) was widespread in the Ancient Near East, including Egypt (Exod. 7:11), Canaan (Deut. 18:9–10,14), Babylon (Isa. 47:9,12; Dan. 2:2), and even Israel (2 Kgs. 17:17; 21:6). The practice continued into New Testament times (Acts 8:9; 13:6,8; 19:19). All occult practices are categorically condemned in the Bible and are extremely dangerous yet ironically seem to be gaining in popularity in our so-called scientific and enlightened world. Lack of respect **(fear)** for God (Ps. 36:1) is the root sin of all the others listed in this verse.

3:6. Judgment was coming on Israel and the world (3:2–5). Does this mean the end for Israel? No. God has made covenant promises about the nation's future that are unchangeable. But promises are only as trustworthy as the character of the one who makes them. Thus, God solemnly declared, **I the Lord do not change. So you, O descendants of Jacob, are not destroyed.** God's holy, just, and faithful character does not, and cannot, change. The apostle Paul wrote, "If we are faithless, he will remain faithful, for he cannot disown himself" (2 Tim. 2:13). Because God is holy and just, he will judge sin. Because God "does not lie" (Titus 1:2), he would purify Israel but not totally destroy it (Ps. 89:34). Undoubtedly, the name Jacob ("heel grabber, supplanter" = deceiver) is chosen as an appellation for the nation here as a reminder that, like their scheming ancestor (Gen. 27:1–36), Israel did not deserve God's grace.

"I the Lord do not change" is one of the most important theological statements in the Bible (Jas. 1:17), refuting claims by some people that God is in process of growing and developing. God cannot become better because he is already perfect. God cannot learn more because he is already omniscient. God cannot become more powerful since he is already omnipotent. According to Kaiser, "With respect to God's essence, attributes, moral character and determination to punish sin and reward goodness, there can be no variation or inconsistency. With regard to these characteristics, there is absolute and unconditional dependability" (Kaiser, *More Hard Sayings of the Old Testament,* 266). *Immutability* is the theological term for God's changelessness.

B Robbing God (3:7–12)

SUPPORTING IDEA: *People may rob God by withholding what rightfully belongs to their Creator. Faithfulness in giving brings divine blessing.*

3:7. Israel had a history of waywardness—turning from God's **decrees** (the law), but **the Lord Almighty** still loved his people and entreated them to **return to me, and I will return to you** (cp. Zech. 1:3). If they would repent of their sins, God's special presence and blessing would come to rest on the nation as it had in times past. Perhaps the people's question, **How are we to return?** was sincere; but in light of the attitude expressed throughout the book, it was likely a cynical response. Contrary to his usual pattern, Malachi did not follow the question with a specific explanation because in reality the whole book points the way for the people to get right with God. Verse 7 could stand alone, but most commentators connect it with verses 8–12, a transition from the general charge of disobedience to the specific charge of robbing God.

3:8. In verses 8–12 we have Malachi's treatise on tithing, probably the most familiar passage in the book. Malachi's opening question is shocking—**Will a man rob God?** Even most unbelievers would be too frightened (if merely out of superstition) to steal from God. Yet, in addition to all their other offenses, the people were now charged with this heinous crime. Understandably, they wanted God to explain, **How do we rob you?** God replied, **In tithes and offerings.** The word *tithe* (also v. 10) is a translation of the Hebrew word *ma'aser,* which literally means "tenth part," defining the tithe as 10 percent of one's material increase. *Offering* is a more general term, specifying contributions for a sacred purpose. Tithes were given to support the priests and Levites, since the tribe of Levi received no allotment in the land of Canaan like the other tribes (Num. 18:21,24–29).

3:9–12. As a result of Judah's sin, **the whole nation** was **under** the **curse** outlined in Deuteronomy 28:15–42—drought, poor crops, and so forth. The remedy was to **bring the whole tithe into the storehouse.** The words "the whole tithe" may intimate that some people were giving a partial tithe. The phrase **food in my house** (the temple) refers to the provisions for the priests' sustenance and the offerings. Tithing can be a frightening commitment. "How will we ever survive financially if we give so much to God? Our children will starve!" To allay such fears, God challenged Judah (and us) to **test** him in this matter. In other words, God says, "Give tithing a try and see what happens."

If the people would trust him in the matter of tithing, God promised to lift the curse and send **so much blessing that you will not have room enough for it.** Rain would fall (heaven's **floodgates** opened), and they would have bountiful crops (not **room enough** to store it all). God would **prevent pests** (literally, "will rebuke the devourer"; probably locusts, Deut. 28:38) from destroying the grain, and the **vines** would produce abundantly. Even pagan **nations** would observe God's blessing on Judah and label it **a delightful land** (cp. Isa. 62:4). No doubt God blesses people spiritually when they obey him, but here we see that God often blesses us economically as well.

Ⓒ Insulting God (3:13–15)

SUPPORTING IDEA: *People insult God when they claim that serving him is a waste of time. Ultimately, the righteous will be rewarded.*

3:13. The phrase **you have said harsh things against me** (literally, "your words have been strong against me") is the most serious indictment in the book. As usual, the people claimed to be innocent. **What have we said against you?** is the last of the prophecy's six key (foolish) questions (1:2,6; 2:14,17; 3:8,13), around which the book seems structured.

3:14. God explained that these insolent people had grumbled, **It is futile to serve God.** The word *futile* (Heb. *shaw'*, "emptiness, nothingness, vanity"; "vain" in Exod. 20:7 KJV) speaks of that which is useless, a waste of time. The word **gain** suggests a selfish, financial incentive. For example, in Genesis 37:26 we read, "Judah said to his brothers, 'What will we gain if we kill our brother [Joseph] and cover up his blood? Come, let's sell him to the Ishmaelites" (cp. Jer. 8:10). Malachi's countrymen were crassly saying that serving God was a waste of time and did not pay financially! Their attitude was, "What is in it for me?" Their worship was insincere—not from the heart. They claimed to have faithfully carried out God's **requirements** and even to have gone about **like mourners** [fasting] **before the LORD Almighty.** Their fasting and tears did not bring the favor of God because their lives were filled with sin (cp. 2:13–14).

3:15. Although these whiners professed to serve God faithfully, they were not doing well economically ("gain"). On the other hand, **the arrogant** (rebellious, godless; cp. Ps. 86:14), **the evildoers, and even those who challenge God** seemed to be prospering. Earlier the people had called God unjust because evildoers seemed to flourish and go unpunished while they (the so-called "righteous") lacked (2:17). Now they moved to a new level and decided that serving the Lord was a waste of time and energy. The Lord will reply to their charges in 4:1–3.

𝔻 Honoring God (3:16–4:6)

SUPPORTING IDEA: *God desires that we revere and honor him. Believers have a joyous future and will be spared the coming judgment.*

3:16. Many people in Judah no doubt viewed Malachi as a pest and did not welcome his condemnation of their sins. However, some of the prophet's audience (**those who feared the LORD**) were convicted of their wrongdoing and repented. In ancient Judah (as today) we find two groups of people— believers and nonbelievers. The phrase **talked with each other** probably means they discussed Malachi's sermon and agreed the crusty prophet was right. God **heard** when they repented of their sins and a permanent record was made of it—**a scroll of remembrance** [phrase only here in Scripture] **was written in his presence.**

According to Alden, "This idea of God's keeping written records appears occasionally in the Old Testament (cp. Exod 32:32; Ps 69:28; Isa 4:3; Dan 12:1). The New Testament mentions it many times, especially in Revelation (cp. Luke 10:20; Phil 4:3; Heb 12:23; Rev 3:5; 13:8; 17:8; 20:12,15; 21:27)" (Alden, *Expositor's Bible Commentary*, 723). **Honored** means to "think on" or "regard with esteem." Earlier, we met people who showed contempt for and did not honor God's **name** (1:6,12,14; 2:2). Now "those who feared the Lord" honored God's name as worthy and wonderful because they loved and honored God himself.

3:17. God made two wonderful promises to believers. First, **they will be mine** indicates a special relationship to God—part of his spiritual family (John 1:12). Followers of the true God are precious to him, like treasures of gold and silver (Exod. 19:5; 1 Chr. 29:3; Eccl. 2:8). Believers should never feel unloved or insignificant. Second, God would **spare them** from the wrath to come (4:1).

3:18. This verse is a direct reply to those who insulted the Lord by complaining that serving God was a waste of time and that the wicked were blessed (2:17; 3:14–15). In the coming day of the Lord (4:1), accounts would be settled and justice would be done. The **righteous** would be spared judgment and enjoy messianic kingdom blessings, whereas the **wicked** would reap wrath and eternal separation from God. A **distinction** would indeed be made between the just and the unjust! Then all would **see** that it pays to serve the Lord. The phrase **again see the distinction** refers to examples of God's sparing the righteous and judging the wicked throughout the course of history (Gen. 6:7–8; 19:29; Exod. 11:7).

4:1. The "distinction" (3:18) between God's followers and others is vividly set forth in 4:1–3. **The day** in view is the "day of the LORD" (4:5), a time of judgment for the wicked and blessing for the righteous (vv. 2–3). (For a discussion of the day of the Lord, see the "Deeper Discoveries" section for the Book of Zephaniah.) The word **surely** emphasizes the certainty of this coming day, a rebuttal to the charge of divine injustice in 3:15 and unconcern in 2:17. The fire of God's wrath would leave **the arrogant** and **evildoer**, the very ones the skeptics complained sinned with impunity (3:15), without **root or a branch**. There would be a payday for sin after all.

4:2–3. By way of contrast, those **who revere** God's **name** would experience unimaginable joy (**leap like calves released from the stall**) and a permanent, complete victory over their **wicked** oppressors. This new world would be ushered in when **the sun** [a figure for deity in Ps. 84:11] **of righteousness** rises, a grand picture. Upon the darkness of a sinful world (in fact, at its darkest hour), spiritual light would suddenly burst forth like the dawn, and righteousness would prevail. We agree with Kaiser: "While there is little agreement among scholars as to the meaning of the phrase 'sun of righteousness,' those scholars are closer to the mark who regard the sun as pointing to the Messiah as the One characterized by righteousness and acting in righteous ways so as to produce righteousness" (Kaiser, *The Messiah in the Old Testament,* 230).

Jesus the Messiah, the light of the world (John 8:12; 9:5), will return and bring in everlasting righteousness (and justice) to earth. The word **healing** apparently alludes to the deliverance of God's people from destruction as in Psalm 107:20 (see KJV, NASB, NRSV). The phrase **in its wings** has been interpreted as: (1) a figure for the winged solar disc of Egypt, Assyria, Babylon, or Persia; (2) the warm rays of the sun (Ps. 139:9); (3) the "folds" (same Hebrew word rendered "wings" in Mal. 4:2) of a robe where possessions were stored (Ezek. 5:3); and (4) the protective wings of a bird. Views 2 and 4 seem most likely, and it is difficult to choose between them. In summary, at his coming Jesus the Messiah will bring spiritual light to a sin-darkened world, righteousness (justice), and deliverance ("healing") for his people. This is the last messianic reference in the Old Testament.

4:4. Heartfelt obedience to the word of God is the key to escaping judgment (v. 1) and enjoying the blessings of the messianic kingdom (vv. 2–3). **The law of my servant Moses** was the basic corpus of the Old Testament's religious teaching, and prophetic preaching was essentially an exposition of the law. **Horeb** is another name for Mount Sinai (Exod. 34:4; 1 Kgs. 8:9), traditionally identified as Jebel Musa located in the southern part of the V-shaped Sinai Peninsula.

4:5. That the Lord would send a messenger to prepare the way for Messiah's coming was prophesied in 3:1. Here this forerunner is called **the prophet Elijah,** not the ancient prophet reincarnated but one with the same prophetic power and mission—calling the nation back to God (v. 6). In Matthew 17:10–13, Jesus explained that John the Baptist was the Elijah who prepared the way for his first coming (cp. Matt. 11:13–14) but made clear that another Elijah was yet future. This future Elijah would prepare the way for Messiah's second coming—**before that great and dreadful day of the LORD comes.**

4:6. Turning **the hearts of the fathers to their children, and the hearts of the children to their fathers** seems to be the result of people getting right with God. Reconciliation with others always follows true revival. An alternative interpretation is that "the fathers" are Israel's godly ancestors (like Abraham,

Moses, and David) and "the children" are their wayward descendants, being called to turn back to their fathers' faith. The difficulty with this view is in explaining how Elijah could turn the hearts of the fathers (Moses, etc.) to their children.

In these last verses God entreated the human race to obey his word and promised to send an Elijah to warn Israel and the world to repent before Messiah's coming. The alternative for those who obstinately refuse to repent is almost too horrible to contemplate—**or else I will come and strike the land with a curse.** Three times before (1:14; 2:2; 3:9), Malachi had spoken of curses, but the Hebrew term used here (*cherem*) is different from the others and is frightening in its severity. Often *cherem* refers to something set apart for total destruction (Deut. 7:26; Josh. 6:17), and that is its meaning here. Failure to repent would result in complete devastation for the people and their land. Malachi's focus (as a Jew) was on **the land** of Israel, but the "day of the LORD" (v. 5) judgment in view here will affect the whole earth (Joel 3:12–14; Obad. 15).

Wolf notes: "The Masoretes, Jewish scholars who preserved the Hebrew Bible during the Middle Ages, repeated verse 5 after verse 6, lest the book of the twelve minor prophets end on the harsh note of a curse. This attempt to soften the message does not alter the grim reality" (Wolf, 126).

Actually, the whole of 3:16–4:6 is the divine response to those who charged that serving God was a waste of time and did not pay (3:13–15). Is following God worth it? Absolutely! Receiving Jesus the Messiah means that we become part of God's family (3:17), will escape the judgment ("the curse") to come (4:1,6), and will experience the blessings of Messiah's wonderful kingdom (4:2–3). It pays to serve Jesus now and in eternity!

MAIN IDEA REVIEW: *People may mistreat their Creator in various ways, but God desires that we treat him with reverence and honor. Following God pays eternal dividends.*

III. CONCLUSION

Famous Last Words

When people die, a question often asked is, "Did they have any last words?" We think that surely what someone says just before he goes out into eternity is worth hearing. Sometimes that is true but sometimes it is not, as we discover through the following samples of famous last words from Mark

Water's *The New Encyclopedia of Christian Quotations* and the *Reader's Digest Book of Facts:*

- "I've never felt better" (Douglas Fairbanks Sr.).

- "This is the fourth?" (Thomas Jefferson).

- "I am about to—or I am going to—die; either expression is used" (Dominique Bouhours, French grammarian).

- "Go on, get out. Last words are for fools who haven't said enough" (Karl Marx, dying words to his housekeeper).

- "So little done, so much to do" (Cecil Rhodes).

- "Ah, well, then I suppose I shall have to die beyond my means" (Oscar Wilde).

- "Why yes: a bulletproof vest" (James Rodges, murderer, when asked for his final request before facing the firing squad).

- "They couldn't hit an elephant at this dist . . ." (John B. Sedgwick, Union general, 1864).

- "Don't let it end like this. Tell them I said something" (Pancho Villa).

- "I am abandoned by God and man. . . . I shall go to hell" (Voltaire).

- "Go away. . . . I'm alright" (H. G. Wells).

- "See in what peace a Christian can die" (Joseph Addison).

- "I shall hear in heaven" (Ludwig van Beethoven).

- "Do not pray for healing. Do not hold me back from the glory" (D. Martyn Lloyd-Jones).

- "Earth is receding; heaven is approaching. This is my crowning day!" (D. L. Moody).

In the Book of Malachi, we have God's last words in the Old Testament canon—words that are eminently worth hearing. Through his faithful messenger Malachi, God has sharply rebuked the people's sinful attitudes and actions, but he closes the book with a blessed promise that all who will revere and honor him will become part of his spiritual family, escape the judgment to come, and participate in the joyous kingdom of the Messiah (3:16–4:6). Lest anyone take God's grace for granted, the Lord adds a frightful warning in the last half of the Old Testament's last verse: "Or else I will come and strike the land with a curse" (Mal. 4:6). Honor God and receive his Messiah ("the sun of righteousness") as your Lord and Savior. You will never regret it!

PRINCIPLES

- Divine justice will certainly be carried out but on God's timetable not ours.
- Before judgment, God in his mercy sends people a warning to repent.
- By his death on the cross, Jesus the Messiah ("the messenger of the covenant") established a new covenant with all who believe in him.
- At Christ's second coming the righteous will be delivered and the wicked will be judged.
- We may rob God by failing to give our tithes and offerings to him.
- God promises to bless those who tithe.
- It pays to serve God now (in joy, peace, temporal blessings, fellowship with God) and in eternity.
- Those who revere and honor God become part of his spiritual family and will be spared judgment.
- God never forgets his children and their faithfulness to him.

APPLICATIONS

- Do not allow yourself to become bitter over injustices because God will surely reward the righteous and judge the wicked at the proper time.
- Be encouraged by God's promise of Messiah's coming.
- Determine to be faithful in your giving to God.
- Remember that serving God is worthwhile, even when life seems difficult and unjust.
- Rejoice in the truth that those who revere and honor God are part of his spiritual family and will be spared in the judgment to come.
- Obey the teachings of the Word of God.

IV. LIFE APPLICATION

You're Not Home Yet!

Have you ever felt that life is not fair and those who could care less about serving Jesus have it the best? Is serving God really worth it? Ray Stedman shares a touching story about an old missionary couple who had served in

Africa for years and were returning to New York City to retire—with no pension and with broken health. They happened to be booked on the same ship as President Teddy Roosevelt, who had been on a hunting expedition. Everyone wanted to get a glimpse of the president, but no one paid any attention to the faithful missionaries.

As the ship moved across the ocean, the old missionary said to his wife, "Dear, something is wrong. Why should we have given our lives in faithful service for God in Africa all these many years and have no one care a thing about us? Here this man comes back from a big game-hunting expedition and everybody makes much over him, but nobody gives two hoots about us. . . . If God is running this world, why does he permit such injustice?"

When the ship docked, a band was waiting to greet the president. The mayor of New York City was there, along with other leaders of the nation. The papers were full of the president's arrival, but no one even noticed this missionary couple. They slipped off the ship and found a cheap flat on the East side, hoping the next day to see what they could do to make a living in the city.

But that night the man's spirit just broke. He said to his wife, "I can't take this; God is not treating us fairly."

His wife replied, "Why don't you go in the bedroom and talk to the Lord about the whole thing?"

A short time later he came out from the bedroom, but now his face was completely different. His wife asked, "Dear, what happened?"

"Yes," he said, "the Lord settled it with me. . . . I told him how bitter I was that the president should receive this tremendous homecoming, when *no one* met us as we returned home. And you know, when I finished, it seemed as though the Lord put his hand on my shoulder and simply said, *'But you're not home yet!'*" (Ray Stedman, *Talking to My Father*, Portland, OR: Multnomah, 1975, pp. 25–26).

Faithfulness will always be rewarded but not necessarily in this life. When we see Jesus in all his glory and are welcomed to our real home some day, it will be worth it all. Cheer up, because as Frank Huston's hymn says, "It pays to serve Jesus!"

V. PRAYER

Dear God, thank you that you never forget your children. You know those who honor you, and you will reward your followers for their faithfulness. Thank you for the privilege of being a child of God, made possible by the atoning work of Jesus the Messiah on the cross. We look forward to the glorious future you have in store for us. In Christ's name we pray. Amen.

VI. DEEPER DISCOVERIES

A. The Old Testament Tithe (3:8,10)

The Hebrew word translated "tithe" is *ma'aser* (thirty-two times in the Old Testament), which means "a tenth part" or "tithe." *Ma'aser* is related to the Hebrew numerals for "ten," and so a "tithe" is literally 10 percent.

In Genesis 14:17–20 we find the first instance of tithing in the Bible. When Abraham returned from rescuing his nephew Lot from the enemy, he gave a tithe to Melchizedek, the Lord's priest. At Bethel Jacob pledged a tithe to the Lord for a safe return to his homeland (Gen. 28:20–22). These examples demonstrate that tithing was a very early custom. Later the practice was incorporated into the Mosaic Law code and became normative for Israel (Lev. 27:30–32; Deut. 12:6,11).

Israel was by no means the only nation that tithed. Tithing was a widespread practice in ancient times. We find examples among the Canaanites, Phoenicians, Arabs, Carthaginians, Lydians, Greeks, and Romans.

The Israelites were to tithe on everything that they produced from their agricultural pursuits, including crops and livestock (Lev. 27:30,32; Deut. 14:22–23). These tithes were given to the Levites, since the tribe of Levi had received no allotment in the land of Canaan like the other tribes (Num. 18:21,24). In turn the Levites were to present a tithe of the tithes they collected to the Lord for the priests' sustenance (Num. 18:26,28). Tithes were vital to the successful operation of Israel's religious system. If they were not forthcoming, the priests and Levites had to resort to other means of support (Neh. 13:10).

The tithe was presented at the central sanctuary (Deut. 12:6,11), which was first the tabernacle and later the temple. When Malachi exhorted the Israelites to "bring the whole tithe into the *storehouse,* that there may be food in *my house*" (Mal. 3:10, emphasis added), he was referring to the temple in

Jerusalem (Neh. 10:38; 13:12–13). Israelites ate a portion of their tithes, evidently as a kind of fellowship meal, "in the presence of the LORD" at the sanctuary (Deut. 14:23).

Every three years there was a special tithe. This tithe was not taken to the temple but was stored locally for distribution to the Levites, foreigners, orphans, and widows (Deut. 14:28–29; 26:12). Traditionally, Jewish interpreters have held that there were two different kinds of annual tithes, one for the Levites and the other for the prescribed meal at the temple. According to this interpretation, the tithe of the third year was a special use of the second tithe.

Regarding the question of tithing and the Christian, two points seem particularly relevant. First, tithing was practiced before the inception of the Israelite nation and the institution of the Mosaic Law. Second, Jesus endorsed the custom (Matt. 23:23). Consequently, it seems best to view tithing as a timeless moral imperative that modern believers should observe. The fact that Israelites were to present other offerings in addition to their tithes seems to suggest that the tithe is a minimum that we should give to the Lord. James L. Kraft, founder of Kraft Foods, once quipped, "I don't believe in tithing . . . but it's a good place to start."

B. Offerings (3:8)

There were various types of Old Testament offerings. Five are listed in Leviticus 1–7: the burnt offering, the grain offering, the fellowship ("peace," KJV) offering, the sin offering, and the guilt ("trespass," KJV) offering. However, the Hebrew word for "offerings" in Malachi 3:8 is the more general term, *terumah* (seventy-six times in the Old Testament), which basically means a "contribution" or an "offering" for a sacred purpose. *Terumah* is usually taken as a derivative of the Hebrew root, *rum*, "to be high, exalted," or "raised." For this reason some English translations have adopted the ancient rabbinic interpretation that this offering was in certain instances (e.g., Exod. 29:27) ceremonially raised to God ("heave offering," KJV, NASB; "that was raised," NRSV). Recently the view has become widely accepted that, at least in the biblical period, the word always meant "gift." Accordingly, the NIV translators consistently rendered *terumah* with the idea of "gift" ("offering(s)," "contribution(s)," "special gift(s)," so forth).

Terumah denotes various gifts, such as the materials donated by the Israelites for the construction of the tabernacle, its service, and the sacred garments (Exod. 25:2–3; 35:5,21,24; 36:3,6), and the silver half shekel "atonement money" (Exod. 30:13–15; see Neh. 10:32; Matt. 17:24–27). Most frequently the term designates contributions to the Lord that were set apart to provide the needs of the priests, Levites, or both (e.g., Lev. 22:12; Num. 5:9; 18:8,11,19; 2 Chr. 31:10,12,14; Ezek. 44:30).

Undoubtedly, the prophet had in mind the contributions for the priests and Levites when he accused the people of robbing God of "offerings." Nehemiah, who likely lived during the same time period as Malachi, also reported that offerings for sustaining the Levites (and presumably the priests as well) had not been forthcoming (Neh. 13:10–13) in spite of the oath taken earlier (Neh. 10:37–39).

In the New Testament we are likewise taught that God's people should support Christian ministers. For example, Paul wrote, "Anyone who receives instruction in the word must share all good things with his instructor" (Gal. 6:6); and Jesus affirmed, "The worker deserves his wages" (Luke 10:7).

C. Elijah the Prophet (4:5–6)

Elijah was perhaps the greatest prophet of the Old Testament era. He is a mysterious figure who seems to appear out of nowhere and step into the national spotlight. We have no information about his personal background except that he was from Tishbe (1 Kgs. 17:1), a tiny village in Israel (roughly forty miles northeast of Jerusalem).

The prophet lived in a time of national crisis. King Ahab's Phoenician wife, Jezebel, was promoting Baal worship. Believers were persecuted, and the Lord's prophets were being executed (1 Kgs. 18:4). During this dangerous period, the Lord raised up Elijah (whose very name means "the Lord is God") to call the nation back to himself. Elijah courageously stood for the Lord against overwhelming odds and even faced off with hundreds of pagan prophets on Mount Carmel (1 Kgs. 18:19–40). On that day the Lord miraculously sent fire from heaven to consume the offering, demonstrating that he, not Baal, was the true God. This halted the spread of Baal worship in the nation.

After years of faithful service, Elijah was whisked away to heaven without dying, one of only two persons in history known to have experienced this blessing (2 Kgs. 2:11; Gen. 5:24). His greatness is attested by the fact that he appeared with Moses on the mountain during Jesus' glorious transfiguration (Matt. 17:2–3). Moses represented the law and Elijah the prophets. Moses and Elijah are also mentioned together in the closing verses of Malachi.

In Malachi 4:5–6 the Lord promised to send the prophet Elijah to prepare the way for Messiah's coming ("the messenger of the covenant," Mal. 3:1). This Elijah would not be the ancient prophet reincarnated but one with the same prophetic power and mission—calling the nation back to God (4:6).

According to Andrew Hill and John Walton:

> Elijah was deemed the archetype or role model for the prophetic ministry associated with the "forerunner" for several reasons. First, he boldly confronted religious and political leaders on the issues of theological orthodoxy, moral purity, and social justice. Second, he preached a message of repentance from sin in the face of God's impending judgment. Third, his divine commission and message were authenticated by accompanying miraculous signs. And fourth, he was truly "the voice of one crying in the wilderness" in that his ministry stood outside the recognized structures and traditional institutions of Hebrew society. Elijah's role as a herald proclaiming the appointed time of Yahweh's wrath and the inauguration of the messianic age was an important part of later Jewish tradition regarding the prophet (e.g., Sir. 48:10–11; cp. Matt. 17:3,10; 27:47,49; John 1:21) (Hill and Walton, *A Survey of the Old Testament*, 549–50).

John the Baptist was the Elijah who prepared the way for Messiah's first coming (Matt. 11:7–15). Some unknown individual will be the Elijah who will prepare the way for Messiah's (Jesus') second advent—"that great and dreadful day of the LORD" (v. 5; cp. Matt. 17:11). According to Kaiser, "He may well be one of the two witnesses mentioned in Revelation 11:3–12" (Kaiser, *Mastering the Old Testament*, 487). During the Jewish Passover seder, Elijah is welcomed through a door opened for him in hopes that he will usher in the messianic age. We can understand the excitement when some people mistook Jesus' cry from the cross as a call for Elijah (Matt. 27:47–49).

VII. TEACHING OUTLINE

A. INTRODUCTION

1. Lead Story: A Tale of Two Atheists
2. Context: In this final section of the Book of Malachi, God rebukes the following sins: accusations of divine injustice (2:17–3:6), theft of

that which rightfully belonged to him (3:7–12), and the almost blasphemous charge that serving God was a waste of time and effort (3:13–15). Malachi's preaching had not fallen on deaf ears, and the prophet concludes his book with the account of those who repented and honored the Lord (3:16–4:6). These true believers will be spared the coming judgment and will have a joyous future in Messiah's kingdom.

3. Transition: Malachi's message is as up-to-date as this morning's newspaper. People still accuse God of being unfair, fail to tithe, and claim that serving the Lord is a waste of time. Millions today also respect and honor God. In this section Malachi shows that God is perfectly just, that tithing brings blessing, and that serving the Lord pays eternal dividends.

B. COMMENTARY

1. Wearying God (2:17–3:6)

2. Robbing God (3:7–12)

3. Insulting God (3:13–15)

4. Honoring God (3:16–4:6)

C. CONCLUSION: FAMOUS LAST WORDS

VIII. ISSUES FOR DISCUSSION

1. Answer the question in Malachi 3:2, "Who can endure the day of his coming?" In other words, how does a person prepare to meet the Lord?

2. What are some practical applications of God's changelessness (immutability)?

3. Discuss Malachi's teaching about tithes and offerings. What does God promise to do when we tithe? What are the implications of this passage regarding material prosperity?

4. Why is serving God worthwhile—eternally and in this life?

5. How do you explain Malachi's prophecy about Elijah?

Glossary

angel—A messenger from God, either heavenly or human, who delivers God's message of instruction, warning, or hope

Antichrist—Anyone who opposes God or Christ, but especially the evil leader at the end of the age whom Christ will defeat at his second coming

apocalyptic—Symbolic language reflecting belief in two opposing universal powers (God and Satan); two ages of universal history (present age dominated by evil and Satan and age to come under God's rule); and a future judgment giving rewards to the people of God and eternal punishment to the wicked

Babylon—Name of an evil city and empire in the sixth century B.C. (in modern Iraq); a code name for another evil city in Revelation

day of the Lord—God's time of decisive intervention in history and the final day of judgment in the end time

eschatology—The study of last things or the end time when Christ returns

eternal life—The quality of life that Jesus gives his disciples and unending life with God given to those who believe in Jesus Christ as Savior and Lord

evil—Anyone or anything that opposes the plan of God

exile—Israel's life in the Assyrian kingdom after 722 B.C.; Judah's life in Babylon from the fall of Jerusalem in 586 B.C. until the return from Babylon about 538 B.C.

faith—A response which takes God at his word and acts upon it; belief in and personal commitment to Jesus Christ for eternal salvation

forgiveness—Pardon and release from the penalty for wrongdoing; God's delivery from sin's wages for those who repent and express faith in Christ; the Christian act of freeing from guilt and blame those by whom one has suffered wrong

Gentiles—Non-Jewish peoples of the world; all the world's peoples except the Jews

gospel—The good news of the redeeming work of God through the life, death, and resurrection of Jesus Christ

grace—God's undeserved acceptance and love toward us, especially in providing salvation for sinners

heaven—The eternal dwelling place of God and the redeemed

hell—The place of everlasting punishment for the lost

holy—God's distinguishing characteristic that separates him from all creation; the moral ideal for Christians as they seek to reflect the character of God as known in Christ Jesus

Holy Spirit—The third person of the Trinity

idolatry—The worship of that which is not God

incarnation—God becoming human; the union of divinity and humanity in Jesus of Nazareth, qualifying him to be the agent of God's saving plan for humanity

Jerusalem—Capital city of Israel in the Old Testament; religious center of Judaism in the New Testament

Jesus Christ (Messiah)—The eternal Son of God; the Lord and Savior; the second person of the Trinity

justification—The act or event by which God credits a sinner who has faith as being right with him through the blood of Jesus

law—God's instruction to his people about how to love him and others. When used with the definite article "the," law may refer to the Old Testament as a whole but usually to the Pentateuch (Genesis through Deuteronomy)

Messiah—The coming king promised by the prophets; Jesus Christ who fulfilled the prophetic promises; Christ represents the Greek translation of the Hebrew word *messiah* ("anointed one")

minor prophets—The twelve briefer prophetic writings, Hosea-Malachi; labeled "The Twelve" in the Hebrew Bible ("Tanak")

miracle—A supernatural act of God that inspires wonder, displays God's greatness, and leads people to recognize God at work in the world

monotheism—Belief in only one God

Moses—The leader whom God used to bring the Israelites out of slavery in Egypt

omnipotent—God's unlimited power to do that which is within his holy and righteous character

orthodoxy—Holding right beliefs as opposed to heretical beliefs

pagans—Those who worship a god or gods other than the living God to whom the Bible witnesses

polytheism—Belief in more than one god; a heresy prevalent in biblical times

prayer—Communication with God

prophet—One who speaks for God

providence—God's care for and guidance of his creation against all opposition

redemption—The act of releasing a captive by the payment of a price. Jesus' death provided our redemption from sin's power and penalty

repentance—A change of heart and mind resulting in a turning from sin to God that allows salvation and is expressed through faith

revelation—Making known that which has been hidden; God making known his nature and purpose through Scripture and the incarnate Son of God, Jesus Christ

righteousness—The quality or condition of being in right relationship with God; living out the relationship with God in right relationships with other persons

salvation—The experience of life as a believer in Christ; being rescued from condemnation on the judgment day because of Christ's sacrifice and one's trust in him

Satan—The evil angel who leads forces opposed to God and tempts people

second coming—Christ's return in power and glory to consummate his work of redemption

sin—Actions by which humans rebel against God, miss his purpose for their life, and surrender to the power of evil rather than to God

sovereignty—God's freedom from outward restraint; his unlimited rule of and control over his creation

Word of God—The Bible, God's inspired written revelation; God's message in oral form revealed through prophetic or angelic speakers; Jesus Christ, God's eternal Word in human flesh

worship—Reverence, honor, praise, and service shown to God

wrath of God—God's consistent response opposing and punishing sin

Bibliography

General Reference

Brand, Chad, Charles Draper, Archie England, Steve Bond, E. Ray Clendenen, and Trent Butler, eds. *Holman Illustrated Bible Dictionary* (HBD). Nashville: Holman Bible Publishers, 2003.

Harris, R. L., G. L. Archer Jr., B. K. Waltke, eds. *Theological Wordbook of the Old Testament* (TWOT). 2 vols. Chicago: Moody, 1980.

Richards, L. O. *Expository Dictionary of Bible Words.* Grand Rapids: Zondervan, 1985.

Smith, G. *An Introduction to the Hebrew Prophets: The Prophets as Preachers.* Nashville: Broadman & Holman, 1994.

Unger, M. F., and W. White Jr., eds. *Nelson's Expository Dictionary of the Old Testament.* Nashville: Thomas Nelson, 1980.

Walton, J. H., V. H. Matthews, and M. W. Chavalas. *The IVP Bible Background Commentary: Old Testament.* Downers Grove, Ill.: InterVarsity, 2000.

Water, M., compiler. *The New Encyclopedia of Christian Quotations.* Grand Rapids: Baker, 2000.

Nahum

Armerding, C. E. *Nahum.* In The Expositor's Bible Commentary. Vol. 7. Grand Rapids: Zondervan, 1985.

Baker, D. *Nahum, Habakkuk, Zephaniah.* TOTC. Downers Grove, Ill.: InterVarsity, 1988.

Barker, K. L., and W. Bailey. *Micah, Nahum, Habakkuk, Zephaniah.* The New American Commentary. Nashville: Broadman & Holman, 1998.

Craigie, P. *Micah, Nahum, Habakkuk, Zephaniah, Haggai, Zechariah, and Malachi.* Philadelphia: Westminster, 1985.

Johnson, E. E. *Nahum.* In The Bible Knowledge Commentary: Old Testament. Wheaton, Ill.: Victor, 1985.

Kaiser, W. *Mastering the Old Testament: Micah, Nahum, Habakkuk, Zephaniah, Haggai, Zechariah, Malachi.* Dallas: Word, 1992.

Longman III, T. *Nahum.* In The Minor Prophets, ed. T. McComiskey. Vol. 2. Grand Rapids: Baker, 1993.

Maier, W. A. *The Book of Nahum: A Commentary,* 1959. Reprint. Grand Rapids: Baker, 1980.

Patterson, R. D. *Nahum, Habakkuk, Zephaniah*. The Wycliffe Exegetical Commentary. Chicago: Moody, 1991.

Robertson, O. P. *The Books of Nahum, Habakkuk, and Zephaniah*. NICOT. Grand Rapids: Eerdmans, 1990.

Wright, P. *Jonah/Zephaniah*. Shepherd's Notes. Nashville: Broadman & Holman, 1999.

Habakkuk

Armerding, C. E. *Habakkuk*. In The Expositor's Bible Commentary. Vol. 7. Grand Rapids: Zondervan, 1985.

Baker, D. *Nahum, Habakkuk, Zephaniah*. TOTC. Downers Grove, Ill.: Inter-Varsity, 1988.

Barker, K. L, and W. Bailey. *Micah, Nahum, Habakkuk, Zephaniah*. The New American Commentary. Nashville: Broadman & Holman, 1998.

Blue, J. R. *Habakkuk*. In The Bible Knowledge Commentary: Old Testament. Wheaton, Ill.: Victor, 1985.

Bruce, F. F. *Habakkuk*. In The Minor Prophets, ed. T. McComiskey. Vol. 2. Grand Rapids: Baker, 1993.

Craigie, P. *Micah, Nahum, Habakkuk, Zephaniah, Haggai, Zechariah, and Malachi*. Philadelphia: Westminster, 1985.

Kaiser, W. *Mastering the Old Testament: Micah, Nahum, Habakkuk, Zephaniah, Haggai, Zechariah, Malachi*. Dallas: Word, 1992.

Patterson, R. D. *Nahum, Habakkuk, Zephaniah*. The Wycliffe Exegetical Commentary. Chicago: Moody, 1991.

Robertson, O. P. *The Books of Nahum, Habakkuk, and Zephaniah*. NICOT. Grand Rapids: Eerdmans, 1990.

Wright, P. *Jonah/Zephaniah*. Shepherd's Notes. Nashville: Broadman & Holman, 1999.

Zephaniah

Baker, D. *Nahum, Habakkuk, Zephaniah*. TOTC. Downers Grove, Ill.: Inter-Varsity, 1988.

Barker, K. L., and W. Bailey. *Micah, Nahum, Habakkuk, Zephaniah*. The New American Commentary. Nashville: Broadman & Holman, 1998.

Craigie, P. *Micah, Nahum, Habakkuk, Zephaniah, Haggai, Zechariah, and Malachi*. Philadelphia: Westminster, 1985.

Hannah, J. D. *Zephaniah*. In The Bible Knowledge Commentary: Old Testament. Wheaton, Ill.: Victor, 1985.

Kaiser, W. *Mastering the Old Testament: Micah, Nahum, Habakkuk, Zephaniah, Haggai, Zechariah, Malachi*. Dallas: Word, 1992.

Motyer, J. *Zephaniah*. In The Minor Prophets, ed. T. McComiskey. Vol. 3. Grand Rapids: Baker, 1998.

Patterson, R. D. *Nahum, Habakkuk, Zephaniah*. The Wycliffe Exegetical Commentary. Chicago: Moody, 1991.

Robertson, O. P. *The Books of Nahum, Habakkuk, and Zephaniah*. NICOT. Grand Rapids: Eerdmans, 1990.

Walker, L. L. *Zephaniah*. In The Expositor's Bible Commentary. Vol. 7. Grand Rapids: Zondervan, 1985.

Wright, P. *Jonah/Zephaniah*. Shepherd's Notes. Nashville: Broadman & Holman, 1999.

Haggai

Alden, R. *Haggai*. In The Expositor's Bible Commentary. Vol. 7. Grand Rapids: Zondervan, 1985.

Baldwin, J. *Haggai, Zechariah, Malachi*. TOTC. Downers Grove, Ill.: InterVarsity, 1972.

Craigie, P. *Micah, Nahum, Habakkuk, Zephaniah, Haggai, Zechariah, and Malachi*. Philadelphia: Westminster, 1985.

Kaiser, W. *Mastering the Old Testament: Micah, Nahum, Habakkuk, Zephaniah, Haggai, Zechariah, Malachi*. Dallas: Word, 1992.

Lindsey, F. D. *Haggai*. In The Bible Knowledge Commentary: Old Testament. Wheaton, Ill.: Victor, 1985.

Morgan, B. E. *Haggai/Malachi*. Shepherd's Notes. Nashville: Broadman & Holman, 1999.

Motyer, J. *Haggai*. In The Minor Prophets, ed. T. McComiskey. Vol. 3. Grand Rapids: Baker, 1998.

Verhoef, P. A. *The Books of Haggai and Malachi*. NICOT. Grand Rapids: Eerdmans, 1987.

Wolf, H. *Haggai and Malachi: Rededication and Renewal*. Chicago: Moody, 1976.

Zechariah

Baldwin, J. *Haggai, Zechariah, Malachi*. TOTC. Downers Grove, Ill.: InterVarsity, 1972.

Barker, K. L. *Zechariah*. In The Expositor's Bible Commentary. Vol. 7. Grand Rapids: Zondervan, 1985.

Craigie, P. *Micah, Nahum, Habakkuk, Zephaniah, Haggai, Zechariah, and Malachi*. Philadelphia: Westminster, 1985.

Feinberg, C. L. *God Remembers: A Study of Zechariah*. Portland, Oreg.: Multnomah, 1965.

Feinberg, C. L. *The Minor Prophets*. Chicago: Moody, 1976.

Kaiser, W. *Mastering the Old Testament: Micah, Nahum, Habakkuk, Zephaniah, Haggai, Zechariah, Malachi*. Dallas: Word, 1992.

Laetsch, Theo. *The Minor Prophets*. Saint Louis: Concordia, 1956.

Leupold, H. C. *Exposition of Zechariah*, 1956. Reprint. Grand Rapids: Baker, 1971.

Lindsey, F. D. *Zechariah*. In The Bible Knowledge Commentary: Old Testament. Wheaton, Ill.: Victor, 1985.

Luck, G. C. *Zechariah*. Chicago: Moody, 1969.

McComiskey, T. *Zechariah*. In The Minor Prophets, ed. T. McComiskey. Vol. 3. Grand Rapids: Baker, 1998.

Unger, M. F. *Zechariah: Prophet of Messiah's Glory*. Grand Rapids: Zondervan, 1963.

Malachi

Alden, R. L. *Malachi*. In The Expositor's Bible Commentary. Vol. 7. Grand Rapids: Zondervan, 1985.

Baldwin, J. *Haggai, Zechariah, Malachi*. TOTC. Downers Grove, Ill.: InterVarsity, 1972.

Blaising, C. A. *Malachi*. In The Bible Knowledge Commentary: Old Testament. Wheaton, Ill.: Victor, 1985.

Craigie, P. *Micah, Nahum, Habakkuk, Zephaniah, Haggai, Zechariah, and Malachi*. Philadelphia: Westminster, 1985.

Hill, A. *Malachi*. AB. New York: Doubleday, 1998.

Isbell, C. D. *Malachi: A Study Guide Commentary*. Grand Rapids: Zondervan, 1980.

Kaiser, W. C., Jr. *Malachi: God's Unchanging Love*. Grand Rapids: Baker, 1984.

Kaiser, W. *Mastering the Old Testament: Micah, Nahum, Habakkuk, Zephaniah, Haggai, Zechariah, Malachi*. Dallas: Word, 1992.

Stuart, D. *Malachi*. In The Minor Prophets, ed. T. McComiskey. Vol. 3. Grand Rapids: Baker, 1998.

Verhoef, P. A. *The Books of Haggai and Malachi*. NICOT. Grand Rapids: Eerdmans, 1987.

Wolf, H. *Haggai and Malachi: Rededication and Renewal*. Chicago: Moody, 1976.